Law and Trade Issues
of the Japanese Economy

Law and Trade Issues of the Japanese Economy

American and Japanese Perspectives

Edited by

GARY R. SAXONHOUSE

and

KOZO YAMAMURA

University of Washington Press
Seattle and London

University of Tokyo Press

This book is sponsored by
The Committee on Japanese Economic Studies and published with
the assistance of a grant from the Japan Foundation.

Published in Japan by University of Tokyo Press
ISBN 4-13-047030-2   UTP 47301

Library of Congress Cataloging in Publication Data

Law and trade issues of the Japanese economy.

   Based on a workshop held in Sept. 1983, sponsored by
the Committee on Japanese Economic Studies.
   1. Foreign trade regulation—Japan—Congresses.
2. Foreign trade regulation—United States—Congresses.
3. United States—Foreign economic relations—Japan—
Congresses.   4. Japan—Foreign economic relations—
United States—Congresses.   I. Saxonhouse, Gary R.
II. Yamamura, Kōzō.   III. Committee on Japanese
Economic Studies (U.S.)
KF1976.A5L38   1986   343'.07   85-40975
ISBN 0-295-96343-3   342.37

Foreword

One important contribution the Japan-United States Friendship Commission can make is to encourage dispassionate, scholarly studies of the difficult and complex issues that continue to cause serious discord in the economic relations between these two staunch allies. Our sincere hope is that increased mutual understanding can help minimize this discord, which unfortunately appears to have intensified during the past few years. In pursuit of such understanding, we are pleased to have supported the binational efforts that made the publication of this book possible. We are confident that the essays that follow on legal and economic issues affecting bilateral trade will be useful in taking the necessary steps toward building more harmonious economic relations between Japan and the United States.

GLENN CAMPBELL, CHAIRMAN
Japan-United States Friendship Commission

Contents

Introduction

The United States–Japan economic relationship is under great pressure, and it seems unlikely that this pressure will ease in the foreseeable future. Such pressure is in considerable measure the almost unavoidable consequence of the scope and continuing rapid transformation of the largest overseas bilateral trading relationship in the history of the global economy. This unprecedented bilateral economic intimacy, however, is occurring between two large nations with very different economic institutions and traditions. These differences work to exacerbate what are already extremely complicated diplomatic relations between the two nations.

The experience of the past twenty years suggests the importance of the domestic legal frameworks of both Japan and the United States in framing institutional differences, thereby shaping the character of bilateral economic negotiations and the very nature of the relationship itself. Unhappily, for all this importance, the nexus between legal framework, economic behavior, and bilateral U.S.-Japan relations has been too little analyzed.

In an effort to throw more light on these complicated issues, the Committee on Japanese Economic Studies sponsored a workshop in September 1983 on legal institutions and U.S.–Japanese economic relations. Three related issue areas were considered. First, attention was given to how Japan's legal framework influences selected significant domestic features of Japan's economy. Under this heading, Japanese savings behavior, the character of domestic competition, the reasons for ministerial "administrative guidance," and Japanese treatment of product liability were examined. As will be seen, while each of these areas has profound consequences for the character of U.S.–Japan relations, the consequences tend to be indirect. It is true that domestic policy instruments, including legal rules, can always be good functional substitutes for foreign economic policy instruments, but the character of the traditional international regime is such that only rarely will these instruments become the object of international diplomacy. By contrast, when Japan's legal framework directly affects foreign (and particularly U.S.) access to the Japanese economy, diplomatic interest can be intense.

The workshop had the good foresight to also focus on that portion of the Japanese legal framework governing (1) foreign access to Japanese financial markets and (2) treatment of foreign intellectual property rights in Japan. With some hindsight it is now apparent that no two single issues have been in more contention bilaterally or more in need of good explication and analysis.

As a truly bilateral exchange, this workshop dealt not only with the Japanese legal framework, but also with how the U.S. legal framework affects U.S.–Japanese economic relations. In particular, the workshop examined the application of U.S. antitrust statutes to Japanese industry. Attention was also paid to the impact of the national security clause of the Trade Expansion Act of 1962 on Japanese access to American markets for high technology products. Finally, the presence at the workshop of Paula Stern, now chair of the United States International Trade Commission, allowed a firsthand reconsideration of the application of the escape clause of the Trade Act of 1974 in three significant instances of U.S.–Japanese friction.

From the lively proceedings of the workshop, nine essays have been culled for inclusion in this volume. Reflecting the organization of the workshop discussions, this volume is divided into three parts. Part 1, "Japanese Legal Framework and Domestic Economic Institutions," includes essays by Kazuo Sato of Rutgers University; Hiroshi Iyori, secretary general of Japan's Fair Trade Commission; a study team headed by Koichi Hamada of Tokyo University; and John O. Haley of the University of Washington School of Law.

Sato's essay surveys interactions between economic laws, especially tax laws and household wealth formation in Japan over the last three decades. He finds that the Japanese tax system that was developed in the late 1940s and early 1950s showed little concern for distributional equity but was designed to encourage private savings and investment for the goal of economic growth. As Sato points out, this system was compatible with the economic climate of the high-growth period that lasted until the early 1970s. However, since then Japan's policy-induced high household savings has spawned macroeconomic dilemmas even as it has greatly complicated Japan's relationship with the global economy.

Neither the Japanese government's large fiscal deficit nor the reduced financing needs of the slower growing Japanese corporate system have been sufficient to fully utilize within the Japanese economy the very large savings of the household sector. In consequence, these savings must be put to use outside Japan. For Japan to export these savings and thereby run a capital account deficit, it must run a surplus in its current account on international transactions in goods and services. This means selling more to its trading partners than it buys from them. In this way, the mundane facts of household economy translate into the structural trade imbalances that bedevil the bilateral negotiators.

Sato emphasizes that the Japanese tax system and the legal framework governing Japanese savings have been slow to respond to changes in Japan's economic structure. Not only Japan's current account surplus, but also its government budget deficit and its undue reliance on revenues drawn from taxation of wage and salary earners all indicate that an overhaul of Japan's tax system is in order. Sato surveys four attempts to change the government's regulation insofar as it affects Japanese household finances. First, Sato examines the inequitable treatment of wage and salary workers relative to farmers, nonfarm business proprietors, self-employed professionals, medical and dental practitioners, rentiers, and landowners. Japanese wage and salary workers, like their American counterparts, have their income taxes withheld at the source. In consequence, their earned incomes are almost wholly reported to the tax offices. By contrast, individuals who are not on company payrolls turn in self-assessed income tax returns. In addition to uniquely generous business-expense deductions, Japanese taxpayers in this category have many legal and illegal means for evading taxes. Such evasion has been made especially easy by the National Tax Agency's devoting relatively few resources to auditing noncorporate, nonwage, and non-salaried taxpayers. Despite the notoriety of this problem, farmers' groups and associations of small and medium-sized businesses have been successful in preventing any changes at all in a system that is clearly to their benefit. The only outcome of fifteen years of criticism to date has been the sponsorship of one relatively inconclusive study by the National Tax Agency.

While the Ministry of Finance has been unwilling to act on the evasion of taxes on the earned income, it has made an elaborate, if until now unsuccessful, effort to curb tax evasion from property income. In 1979, the Ministry of Finance's Tax Advisory Commission recommended that all individuals opening a savings account be issued a "Green Card." The Green Card system was designed to prevent the evasion of Japanese taxes on savings by insuring that all multiple savings accounts issued under all names, fictitious and otherwise, could be traced to their actual owners. This would end the widespread practice among middle- and upper-income Japanese households of opening multiple postal-savings accounts so that the interest income from any given account could always be maintained below the individual tax-exempt level.

A bill embodying the Green Card proposal did pass the Diet in March, 1980. As the Ministry of Finance made plans to implement the system, public opposition fanned by Japan's Ministry of Posts and Telecommunications, which stood to lose considerable influence under the Green Card system, grew sufficient to delay its implementation. Sato believes this particular initiative for greater equity in the Japanese tax system is now effectively dead.

Unlike its problems in taxing interest income, the Ministry of Finance has maintained a high effective tax rate on capital gains from land transactions. Ironically, while this tax had been designed to mitigate the influence of one of the most important sources of Japanese income inequality, it has had perverse social consequences. In particular, a high capital gains tax without a high effective property tax on lightly used urban and suburban real estate (e.g., farmland) has left most densely populated areas in Japan with only very limited supplies of newly available residential land.

Having examined a number of the features of Japan's regulatory environment as they influence household accumulation of assets, Sato also turns his attention to the liability side of the household balance sheet. Coping with emergencies remains a major motivation for Japanese savings. Doubtless, such motivation remains strong because of the absence of a fully competitive, unsecured consumer loan market in Japan. With Japan's banks unwilling and perhaps unable to enter this market, real interest rates are some four to five times what they are in the United States.

Sato's analysis of these four cases makes it abundantly clear that while the path that might be taken to resolve social tensions at home and diplomatic problems abroad is well known, a kind of pluralistic gridlock often makes even the timid changes in Japan's regulatory environment very difficult to undertake. The delicate balance between the interests of the Ministry of Finance, the Ministry of Post and Telecommunications, the banking system, farmers, and small businessmen is upset only at very great cost to Japanese political and economic stability. The possibility of change is further diminished by the nature of the issues involved. Despite the very clear foreign interest in the character of constraints on the Japanese household acquisition of assets and liabilities, the issues are too much the traditional stuff of domestic politics for foreign pressure to be usefully exerted.

By contrast with Sato's work both Haley and Iyori find the legal framework governing the relationship between Japanese ministries and Japanese business neither so successful in accomplishing its stated purpose of structural transformation nor so inflexible as conditions changed. Haley stresses that the Japanese government uses administrative guidance—informal means to regulate the behavior of Japanese business either because it lacks the formal statutory authority to proceed otherwise or because the costs of using a more formal approach are too great. In this respect, Haley's outlook is bolstered by Sato's evidence. With the notable exception of where agricultural interests are concerned, new statutory guidance from the Diet in the face of changed circumstances is exceedingly difficult to obtain. Notwithstanding a parliamentary form of government, Japan's Diet remains a blunt instrument for policy formation.

Not entirely unsurprisingly Haley finds that because regulation was largely informal, it was mostly ineffective and/or unimportant. According to Haley, this meant much of Japanese business was subjected to the full impact of market forces. This, in turn, fostered rapid growth and ultimately international competitiveness. However, where formal statutory authority and extralegal sanctions have permitted effective implementation of government policies, either through administrative guidance or mandatory controls, Haley finds the consequences have often been less positive. In illustrating the nature of Japanese administrative guidance Haley draws some useful parallels between the work of the Antitrust Division of the U.S. Department of Justice and the Federal Trade Commission on the one hand and Japan's Ministry of International Trade and Industry and Fair Trade Commission on the other. All four agencies practice administrative guidance with increasingly similar ineffective outcomes. In the perspective of Haley's paper, it is difficult to believe that the financial practices that Sato finds so impervious to change are being maintained in the interest of making the Ministry of International Trade and Industry efforts to influence the sectoral allocation of resources more effective.

Iyori, writing with the authority and perspective of a high official of the Japan Fair Trade Commission, takes a more positive view of the role of the Japanese government. He finds that both the special statutory authority that Japanese ministries have often sought to implement their industrial policies and administrative guidance have played a significant role in the development of such industries as steel, computers, and semiconductors. These policies have been implemented using instruments including import restrictions, tariffs, allocation of raw materials, subsidies, special financing arrangements, and the promotion of cartels and mergers.

In discussing the promotion of cartels and mergers, Iyori is in close agreement with Haley. Among the instruments used by the Japanese government, pro-merger-collusion policies were particularly ineffective. Unlike Haley, Iyori, in explaining these failures, stresses not so much the lack of specific statutory authority as the tenacious opposition of the Fair Trade Commission. In Iyori's view, the Fair Trade Commission has consistently opposed and criticized special legislation and administrative guidance to achieve anticompetitive ends. In this way, the Japanese economy has remained competitive and in being competitive has been able to grow rapidly and successfully.

In looking to the future, Iyori finds the need to maintain competition through the Antimonopoly Law more important than ever before. In an earlier era, rapid economic growth worked against inefficient allocation of capital, inflexible industrial structure, and stagnation. In an era of slower growth, it is Iyori's view that a competitive market structure must now shoulder this burden.

Quite apart from the benefits to Japan's domestic economy from strong pro-competitive policies, Iyori notes that Japan's international economic diplomacy will increasingly require competition at home. While trading among nations with very different economic institutions will in all likelihood be mutually beneficial, the continuing legitimacy of the growing intrusive international economic order from which Japan draws such great benefits appears to require institutional harmonization among its major actors. Given the liberal auspices of the international economic system, competitive domestic markets are a requirement for the competitive international markets that will insure for Japan in the future the ready market access abroad it has enjoyed in the past.

However central to Japan's global position the Fair Trade Commission's agenda may become in the future, the means to accomplish it remains extremely limited. For example, Sato identifies the absence of competition in the consumer loan market as a major problem for the Japanese economy. In the absence of Ministry of Finance connivance, is there really any chance that the Fair Trade Commission might seriously influence the character of competition in this market?

In common with other elements of Japan's domestic legal framework, Japan's treatment of product liability varies sharply with American practice. This variance reflects the paradigmatic qualities of both systems. As Hamada, Ishida, and Murakami note, despite Japan's having had a number of extremely serious product liability cases including the Kanemi Rice Oil, the SMON, the Morinaga Powdered Milk, and the thalidomide cases that have caused as much serious injury and have involved as many individuals as any of the well-known cases in North America and Europe, on the whole there is little product liability litigation in Japan and the amount of compensation awarded in successful litigation is relatively small.

In explaining these substantial differences in outcome, Hamada et al. point out that while in the United States there are at least four causes for damages due to defective products including negligence, breach of expressed or implied warranty, strict liability, and misrepresentation by the seller to the consumer, in Japan, by and large, only negligence is actionable. Moreover, in Japan, (1) there is no practice of punitive damages; (2) allowance is seldom made for inflationary expectations in determining future loss of income for plaintiffs; (3) the jury system is not used; (4) it is professionally most difficult for Japanese attorneys to take cases on a contingency basis; (5) class action complaints do not exist; (6) when an action is brought before a court, a tax is imposed on the plaintiff that varies with the size of the claim being made; and (7) the number of attorneys is so carefully controlled by Japan's Ministry of Justice that the Japanese legal profession is one-fiftieth the size of its American counterpart. All of these factors work to discourage product liability suits in Japan.

While the preceding analysis does suggest that Japanese producers compared to American producers may face fewer economic incentives to build safety into their products, Hamada et al. do note that Japanese practice is once again moving closer to American precedent. Regardless of strict legal basis, strategies pursued by Japanese lawyers, decisions made by Japanese judges, and commentaries made by Japanese scholars on product liability issues have drawn very heavily on the American example. Practices in the United States, where product liability cases are numerous and where case law is highly developed, have almost inevitably influenced Japanese outcomes. In this way, Hamada et al. find, despite differences in the basic legal framework, actual treatment of specific cases has been quite similar between Japan and the United States. In common with Sato and Haley, Hamada et al. conclude that statutory changes are among the most sluggish elements of Japan's complex political economy. Unlike Haley, however, they do find that effective action is often possible even in the absence of specific statutory authority.

Part 2, "Japan's Legal Framework and Foreign Access to the Japanese Market," contains papers by Dan Henderson of the University of Washington School of Law and by Waseda University's Teruo Doi. Henderson reviews the operation of Japan's old Foreign Exchange and Foreign Trade Control Law (FECL) and tries to assess what differences the widely publicized revisions of 1980 and thereafter have made for foreign access to the Japanese market. Contrary to the view of many observers, Henderson is doubtful that the 1980 changes represent a landmark in the liberalization of the Japanese economy. Henderson views the revised statute as still "pure administration," its hallmark being unchallengeable discretion in practically every provision. He feels this continued discretion will be used to frustrate unfettered foreign access to the Japanese market.

Henderson places particular emphasis on the continuation of the virtual prohibition of unwanted foreign takeovers of Japanese firms. The purchase of an existing company is the most common means by which American-based multinationals have expanded into Europe. Given the nature of the Japanese real estate and labor markets and the character of the Japanese distribution system, it would seem that this means would be still more useful for foreign corporations wishing to enter the Japanese market. If Henderson is correct, and the 1980 law has had no influence on the ease with which such takeovers may be accomplished, then a decade of American diplomatic effort in this area may well have come to naught.

Unlike Iyori, Henderson does not envision the gradual harmonization of Japanese and American institutions in the context of a liberal economic framework. Henderson believes that given the Japanese tradition and the current structure and operation of the Japanese economy, it is unrealistic to expect the Japanese government to allow the transfer of control of a Japanese company simply because of foreign (or for that matter domestic) majority purchase of shareholder equity. Henderson does not dispute that the revised FECL has had an effect on international interest rate differentials, exchange rates, and capital movements, but he feels it has done little to make it easier for foreigners to compete in Japan.

If, according to Henderson, American firms have little access to the Japanese economy other than through technology sales, it is not so surprising that Japan has for many years been the United States' largest market for technology and that for no other major industrialized economy has the U.S. technology trade surplus been proportionately so large. Much of this trade in technology is conducted through patent, copyright, and trademark licensing agreements, through franchise arrangements, and through consulting contracts.

However much technology is transferred through such market means, it is also abundantly clear that far more technology is transferred by nonmarket means. The few hundred million or even one billion dollars in transfer of technology payments that Japan has annually made throughout the postwar period reflect only a small part of the foreign technology that Japan has imported and from which Japan has so greatly benefited.

It is in the nature of technological knowledge that its benefits cannot be fully appropriated by its producers. Even excluding the presumably rare instances where illegal activities are undertaken, Japanese overseas technological information gathering activities are elaborate and highly successful. Through freely disseminated university research, through professional meetings, trade journals, and factory tours, Japanese industry throughout the past forty years has had nonmarket access to much of the benefits of American research and development.

In reviewing the above circumstances and in common with Hamada et al. Doi reminds us that while the Japanese legal system being based on civil law and the

American legal system being based on common law makes for many differences in form, in practice the two systems are converging. Japanese intellectual property law has for many years drawn heavily on American practice. As rapid technological change raises new challenges for intellectual property law it can be expected that this dependence will grow. Even as Japan becomes a major producer of technology, purchases of technology from the United States will increase. Doi argues persuasively that the Japanese legal system will continue to offer American licensors of technology protection for their property rights substantially equivalent to what they might expect at home.

Doi's finding is particularly interesting in view of the current controversy over how much protection will be afforded American-created computer software under Japanese copyright laws. In all likelihood Henderson would argue that such software will not be given any effective statutory protection and American programmers will be at the mercy of the Ministry of International Trade and Industry. Doi would not agree at all with such an analysis. He would probably project that the Ministry of Education interest in having software protected under the international standards maintained under copyright law will prevail over a belated initiative by the Ministry of International Trade and Industry to assert its authority in this area. On the basis of evidence to date such a projection is correct, but one might agree with Henderson that this outcome owes a great deal to a vigilant American diplomacy.

Turning from the terms of American entry into the Japanese market to the terms of Japanese entry to the American market, the final section of this volume, "The American Legal Framework and Bilateral Issues," contains papers by Paula Stern and Andrew Wechsler of the United States International Trade Commission (USITC), by Gary Saxonhouse of the University of Michigan, and by Kozo Yamamura and Jan VanDenBerg of the University of Washington.

Stern and Wechsler begin this section by examining the operation of the escape clause within the American system of trade law, which is designed to offer relief to American industries hard hit by import competition. Where once escape clause action required the petitioning industry to demonstrate a direct causal link between American trade concession and industry distress, since 1974 it has only been necessary to show that imports entering American markets for whatever historical reasons are a substantial cause of economic injury to the industry.

The 1974 escape clause formula has come under increasing criticism following the denial by the USITC of relief in 1980 to the American automobile industry. Is it possible that the escape clause denies general import relief to cyclical industries during the depths of a recession when they may need such aid the most? This might happen because the recession replaces import competition as the main problem facing the industry.

Stern and Wechsler argue that an analysis of the USITC's handling of the Automobile, Motorcycle, and Specialty Steel cases, all of which involve Japanese import competition, demonstrates that there is no barrier in the present statute to offering relief to cyclical industries beset by serious recessions. A majority of the USITC has never argued that a decline in demand due to a general recession should be treated as a single cause to be set against imports in deciding whether the escape clause should be applied. Indeed, the USITC has never adopted a uniform approach at all.

Reviewing these three major cases, Stern and Wechsler identify an approach they feel is consistent with and embodies these USITC decisions. Starting from the presumption that Congress intended that cyclical industries have as ready an access to relief as noncyclical industries, they suggest that the difficult effort must be made to remove from consideration the usual consequences of a recession. After that step is taken, what is left from the impact of a recession should be compared with the effect of import competition in making a decision on import relief.

The Stern and Wechsler chapter is fascinating not only as an analysis of how U.S. regulatory bodies cope with the problems fostered by aggressive Japanese competition, but also in perspective of the Japanese experience. Consistent with Henderson's analysis, there is no analogue to the International Trade Commission within the Japanese government. Since Japan has been a signatory to the General Agreement on Tariffs and Trade (GATT) for decades its import competing industries are afforded escape clause protection. Like antidumping proceedings, no Japanese industry has ever attempted to get protection for itself under the escape clause. In part, this is because Japanese industries do not have standing under Japanese law to initiate such legal proceedings. More important and consistent with Henderson's analysis, the Japanese government has far more effective means to protect its industries when and where it wishes.

The escape clause has been frequently and successfully used as a vehicle to gain relief for American industries from Japanese import competition. By contrast, the national security clause that appears in most of the major pieces of U.S. trade legislation has never been successfully used as a means of getting relief from Japanese competition or for that matter from any other foreign manufactured good competition. In 1983, however, the National Machine Tool Builders' Association petitioned the U.S. Department of Commerce alleging that the U.S. machine tool industry was suffering from Japanese machine tool competition to such an extent that national security was being impaired.

Saxonhouse, in reviewing this case, discusses the development of the Japanese machine tool industry and the plight of its American counterpart. He finds that the difficulties of the American machine tool industry are more the result of the sharp cyclical downturn of the American economy than of any other single factor, including import competition. What import competition the machine tool industry does face comes not from a monolithic Japanese cartel nurtured by large doses of Japanese government aid. Tariff protection, subsidies and grants, tax expenditures, and low interest rate loans from government financial institutions are comparable to or less than aid received by the American machine tool industry from the American government.

Because of the extremely large impact the early 1980s recession had on the machine tool industry and in light of the considerations raised in the Stern and Wechsler essay, it is not surprising that the industry and its members have avoided going to the USITC for relief. Rather, by invoking the aid of the national security clause, the machine tool industry sought a favorable recommendation from the U.S. Department of Commerce, an agency not as subject as the USITC to the burdens of precedent and routinized procedure.

Saxonhouse points out that the industry's argument that present machine tool capacity is insufficient to meet the demand of a mobilization for a large-scale conventional war rests on the assumption (1) that civilian demands on machine tool capacity will not be suppressed in any major way in the event of such a mobilization; (2) that the United States will respond only by conventional means in the event of Soviet domination of Western Europe and Japan; and (3) that the entire locus of future technological progress in the machine tool industry is producer-based and financed rather than user-based and financed. None of these assumptions seems very plausible.

Even if it were true that present American machine tool industry production and technological capacities were insufficient to meet future national security needs, Saxonhouse notes that the quota protection asked by the National Machine Tool Builders' Association is a poor instrument to use to build up such capacity. Japanese government aid to the machine tool industry and to many of its other industries looks extremely small when compared with American government programs, precisely because so much U.S. aid is defense related. This suggests to Saxonhouse that the American government has already assembled a sophisticated array of instruments to encourage the American industrial base to prepare to meet national security needs. If a question exists as to American industrial preparedness, Saxonhouse maintains these very large programs need to be reviewed and adjusted.

Prior to the National Machine Tool Builders' Association petition to the U.S. Department of Commerce, Houdaille Industries also petitioned Commerce asking, under the Revenue Act of 1971, that the eligibility of purchasers of Japanese machine tools to qualify for the investment tax credit be denied because the Japanese industry was a government-aided cartel. This petition was rejected in April 1983 on grounds that were never fully specified, but the great difficulty Houdaille had in establishing not only the existence of substantial Japanese government aid but also any evidence of industry collusion undoubtedly had an important effect on the outcome.

Many of the same allegations regarding the role of the Japanese government and the collusive strategies employed by Japanese industry have been made against Japanese television set producers and are reviewed by Yamamura and VanDenBerg in the final paper in this volume. Yamamura and VanDenBerg address the influence of Japanese government policies, especially the control of the capital market and the lax enforcement of the antitrust statute, on the rapid growth of the export of Japanese television sets to the United States in the 1960s and 1970s. The authors focus their attention on this well-known bilateral trade issue because it has given rise to a series of trade problems that involved various branches of the U.S. government and to a complex and protracted antitrust case between the Japanese and the American firms. In the latter, two American firms charge that the Japanese firms had cartelized their domestic market for electric and electronic appliances and were using profits realized there to mount a collusive predatory campaign against the U.S. industry.

Based on close examination of the seven Japanese firms' internal cost structures, collusive marketing practices both at home and in the United States, and export strategies, Yamamura and VanDenBerg argue that the firms seem to have had the incentive and capabilities to export their products at prices far below those charged in Japan and even below the cost of production. Thus, they argue that while predatory intent was not a necessary precondition to such injurious "dumping," it cannot be lightly dismissed as a contributing factor. Unlike the cases examined by Haley, Iyori, and Saxonhouse, Yamamura and VanDenBerg conclude that the television set case is an example where Japanese industrial policy has been effective in accomplishing its goals. Rather than uncritically recommending such policies for adoption in the United States, however, Yamamura and VanDenBerg are quick to point out their costs. They suggest that the costs imposed on consumers by the long-term virtual abrogation of antitrust statutes are likely to exceed the benefits such policies provide the firms. They also suggest that the insights gained from their study can be useful in examining the bilateral trade issues that appear to be intensifying involving the products of the semiconductor and other high technology industries.

This volume and the workshop that preceded it are the second in a series being sponsored by the Committee on Japanese Economic Studies. The preceding volume, *Policy and Trade Issues of Japanese Economy*, was edited by Kozo Yamamura and was published by University of Washington Press in 1982. A third workshop concerning Japanese industrial policy was held in March 1984 and the papers from that workshop are currently being edited for publication by Hugh Patrick.

Currently, the Committee on Japanese Economic Studies consists of Masahiko Aoki, Hugh Patrick, Henry Rosovsky, Kazuo Sato, and the two editors of this volume. Other activities of the committee include organizing symposia and seminars for government officials, business leaders, and academic specialists; holding seminars for graduate students interested in the Japanese economy; assisting young American specialists of the Japanese economy in finding an appropriate Japanese or American government agency or a university where they can most profitably continue their research; and carrying out other similar activities that can increase American knowledge of the Japanese economy.

The committee wishes to express its appreciation to the Japan–United States Friendship Commission for the financial assistance it provided in holding the original workshop for this volume. The editors of this volume are most grateful to Professor Hugh Patrick of Columbia University who generously contributed his time and talents to make this volume possible. And the editors thank Professor Michael Young, also of Columbia University, who was an active participant in the workshop.

Further, the committee, and especially the editors, also wish to thank Martha L. Lane for most ably assisting in all aspects of the difficult administrative and editorial work that was involved in organizing and publishing a volume that included many essays by nonnative speakers of English. Finally, Gary Saxonhouse wishes to thank the Center for Advanced Study in the Behavioral Sciences and the National Science Foundation for providing the funding so he might have the time and resources to complete the editing of this volume.

Gary Saxonhouse

Kozo Yamamura

Part 1

JAPANESE LEGAL FRAMEWORK

AND DOMESTIC ECONOMIC INSTITUTIONS

Economic Laws
and the Household Economy in Japan:
Lags in Policy Response to
Economic Changes

KAZUO SATO

This study examines the relationships between economic laws, particularly tax laws, and the household economy, especially income, saving, and wealth, in Japan over the last three decades. In 1950, the Japanese government was provided with the Shoup Mission blueprint for its tax reform. But the Japanese tax system that was ultimately born was in spirit quite the opposite of the Shoup Mission's conception. It was principally designed to encourage private saving and investment for the goal of economic growth, which has been achieved at the expense of distributional equity.

This tax system was compatible with the economic climate of the high-growth period, which lasted for more than two decades until the early 1970s. Rapid economic growth kept inequities suppressed during that time. In the low-growth period that followed, macroeconomic contradictions surfaced and problems of inequity became glaringly apparent. The tax system now needs wholesale overhaul to meet the new economic conditions. Yet, politically powerful vested interests have proven highly resistant to any reform that would diminish their economic power.

It is this process of developing need and efforts for reform against counterposed resistance that I wish to describe here. To establish a point of departure for my analysis, part one reviews the Shoup Mission blueprint and its aftermath and then outlines economic changes that took place over the next three decades. Part two describes the current tax system as it concerns the household economy. Part

The author benefited from discussions at the conference as well as at a meeting in Washington, D.C., of the Japan Economic Seminar. I wish to thank the participants of these meetings, especially Jack Lucken, James Nakamura, and Hugh Patrick for their detailed comments.

3

three discusses the relationship of the tax laws to household saving, and part four examines the evolution of Japan's household wealth. Part five surveys four recent cases as examples of powerful resistance to reform on the part of vested interests and part six examines implications for U.S.–Japan economic relations.

1. TAXATION, GROWTH, AND HOUSEHOLD SAVING: A HISTORICAL OVERVIEW SINCE 1950

The Shoup Mission and Its Aftermath

In 1949, toward the end of the Allied Powers' occupation of Japan, a tax mission headed by Professor Carl Shoup (Columbia University) was invited by the supreme commander of Allied Powers to draft a blueprint of a tax system for Japan.[1] After a stay of five months in Japan, the mission reported back with detailed recommendations that were to form "the best tax system in the world," in the mission's opinion. As such, this system contained many ideas that were radical or idealistic. Let us examine a few major features of the Shoup Mission recommendations as regards the household economy.

(1) The personal income tax was to become the mainstay of the national tax system. All incomes, including capital gains, were to be taxed collectively under a progressive income tax schedule. Separate taxation of interest and dividend income was to be discontinued. The system of anonymous and fictitious accounts that were tax free except at source was to be abolished to eliminate a major source of abuse. The earned income credit was to be reduced.

(2) As a compromise with the need for promoting capital formation, land and fixed capital assets were to be revalued and adequate depreciation reserves to be set up. Capital gains were to be taxed as fluctuating income.

(3) The valued-added tax was to be introduced as a major source of local government revenue.

(4) The net-worth tax would be imposed on high levels of individuals' net worth while keeping the marginal income tax rate on top income brackets at a moderate level. It was thought that this tax would provide a double check on the accuracy of top income earners' tax returns. The accession tax would be imposed as a cumulative tax on gifts and bequests.

The Japanese Diet accepted and passed the new tax laws in 1950, albeit with some important modifications. Following the signing of the peace treaty in 1952, however, these tax laws were reviewed. Many of the most radical ones were repealed and others significantly modified[2] by 1953, on the grounds that they were unsuitable for Japan's economic conditions. Japan needed to promote capital accumulation to achieve economic growth.

This reform and counterreform of the tax system at the very beginning of Japan's postwar growth clearly reveal Japan's national attitudes on private saving, capital formation, and wealth. After all the dust had settled, a tax system finally emerged.

For personal income tax, exemptions were raised; earned income credit was cut less than recommended. The income tax schedule was made very progressive. Income tax on wages and salaries was withheld at source, and most wage and salary workers were not required to file tax returns, thus minimizing the cost of tax collection. Individual proprietors filed self-assessed returns with deductions allowed for business expenses.

Separate taxation of interest and dividend income, which had been in practice since 1899, was retained, using a separate schedule. Anonymous accounts were never abolished since banking and securities interests resisted, arguing that a ban on anonymity of accounts and securities would eliminate the attractiveness of saving and investment relative to consumption.

Capital gains on sales of securities remained tax exempt. No revaluation gains tax was imposed. As for capital gains on sales of real estate, the earlier procedure of treating one half of capital gains above a special deduction as income for the year was retained.

The net-worth tax was initially accepted with tax rates up to 3 percent on net worth in excess of five million yen, but it was repealed in 1953 since it proved to be extremely difficult to assess values of real estate and other private properties. The accession tax was also repealed in the same year, while the inheritance tax was retained. Thus, as Pechman and Kaizuka summarize it, "Japan began its postwar recovery with a blueprint by the Shoup Mission that would have made its tax system a model for the rest of the world. But the Shoup blueprint was quickly discarded, and a Japanese brand of taxation was substituted. Thereafter tax policy was oriented toward growth. . . ."[3]

The Shoup Mission blueprint emphasized equity, that is, sharing the tax burden equitably according to the taxpayer's ability to pay. But equity was an ideal far from the minds of Japanese policymakers at the time. The most imperative task on the agenda was the nation's reconstruction and growth. Indeed, as early as September 1, 1945, the cabinet adopted a resolution entitled "On Strengthening National Saving in the Postwar Period," emphasizing the unchanged role of saving in the new milieu following the end of the war.[4] The resolution was drafted by Ministry of Finance (MOF) bureaucrats. Though political parties in power zigzagged between the right and the left, the MOF bureaucracy remained stable, and pro-saving policy was the basic tenet of the postwar reconstruction plan.[5] Needless to say, this philosophy flourished after the peace treaty. To achieve the professed goal, saving and investment had to be encouraged by various fiscal and financial measures. The hegemony of the national government was now in the hands of the Liberal Democratic party (LDP), which was the spokesman for the business community. The finance minister at the time was Ikeda Hayato, a former MOF bureaucrat and later a prime minister, who is best remembered for his growthmanship in the then ambitious Income Doubling Plan for the 1960s. To encourage saving, it was deemed necessary to alleviate the tax burden on property. Property income was treated generously, and capital gains on securities were tax exempt. Financial interests lobbied successfully for counterreforms such as these. The Japanese tax system emerged from the Shoup Mission blueprint as "political compromises between the personal and subjective preferences, reflecting the economic interests of at least the most powerful and best organized individuals and groups concerned."[6] It was this tax system that was to prevail for the next three decades with relatively minor modifications.[7]

Economic Changes over the Subsequent Three Decades

We have seen that in the period immediately following the occupation, Japanese tax laws were geared to encourage capital accumulation, and considerations of distributional equity were ignored. There are conflicts between the two objectives, and to see how such inherent conflicts emerged, let us take an overview of Japan's economic changes since 1952. The period is conveniently demarcated at 1973–74.

The High-Growth Period: 1952–73. By the time the Japanese tax system had come into being, the Japanese economy had entered a growth orbit it was to follow at full tilt for the next two decades. Economic growth accelerated from the 1950s to the 1960s. The need for capital accumulation intensified (see table 1 for data). A salient feature of Japanese growth in this period was the match between capital formation and saving on an expanding scale without much strain on the economy.

As there was "wide agreement in Japanese government and business circles that the tax system should be actively used to promote economic growth,"[8]

TABLE 1
Japan's Economic Growth,
Gross Capital Formation (GCF),
and Household Saving
(*In percentages*)

Period	Economic Growth Rate[a]	GCF (total) GNP	GCF (private) GNP	Household Saving Rate[b]
1952–59	6.4	27.3	20.1	10.3[c]
1960–73	11.0	36.1	27.4	17.4[c]
1974–81	3.8	32.7	23.2	20.9

[a]Average annual compound rate of growth of GNP in constant prices for 1951–59, 1959–73, and 1973–81.

[b]Household savings divided by household disposable income where households exclude nonprofit institutions.

[c]Before 1964, extrapolated from the old series.

SOURCE: Keizai Kiakkuchō, *Kokumin shotoku tōkei nempō* (Annual report on national income statistics) (Tokyo: Government Printing Office, 1978 and 1983).

measures were taken to encourage capital accumulation on both the investment and saving sides.[9] On the saving side, which is the concern of this study, measures included zero or low tax on interest and dividend income, low property tax, tax exemption of capital gains on sales of securities, and tax preferences on farm and nonfarm business income.

Among households, wage and salary workers received the fewest tax preferences. Their incomes were most accurately captured by the tax authorities. Further, as their nominal incomes rose with economic growth, they moved into higher tax brackets. Fortunately, the fiscal scale of the government remained small in Japan (see table 2). By renouncing national defense, the government was exempted from spending much on unproductive armaments. The social security system was still underdeveloped and accounted for a relatively small fraction of public expenditure. The civil service was relatively small, and the pay scale for government workers remained more modest than that in the private sector. As economic growth tended to raise government revenue faster than government expenditure under progressive personal income taxation, the government was able to pay back fiscal dividends in the form of personal income tax cuts, especially by raising standard deductions. Tax cuts became an almost regular annual ritual in the high-growth period. This helped to keep tax inequities at bay.

Slow but steady changes took place in government finance through this period. As shown in table 3, there was a steady shift of national tax revenue from indirect to direct taxes. By the end of the period under study, national tax revenue consisted of three broadly equal parts of personal income tax, corporate income tax, and indirect tax. This outcome was a deliberate choice of the Ministry of Finance.[10]

Local tax revenue must be added to national tax revenue to get the total tax burden. As shown in table 4, the latter was rising slightly relative to national tax revenue, reaching about one half of national tax revenue by the early 1970s. The major source of local tax revenue collected by prefectural and municipal governments is local income tax on households and corporations; property tax forms a relatively minor portion.

The Low-Growth Period since 1974. The high-growth period came to an end in 1973, coincident with the first oil shock. A severe inflation in 1974 and a recession in 1975 opened the new period. Compared with other countries, Japan recovered from the stagflation fairly quickly, but the growth rate decelerated considerably, giving rise to structural disequilibria in the economy.

First, the need for capital formation declined in the private sector, especially in the corporate business sector. While the household saving rate was falling from its peak of 24 percent in 1974, it still hovered around 20 percent in the early 1980s. Since households' capital formation was also falling due to weakened demand for housing investment, the household sector remained a net lender to the rest of the economy. Thus, the Japanese economy found itself for the first time with an excess of private saving.[11]

This situation would have thrown the Japanese economy into a Keynesian unemployment situation unless excess saving in the private sector had been

TABLE 2

General Government Account

Percentage of Gross Domestic Product

Period	1951–54ᵃ	1955–59ᵃ	1960–64ᵃ	1965–69ᵃ	1965–69ᵃ	1970–74	1975–79	1980–82
Current receipts								
indirect tax	9.5	8.8	8.3	7.5	7.1	7.0	6.9	7.5
direct tax	8.6	6.7	7.7	7.8	7.4	9.2	9.4	11.2
on households	4.8	3.4	3.4	3.9	3.8	4.8	5.1	6.5
on corporations	3.8	3.3	4.3	3.9	3.6	4.4	4.3	4.7
social security contributions	1.9	2.3	2.7	3.5	4.0	4.7	6.8	7.7
property income receivable	.6	1.1	1.3	.7	.7	1.0	1.4	2.1
Subtotal	20.6	18.9	20.0	19.5	19.2	21.9	24.5	28.5
(1) Total	21.1	19.4	20.7	20.2	19.4	22.1	24.7	28.7
Current disbursements								
government final consumption	10.7	9.6	8.8	8.7	7.7	8.2	9.9	10.1
social security benefits	} 2.8	1.7	2.2	2.8	3.2	3.9	6.9	8.3
social assistance grants		2.0	1.6	1.5	1.4	1.4	2.1	2.2
subsidies	.8	.3	.5	.8	.9	1.2	1.3	1.5
property income payable	.4	.5	.4	.5	.5	.8	1.9	3.4
Subtotal	14.7	14.1	13.5	14.3	13.7	15.5	22.1	25.5
(2) Total	14.8	14.4	13.6	14.4	13.9	15.6	22.5	25.9

(3) Saving = (1) – (2)	6.7	5.5	7.5	6.3	5.5	6.5	2.3	2.8
Consumption of fixed capital	.8	.9	.8	1.1	.5	.4	.5	.6
Subtotal	7.5	6.4	8.3	7.4	6.0	6.9	2.8	3.4
Gross accumulation	…	…	…	…	…	6.7	2.4	3.2
of which:								
(4) Gross capital formation	4.3	3.8	4.8	4.9	4.5	5.2	5.7	6.3
Purchases of land, net	…	…	…	…	…	.7	.8	1.0
(5) Net lending	…	…	…	…	…	.9	–3.9	–4.2
(6) Saving – gross capital formation = (3) – (4)	2.4	1.7	2.7	2.4	1.0	1.8	–3.4	–3.5

[a]Percent of gross national product.
SOURCE: See table 1.

TABLE 3

Composition of National Tax Revenue by Source,
Selected Fiscal Years, 1950–1983

(In percentages)

Year	Total revenue[a]	Direct taxes	Personal income tax	(Withheld at source)	(Self-assessed)	Corporate income tax	Inheritance tax	Indirect taxes[b]
1950	100.0	53.7	38.6	22.3	16.3	14.7	.5	46.3
1955	100.0	50.8	29.7	22.8	6.9	20.5	.6	49.2
1960	100.0	54.2	21.7	16.3	5.4	31.8	.7	45.8
1965	100.0	59.5	29.9	22.0	7.9	28.3	1.3	40.5
1970	100.0	66.0	31.2	22.2	9.0	33.0	1.8	34.0
1975	100.0	69.3	37.8	27.3	10.5	28.5	2.1	30.7
1980	100.0	71.1	38.7	29.1	9.6	30.8	1.6	28.9
1981[c]	100.0	70.1	38.7	29.2	9.5	31.0	1.6	29.9
1982[c]	100.0	70.4	39.3	29.3	9.9	31.3	1.8	29.6
1983[d]	100.0	70.7	40.5	31.7	8.8	27.8	2.3	29.7

[a]Tax revenue plus stamp receipts plus government monopoly profits.
[b]Including stamp receipts and government monopoly profits.
[c]Budgetary figures (including supplementary budget).
[d]Budgetary figures (initial budget).
SOURCE: Ministry of Finance, as reported in Tōyō Keizai Shimpō Sha, ed., *Keizai tōkei nenkan (Economic statistics yearbook)* (Tokyo: Tōyō Keizai Shimpō Sha, 1983 *and earlier issues*).

siphoned off by government deficits. It was therefore fortuitous that the government was forced to go heavily into deficit spending at this time.

Even though the Japanese government remained small in fiscal scale compared with other advanced countries, it was succumbing to the pressure of expenditure rising faster than GNP. One cause was an expansion of welfare programs, including social security and medical insurance schemes. Initially, the social security fund was able to maintain a surplus as contributions exceeded benefits paid while the fund was being built up. However, as time went on, more and more contributors became old enough to be eligible for benefits, and the fund's balance began to shift the other way. Other expenditures also tended to increase, in large part due to the government wage bill. Both the government work force and the government worker wage rate were rising faster than their private-sector counterparts. Thus, as seen in table 2, government expenditures started to rise sharply in the late 1970s.

But the government revenue was not able to keep pace: revenue from corporate income tax was depressed while the economy was not growing rapidly and revenue from indirect taxes fell below the one-third benchmark. This slack in revenue had to be taken up by the personal income tax, particularly by wage and salary workers who could not evade tax withheld from their paychecks. The trend since 1974 is clear in table 3. The government could no longer afford tax cuts. After some nominal cuts, it froze the personal income tax schedule as of 1978. Thus, the tax burden continued to increase on worker households in the form of both income tax and social security contributions.

Yet government revenues still fell short of expenditures. The national government financed the shortfall by selling "deficit" bonds, which now total one-third of annual GNP.[12] To balance the budget under these circumstances is a stupendous task, and the government has to maintain a pretense of achieving a balanced budget in the near future.

Thus, the Japanese economy has been playing an entirely new ball game. But the rules have not changed. Private saving is not needed as much as it was in the high-growth period. Yet the same tax laws prevail that have encouraged and protected savings. Consequently, inequity in sharing the tax burden has been rising.

2. MAIN FEATURES OF THE CURRENT TAX SYSTEM
FOR THE HOUSEHOLD ECONOMY

Taxes on Income

Personal income consists of many types, the most important of which are wage and salary income, proprietors' business income, property income (interest, dividends, and real estate), and realized capital gains on sales of property. The most prominent feature of Japan's personal income taxation is that incomes from different sources are often taxed on different schedules instead of being added up into total household income.

There are two types of tax collection—those withheld at source and those paid on annual self-assessed returns. In the main, a single personal income tax schedule applies to both. The following description is based on the tax schedule in force from 1974 to 1983.[13]

Wages and Salary Income. Both national and local income taxes are withheld from workers' monthly paychecks, and any necessary adjustments for the year are made on the final paycheck of the calendar year. Workers are not required to file tax returns unless their taxable income exceeds 10 million yen (15 million yen in the 1984 revision). When a household contains more than one wage earner, each worker is taxed separately.

Taxable wage income is arrived at by subtracting from gross earnings (1) a standard deduction (*kyuyo shotoku kōjo*), which varies with earnings, (2) exemptions which are 0.20 million yen (0.33 million yen in the 1984 revision) times the household size (the income earner, the spouse, and other dependents), and (3) other special deductions including employee contributions to social security schemes.

During the rapid-growth period, annual tax cuts were introduced mainly through improved deductions and exemptions. For a standard family of four (one earner, a nonworking spouse, and two children), zero taxable income after (1) and (2) corresponds to gross income of 0.40 million yen in 1963 and 2.015 million yen since 1978 (2.357 million yen in the 1984 revision). This nontaxable limit is relatively favorable to low-income households.

Japan's income-tax schedule is very progressive: the highest marginal tax rate

TABLE 4

The Tax Burden

Percent of Net National Product

Selected Fiscal Years, 1950–1983

Year	Total	National tax	Local tax
1950	22.4	16.9	5.6
1955	18.1	12.8	5.2
1960	19.2	13.6	5.6
1965	18.2	12.3	5.8
1970	18.9	12.8	6.2
1975	18.4	11.8	6.6
1980	22.8	14.6	8.2
1981	23.6	15.0	8.6
1982	23.7	15.0	8.7
1983[a]	23.7	15.	8.6

SOURCE: See table 3
[a]Budgetary (projection).

TABLE 5
Maximum Marginal Tax Rates
(Personal Income Tax)

Personal income tax	Taxable income in excess of (million ¥)	Marginal tax rate (%)	
		(1974–83)	1984–)
Central government	80	75	70
Prefectural government	1.5	4	4
Municipal government	49	14	14
Total		93	88

SOURCES: *Yomiuri Shimbun*, Jan. 11, 1984, and Pechman and Kaizuka, "Taxation," table 5–16, p. 376.

(in excess of taxable income of 80 million yen and over) has been 93 percent (to be lowered to 88 percent in the 1984 revision) (see table 5). As far as wage and salary income is concerned, this feature is not particularly relevant. In Japan, the distribution of labor income is relatively equal. In 1981, average worker earnings (gross income) were 3.35 million yen according to the *Basic Wage Survey*, while those of a chief executive (president) of a company with equity above 100 million yen were 29.17 million yen on average. Thus, with separate taxation of property income, even the highest paid salary earner would not be subject to the confiscatory marginal tax rate. Income-tax payers with taxable income in excess of 40 million yen make up less than 0.5 percent of all income-tax payers.

For an international comparison of the income-tax burden on wage earners, see table 6. The data in the table are limited to the national (federal) tax, and the date of comparison is January 1982. The household is a standard four-person family with one income earner. The table reveals that, with the exception of France, Japan's personal income tax on wage earners is lighter than others in terms of both the zero taxable income level and the starting marginal tax rate.

The American tax schedule is similar to Japan's. The marginal tax rate (t) is seen to be a linear function of gross income (Y in million yen) for both Japan and the United States. For Y<10 million yen, the following equations approximate the relation:

$$t = \begin{cases} .028\,Y + .0440, & Y \geq 2.015 \text{ (Japan)} \\ .034\,Y + .0625, & Y \geq 1.695 \text{ ($7400 at ¥229/$) (U.S.)} \end{cases}$$

Integrating the above equations, we approximate the average tax rate ($\bar{t}$), i.e., tax payment/gross income, as follows:

$$\bar{t} = \begin{cases} .014\ Y + .0440 - .146/Y\ \text{(Japan)} \\ .017\ Y + .0625 - .154/Y\ \text{(U.S.)} \end{cases}$$

In 1980, wages and salaries per employee were 2.75 million yen in Japan and 3.62 million yen in the United States (both based on the National Income and Product Accounts [NIPA]). From the $\bar{t}$ functions above, we obtain

	$\bar{t}$	
Y	Japan	U.S.
2.75	.030	.053
3.62	.055	.082

Three factors account for the higher U.S. tax burden: the lower exemption level, the stronger tax progressivity, and the higher average income.

Interest and Dividend Income. Wage and salary workers are the majority of individual taxpayers. Withholding income tax at the source for this group leads to tremendous cost savings for the tax administration, especially since most members of the group are not required to file tax returns. Their status as exempt from the filing requirement is feasible only because other types of income that worker households may receive are not taxed together with wage and salary income.

Even when property income is subject to income tax, interest and dividend income are virtually tax free as far as most worker households are concerned

TABLE 6
Personal Income Tax Schedule (Central Government)
for a Standard Worker Household as of January 1982

	Japan	U.S.	U.K.	West Germany	France
Minimum gross income before taxation (million ¥)	2.015	1.694	.918	1.254	2.323
Marginal tax rate (%)					
Minimum	10	12	30	22	5
Maximum	75	50	60	56	60
Income steps (number)	19	12	6	na	12
Tax returns	separate	separate or joint	joint	separate or joint	joint

NOTE: A worker household consists of one income earner, a spouse, and two dependent children.

SOURCE: Ministry of Finance, as quoted by H. Ishi, "Zaisei kaikaku no shiten" (Focus of tax reform), *Keizai Hyōron*, vol. 32 (Jan. 1983), table 5, p. 47.

because of a special tax-exemption system that qualifies each *individual* (not each household) for tax-exempt status up to certain ceilings on principals.

Interest on postal savings is nontaxable (since 1920) up to a principal amount of 3 million yen. In addition, a system of tax-exempt small savings treats as tax exempt the interest on small bank accounts up to a principal of 3 million yen, on securities such as public bonds (purchased within a year of issue) up to a principal of 3 million yen (*toku-yu*), and on "Savings for Worker Asset Formation" (instituted in 1971) up to a principal of 5 million yen. This is the *maru-yu* system, which dates back to 1941 and was started to encourage small savers to help finance the war. To obtain the advantages the system offers, individuals are required only to file applications with the tax office via depository financial institutions.

Table 7 shows the total and tax-exempt amounts of personal savings for 1971–81. In per capita terms, personal savings are below the tax-exempt ceiling.[14] Most households pay no tax on interest income. Thus, though the nominal interest rate on savings has been low (5 to 7 percent), the after-tax interest rate has been at an internationally comparable level.

Beyond the legal limit on tax-exempt interest, households may either have income tax withheld at the source at a flat rate of 35 percent or pay income tax on self-assessed tax returns after the withholding of tax at the source at a flat rate of 20 percent.[15] A special form of the former is anonymous time deposits, which require no identification of depositors.[16]

Dividend income is treated similarly; it is nontaxable up to 0.1 million yen per account. Although, unlike wage income, the property income of household members must be added to the taxable income of the principal household income earner when in excess of the sum of 10 million yen (to be raised to 15 million yen in the 1984 revision), it is apparent that a very substantial part of interest income is untaxed and a remaining small portion is taxed at a moderate rate, nowhere near the maximum marginal rate of 93 percent.

This aspect of the tax code makes tax evasion easy in Japan. First, individuals can hold multiple tax-exempt accounts enabling them to exceed the tax-exempt limits in the aggregate. Moreover, the tax authorities have thus far been unable to process the millions of applications for tax-exempt accounts they receive.[17] Further, individuals can set up these accounts under fictitious names with false addresses. All that depositors need to withdraw cash from such an account is the seal that was used to open it. Taxable deposits may also be opened in fictitious names although tax is withheld at the source at a flat rate of 20 percent. Anonymous accounts are perfectly legal. Since tax offices are understaffed, they can detect only flagrant cases of tax evasion.

It appears that worker households account for no more than 40 percent of personal savings, both total and nontaxable.[18] Thus, this generous tax treatment of property income greatly benefits high-income households.

Business Income. Entrepreneurial income from an unincorporated business is an important category of personal income in Japan since individual proprietors are still an important fraction of the labor force[19] although their importance has

TABLE 7

Personal Savings by Taxable Status

(A) Personal savings and household disposable income (*In trillion* ¥)

Fiscal year	Household disposable income (1)	Personal savings[a] (end of year) (2)	of which: tax-exempt (3)	(2)/(1) (%) (4)	(3)/(1) (%) (5)	(3)/(2) (%) (6)
1972	62.6	90.5	39.0	144.5	62.3	43.1
1973	78.4	108.2	48.6	138.1	62.0	44.9
1974	98.4	128.9	64.8	131.0	65.8	50.3
1975	110.7	154.6	81.4	139.7	73.6	52.7
1976	123.7	180.6	98.8	146.0	79.9	54.7
1977	136.0	210.2	116.5	154.6	85.7	55.4
1978	146.1	242.0	136.7	165.6	93.5	56.5
1979	157.9	274.3	155.6	173.7	98.5	56.7
1980	170.7	307.8	180.0	180.3	105.4	58.5
1981	180.6	343.7	202.2	190.3	112.0	57.3

(B) Tax-exempt savings as percent of total personal savings, end of fiscal year

Fiscal year	Small savers (maru-yu)		Small public bonds (toku-yu)	Zaikei savings[b]	Deposits for tax payment	Postal savings	Total tax-exempt
	Deposits	Securities					
1972	27.8	1.3	.3	.06	.10	13.6	43.1
1973	28.6	1.6	.3	.2	.10	14.2	44.9
1974	32.6	1.9	.3	.3	.07	15.1	50.3
1975	33.7	2.0	.5	.5	.08	15.9	52.7
1976	34.0	2.1	.9	.7	.07	16.9	54.7
1977	33.3	2.1	1.1	.9	.06	17.9	55.4
1978	33.4	2.1	1.2	1.1	.05	18.6	56.5
1979	33.3	2.0	1.5	1.3	.06	18.9	56.7
1980	33.2	1.8	1.9	1.4	.05	20.1	58.5
1981	33.0	1.8	2.1	1.5	.05	20.2	57.3

[a]Personal savings are the outstanding balance (personal accounts) of deposits and savings (at ordinary banks, sōgo (mutual) banks, shinkin (credit association) banks, credit cooperatives, agricultural cooperatives, fishery cooperatives, post offices, and labor credit associations), trusts, insurance, and securities.

[b]Worker savings for asset formation (excluding those included in postal savings).

SOURCES: Nihon Ginkō, Keizai tōkei nempō (Economic statistics annual) (Tokyo: Bank of Japan, 1982), tables 80 and 82, pp. 157–58, except A(1), which is from Keizai Kikakucho, Kokumin shotoku tōkei nempō.

continued to decline with the contraction of the farm sector. Proprietors are required to file self-assessed tax returns. They may file ordinary "white" returns, which allow certain itemized deductions. The standard personal income-tax schedule applies to taxable business income. Business owners, however, can get a better break by filing "blue" returns, which entitle them to a number of business-expense deductions in return for meeting the minimum bookkeeping requirement. The best tax break is a clause that allows a business owner to separate wages paid to family members, including his spouse, who are engaged in full-time work in the business. This measure became effective in 1967. Since lower rates apply when these wages are taxed separately, the proprietor can allegedly save as much as 26 percent on his tax bill. An even better break was introduced in 1974. Proprietors who file blue returns have been allowed to treat themselves as quasi-corporations (*minashi hōjin*), which means that, in addition to the family wage bill, a proprietor can now separate his own remuneration from business income. What is left over as taxable business income is taxed at the national level as corporate income at a rate of 23.9 percent up to 7 million yen and 34.1 percent above that limit, a rate comparable with the corporate income tax on distributed profits. Thus, private business owners receive very generous tax treatment.[20]

Realized Capital Gains. Capital gains on sales of securities have been tax exempt except for professional traders. Capital gains on sales of real estate have been subject to frequent changes in taxation in the last dozen years, reflecting the importance of real estate, especially land, as a form of household wealth. There were substantial tax-rate increases in the 1970s. The March 1982 revision reduced this tax to some extent. At the moment, the tax rates are as follows: A property acquired ten or more years ago is considered to have been under "long-term" ownership. For the former, capital gains up to 40 million yen are taxed separately from other incomes at flat rates of 20 percent (national) and 8 percent (local). Above 40 million yen, one half of capital gains are added to the total taxable income of a seller household.[21] For the latter, capital gains are taxed at whichever is larger: separately taxed at 40 percent (national) and 12 percent (local), or 110 percent of the tax liability attributable to the capital gain when taxed together with other taxable incomes.

Putting all these together, the following has been the general picture regarding the incidence of personal income tax in Japan. A substantial portion of wage earners used to be entirely exempt from tax liability (about 30 percent in the early 1970s). Those who paid taxes were taxed lightly. Farmers and nonfarm business proprietors have managed to pay relatively little tax by virtue of the popular blue returns. Property income is either wholly tax exempt or taxed lightly. Capital gains on sales of land have been taxed relatively heavily, but they are unearned income enjoyed only by a handful of wealthy households.

Self-assessed taxpayers[22] are (1) earners of high salaries, (2) owners of non-corporate businesses, including private medical practitioners, (3) rentiers, and (4) sellers of real estate. In recent years the majority of top taxpayers has belonged to category 4,[23] supplemented by combinations of 1 and 3, namely, chief executives who are founders of their own rapidly expanding corporate businesses.

Taxes on Property

Property Tax. The tax on real estate is collected by the municipal government at the standard rate of 1.4 percent on its officially assessed value. Since the assessed value is said to be about one-third of market value, the effective tax burden is relatively minor. In 1980, for instance, the total amount of the property tax was 2.8 trillion yen while the market value of privately owned land (beginning of the year) was 544 trillion yen (National Income and Product Accounts [NIPA] estimate), which implies an effective tax rate of 0.5 percent. The property tax is a relatively small fraction of local tax revenue.[24]

Farmland in metropolitan suburbs has been especially favorably treated in this regard. Farmers hold onto their farms in anticipation of further land price increases. Meanwhile, the property tax they pay is based on their property's assessed value as farmland, which is far below its potential value as residential land. Despite a number of measures taken to change this situation, their actual impact has been limited.

Inheritance Tax. Another tax on property (not limited to real estate) is the inheritance tax. The taxable value of an inheritance is obtained by subtracting a base deduction of 20 million yen and exemptions equal to 4 million yen times the number of statutory heirs.

The inheritance tax is as light in Japan as elsewhere. The White Paper on Inheritance Tax for 1981, prepared by the National Tax Agency, reports 32,000 persons who declared inheritance tax returns, 4 percent of a total of 720,000 deaths in that year. The aggregate value of reported inheritances was 3,808 billion yen or 110 million yen per inheritor. (Compare with the average net worth of 25 million yen per household at the end of 1980 [NIPA].) The inheritance tax amounted to 538.7 billion yen or 14.1 percent of inheritances. Land accounts for 68 percent of inheritances, showing the overwhelming importance of land ownership in the wealth of Japan's richest families (*Yomiuri Shimbun,* June 18, 1983).

3. TAX LAWS AND THE SAVING RATE

It is one thing to note that Japanese tax laws were geared to encouraging saving and investment. Whether they really contributed to keeping Japanese household saving and business capital formation at a high level is another question. Indeed, one can find contrasting views on the effectiveness of the tax laws. Pechman and Kaizuka,[25] after reviewing possible effects of tax measures on private saving and investment, concluded that "there is little evidence that the tax structure contributed significantly to the remarkable economic record of the

1950s and 1960s." However, there are those who believe otherwise. For instance, the writers of the *Economic Report of the President*[26] think that it is governmental encouragement of saving and investment that enabled Japan and continental Europe to maintain higher growth with higher proportions of capital formation than the United States in the 1970s. President Reagan repeated the same opinion in his address to Japan's National Diet on November 11, 1983. This view seems to be shared by many, especially by noneconomists.

We have already reviewed changes in the household saving rate in Japan (table 1). The average saving rate continued to rise until 1974, when it peaked at 24 percent. Even in the low-growth period following the first oil shock, the rate remained as high as 20 percent. Over time, saving rates of earners of various types of income seem to have undergone broadly similar changes, changes due to the influence of macroeconomic forces.[27] These forces include varying rates of economic growth and inflation coupled with persistent structural changes in the economy. Examples of these structural changes are the shrinking of the farm sector as steady migrations from the countryside to the cities proceeded, and the rapid aging of the population with attendant effects on labor market conditions. By and large, these kinds of macroeconomic influences are, indeed, independent of tax laws. In this regard, Pechman and Kaizuka are right.

Let us consider this point in a little more depth, however. From the *Family Income and Expenditure Survey* we can confirm that worker households save as much of their disposable income as do all other households.[28] The same source reveals that 94.5 percent of their income is wages and salaries. Of the remaining 5.5 percent, property income is about 1 percent.[29] Thus, even if property income is wholly tax free *and* saved, it does not explain worker households' high propensity to save. Ordinary worker households save mainly for their retirement in addition to meeting the more immediate needs of purchasing houses and durables and also preparing for anticipated heavy future expenses such as children's education. If taxes become heavier, they readjust their consumption-saving plans over their lifetimes. The result is a reduction in current saving while current disposable income is also reduced. Hence, for workers households, the saving/disposable income ratio is not likely to be very sensitive to taxes. However, we have attributed roughly 60 percent of taxable and nontaxable personal savings to nonworker households. Their propensity to save may be quite sensitive to income-tax provisions. They are relatively affluent, and what they save may be mainly passed on to their progeny. A heavier tax reduces their disposable income from property. If they give priority to their current consumption over bequests, saving takes the brunt of the consumption-saving realignment. Their saving/disposable income ratio would thus be adversely influenced by taxation.[30] Japan's low tax on property income may therefore have contributed to raising rentiers' propensity to save.

Now let us look at the functional distribution of household income. Table 8 compares this distribution in Japan and the United States for the year 1978 (chosen for its relative normality), based on the NIPA data. Broadly speaking, the two economies exhibit similar economic structures in terms of functional dis-

TABLE 8
Composition of Household Income, 1978
(*In percentages*)

	Japan	U.S.
Wages and salaries	62.9	66.5
Employers contributions to social security	4.8	5.5
Employers' contributions to private pension funds	2.7	6.0
Proprietors' income	14.6	7.1
Property income	12.0	10.9
Interest	6.9	8.9
Less interest on consumer debt	−0.2	−2.2
Dividends	1.6	2.7
Rent, net	0.8	1.1
Imputed rent on owner-occupied dwellings	3.0	0.5
Social security benefits	9.6	9.3
Less social security contributions	−9.0	−9.6
Social assistance grants	3.3	2.9
Casualty insurance claims	0.5	1.0
Less net casualty insurance premiums	−0.5	. . .
Current transfers, received	6.4	0.6
Less current transfers, paid	−7.3	−0.1
Household income	100.0	100.0
Taxes and nontax payments	6.4	13.9
Consumption expenditure	74.3	80.3
Saving	19.2	5.8

SOURCES: Organization for Economic Cooperation and Development (OECD), *National Accounts of OECD Countries, 1963–1981* (Paris: OECD, 1983), supplemented by Keizai Kikakuchō, *Kokumin shotoku tōkei nempō*, 1983, and *Survey of Current Business*, July 1982.

tribution, especially when proprietors' income is split between labor and capital. Proprietors' income accounts for a much larger part of total income in Japan, showing that small unincorporated businesses are still thriving in Japan. Property income in large part comes in the form of interest received on savings accounts, while dividends make up a smaller fraction in Japan because individual stock ownership has been steadily falling there. As we have seen, interest income is either untaxed or taxed relatively lightly in Japan. Thus, Japan's lighter tax on business and property income may also have contributed to general households' high propensity to save in Japan as compared with the United States. However, nearly two-thirds of household income is accounted for by wages and salaries, and for this component, income tax may have very little effect on saving.

A related point worthy of mention in this connection is that there is much less double taxation of capital income in Japan than in the United States. The tax burden on corporate profits has been roughly similar in the two countries, though it has risen in Japan and fallen in the United States since the mid-1970s.[31] However, debt/equity structure has differed significantly between the two, as shown by the data in table 9 for nonfinancial corporations in 1978. In book value, the debt/equity ratio was 86/14 in Japan and 41/59 in the United States. Interestingly, the overall rate of return on the book value of total assets was similar in the two countries. Income (profits, rent, and interest) was 10.44 percent in Japan and 10.89 percent in the United States, before depreciation and tax liability, and 4.81 percent and 4.37 percent, respectively, afterwards. However, the disposition of after-tax income was quite different. For net profits and interest, we have the following (as percentages of total assets):

	Japan	U.S.
Undistributed profits	1.30	2.65
Dividends	.43	1.32
Interest	3.13	1.30
Total	4.87	5.27

It thus follows that in Japan a substantial part of corporate income is paid out as interest that is free of the corporate tax and relatively little is paid in dividends. Double taxation of capital income is therefore a minor issue in Japan.

Thus, we have seen that the saving rate for worker households is unlikely to be sensitive to tax laws, but nonworker households, which account for roughly 60 percent of taxable and nontaxable personal savings may be quite sensitive to taxes on property income. In addition, low to zero tax on interest income contributes to households' high propensity to save, although business and property income is admittedly not the major component of household income. Furthermore, Japanese corporations are not saddled with the double taxation of capital income as are their U.S. counterparts.

4. THE EVOLUTION OF HOUSEHOLD WEALTH

Savings accumulate as wealth. Let us therefore look at the stock of household wealth. Table 10 compares Japan and the United States at the end of 1980 for composition of household wealth as multiples of household disposable income. Though care must be taken in comparing the two countries because of differences in definitions and coverages, the table suffices for broad comparisons. First, a few well-known features are worthy of comment.

In Japan, net worth is some five times as large as household disposable income. In the United States, the ratio is a little over four. But when land is excluded from wealth, the ratio is 2.4 versus 4.0. Japanese households still have some distance to go in wealth accumulation compared to U.S. households.

It is evident that land is an extremely important component of household assets in Japan, accounting for more than half of household net worth. By contrast, land is only 8 percent of net worth in the United States.[32]

About 20 percent of Japan's net fixed assets are noncorporate business assets.[33] Thus, dwellings and structures are about 75 percent of disposable income in Japan compared with a little over 100 percent in the United States.

The net stock of consumer durables is also relatively low in Japan in relation to income, reflecting, among other things, limited housing space. Of this stock, motor vehicles account for 28 percent in Japan and 36 percent in the U.S.[34]

As is well known, Japanese households keep most of their financial assets in fixed-claim assets, most prominently in savings accounts at banks and post offices. Corporate equity is only a very small fraction of total net worth.

Having ascertained the current state of Japanese household wealth, let us now see how it has evolved over the last three decades (see table 11). Here we must emphasize the critical role of land in the dynamics of household asset formation.

First of all, while household saving accumulates as household wealth, household wealth is more than the cumulative sum of past savings. Some assets appreciate in market value and bring about windfall gains to their owners. In Japan, since households own little corporate equity, capital gains are realized largely on privately owned land and to a smaller extent on dwellings. As is readily apparent from table 11, which traces changes in the relative importance of various types of assets and liabilities since 1953, land has been the single most important item in the portfolio of household wealth. Let us now review how land prices have changed since the end of World War II.[35]

When World War II ended, land prices were depressed relative to the general price level. Houses, factories, offices, and stores in metropolitan areas had been razed by air raids. The population moved en masse to villages for temporary shelter, swelling the farm population to more than half the total population. Urban land prices were thus kept low. The situation with respect to farmland was galvanized by a sweeping land reform introduced as a pillar of the occupation forces' democratization measures. Farm landowners were forced to sell their landholdings to tenants at nominal prices. Hence, farmland prices were also kept low. The land/income ratio was very depressed at this time. The distribution of wealth in 1949, which was also deeply affected by the dissolution of the zaibatsu, was no doubt the least unequal in Japan's modern economic history.

When the Japanese economy recovered and started to grow, slowly at first in the 1950s and then rapidly in the 1960s, the population began to move back to the cities, especially the three metropolitan areas (Tokyo-Yokohama, Kyoto-Osaka-Kobe, and Nagoya) which are the major centers of the country's industrial and administrative activities. The rising demand for urban land that accompanied this trend was exacerbated in the extreme by only a very small proportion of

TABLE 9

Returns on Total Assets (book value)
Nonfinancial Corporations, 1978
(*In percentages*)

	Japan		U.S.	
Capital consumption allowance	3.91		4.60[a]	
Corporate profits	3.17		4.99	
Profits before tax	3.45		6.26	
Tax liability	1.72		2.35	
Profits after tax	1.73		3.92	
Dividends, net	.43	.63 (paid)	1.32	2.02 (paid)
		−.20 (received)		−.71 (received)
Undistributed profits	1.30		2.65	
Inventory valuation adjustment	−.29		−.84	
Capital consumption adjustment	. . .	.32 (received)	−.43	
	.23	−.09 (paid)		
Rent, net			. . .	
Interest, net	3.13	4.21 (paid, monetary)	1.30	2.70 (paid, monetary)
		−1.08 (rec'd, monetary)		−1.11 (rec'd, monetary)
				−.39 (rec'd imputed)
Total	10.44		10.89	

Assets	100.0	100.0
Tangible	52.3	73.4
Reproducible	46.2	65.2
Land	6.1	8.2
Financial	47.7	26.6
Liabilities	85.7	41.2
Net worth	14.3	58.8

SOURCES: *Japan.* Keizai Kikakuchō 1982 for returns and assets (in current values); Ministry of Finance, *Hōjin Kigyō Tōkei Nempō* for assets (in book values). *United States Survey of Current Business,* July 1982 for returns; Department of Commerce (U.S.), *Satistical Abstract of the United States,* 1981 (Dec. 1981), table No. 915, p. 541 for assets (in book values).
aIncludes capital consumption adjustment.

TABLE 10
Household Assets, Liabilities, and Net Worth
Percentage of Household Disposable Income, 1980

	Japan		U.S.
Reproducible assets	117.8	*Reproducible assets*	177.5
Net fixed assets	92.9	Net household structures	109.9
Consumer durables	19.6	Consumer durables	55.6
Inventories	5.3	Inventories	12.0
Nonreproducible			
tangible assets	290.0		
Land	273.9	Land	32.6
Urban	206.1		
Farm	67.8		
Forests	15.6		
Fisheries	.5		
Financial assets	199.3	*Financial assets*	306.0
Fixed-claim assets	158.1	Fixed-claim assets	122.6
Currency	8.9	Currency and	
Demand deposits	16.3	checkable deposits	14.8
Time deposits	114.3	Time deposits &	
Long-term securities	16.6	money market	
Others	2.0	fund shares	76.1
		Credit market	
		instruments	27.2
		Security credit	.7
		Others	3.8
Equities held	41.1	Equities held	183.4
Corporate equities		Corporate stock	55.6
(market value)	16.4	Noncorporate nonfarm	
Life insurance equities	24.7	equity	62.6
		Farm business equity	37.5
		Estates & trusts	15.7
		Others	12.0
Total assets	607.1	Total assets	516.1

Japan's land area being habitable, and most of the population was concentrated in the very narrow strip where these three metropolitan areas are located. Urban land prices skyrocketed, rising by a factor of 78 from 1950 to 1970 according to the Japan Real Estate Institute's average residential land price index. Farmland prices rose commensurately in metropolitan vicinities.

Consequently, the aggregate value of urban land continued to rise relative to income toward the end of the rapid-growth period of the last two decades. The

TABLE 10 (continued)

	Japan		U.S.
Liabilities	76.4	*Liabilities*	80.8
Private loans	45.4	Credit market	
Government loans	16.1	instruments	78.8
Current credit	14.9	Home mortgages	52.6
Others	.1	Current credit	21.5
		Bank loans, nec	1.6
		Government & policy	
		loans	3.1
		Security debt	1.3
		Others	0.7
Net worth	530.7	*Net worth*	435.2
Net worth per capita	$32233[a]	Net worth per capita	$34212
Household disposable		Household disposable	
income per capita	$6072[a]	income per capita	$7859

SOURCES: *Japan:* Keizai Kikakuchō, 1982, end-of-year values. United States: R. Ruggles and N. Ruggles, "Integrated Economic Accounts for the United States, 1947–80," *Survey of Current Business*, May 1982, p. 43, for asset values (end-of-year), and *Survey of Current Business*, July 1982, for household disposable income (the sum of personal consumption expenditure and saving).
[a] At ¥240/$1.

last two years of the high-growth period witnessed a particularly violent speculative land boom, but after this last fling, the low-growth period set in and land price increases have been relatively modest under the depressed macroeconomic conditions.

Taking a broad view, we observe that as a historical rule of thumb, the land/income ratio fluctuates at around 2.5–3.0. Thus, as a trend, the real price of land tends to grow at the same rate as the real economy. This is the trend for capital gains on land after allowing for general inflation. A little calculation shows how tremendous such gains have been.[36] Thus, landowners pocketed truly unearned wealth merely by virtue of their birthrights to pieces of land, especially when these were located in metropolitan areas. On the other hand, unless they owned their residences,[37] ordinary worker households suffered capital losses in real terms as their liquid assets depreciated under inflationary conditions.

So long as land was held by the orginal owners, its appreciation in value existed on paper. But when farmers sold land for residential conversion, they made large capital gains even after a relatively stiff tax on land sales in the 1970s. In Japan, normal practice since World War II has been to sell a house and its site as a package[38] in which the predominant proportion of the cost is the land value.

TABLE 11
Household Assets, Liabilities, and Net Worth
Percentage of Household Disposable Income in Selected Years

	1953	1955	1960	1965	1970	1975	1980
Assets, total					514.3	506.8	607.1
Tangible assets					363.3	345.9	407.8
Reproducible					83.1	100.2	117.8
Net fixed assets				44.2 {	55.3	74.3	92.9
Inventories					6.9	5.8	5.3
Consumer durables					20.9	20.1	19.6
Nonreproducible	251.5[a]	276.8[a]	342.0[a]	271.1[a]	280.2	245.7	290.0
Land	233.4	259.1	312.7	251.6	265.0	229.0	273.9
Urban	52.8	57.3	132.3	155.5	184.7	162.9	206.1
Farm, etc.	180.6	201.8	180.4	96.1	80.3	66.1	67.8
Forests	18.1	27.7	29.3	19.5	14.5	16.2	15.6
Fisheries	...	...	...	...	.7	.5	.5
Financial assets	68.4	77.1	121.5	136.5	151.1	160.8	199.3

Currency	9.9	8.2	8.4	8.5	9.6	9.2	8.9
Demand deposits	13.1	13.0	15.4	16.9	18.1	17.8	16.3
Time deposits	29.0	36.4	57.1	64.8	76.0	86.5	114.3
Long-term securities	2.4	3.1	5.0	7.4	10.3	11.7	16.6
Corporate stock (market value)	10.0	9.4	23.6	21.1	17.2	15.4	16.4
Life insurance equity	3.8	5.5	10.9	15.5	18.6	18.4	24.7
Other	.0	1.4	1.0	2.2	1.3	1.7	2.0
Liabilities, total	17.9	21.1	36.6	50.2	58.5	62.8	76.4
Private loans	11.2	13.1	23.7	30.6	31.6	37.6	45.4
Government loans					7.9	9.8	16.1
Current credit	6.7	8.0	12.9	19.6	19.0	15.3	14.9
Other					.0	.1	.1
Net worth					455.8	444.0	530.7

NOTE: Households include noncorporate business households and nonprofit institutions serving households.
[a]Excludes fisheries.

SOURCES: Keizai Kikakuchō, 1982 for 1970–80. For 1953–65, see Kazuo Sato, "Why Have the Japanese Saved So Much? On Determinants of Japanese Household Saving," unpublished paper, January 1982.

Thus, workers must part with the nest eggs they have accumulated out of their earned income in exchange for small housing sites. Sellers of land, on the other hand, dispose of illiquid assets that usually don't pay much as long as they are in use as farmland. The financial assets they receive in return for their land promise at least a fair rate of return if invested judiciously. The upshot of this exchange is that not only land and money change hands but income is redistributed within the household sector as well—from the relatively less affluent to the more affluent. As the latter are more prone to save, the average saving rate is kept high and the tendency for the rich to get richer is reinforced.

While the aggregate value of household wealth is now part of the NIPA statistics, there are no comprehensive data on its distribution among individuals. It is known that, with respect to reported incomes, inequality has been decreasing in Japan. Such measures of inequality as the Gini coefficient show Japan's income distribution to be very favorable compared with other advanced countries.[39] As far as accumulated wealth (financial wealth) is concerned, the same observation may apply. It is, however, apparent that when landownership is taken into account, the situation is completely reversed.[40]

5. THE LEGAL FRAMEWORK: RESISTANCE TO CHANGE

For a decade Japan's public finance has been in a state of imbalance. Behind this situation lies the Japanese tax system, which is geared to promote saving and investment while neglecting the issue of distributional equity. It appears that the tax system requires a fundamental overhaul in the light of new economic conditions. But such a reform has been slow in coming, not because of a want of attempts at reform but because of the strong resistance to it. In this section, we review four cases that have attracted a great deal of attention in Japan recently.

Unequal Tax Burden Depending on Occupation

Wage and salary workers have their income taxes withheld at the source, so their earned incomes are almost wholly reported to the tax offices. By contrast, individuals who are not on company payrolls turn in self-assessed income-tax returns. In addition to relatively generous business-expense deductions, they have many legal and illegal recourses for evading taxes. These individuals are farmers, nonfarm business proprietors, self-employed professionals, medical and dental practitioners, rentiers, and landowners. The alleged inequity between wage earners and other occupations has given rise to the folklore of *kuroyon* or 9-6-4, sometimes called *toh-goh-san-pin* or 10-5-3-1. The numbers, on a scale of ten, represent the proportions captured by the tax offices of what should constitute correctly measured incomes in various occupations (see table 12).

When farmers were a very important part of the labor force, it was believed difficult to assess farmers' income correctly. To a lesser extent, the same applies to nonfarm proprietors' income. As we have seen, blue returns were introduced to improve the record keeping of small businesses, which, in exchange, were allowed business cost deductions, especially wages supposedly paid to spouses and other family workers in businesses. Spreading business income in this way saves taxes—reportedly as much as 26 percent. When noncorporate enterprises are treated as quasi-corporations, they can deduct proprietors' remuneration as well, and the remainder of business income is taxed as corporate profits. In the last several years, blue returns have been submitted by 53 percent of noncorporate businesses as well as by 90 percent of corporations. Furthermore, as only one twentieth of proprietors' tax returns are currently audited and the statute of limitation on tax evasion is five years, lax bookkeeping and tax cheating have become endemic among business proprietors.[41]

Despite its longstanding popularity, the proportions 9-6-4 are merely conjectural. There has been no quantitative investigation of the issue. In March 1981, the point was raised by a Kōmeitō member in the National Diet, and the National Tax Agency was commissioned to make an official inquiry. Its report of a year later does not deal directly with the issue due to the lack of appropriate data, but it contains a table showing incomes by source for average households of each of four occupational types (see table 13). Incomes are gross income before adjustment.

Sources of income, of course, differ considerably among different types of households. As the tax burden on incomes differs by source, the overall tax burden should differ considerably even though average gross incomes are similar among these different types of households (except farmer households). The table does not report the effective tax rate but shows the proportion of households that paid taxes—83 percent for wage earners, 38 percent for nonfarm proprietors, and 10 percent for farmers. This finding seems to give some support to the 9-6-4 contention.

TABLE 12

The Proportion of Income
Allegedly Reported to Tax Authorities by Occupation

The proportion		Occupation	Remark
(A)	(B)		
9/10	10/10	Wage and salary worker	Income tax withheld at source
6/10	5/10	Nonfarm proprietor	Self-assessed return
4/10	3/10	Farmer	Self-assessed return
. . .	1/10	Politician	Most revenue un-reported

NOTE: (A) = *Kuroyon*; (B) = *toh-goh-san-pin*

TABLE 13
Annual Income by Type of Household

Type of Income	Wage and Salary Earner		Nonfarm Proprietor		Farmer		Other	
	¥000	%	¥000	%	¥000	%	¥000	%
Business income								
nonfarm	48	1.4	1696	56.4	30	1.4	12	.3
farm	20	.6	14	.5	520	23.0	14	.4
Real estate income	202	5.9	122	4.1	29	1.3	1131	32.0
Interest-dividend income	48	1.4	16	.5	1	.0	42	1.2
Wages and salaries	2922	85.3	954	31.7	1187	52.5	795	23.0
Gifts, timber income, etc.	173	5.1	200	6.6	493	21.8	1402	40.6
Miscellaneous	11	.3	5	.2	1	.0	58	1.7
Total	3424	100.0	3007	100.0	2261	100.0	3454	100.0
No. of Taxpayers (%) No. of all households	82.9		37.5		9.8		· · ·	

SOURCE: National Tax Agency, as reported in the *Yomiuri Shimbun*, Feb. 17, 1982.

The tax burden on wage earners has been steadily rising. In the low-growth period since 1974, the Japanese government could no longer afford annual cuts in personal income taxation. The personal income-tax schedule has been frozen since 1974, and no improvement was made in deductions and exemptions from 1978 until 1983. As nominal income continues to increase, albeit at a relatively modest rate thanks to Japan's low inflation, individuals move into higher tax brackets, and the tax burden on wage income consequently has been rising.[42] In late 1983 the government found it necessary to placate the general discontent among wage-earning taxpayers on the rising inequity in the tax burden. It raised deductions and exemptions by a small amount for 1983 and has proposed a revision of the income-tax schedule to alleviate the tax burden among low and middle-income worker households. This action was thought to be a necessary prelude to a general tax increase, which may be proposed in the near future. However, a basic change in this area is yet to come. There has been a great deal of talk, but very little has been achieved. Associations of small businesses, for one, have been vocal and adamant in opposing any steps that will diminish tax preferences they have already won.

The Green Card Fiasco

To replace the expiring special tax measure on interest and dividend income, a new system was drafted by the Ministry of Finance in late 1979 based on a proposal by the government's Tax Advisory Commission. With the approval of the tax committee of the Liberal Democratic party, the bill was passed by the Diet in March 1980. This so-called Green Card system was to herald a new era in Japanese income taxation by enforcing strict vigilance over tax-exempt small savings to eliminate present abuses and by discontinuing separate taxation of property income.

The essence of the new law was as follows: The system of tax-exempt small savings would be retained. But, to facilitate strict enforcement of the nontaxable ceiling as well as to eliminate fictitious and anonymous accounts, a small savings user card or Green Card[43] was to be issued to individuals on application. The card would record the individual's tax-exempt accounts, and records would be stored in a government computer. Interest income above the tax-exempt limit would be added to incomes from all other sources, and income tax calculated from a single total income.

The law was to become effective in January 1984. Preparations were to begin in November 1982 for issuance of the Green Card, while the construction of a National Computer Center was to start in May 1981 (for completion in September 1982).

In substance, most worker households were not to be affected by the Green Card system as their savings would fall short of the maximum tax-exempt principals. They could continue to enjoy tax-free interest income. But the impact on the propertied class including business proprietors would be substantial. Banking and securities companies feared serious repercussions on their business. Local postal administrators became wary of possibly unfavorable effects on the postal savings they handle.[44] Thus, belatedly, after the bill was passed, political pressures began to mount, and vigorous campaigns against the Green Card system were started by various interested parties.

How and why was a law of such crucial importance allowed to pass the Diet without much scrutiny? The bill had been drafted by the Ministry of Finance and had sailed through the Lower House after seven days' deliberation and passed the Upper House with a week's discussion. The law was proposed as a second-best solution after a tax increase proposal was defeated and the taxpayer identity card system was aborted. With an impending Upper House general election in 1980, the LDP was impatient to find some measures with strong public appeal. The Green Card proposal came along at this juncture, a measure supposed to rectify tax inequities. The LDP grasped it without giving much thought to the potential effect on its constituency.

By August 1980, financial interests began rallying to stage a campaign against the Green Card system. Small business owners who were influential in local politics started exerting pressure on Diet members from their local areas. They feared loss of their vested interests in fictitious accounts for tax avoidance. Further, the national association of specially designated post-office franchisees began its own campaign directed at Diet members within its sphere of influence to minimize the impact of the Green Card system on postal savings.

By May 1981, influential Diet members of the LDP got together to create a Green Card Countermeasure Diet Member League. Momentum gathered, and from then on a rather bizarre and comical sequence of events followed over a period of close to two years during which negotiations took place among the various interest groups. Finally, a special tax measure was approved by the Diet in February 1983 granting a three-year postponement of the Green Card system to January 1987. In a public statement issued on that occasion, the cabinet explained this unusual step by noting that although the Green Card system was devised in the interest of more equitable taxation, appropriate consideration had not been given to nontax aspects of the system.[45] It is generally agreed that this three-year postponement is a de facto repeal of the law. There is almost no precedent for a law being scrapped before it is put into force. The MOF, it is reported, has opted for keeping the law in abeyance for the time being instead of repealing it outright with the intention of using it as a bargaining chip to be exchanged for tighter vigilance on the maximum ceiling for tax-exempt savings, a measure contemplated in its revision of the Income Tax Code scheduled for 1985.

One popular argument mounted against the Green Card System during the debate was that the system would dampen people's willingness to save, thereby leading to reduced economic growth and a loss of economic vitality. This conventional wisdom is ten years out of date in Japan. There is little recognition that too much saving can be as bad as too little. Conventional wisdom, once accepted, entrenches itself as a truism.

Banking and securities interests, which have a vital stake in retaining deposits, took advantage of this and other conventional views on the subject. This is none too surprising, and their arguments did not materially differ from those they advanced in 1950 against the Shoup Mission proposal. However, a new force that has emerged on the scene is the political power that the propertied class has amassed. Note that the Green Card system keeps the personal income-tax schedule intact. Thus, when interest and dividend income is to be taxed along with all other incomes, it must be taxed at progressively high marginal tax rates, the maximum at 93 percent (as of 1983). The Green Card system pays no attention to this important feature of the income tax. This leaves little doubt that, should the Green Card system have been put into effect as planned, it would have created a serious inequity in the opposite direction.[46] Hence, the propertied class put up vehement opposition to it.

This is clearly not a time for piecemeal changes in the tax system. A system-wide overhaul is needed. The problem at the moment is the absence of consensus on what that reform should be. Indeed, there is a plethora of alternative proposals on taxation of property income, ranging from one that proposes abolition of separate taxation of interest and dividend income while raising the tax-exempt limits on principals, to another that insists on keeping tax preferences on interest income but abolishing the system of tax-exempt small savings altogether. Both views have been entertained inside and outside of the government, though the MOF seems to be inclined to keep the system as is (because it is not feasible to abolish it in its view) while reducing its abuses. It is clear, however, that any proposal is tenable and successful if and only if it is placed in a broader perspective of a system-wide reform. As of this writing, no clear consensus has yet emerged.

The Land Problem

From the viewpoint of raising economic welfare, the most serious problem Japan has encountered in its postwar growth process is related to housing and commuting. Overconcentration of population in the three metropolitan areas— nearly half the population living in 14 percent of the total national land area— implies that people must live in "rabbit hutches" (as an EC report called them) because of the lack of space. Even that small living space is located far away from the place of work. Thus, many metropolitan workers must spend a substantial part of their workday riding on crowded commuter trains. This makes it difficult to compare the living standard of Japanese households with that abroad.

The poor housing and commuting conditions are inevitable consequences of Japan's rapid industrialization after World War II. But the government failed to provide an effective, systematic policy in this field, especially in creating residential areas at low cost and under orderly urban planning. The new urban land supply has been left by and large to private initiative, the market mechanism. The market mechanism has worked but at a cost of soaring land prices. As workers moved into cities, the demand for housing sites rose. Farmland was converted into residential uses while residential land prices increased sharply.

High land prices could be paid because of highly efficient use of land (e.g., very small houses with little spare space). In the process, landowners made tremendous capital gains. The trouble is that something like the Wicksellian cumulative process works in the land market. In metropolitan suburbs, owners of farmland withhold their landholdings from the market of new residential sites in anticipation of further price increases. As the short supply raises the market price while the demand for land remains unabated, landowners' expectations prove to be self-fulfilling. Heavier taxes on realized capital gains of land sales may result in aggravating the situation because landowners postpone sales to more distant dates.

Considering that houses (with their sites) in Japan are far more expensive relative to income and other goods, the Japanese have a surprisingly strong penchant for owning their dwellings.[47] Even so, the continued rises in land prices have made the acquisition of a dwelling beyond the reach of the ordinary worker household. A rule of thumb in the last few years has been that a new house in a reasonable metropolitan suburban neighborhood is equivalent to a little over seven times the annual income of an ordinary household. Because of this, housing investment has been relatively depressed in the last few years, contributing to depressed aggregate economic activities.

The housing problem is ipso facto the land problem. There are two major aspects of the latter—land as stock and land as flow. There are serious conflicts in policy when dealing with the two simultaneously.

As a stock, land is a store of value to landowners. We have already noted that growing inequity in the distribution of wealth owes a great deal to the appreciation of land value. From the point of view of social equity, it is desirable to impose a stiff tax on land. But the property tax and the inheritance tax have been relatively low in Japan.[48]

However, land is also a flow in the context of contemporary Japan. New residential sites are supplied and transacted to accommodate new housing space in urban areas. The flow supply is increased by stepping up the conversion of farmland into residential land. This would seem to require a lighter tax on capital gains realized on sales of land, particularly farmland to be converted for residential uses. In reality, this tax has been relatively heavy in recent years.

Thus, policy objectives are in conflict with each other, and policy measures taken actually seem to be opposite to what they should be. Consider the capital gains tax. It was raised substantially in the course of the 1970s, especially after the 1972–73 land speculation boom, with a view to keeping land prices in check. However, as the tax burden became heavier, landowners became increasingly reluctant to sell their holdings; this is the argument put up by real estate interests. Their demand for a lower tax burden led to a reduction in this tax in March 1982. The argument is based on land-sales capital gains tax being high in Japan in comparison with other countries, for example., 40 percent taxable in the United States, 30 percent taxable in the United Kingdom, and none at all in West Germany. Unfortunately, there is no hard evidence of the negative influence of the capital gains tax on new supplies of residential land. The LDP assumes that a lower capital gains tax would stimulate new land supply. The MOF remains skeptical and insists that the tax be kept high to keep wealth inequities at bay. In the fight leading to the 1982 revision, the LDP won.

To promote more orderly urban development, a City Planning Law was promulgated in June 1969. It designated areas covered by city planning, containing two segments—"areas covered by urbanization" (*shigaika kuiki*), that is, city areas to be encouraged to become fully urbanized, especially farmland remaining therein, within the next ten years with the initiative for conversion for residential uses placed on voluntary actions of farm landowners, and "areas adjusted under urbanization" (*shigaika chōsei kuiki*), that is, areas in which urbanization is to be kept to a minimum with legal restrictions on farmers to convert their farms for residential sites.

Despite this law, farmland remains in the former areas even more than ten years after implementation of the law, since farmers have held on to their farms. The result has been urban sprawl or helter-skelter combinations of residential and farm areas in metropolitan suburbs, defying the logic of orderly urban planning.

It was thought the farm-residential land conversion could be expedited by making the cost of holding farmland more expensive by raising the property tax on it through increasing the assessed value of farmland in city planning areas to the level of neighboring residential sites. Various measures have been taken to that effect since the early 1970s, with little avail because of a number of legal loopholes.

Now that Japan's economic growth is reduced and labor migrations to cities have decreased to a trickle, the land problem is in a new phase and more attention should be paid to distributional equity rather than to stimulating new residential land supply. Whether the government can properly respond to the new phase or not is another matter. One must take into account the strong vested interests of the landed gentry.

The Consumer-Finance or Sarakin Problem

The consumer loan market had long been underdeveloped in Japan. However, a rapid change started in the mid-1960s. On one hand, the demand for house mortgages was rising. On the other, installment credit became popular for buying big-ticket items like consumer durables and automobiles. Later on, credit cards and especially cash cards were popularized.

In the last few years, short-term consumer loans have been expanding very rapidly. The outstanding balance increased from 1.0 trillion yen in 1977 to 2.5 trillion yen in 1981, and is still growing. The share of financial institutions in this balance has been falling. In the meantime, large-scale consumer finance companies have entered the market.

Consumers, especially low-income consumers, have always been in need of money to meet unexpected emergencies. The traditional means of finance used to be pawnshops. The general affluence has brought even these consumers face to face with new needs—paying for leisure-related activities such as gambling, bar-hopping, and vacation trips. Such borrowers want quick service and ready credit without putting up collateral. When there is demand, there is supply. There is now a multitude of finance businesses (reported variously between 25,000 and 200,000), ranging from a few large consumer finance companies with a nationwide network of branches with a size comparable to a medium-sized bank to a horde of very small moneylending establishments that cater to their limited local clientele. Individuals can obtain almost instant loans from them, provided they are willing to pay exorbitant rates. All they need is some sort of an identification document, very often health insurance papers. Because of its popularity, especially among low-wage workers, this type of a loan is called *sarakin* in Japanese, short for "salaryman's loan."

The principal problem with the *sarakin* is that terms of credit are very stiff. There has been no government control except for the maximum legally chargeable loan rate of 109.5 percent per year as stipulated in the "Investment" Law (Shusshi Hō).[49] Article 5 of this law states: "A lender who makes a contract for, or receives, interest that is more than 109.5 percent per annum (or 0.3 percent per day) is punishable by penal servitude of no more than three years and/or a fine of no more than 0.3 million yen (3 million yen in the 1983 revision)." Under the protection of this law, many small moneylenders charge rates as high as 70 percent per annum. As most borrowers are low-income individuals, they have trouble repaying their loans on time. Lenders are notorious for harassing delinquent borrowers with strong-arm as well as psychological tactics. Hence, cases of *sarakin jigoku* (consumer loan hell) have mushroomed.

It is not that there has been no usury law in Japan. Indeed, the Interest Restrictions Law (Risoku Seigen Hō), dating back to 1877, set the maximum interest rates applying both to financial institutions and moneylenders until World War II.[50] After the war, a new law called the Temporary Interest-Rate Adjustment Law (Rinji Kinri Chōsei Hō) was promulgated in 1947 for financial institutions to enforce the government's low-interest rate policy for postwar reconstruction. But moneylenders were outside of this law as they were not financial institutions. For them, the Interest Restrictions Law was revised in 1954. Its Article 1 limits the maximum loan rate to 20 percent on a loan whose principal is less than 0.1 million yen, 18 percent on a loan whose principal is between 0.1 yen and 1.0 million, and 15 percent on a loan whose principal is above 1.0 million yen. This law has never had a penalty clause since 1877.

Thus, there have been two laws, one declaring it illegal to charge more than 109.5 percent interest per year and another setting the upper limit at no more than 20 percent per year. What happens when a moneylender charges a rate in between, in the so-called gray zone? In 1964, the Supreme Court ruled that, when interest was voluntarily paid in excess of the rates prescribed in the Interest Restrictions Law, that excess should be apportioned to payment of the remaining principal. In a followup judgment of 1968, the court ruled that the payor could demand a refund of the excess payment.[51]

Thus, a schizophrenic situation has existed in Japanese laws on consumer loans. It is necessary to determine which law is binding. As short-term consumer loans have been expanding at a sharp rate and injurious cases have been increasing at an alarming rate, the government was forced to move to protect consumer interests against usurious moneylending businesses. The government started to deliberate on it in1977, but the bone of contention proved always to be where to set the upper limit on interest rates. Opinion was sharply divided among and within political parties. A bill was put before the Diet for revising the Interest Restriction Law. After six submissions, the bill passed the Lower House in August 1982 and the Upper House in April 1983. The new law, called the Moneylending Regulation Law (Kashikingyō Kisei Hō, or more popularly Sarakin Kisei Hō), went into force in November 1983.

While expanding the government's power to regulate the moneylending business, the new law reduces the maximum rate from 109.5 percent to 73 percent for the first three years, to 54.75 percent in the fourth year, and finally to 40.004 percent at an as yet unspecified date. In doing this, in its Article 43, the law altered the aforementioned Supreme Court decisions, making it legal for a moneylender to accept a voluntary payment of interest in excess of the maximum stipulated in the Interest Restriction Law. The latter law is still in force, however, and recourse to it can be had by borrowers if they wish.

Consumer loan rates are high. Even large consumer finance companies charge nearly 50 percent per annum, as shown in table 14. What determines these rates? Moneylenders, including consumer finance companies, are not banks. They cannot create credit. Thus, the full cost of funds must be passed on via loan rates. By its nature, moneylending is full of default risk. Any cost of bad loans must be spread over good loans. Operating costs must also be covered, including the cost of bill collections. Thus, even a fair rate is high.[52]

Yet there has been strong competition among large consumer finance com-

TABLE 14
Small Consumer Loans: Terms of Credit

Lender	Annual Interest (%)	Maximum Principal (million ¥)	Terms of Repayment
City banks (small loan)	13.5	.3	2 years
Mutual banks (small loan)	18	.3	2 years
Bank-related (loan)	17.4	.3	. . .
Credit card companies ("cashing")	19.9–43.8	.1	55–25 days
Credit sales companies	26–28	2.0	5 years
Retailers' card companies	27–29	.3–.5	2 years
Major consumer finance companies	42–48	1.0	4 years

SOURCE: *Yomiuri Shimbun*, April 21, 1983.

panies. They have been expanding their scale of operations by setting up many branches all over the country. This has not led to a lowering of loan rates, however. It is rather an attempt at product differentiation via locational advantages while the product itself is homogeneous. To support this expansion of facilities, these companies lower the standard of borrower screening, and less sound loans are solicited, resulting in increasing default (allegedly about 20 percent). The loan rates must be set high to compensate for the increased default risk.

Why then don't commercial banks enter the market at lower rates? If they lend at their maximum loan rates, they can still make a profit because their prime rates are about 10 percent and lately they have had sufficient idle funds to invest. They don't follow this course of action because they do not like small, high-cost transactions. Thus, banks do not wish to go "retail" in the small consumer loan market and have instead found an alternative solution, to go "wholesale" by lending to consumer finance companies at rates close to prime rates. A recent MOF survey reports that banks and insurance companies had a total balance of 1.1 trillion yen with consumer finance companies as of March 1983, with the active participation of foreign banks.[53] This means that the rapid, overcompetitive expansion of consumer finance companies has been made possible with the general support of financial institutions. It is thus not difficult to imagine the influence of vested financial interests in moderating the acceptance of revising legal control over usury rates. Consumer welfare is of secondary importance.

6. IMPLICATIONS FOR U.S.-JAPAN ECONOMIC RELATIONS

Pro-saving tax policy no doubt has reinforced the Japanese economy's fundamental tendency toward oversaving. We may ask what this feature implies for U.S.-Japan economic relations.

When a country tends to save too much, its aggregate demand, which is domestically generated, tends to be weak. Hence, there is a strong push for its producers to export their surplus abroad. For Japanese manufacturers who find themselves in this position, the "export drive" is directed very much toward the United States, which is still the largest market for Japan's manufactured exports. In combination with Japan's protection of domestic markets, especially in the internationally noncompetitive agriculture sector, this creates an unfortunate situation that gives rise to recurrent trade friction between Japan and the United States. One solution to the impasse is to promote consumption rather than saving in Japan, and revising current pro-saving tax laws is one such measure.

A related facet of the same issue is Japan's capital exports. A country's tendency to oversave in the private sector has to be offset either by the government running deficits or by the private sector investing the excess saving overseas. (For the latter, however, the country must maintain a surplus in the current account of its balance of payments, provided that foreign countries allow it to run a persistent surplus.) Japan's overseas investment has been growing rapidly, especially since Japan's capital market has been substantially liberalized. Since the U.S. government developed a large deficit in 1982 and 1983 and is expected to remain in this situation for some time to come, the United States may find it expedient to rely on Japan's excess saving as a source of foreign funds.

An interesting phenomenon, however, is that as Japan's capital outflows have expanded, its capital inflows have also increased almost *pari passu*. An economic reason for this phenomenon must be that, apart from short-term speculative investments, there have been long-term investments because of fairly reasonable returns in Japan. While interest rates have been relatively modest, taxes on property income have remained low. Hence, after-tax rates of return can be internationally competitive. It must also be noted that the yen tends to appreciate over time because of differentials in inflation (inflation against the United States) and productivity growth in manufacturing. Combined with political stability in Japan, investing in Japan remains attractive despite various restrictive measures on capital inflows into Japan that may still be pronounced. Revisions of tax laws that will significantly affect after-tax returns must take this point into account.

7. CONCLUDING REMARKS

This study has surveyed interactions between economic laws, especially tax laws, and household wealth formation in Japan over the last three decades.

Because of its preoccupation with the goal of economic growth, Japan's tax system has been generous to the more affluent members of the population. Fortunately, inequity in the tax burden was kept suppressed while Japan's rapid economic growth went on, though the distribution of wealth continued to become increasingly unequal.

The inherent inequity in the tax system became apparent when the Japanese economy could no longer maintain high growth. The burden of the government's rising need for revenue has been primarily borne by wage and salary earners. Their real disposable income has been growing at a negligible rate over the last few years. Nevertheless, private saving has declined only slightly as a fraction of disposable income. As private capital formation has become much weaker due to lower economic growth, an excess of saving over investment has emerged in the private sector. In the meantime, the public sector has been faced with a sizable imbalance between revenue and expenditure due primarily to structural causes. The persistent budget deficits of the national government have been financed by new issues of public bonds, which fortuitously helped to absorb the excess of saving in the private sector.

In Japan, it has been increasingly recognized that its current fiscal situation cannot be sustained indefinitely. To balance the budget, Japan's public finance system must be restructured, including a wholesale overhaul of its tax system. Among other things, the latter's pro-saving stance must be reexamined. So far, it has proven difficult to introduce such a restructuring, as seen in the few cases reviewed. Changes that are now required are not piecemeal changes but global and systemic. In Japan where any large-scale changes must be based on consensual agreement, such changes, if any, can only be adopted followed by a very long lag in response.

International attention has recently been focused on the weakness of effective domestic demand in Japan because of its strong propensity to save. A few commentators argue that this element is in no small measure responsible for the increasingly severe trade frictions felt between Japan and its trading partners, especially the United States. Those economic laws that influence Japanese households' consumption-saving decisions are particularly pertinent in this context.

Thus, an extensive revision of the economic laws in Japan, which is anticipated for the future, will not only have domestic, but international impact as well. For this reason, any changes and their resultant impact must be carefully monitored.

NOTES

1. For a critical assessment, see M. Bronfenbrenner and K. Kogiku, "The Aftermath of the Shoup Tax Reforms, Part I and Part II," *National Tax Journal* 10 (Sept. 1957): 236–54 and (Dec. 1957): 345–60. For detailed accounts of Japan's fiscal system during the occupation period, see the 20-volume history, *Shōwa Zaiseishi*, sponsored by the Ministry of Finance, which has been published since the late 1970s.

2. For a list of emendations, see the appendix of Bronfenbrenner and Kogiku, "Aftermath of the Shoup Tax Reforms."

3. J. Pechman and K. Kaizuka, "Taxation," in Hugh Patrick and Henry Rosovsky, eds., *Asia's New Giant* (Washington, D.C.: Brookings Institution, 1976), p. 371.

4. See *Shōwa Zaiseishi* 17 (1981): 181–82.

5. See successive finance ministers' state-of-the-economy speeches reported in the same source.

6. Bronfenbrenner and Kogiku, "Aftermath of the Shoup Tax Reforms," p. 354.

7. These modifications were introduced successively as special measures in the Special Tax Measures Law. For measures up to 1960, see J. Teranishi, *Nihon no keizai hatten to kin'yū* (Money, capital, and banking in Japanese economic development) (Tokyo: Iwanami Shoten, 1982), p. 427. For a list as of 1976, see H. Ueno, *Nihon no keizai seido* (Japan's economic institutions) (Tokyo: Nihon Keizai Shimbun Sha, 1978), pp. 138–49.

8. Pechman and Kaizuka, "Taxation," p. 328.

9. The relation between tax and growth in this period is discussed in R. Komiya, "Japan," in E. Gordon Keith, ed., *Foreign Tax Policies and Economic Growth* (New York: National Bureau of Economic Research 1966), and in Pechman and Kaizuka, "Taxation."

10. Pechman and Kaizuka, "Taxation," p. 327.

11. Kazuo Sato, "Japan's Savings and Internal and External Macroeconomic Balance," in Kozo Yamamura, ed., *Policy and Trade Issues of the Japanese Economy* (Seattle: University of Washington Press, 1982).

12. Earlier, the national government was engaged principally in issuing bonds for financing public projects ("construction" bonds). In 1975, with the authorization of the Diet, the government began to issue, on a large scale, "deficit" bonds to finance government deficits.

13. The tax-rate schedule remained unchanged from 1974 to 1983. See Pechman and Kaizuka, "Taxation," p. 376. Deductions and exemptions were raised in 1978. A small tax cut was introduced for 1983. A new schedule has been adopted for 1984 and subsequent years.

14. The 1980 population was 117 million in 36 million households.

15. Of taxable personal savings, a little over 10 percent are separately taxed at 35 percent. Nearly 90 percent are jointly taxed with other incomes after tax withholdings of 20 percent at source. *Yomiuri Shimbun*, Sept. 29, 1982.

16. At the end of the 1981 fiscal year, there were 639,000 anonymous accounts with a total balance of ¥927 billion in ordinary banks, *sōgo* banks, and *shinkin* banks. Nihon Ginkō, *Keizai tōkei nempō* (Economic statistics annual), 1982 (Tokyo: Bank of Japan). Anonymous accounts are alleged to be a haven for dirty money.

17. It is reported that there were 318 million nontaxable postal savings accounts and 208 million tax-exempt small deposit accounts at the end of the 1981 fiscal year. *Yomiuri Shimbun*, Mar. 9, 1983.

18. According to the *Household Saving Survey*, as percentages of worker household income, the balance of financial savings at the end of 1980 consisted of demand deposits (10%), time deposits (52%), life insurance (21%), and securities (18%). As total wages and salaries reported in the NIPA were ¥114 trillion for that year, personal savings attributed to worker households are ¥114 trillion (total) and ¥71 trillion (deposits). We may consider the latter nontaxable. Then, the former is 37 percent of total personal savings and the latter 39 percent of tax-exempt personal savings (see table 7).

19. Of the labor force, proprietors without employees were 3.7 percent, proprietors with employees 13.2 percent, and family workers 11.3 percent as of Oct. 1, 1980, according to the 1980 Population Census.

20. Tax auditing has also been lax. Only one-twentieth of noncorporate blue returns are audited now as compared to one-third in 1960 (and one-tenth for corporate blue returns now). As the statute of limitations on tax evasion is five years, there is a strong inducement for tax cheating by underreporting income and overstating expenses.

21. Before the recent tax revision, three-quarters of capital gains in excess of ¥80 million were treated as taxable income.

22. The average national tax rate on wage income withdrawn at source was 5.4 percent and that on self-assessed returns was 10.3 percent in 1980–81 (Tōyō Keizai Shimpō Sha, ed., *Keizai tōkei nenkan* [Economic statistics yearbook], 1983, and earlier issues [Tokyo: Tōyō Keizai Shimpō Sha]).

23. In several recent years about 70 of the top 100 income-tax payers belonged to (4). In fiscal 1982, the number was 68. In that year, the lowest taxable income of the top 100 taxpayers was ¥413 million (*Yomiuri Shimbun*, May 2, 1983).

24. Of local tax revenue (both prefectural and municipal) in 1980, the property tax accounted for 17 percent and personal and business income taxes for 57 percent (Nihon Ginkō, *Keizai tōkei nempō*, 1982).

25. Pechman and Kaizuka, "Taxation," p. 371.

26. February 1983, p. 81.

27. Kazuo Sato, "Why Have the Japanese Saved So Much? On Determinants of Japanese Household Saving," unpublished paper, January 1982.

28. Kazuo Sato, "Supply-Side Economics: A Comparison of the U.S. and Japan," *Journal of Japanese Studies* 11, no. 1 (Winter 1985): 105–28.

29. The proportion of property income may be understated. With the balance of personal savings owned by worker households (see n. 18), interest income may be 3 to 4 percent of their income (at interest rates of 2 percent on demand deposits and 6 to 7 percent on time deposits).

30. However, it is also plausible that they would keep the saving ratio at a high level to maintain their social status by not unduly lowering their relative wealth position.

31. Sato, "Supply-Side Economics."

32. The aggregate market value of land owned by households was $583 billion in the United States and $2,062 billion in Japan (at ¥240/$1). The Japanese population is one-half of the U.S. population, and the Japanese land area (including nonhabitable) is 4 percent of the U.S. land area. The average residential land price per square meter for 1979 is reported to have been: Japan, ¥44,800; U.S., ¥2,900; U.K., ¥3,600; and West Germany, ¥8,300. Kokudochō, *Kokudo riyō hakusho* (White paper on land utilization) (Tokyo: Government Printing Office, 1981).

33. Sato, "Why Have the Japanese Saved So Much?"

34. *Survey of Current Business*, October 1982, p. 36.

35. Kazuo Sato, "Japan's Land-Price Determination: A Longitudinal Study," unpublished paper, June 1982.

36. As a percentage of GNP, nominal gains on land (per annum) were 45 percent (1970–74), 25 percent (1975–79), and 41 percent (1980–81) according to the NIPA estimates.

37. Owner-occupied dwellings account for 60 percent of all dwellings in Japan.

38. This is partly due to the legal protection of tenants with continuing leases against eviction.

39. See, for example, T. Mizoguchi, "Size Distribution of Household Income in Postwar Japan," JERC-CAMS, *Income Distribution, Employment, and Economic Development in Southeast and East Asia* (Tokyo: Hitotsubashi University Press, 1975).

40. See N. Takayama and M. Togashi, "A Note on Wealth Distribution in Japan," *The Philippine Economic Journal* 19 (July 1980): 163–88.

41. The 1981 audit revealed that 94 percent of the audited proprietors underreported their business income (by ¥3 million on average). *Yomiuri Shimbun*, July 21, 1983.

42. The proportion of private-sector employees who paid income tax rose from 71 percent in 1970 to 75 percent in 1974 and 88 percent in 1980 (*Keizai tōkei nenkan*, various issues). In addition, there has been a steady increase in female labor force participation as housewives have begun to enter the labor market in large numbers to supplement family income, which has ceased to improve in real terms. This has given rise to the problem of the two-paycheck family.

43. Earlier, a proposal was made to issue a taxpayer identity card so as to computerize all tax returns. It was aborted by strong public resistance for fear of police-state misuse of the ID system. The Green Card made its debut as a compromise. The name was invented to give it a soft image.

44. Small local post offices are run as franchises (called specially designated post offices). The national association of their franchisees, with a membership of 17,500, has a strong lobby in local and national politics.

45. *Yomiuri Shimbun*, Feb. 9, 1983.

46. In mid-1982, the then minister of finance, Watanabe Michio, suggested a need for lowering the maximum marginal tax rates to 55 percent (national) and 5 percent (local) to be comparable with other countries when the Green Card system would go into effect. His suggestion was not taken too seriously at the time as the minister was known for off-the-cuff statements.

47. The proportion of owner-occupied dwellings to all dwellings has been 60 percent in Japan (*Housing Survey*, 1983 and 1978), which is below the ratio in land-rich countries like the United States (63 percent in 1970), Canada (62 percent in 1975), and Australia (67 percent in 1971), but above Western Europe—Great Britain (50 percent in 1971), Italy (51 percent in 1971), France (42 percent in 1975), Sweden (35 percent in 1970), and West Germany (34 percent in 1972). (Data from Economic Planning Agency's *Kokusai Keizai Yōran*, 1977, as quoted in N. Maruo, "The Levels of Living and Welfare in Japan Reexamined," *Japanese Economic Studies* 8 [Fall 1979]: 42–93).

48. The burden of the property tax as a percentage of national income is reported as follows: Japan (1.8 percent in 1983), U.S. (3.8 percent in 1978), U.K. (4.6 percent in 1978), West Germany (1.1 percent in 1973), and France (0.7 percent in 1978). *Yomiuri Shimbun*, Mar. 30, 1983. In comparing these percentages, one must take note of the land/income ratio, which is inordinately high in Japan.

49. "Shusshi no Ukeire, Azukarikin, oyobi Kinri no Torishimari nadoni kansuru Hōritzu" (1954). This law was introduced in the wake of the 1953 incident in which an investment company called the Hozen Keizai Kai went bankrupt. The company solicited deposits from households with a promise of high interest rates to be obtained by operating Ponti's game. The law was intended to prevent any further dishonest financial practices.

50. For this law and its changes, see Teranishi, *Nihon no keizai hatten to kin'yū*, p. 205.

51. See *Saikōsai minji hanrei shū* (A comparison of decisions on civil cases by the Supreme Court), 18, no. 9: 1868, which reports a decision rendered by the Grand Court of the Supreme Court on Nov. 18, 1964: "When a debtor has voluntarily paid interest in excess of the maximum stipulated in the Interest Restrictions Law, should the excess payment be naturally assigned to the remaining principal?" For civil cases subsequent to this decision, see those reported in *Hanrei Jihō* in the late 1960s.

52. The fair rate estimated by the Japan Bar Association is 36 percent (*Yomiuri Shimbun*, Apr. 20, 1983).

53. The total consists of ¥243 billion from foreign banks in Japan, ¥265 billion from Japanese banks and insurance companies, and ¥592 billion from their subsidiaries. This should be compared with the total loan balance of the big five consumer finance companies, which was ¥1.0 trillion at the end of 1982 (*Yomiuri Shimbun*, July 3, 1983).

APPENDIX

DIRECT TAXES ON THE HOUSEHOLD ECONOMY

The following reviews Japan's tax system on the household economy that was in force from 1974 to 1983.[1] The 1984 revision is also described. Our study is limited to direct taxes that are levied on household income and property.[2]

TAXES ON INCOME

Tax Units

The tax unit is a household consisting of the head of the household, spouse, and dependents. Household members' incomes are either taxed separately (wage and salary income) or taxed jointly (property income in excess of a certain limit).

Tax Jurisdiction

There are three levels of tax administration—the central government for national tax, the prefectural government for prefectural tax, and the municipal government for municipal tax. The last two together are called local tax. There is a substantial transfer of national tax revenue to local governments.

Types of Taxpayers and Tax Returns

There are two major types of income taxpayers. (1) Wage and salary earners, whose national and local taxes are withheld at the source and the necessary annual adjustment undertaken by their employers at the end of the tax year (which is the calendar year). They file no tax returns. (2) All other taxpayers, including wage and salary workers with annual taxable wage income in excess of ¥10 million yen (¥15 million yen in 1984 on). They may file ordinary "white" returns or, in the case of business proprietors, "blue" returns.

Some incomes other than wage and salary income are also taxed at the source and need not be reported on tax returns. Of total national personal income tax revenue in 1981, 53% was withheld from payrolls, 23% withheld from interest, dividends, etc., at the source, and 24% paid on self-assessed returns.

Income Tax Schedules

Taxable income is arrived at by subtracting exemptions and deductions from gross income. Exemptions and deductions differ slightly in amount for national and local tax purposes.[3]

In the national income tax, taxable income was divided into 19 steps, with the marginal tax rates ranging from 10 to 75%. The 1984 revision has reduced the number of steps to 15 and revised the marginal tax rates to range from 10.5 to 70%.

Prefectural income tax is simple in structure, with only two marginal rates, 2 and 4%. Municipal income tax is more complex; the marginal rates ranged from 2 to 14%. The 1984 revision has raised the starting rate to 2.5%. This tax is relatively heavy on low-income households. Thus, local income tax can be as much as two-thirds of national income tax for a standard household with an average income. See table A.1 for the old and new income tax schedules.

Kinds of Income

The Personal Income Tax Code distinguishes several types of personal incomes: wage and salary; interest; dividends; from real estate; from business; retirement; from timber; capital gains; temporary; miscellaneous.

Of these, the law treats wages and salaries and businesses as two major sources of income. Other incomes are either tax exempt or taxed mostly on separate schedules unless they exceed certain limits.

(1) *Wage and salary income.* For wage and salary workers, taxable income (*shotoku*) is arrived at by subtracting exemptions and deductions from gross income (*shūnyū*).[4] In 1978–82, exemptions and deductions were as follows:[5]

  (i) standard deduction (*kyūyo shotoku kōjo*): the following (marginal) percentages of gross wage income are excluded from gross income.

Gross income (million ¥)	Percent excluded
0–1.5	40 % (or ¥0.5 million,
1.5–3.0	30 whichever is larger)
3.0–6.0	20
6.0–10.0	10
10.0 and over	5

  (ii) dependent exemptions:
     a. spouse exemption − ¥.29 million times 1 (¥.35 if aged 70 and over)
     b. dependent exemption − ¥.29 million times the number of dependents other than the spouse (¥.35 million if aged 70 and over)
     c. basic exemption − ¥.29 million times 1
     d. special exemption − ¥23 million times 1 for a handicapped (¥.31 million for specially handicapped), an aged (70 and over) person, a widow, or a self-supporting student.
  (iii) social insurance premiums including contributions to social security
  (iv) life insurance and casualty insurance premiums up to a certain limit
  (v) other special deductions (including medical expenses in excess of ¥.05 million or 5% of income)[6]

The case of a working wife has become prominent recently as more and more housewives have begun to work—often as part-time workers. Her gross wage income is nontaxable up to ¥.79 million, which is the sum of the standard deduction of ¥.50 million and the basic exemption of ¥.29 million. She is still treated as a dependent from the point of view of her husband's payroll, qualifying for the spouse exemption. Beyond the nontaxable limit, she is taxed separately from her husband and is taken off her husband's dependent list as well as his health insurance.

For the 1983 tax year, an interim tax cut measure was introduced late in the year, raising each of the dependent exemptions (a, b, and c of (1)ii above) by ¥.01 million to ¥.30 million. A more liberal change that was brought before the Diet in January 1984 for the 1984 tax year and thereafter is as follows:

(i) standard deduction. Exclusions from gross income below ¥3.0 million are revised as follows:

Gross income (¥)	Percent excluded
0–1.65	40% (or ¥.55 million
1.65–3.30	whichever is larger)

(ii) dependent exemptions:
   a. spouse exemption − ¥.33 million times 1 (¥ million if aged 70 or over)
   b. dependent exemption − ¥.33 million times the number of dependents (¥.39 million if aged 70 or over)
   c. basic exemption − ¥.33 million times 1
   d. special exemption − ¥.25 million times 1 for a handicapped (¥.35 million for specially handicapped), or aged (70 or over) person, a widow, or a self-supporting student

(v) other special deductions: medical expenses in excess of ¥.07 million

These increases in exemptions and deductions raise the maximum nontaxable gross income for a standard married couple (one income earner, a spouse, and two dependent children) from ¥2.015 million (up to 1982) to ¥2.357 million. A working wife's gross wage income is to be nontaxable up to ¥.88 million.

(2) *Other earned income.* Honoraria, royalties, professional fees, social-insurance medical fees (received by physicians), tips, prizes, etc. are separately taxed at the source at a flat rate of 10% (20% in excess of ¥1 million for each item).

(3) *Business income.* Business income is income that accrues from an unincorporated private business. A business proprietor must file a self-assessed return, and business income together with other types of income is taxed on the personal income tax schedule. There are two forms of tax returns—"white" and "blue." White returns are ordinary returns. In addition to exemptions already mentioned for wage income, deductions such as casualty and theft losses, charitable contributions, and so on are allowed on white returns. Proprietors are also entitled to deduct business expenses.[7]

Business owners are allowed to submit blue returns,[8] which entitle them to special business expense deductions in return for meeting the minimum bookkeeping requirement.[9] The most important of these deductions is wages and salaries paid to family workers including the spouse as regular employees of a business. They pay income tax on their wage incomes at a lower rate than when

TABLE A.1
Personal Income Tax Schedules:
National, Prefectural, and Municipal

National income tax

Taxable income (Million ¥)	Marginal rate (%)	
	(A)	(B)
0 – 0.5		10.5
0.5– 0.6	} 10	} 12
0.6– 1.2	12	
1.2– 1.8	14	} 14
1.8– 2.0	} 16	
2.0– 2.4		} 17
2.4– 3.0	18	
3.0– 4.0	21	21
4.0– 5.0	24	} 25
5.0– 6.0	27	
6.0– 7.0	30	} 30
7.0– 8.0	34	
8.0–10.0	38	35
10.0–12.0	42	40
12.0–15.0	46	45
15.0–20.0	50	50
20.0–30.0	55	55
30.0–40.0	60	} 60
40.0–60.0	65	
60.0–80.0	70	65
80.0 and over	75	70

Prefectural income tax

0–1.5	2
1.5 and over	4

included in business income. The net effect is reported to be a 26% tax saving. This provision was made legal in 1967. Further, in 1974, noncorporate businesses were allowed to treat themselves as quasi-corporations (*minashi hōjin*). A quasi-corporate business can deduct the proprietor's remuneration from business income, and business income itself is taxed at a rate of 23.9% up to ¥7 million and 34.1% in excess of ¥7 million (national tax rates), roughly the rate that applies to distributed corporate profits.[10] Private medical practitioners are given special tax preferences.[11]

Municipal income tax

(A)		(B)	
Taxable income (Million ¥)	Marginal rate (%)	Taxable income (Million ¥)	Marginal rate (%)
0– 0.30	2	0–0.20	2.5
0.30– 0.45	3	0.20–0.45	3
0.45– 0.70	4	0.45–0.70	4
0.70– 1.0	5	0.70–0.95	5
1.0 – 1.3	6	0.95–1.2	6
1.3 – 2.3	7	1.2 –2.2	7
2.3 – 5.3	8	2.2 –3.7	8
3.7 – 5.7	9		
5.7 – 9.5	10		
9.5 –19.0	11		
19.0 –29.0	12		
29.0 –49.0	13		
49.0 and over	14		

NOTES AND SOURCES: (A) the schedules in force, 1974–83. (B) the schedule proposed to the Diet as of Jan. 11, 1984. (1) and (3) from *Yomiuri Shimbun*, Jan. 11, 1984; (2) from Pechman and Kaizuka (1976), table 5–16, p. 376.

(4) *Interest and dividend income*. In principle, a household must be taxed on the sum of property income received by its members if the sum is in excess of ¥10 million (¥15 million in the 1984 revision). However, many tax exemptions apply to interest and dividend income. Interest on postal savings is nontaxable up to a principal of ¥3 million. In addition, the system of tax-exempt small savings allows the following tax exemptions per person on interest received: small bank deposits—up to a principal amount of ¥3 million (limit effective since 1963); securities (such as public bonds)—up to a face value of ¥3 million; worker savings for asset formation (*zaikei chochiku*)—up to a principal of ¥5 million (effective since 1971). To qualify for this exemption, a depositor makes application to the tax authorities via a depository financial institution.[12]

For interest on taxable deposits (in excess of the exemption limit) and dividend income (in excess of annual dividend of ¥0.1 million per account), income tax is collected at the source at a flat rate of 20%, and taxpayers report such income together with other incomes.[13] Depositors may elect to be taxed at a flat rate of 35% separately from other incomes.

(5) *Retirement income*. Retirement or severance allowances paid in a lump sum at the time of workers' retirement often amount to a few years' wage income. Retirement income is taxed separately from regular annual income though the

same income tax schedule applies. The taxable amount of retirement income is determined as follows:

½ (gross retirement income—exemption), where exemptions are determined as follows:

$$T < 2, ¥0.5 \text{ million}$$
$$2 \leq T < 20, ¥0.25 \text{ million times T}$$
$$T \geq 20, ¥5 \text{ million} + ¥0.5 \text{ million times (T–20)}$$

(T is the number of years of service.)

(6) *Timber income.* Income from sales of timber in forests acquired more than five years ago is taxed separately from other incomes. Timber income is defined as gross proceeds minus necessary expenses and a special deduction of ¥0.5 million. The tax is computed by applying the personal income tax schedule to one fifth of timber income and then multiplying the amount thus obtained by 5.[14]

(7) *Capital gains on sales of securities.* Capital gains realized on sales of securities are tax exempt for professional traders.[15]

Redemption gains on "discount" bonds to be realized at the time of maturity are to be taxed not as interest income or capital gains but as miscellaneous income at a flat rate at the source. The tax rates are to vary by date of issue: 16% for those issued by and within 1983, 35% for those to be issued in 1984 and 1985, and 42% thereafter. Along with the Green Card system, these increases have also been postponed. Note that if these bonds are sold before maturity, capital gains are tax exempt.

(8) *Capital gains on sales of real estate.* Real estate, especially land, is the most important component of household wealth. And the tax law on capital gains realized on sales of real estate has changed several times in the past. We limit our review to major changes since 1969. To begin with, note that real estate is classified by duration of ownership as short-term and long-term. The tax rate on the former is, as a general rule, twice as high as the rate on the latter. Also, both national and local taxes are levied.

In 1969, capital gains on land sales were made taxable separately from other incomes. In 1969–71, the tax rate was very low—10% for national tax and 4% for local tax, so as to encourage the conversion of farmland to residential uses. The rate was to rise to 15% and 5% respectively in 1972, and again to 20% and 6% in 1974. These figures apply to real estate under long-term ownership, defined as five years or more. They were double for real estate under short-term ownership.

The land speculation boom of 1972–73 led to a rethinking of this tax within government circles, and the tax was made stiffer. The national tax rate on land sold under long-term ownership (redefined to mean land acquired prior to Jan. 1, 1969) was changed to 20% for capital gains of up to ¥20 million, and three-fourths of capital gains in excess of ¥20 million was added to total household taxable income and taxed on the personal income tax schedules. The latter fraction was reduced to one half in 1979. Land sold for short-term ownership was taxed more stiffly. However, to encourage the conversion of farmland to residential sites in areas subject to city planning, the tax rate was 15% on gains up to ¥40 million and 20% beyond that amount.

The following shows the tax rates in force before the revision in March 1982: On land sold for long-term ownership (acquired before Jan. 1, 1969):

Capital gains (million ¥)	Tax
0–40	separately at 20% (national) 6% (local)
40–80	½ of capital gains added to total household taxable income
80 and over	¾ of capital gains added to total household income

On land sold for short-term ownership (acquired after Jan. 1, 1969), whichever is the larger of the two: (i) taxed separately at 40% (national) and 12% (local), or (ii) 110% of the tax attributable to capital gain when included in total taxable household income.

For a large capital gain, these taxes are quite high. Assuming that the household has no other income, the effective tax rate on the sum of ¥500 million is estimated at 63% (combining national and local taxes) for a long-term estate and 88% for a short-term estate.

In March 1982, with a view to reduce the tax burden on land sellers so as to stimulate the creation of a new supply of residential land, the distinction between long-term and short-term ownership was shortened to ten years. For long-term ownership, the higher rate in excess of ¥80 million was eliminated. This has resulted in a reduction of the effective tax burden to 43%. In addition, farmland to be converted to residential sites in city-planning areas was taxed at a flat rate of 25% in 1982–84.

From 1952–1969 a special exemption could be claimed when a household changed place of residence. This provision was replaced by a special deduction amount to ¥10 million in 1970–72, ¥17 million in 1973–74, and ¥30 million from 1975 on.

TAXES ON PROPERTY

Direct taxes on property are the real estate tax and the inheritance and gift taxes.

Property Tax

The municipal government collects property taxes at the standard rate of 1.4% (2.1% maximum rate on the assessed value of a fixed asset). A tax preference is given to residential land: for a house site less than 200m², the taxable value is 1.4

of the assessed value; for a site in excess of 200m², the taxable value is ½ of the assessed value.

The property tax burden is low in Japan because assessed value has been only a fraction of market value (see below). Especially low has been the property tax on farmland located in urban areas subject to city planning. There are three types of farmland in metropolitan areas, based on assessed value: *Class A*—assessed at more than ¥50,000 per 3.3m² (*tsubo*) or the average residential site price in the area; *Class B*—assessed at between 50% and 100% of the average residential site price in the area; *Class C*—assessed at less than ¥10,000 per 3.3m² or ½ the average residential site price in the area.

Owners of farms are reluctant to sell their land because they anticipate continued increases in residential land prices. While monetary returns on their farms are low, the property tax burden is also low, thus enabling farmland owners to hold on to their properties. The government decided to increase the tax burden on farms remaining in metropolitan areas by raising their assessed values to levels equivalent to neighboring residential land values. The measure was put into effect in 1973 for Class A farmland and in 1974 for Class B farmland. Even so, the effective tax rate has been limited because the tax is reduced as municipal governments apply central government grants-in-aid. Farmers strongly resisted putting Class C farmland under the same system. It was only in march 1982 that the measure was finally extended to cover this class of farmland. However, farms

TABLE A.2
Inheritance and Gift Tax Rates

Taxable Value		Marginal rate (%)
Inheritance (Million ¥)	Gift (Million ¥)	
0– 2	0– 0.5	10
2– 5	0.5– 0.7	15
5– 9	0.7– 1.0	20
9– 15	1.0– 1.4	25
15– 23	1.4– 2.0	30
23– 33	2.0– 2.8	35
33– 48	2.8– 4.0	40
48– 70	4.0– 5.5	45
70–100	5.5– 8.0	50
100–140	8.0–13	55
140–180	13 –20	60
180–250	20 –35	65
250–500	35 –70	70
500–	70 –	75

SOURCE: Inheritance Tax Law, Article 16 and 21-7 (rev. March 1975), in *Genkō Hōki Sōran*, vol. 43.

with assessed values less than ¥30,000 per 3.3m² are exempt. Further, a farmer who files a declaration of intent to maintain his farm as a farm for the next ten years is also exempt. Since he will not be penalized if he changes his mind after five years, the measure will actually remain ineffective for five years.[16]

Inheritance and Gift Taxes

The inheritance tax is imposed on the taxable value of inheritances. The tax schedule as revised in 1975 is shown in table A.2. The taxable value of an inheritance is defined as: (total inheritance—base exemption of ¥20 million—¥4 million times the number of statutory heirs). Some exemptions have already been applied prior to obtain the figure for the total inheritance, i.e., up to ¥2.5 million per heir for life and casualty insurance, and up to ¥2 million per heir for retirement allowances acquired due to the benefactor's death. The inheritance tax is allocated among heirs according to their individual shares of the inheritance. There are special preferences for heirs who are spouses, juveniles, and handicapped.

The gift tax has a base exemption of ¥0.6 million per recipient. This tax schedule is also shown in table A.2. There are various special preferences associated with this tax.

Assessment of Land Values

The burden of the property tax and the inheritance tax depends very much on the land value assessment employed by the tax offices. So far, their assessments are loosely based on two major government-sponsored appraisals of land value.

(i) *Publicly appraised land value (chika kōji kakaku)*. The National Land Agency conducts a national survey of land values as of January 1 every year (since 1970). Land sites selected for appraisals are standard residential sites (17,600 in 1982), which are assessed by real estate appraisers (1,821 persons in 1982) who report to the Agency's Land Appraisal Committee. The assessed values are tallied by region and other categories and published annually.

A major and serious complaint about this exercise is that appraisals are not only understated (reportedly 0.5 to 0.7 of market value), but also contain longitudinal distortions due to changes in personal judgment and to political and other external influences.

Following the same general procedure, the land agency conducts another survey as of July 1 every year under the Land Utilization Planning Law on a larger number of sites (27,810 in 1982). This series is called standard land prices (*kijun chika*).

(ii) *Highest residential site prices (saikō rosenka)*. The National Tax Agency conducts a survey as of July 1 every year on standard prices of residential sites per m² facing the main thoroughfares of prefectural capital cities. The highest price for each capital is publicly reported as the highest price of land adjacent to a thoroughfare (*saikō rosenka*). This series yields even lower prices than the series in (i). The ratio (ii)/(i) is reported to have been 51% in 1975 and 63% in 1981 (*Yomiuri Shimbun*, Apr. 11, 1982). In estimating (ii), the tax agency takes (i) into consideration, however.

Series (ii) is consulted in assessing land values for both the inheritance tax and the property tax. For the inheritance tax, the National Tax Agency professes that assessed values should eventually be raised to 70% of (i). Land values for the property tax are revised every three years. Residential land values within a prefecture are aligned with series (ii). The Ministry of Home Affairs advocates that land values for property tax purposes eventually be raised to 40% of (i) (*Yomiuri Shimbun*, Apr. 11, 1982).

NOTES TO APPENDIX

1. For the tax system in force in the earlier period, see Pechman and Kaizuka, "Taxation."
2. The principal relevant tax laws are the Personal Income Tax (Shotokuzei Hō), the Inheritance Tax Code (Sōzokuzei Hō), the Local Tax Code (Chihōzei Hō), the Special Tax Measures Law (Tokubetsu Sozei Sochi Hō), and their enforcement orders. See the Legal Bureaus of the Diet, *Genkō Hōki Sōran*, vols. 17, 19, 20, and 21.
3. Local taxes are largely uniform throughout the country. National income tax is levied on the current year's income, and local income taxes on the previous year's income.
4. Social security and pension benefits are part of gross income. Private pension benefits are tax exempt to the extent apportioned to employee contributions (which are part of taxable income).
5. The following refers to national income tax.
6. To cite a few, the commuting allowance paid by the employer is tax exempt (not counted as part of gross income). There are other deductions, especially as regards private pensions and housing investment. There have been a modest tax credit for the purchase of a newly constructed house, a modest tax credit for mortgage payments (since 1982, tax reduced by mortgage payments less ¥0.3 million times 0.18 up to ¥0.18 million, and a credit for workers' special savings (*zaisan keisei chochibu*). Private pension premiums are not tax exempt, but an IRA system is to be introduced (for pensions administered by employers, a tax exemption was initiated in October 1982 on interest on the sum of principal and accumulated interest up to ¥5 million).
7. The standard deduction on wage income is in lieu of business-expense deductions allowed for business proprietors.
8. Art. 143 of the Income Tax Code states: "A resident who is engaged in a business that yields real estate income, business income, or timber income may submit a blue return when approved by the local tax office director."
9. Art. 149 of the Income Tax Code states: "A blue return must be supported by attachments of a balance sheet, an income statement, or other detailed statements on the amount of real estate income, business income, or timber income." In actual practice, however, this requirement has not been followed by many proprietors.
10. See Art. 25-2, Special Tax Measures Law. The corporate income tax rate (national) was 42% on undistributed profits and 30% on distributed profits (as of 1983).
11. They are allowed as a compensation for low health insurance fees received by private medical and dental practitioners—72% of fees were tax deductible. The rate was scaled down in 1979 as follows (Art. 26, Special Tax Measures Law, rev. March 1979):

Revenue ¥ million	Deduction Percentage
0–25	72
25–30	70
30–40	62
40–50	57
50–	52

12. Art. 10 of the Income Tax Code, which refers to "an individual with a domestic domicile."

13. Art. 96ff. of the Income Tax Code specify that property income (interest, dividends, and real estate income) of household members in excess of their respective dependent exemptions must be added to the taxable income of the principal income earner of the household.

14. This method of tax computation is called the *gobun-gojō hō* (divide by five and then multiply by five). The *nibun-nijō hō* (divide by two and then multiply by two) has been frequently suggested as a method for computing income tax in the case of the two-paycheck family.

15. Art. 10 of the Income Tax Code.

16. The areas of the three classes of farmland in the three metropolitan areas are reported as follows:

Class	as of January 1973 hectares	as of January 1980 hectares
A	3608	2099
B	12817	8114
C	88862	62804

(*Yomiuri Shimbun*, Nov. 29, 1982)

Antitrust and Industrial Policy in Japan: Competition and Cooperation

IYORI HIROSHI

The Japanese Antimonopoly Law of 1947,[1] modeled after antitrust legislation in the United States, today differs in many respects from American law. Evident in provisions for exempt cartels, enforcement procedures, and other features, these differences reflect the influence of the industrial policy pursued by those ministries that have jurisdiction over Japanese industry—including the Ministry of International Trade and Industry, the Ministry of Finance, and the Ministry of Construction. Such differences should surprise no one since antitrust law, like other economic regulations must be adapted to a nation's historical, social, and cultural environment.

This essay will examine some of the factors promoting various competitive and cooperative policies in Japan. Part one describes the development of industrial policy, while Part two discusses the environment for such policies, with particular emphasis on the traditional government-business relationship and collective behavior in Japan. Part three assesses the competitiveness of Japanese markets and offers a brief discussion on the roles that the Antimonopoly Law, the Fair Trade Commission, and administrative guidance play in determining and affecting that competitiveness.

1. THE DEVELOPMENT OF INDUSTRIAL POLICY

As a rule, the ministries of the Japanese government responsible for industrial policy[2] are organized by industry, with individual sections or bureaus exercising jurisdiction over particular industries or lines of commerce. Because the objective of each of these ministries is to protect, modernize, and promote the development of Japanese industry as a whole, their programs and policies tend to further industrial cooperation and concentration and to focus on trade associations and major enterprises rather than fostering competition.

Officials responsible for industrial policy still consider industrial development ultimately to benefit consumers in general, and thus the protection and growth of industry has continued to be their central concern. To be sure, government concern for consumer welfare has increased since the mid-1960s, but antitrust policy designed to foster competition in the interest of consumers is viewed as contrasting with Japanese industrial policy. The fundamental tension between Japanese antitrust and industrial policies is a consequence of the confrontation and compromise between them, and the Japanese Fair Trade Commission (FTC)—the government agency responsible for enforcing the Antimonopoly Law in all fields of industry—remains an independent regulatory agency.

The industrial policy of the Ministry of International Trade and Industry (MITI), which has jurisdiction over commerce, manufacturing, and mining, is the most important in discussing the development of Japanese antitrust policy. MITI's policies with respect to competition have changed over time as summarized below.[3]

Phase One (1950–1960)

During the 1950s the Japanese economy suffered from a shortage of capital, and its industries were not internationally competitive. Thus, MITI considered competition "an impediment to the rational development of the nation's economy as a whole,"[4] and the ministry played a major role in minimizing the effects of the Antimonopoly Law. Intent on removing the obstacles to its policies, MITI was the principal architect of both the 1953 amendments that significantly weakened the Antimonopoly Law and a 1958 bill that attempted to weaken the law even further (but was not enacted by the Diet). During the same period, however, the Diet did pass various statutes drafted by MITI providing for special antitrust exemptions. Moreover, with increasing frequency the ministry resorted to administrative guidance such as official recommendations to curtail production to restrict competition. MITI policy was modeled after the industrial rationalization policy of 1931, which cartelized all major industries in order to rationalize them, that is, to eliminate excessive competition. This first phase thus represented the period of sharpest confrontation between MITI and the FTC over relaxation of the Antimonopoly Law. After the defeat of the 1958 bill to amend this law, MITI gave up efforts to weaken existing legislation but continued to use administrative guidance.

Phase Two (1960–1970)

During this period of high economic growth following the liberalization of trade and investment, MITI revised its views and acknowledged the need for an antitrust policy as a means of "protecting the function of competition to stimulate efficient industrial activity and creativity and innovation in the enterprise." The Japanese economy, MITI stated, "is based on recognition of the fact that free enterprise is the motivating force for industrial creativity and innovativeness." However, because Japanese firms were generally small and unable to take advantage of economies of scale relative to West European and American en-

terprises, MITI officials have engaged in an array of activities aimed at strengthening the international competitiveness of Japanese industry.[5] They have
advocated mergers, industry cooperation, and rationalization cartels as well as
actively promoting government and business cooperation. The same motives
prompted MITI to propose the enactment of Special Measures for the Promotion
of Designated Industries in 1963 (ultimately defeated in the Diet[6]), to promote
such major mergers as that between Yawata Steel and Fuji Steel, and to use
government-business cooperation to effect an "adjustment" of investment in the
petroleum and chemical industries. Several groups of economists and legal
scholars strongly opposed the Yawata-Fuji merger, and the FTC issued a formal
complaint and ordered the companies to divest themselves of some of their
facilities as a condition for the merger. This prolonged proceeding impressed
upon the Japanese businessmen that a realization of a merger between large
companies is difficult to achieve and the number of large-scale mergers has
decreased sharply.

Phase Three (1970 to the Present)

The Japanese economy achieved a level of performance comparable with that
of the advanced economies of Western Europe and the United States in the
1970s. In response, MITI decided that "the role of industrial policy should be
reexamined to facilitate to the greatest extent possible the effective operation of
the market." "Consolidation of the conditions for competition is essential," MITI
affirmed, "to maintain economic vitality in this period as well." Intervention was
therefore to be used as an exceptional measure when competition failed to
function effectively.[7] Even during this period, however, MITI objected to a bill
drafted by the FTC in 1974 to revise the Antimonopoly Law. Moreover, as
exemplified in the Special Measures for the Stabilization of Designated Depressed Industries enacted in 1978 and renewed in 1983,[8] this shift did not
necessarily eliminate the tendency of MITI's industrial policy to restrict competition. Nevertheless, the principles of a market economy have become generally accepted within MITI. For example, in recent response to foreign criticism
of Japanese protective policies, MITI recently revised its system of approvals and
standards for imports, effective March 26, 1985.

However, not all changes occurred on MITI's initiative. For example, the
Tokyo High Court decision of September 1980 on the oil production cartel case
severely criticized MITI's administrative guidance. In March 1981, the FTC
made public its views on the Antimonopoly Law and administrative guidance.
Also, Western criticism of MITI's industrial policy since 1980 has caused MITI to
adhere more closely to free market principles. All of these developments restricted administrative guidance considerably.

The most recent change in MITI's industrial policy has been to place central
emphasis on the operation of market forces, at least in principle. This shift in
policy was caused by such factors as the greater independence and autonomy
Japanese firms have achieved as a result of rapid growth, the theoretical support

for a competitive market economy provided by economists and legal scholars, the desirability of adopting consumer-oriented policies, and the liberalization of trade and investment, as well as the influence of the FTC's antitrust policies. In short, MITI's industrial policy has been forced to become more flexible to meet the changing conditions of the economy and its needs.

2. THE ENVIRONMENT FOR
A COOPERATIVE GOVERNMENT-BUSINESS RELATIONSHIP

From an American or West European perspective, one may ask why MITI's industrial policy has been so anticompetitive. The answer can be traced at least in part to the traditional relationship between government and business and to the influence of a Japanese proclivity for collectivism. These two factors in combination have tended to result in the restriction of competition.

The Government-Business Relationship

Americans appear to view the purpose of government as limited to the preservation of order and the protection of the rights and safety of the people. The three branches of government (legislative, executive, and judicial) are separate, with administrative agencies operating only under express statutory authorization. In principle, government should resist intervention in the economy. By protecting the freedom of economic activity and maintaining a competitive economic order, the government can protect both business and consumers.

Japan, by contrast, has been endeavoring since the beginning of the Meiji period (1867–1911) to acquire national economic and military power comparable to that of the industrial states of the West. For Japan to attain the status of an industrial power, positive leadership by a strong government vis-à-vis the public and industry was considered essential. Possessing a strong authority and attempting to adopt Western models, the Meiji government provided such leadership in initiating extensive institutional reforms in education, transportation, communication, law, and administration. Established in conjunction with these institutional reforms,[9] the industrial ministries have actively intervened in the economy and provided guidance and assistance to industry. They were restructured and strengthened during the Depression in the 1930s and have continued with some changes in the postwar period. Officials in the industrial ministries have continued to engage in a variety of activities designed to promote individual industries. The means used have included basic planning, the introduction of foreign technology, the establishment of model factories, the dissemination of technical information, capital and financial assistance, special tax treatment, cartelization, and the promotion of mergers and trade associations.

Consequently, government (the industrial ministries) has exerted considerable influence and leadership over private industry. Business has had to accept governmental guidance without the sanction of specific statutes. In most cases, trade associations and major enterprises have tended to seek government direction. Contacts between government and business have usually been informal, and frequently advisory committees established within the industrial ministries have been used rather than open public hearings as in the United States. Important legislative proposals are thus almost always the product of discussion and consultation between the government agencies concerned and affected industries. If, for example, legislation to exempt certain activities from the Antimonopoly Law has the support of both the government officials of the industrial ministries and industries concerned, it is likely to be enacted by the Diet. Such close and closed consultation makes administrative guidance possible and gives rise to the epithet, "Japan Incorporated." Although criticized as harmful to the freedom of individual enterprises and consumer interests, the relationship between government and business is, in Japan, widely believed to be in the national interest so long as it is not abused. The rationale is that industrial growth is thought ultimately to benefit the consumer.[10]

This government-business relationship in Japan has resulted in restriction rather than promotion of competition, and has provided a foundation both for the enactment of special statutory exemptions to the Antimonopoly Law and for anticompetitive administrative guidance, the latter of which the FTC has persistently opposed when inconsistent with the Antimonopoly Law. In the wake of the Tokyo High Court's September 1980 decision in the oil production cartel case,[11] in which MITI was severely criticized, the FTC issued a statement entitled "Concerning the Relationship Between the Antimonopoly Law and Administrative Guidance" and demanded that administrative guidance by the industrial ministries conform to it.[12] Even though administrative guidance may have some merit in specific cases, it is desirable that such guidance at least be expressed in a written, public statement in which its purpose and substance are made clear. We should note in passing, however, that although economic growth weakened the government-business relationship, the relationship has regained some of its lost strength because of the recent recession and decline in international trade.

The government-business relationship in Japan has also been strongly influenced by general attitudes toward business. Bankruptcy produces a sense of panic in Japan. If a major firm or a large number of smaller firms goes bankrupt, officials from the industrial ministries are called to account by the Diet. The officials cannot avoid accountability by pointing out that the firms' managers are the responsible parties. Because of the Japanese system of permanent employment and dependent subcontractors, a major bankruptcy means a devastating loss of jobs and a widening circle of additional bankruptcies. Enterprises are also regarded in Japan as a "community" or *gemeinschaft* to be preserved and not, as in the United States, simply a vehicle for commerce. Consequently, in periods of recession there is a tendency for businesses to form recession cartels with both labor unions and the government providing the necessary support to sustain them.

Although a close government-business relationship may be effective in attaining a certain objective in some instances, obvious problems arise when such a relationship enables government officials and particular industries to decide among themselves on an important course of action that can adversely affect third parties. The relationship can and often does result in a concentration of power in the bureaucracy in violation of the principle of separation of powers and it may restrict individuals' rights and freedoms. Suppliers and other closely related parties may also be injured. Moreover, as economic growth has slowed and markets have contracted, the close relationship maintained between the industrial ministries and individual industries caused the economy to become less efficient, thus making continued growth more difficult.[13] The government-business relationship seems also to have contributed to barriers obstructing foreign access to Japanese markets.

Thus, although such a close government-business relationship might perhaps have been justified when Japanese industry was striving to catch up with industry in Western Europe and the United States, it is difficult to justify such a relationship today when Japan has become a major participant in the international economy. It may even be harmful to a competitive international economic order. These problems remain and thus some rules appear necessary to limit the government-business relationship to insure that it does not impair the market economy.

The Proclivity toward Collective Behavior

The frequently noted[14] collectivist proclivity of the Japanese people manifests itself within and among business enterprises, as well as in society more generally. Trade associations, for example, have been formed in all sectors of Japanese industry,[15] and the level of participation is extremely high. There are nationwide as well as regional associations, industry-wide as well as trade and product-line associations.[16] This tendency plays an important role in the implementation of industrial policy, especially for administrative guidance. Government officials find it difficult to give guidance to individual firms. Trade associations, however, provide a useful conduit through which government policy can be relayed to member firms. These associations also provide a forum for negotiation and cooperation with government officials in formulating policy and the substance of the guidance to be given. Like convoys providing protection for each member, these associations develop industry-wide cooperation but may at the same time be criticized for protecting their members against the discipline of market forces, for allowing them to stagnate and become inefficient.

When carried too far and resulting in cartels as defined by the Antimonopoly Law, collectivist behavior becomes an antitrust violation. Indeed, the majority of all formal FTC decisions on violations of the Antimonopoly Law have involved trade association cartels.[17] To define the legal parameters of such collective behavior, in 1979 the FTC issued a set of "Guidelines for Trade Association Activities under the Antimonopoly Law."[18] In addition, collusion activities by trade associations have been significantly reduced due to passage of the 1977 amendments to the Antimonopoly Law[19] providing for possible surcharges on illegal cartels' activities, and because government conferral of a coveted decoration of honor on the president of a trade association that is involved in an antitrust violation is subject to suspension.[20] Specifically, when an FTC decision finds an association to have violated the Antimonopoly Law, its president is considered ineligible for national honors for a period of three to five years.

Attitudes toward Law

In concluding this section, a note should be added on the author's view of the basic differences between Japan and the West in conceptions of the use of law.

In the West, the law has been viewed as rules or principles that protect freedom and equality. While sharing this principle, the law in Japan is, by contrast, considered primarily an instrument of government control, especially bureaucratic control. Since the government-business relationship in Japan has traditionally involved negotiation and compromise because of the collectivist proclivity described above, resorting to law and litigation is usually regarded as an undesirable or, at best, the least preferred means of resolving disputes. This fact perhaps is one of the reasons why there are only 13,000 practicing attorneys in Japan, as compared to over a half-million in the United States. Moreover, because the number of litigated cases is low, the law often remains ambiguous. Such ambiguity in the law leaves room for flexibility in administrative guidance. Consequently, the separation of legislative, executive, and judicial power in Japan is also quite ambiguous, and the power of the executive branch is not limited to enforcing statutes enacted by the legislature.

Antitrust law in the United States functions in part as a set of rules governing transactions between enterprises. Consequently, there are many private antitrust actions. In contrast, the Antimonopoly Law in Japan is viewed as a regulatory statute to be administered by the FTC. There are few private suits.[21] As a result of these attitudes, the FTC, too, can provide administrative guidance.

These specifically Japanese attitudes toward the nature and function of the law pervade the entire legal environment. For example, the Japanese view contracts quite differently from Westerners. Of course, the Japanese believe that contracts or promises should be honored, but in a strict sense contracts are not considered particularly important, even when concluded.[22] In most instances, a change of circumstances after reaching an agreement is reason enough to modify the contract by mutual consent or in the course of performance. This is considered the "natural" and obvious thing to do. Similarly, few suits are brought if there is a breach of contract, since terms and extent of damages are seldom clear. Even though cartels were legal and enforceable before the war, almost no breach of contract actions were brought against those who broke cartel discipline in Japan—quite unlike the situation in Germany. Moreover, in ongoing relationships, quite often no formal contract is concluded at all.

Nevertheless, the Japanese environment is becoming more similar to that in the West as the use of administrative guidance decreases and there is greater enforcement of regulatory laws such as antimonopoly provisions and those covering consumer protection, pollution control, and product liability. Japanese firms have also become increasingly subject to overseas antitrust and other regulatory laws. As a result of the application of national or foreign antitrust laws, many Japanese firms have created or strengthened their in-house legal departments.

3. THE CONDITIONS FOR COMPETITION IN JAPAN

Despite the collectivist tendencies described above, conditions favoring competition also prevail in Japan. How did the current level of competition develop and how extensive is it? What is the role of antitrust enforcement in maintaining or promoting competition? These are the questions to be addressed in this section.

Competition in Japan

The Allied Occupation carried out reforms to provide strong stimuli for competition just after World War II. The dissolution of the *zaibatsu*, deconcentration of large-scale enterprises, elimination of wartime cartels, and industry control associations all contributed to making the Japanese market structure more competitive as well as directly fostering competition. Other reforms, such as those changing the landholding patterns, labor laws, and taxation, were carried out and had the effect of equalizing the distribution of income. As a consequence, Japan today has one of the lowest income disparities of any country in the world. These reforms benefited the domestic market and also stimulated competition. Wartime and immediate postwar price controls on all but a few commodities such as rice and wheat were also lifted.

After World War II, Japan had even less territory, fewer resources, and a larger and poorer population than before. Moreover, its manufacturing facilities were devastated. But the Japanese worked to restore their economy, and with capital and technological aid from the United States and the competitive postwar environment, Japan was able to achieve rapid economic growth. Because of a competitive environment, many firms such as Sony and Honda grew from small, local factories into major manufacturers; the rapid growth of these firms further stimulated competition.

As in the decade following the Meiji Restoration, after World War II there was again tremendous demand in Japan for Western technology. And it is well known that Japanese industry had the capacity both to absorb and to improve the technology it imported. Competition caused or stimulated the importation, improvement, and diffusion of technology, and thus was an important contributing factor in Japan's economic growth.

During the periods of technological innovation and rapid growth, cartels and other restrictive arrangements to maintain stability were not particularly significant or effective. Except in those sectors of the economy subject to formal government regulation, the anticompetitive industrial policies of the industrial ministries did not greatly reduce the level of competition.

To be sure, foreign pressure has had a significant impact not only on the Japanese economy, but also on its industrial policy. Liberalization of trade in the 1960s and liberalization of investment in the 1970s were undertaken in response to foreign pressure. The government has responded similarly to recent West European and U.S. criticism of barriers to Japanese markets. And the effect of such pressure has been to foster liberalization and competition. Stated differently, liberalization has made industrial policy more responsive to the market economy.[23] Industrial policy that has restricted competition to protect failing firms during periods of temporary recession has often indirectly fostered competition by preserving a sufficient number of firms to provide competition in an industry once the economic conditions have improved.[24]

There is a complex system for the distribution of goods and services—the so-called distribution *keiretsu*—in which large manufacturers dominate both wholesale and retail dealers. This closed and anticompetitive distribution system has been strongly criticized. Although modern, large-scale retailers have developed to counter the system, there are also statutes restricting their activities. The Japanese proclivity for collective behavior noted previously may also have a substantial effect on the distribution sector. Given the facts, the FTC has, for example, conducted studies of various industries including automobiles and consumer electronics. In March 1980 when the results of the studies were published, the FTC-appointed Antimonopoly Law Study Group issued a report, "Problems Concerning the Antimonopoly Law with Respect to the Distribution System," which set forth the FTC's antitrust policies for regulating restrictive practices in the manufacturer-dominated *keiretsu* distribution system.[25]

One problem with respect to market structure in Japan[26] is posed by "enterprise groups" (*kigyōshūdan* or *kigyō keiretsu*), which have appeared since the *zaibatsu* dissolution. These groups of affiliated private business enterprises can be divided into two categories. The enterprise groups consisting of former *zaibatsu*,[27] including Mitsui, Mitsubishi, and Sumitomo, account for 7.4 percent of total sales in Japan; and the non-*zaibatsu* groups, such as Fuyo, Sanwa, and Daiichi Kangyō Bank, for 8.4 percent. The member firms in each group are fixed, and some firms in the former *zaibatsu* groups use their original trade names.

A recent FTC study[28] found that in 1981 the average percentage of stock in each member firm in a *keiretsu* held by another member firm was 2.0 percent for former *zaibatsu* groups and 1.5 percent for non-*zaibatsu* groups. For cross-shareholding ratios—the average proportion of each *keiretsu* member firm's outstanding shares held by all other member firms in the *keiretsu*—the three former *zaibatsu* groups averaged 32 percent, and non-*zaibatsu* groups averaged 19 percent.

This level of intragroup cross-shareholding[29] might provide sufficient control to permit a group to act as a collective unit in carrying out a particular decision, but no group seems to have been able to do so. Member firms can be expected to cooperate only if it is not too burdensome. It is possible, for instance, to establish a jointly held company to engage in a new venture. It is rather difficult, however, for enterprise groups to engage in an intragroup transaction without consensus as to its merits. Although the data on intragroup transactions are considerable, Eleanor Hadley's findings in 1970 seem to hold true: "The answer to the question in the title of this chapter ("Zaibatsu Yesterday, Business Groupings Today: Is There a Difference?") is emphatically yes. . . . Preference for the grouping is still there, but the old exclusiveness is gone."[30]

Another feature restricting competition in the Japanese economy is the number of cartels exempt from the purview of the Antimonopoly Law. Exempt cartels are broadly classified into the following categories: recession cartels, rationalization cartels, export and import cartels, and miscellaneous other cartels.[31] Recession cartels, the most important, are based on Article 24-3 of the Antimonopoly Law, Article 5 of the Special Measures for the Structural Improvement of Designated Industries,[32] and Article 17 of the Medium and Small Enterprise Association Law.[33]

The proclivity to engage in collective and cooperative behavior may result in other, less apparent restrictive practices—in the importation of goods and capital, for example. The causes for such restrictions should be investigated. As an example of what can be achieved in this area, with information received from American government sources, the FTC found in March 1983 that four Japanese caustic soda ash manufacturers had formed an import cartel. The commission concluded that this cartel impeded access to the Japanese market by foreign manufacturers and ordered it eliminated.

The Japanese Fair Trade Commission

The Japanese Fair Trade Commission was created under the Antimonopoly Law (chap. 8) as an independent administrative commission on the model of the U.S. Federal Trade Commission. Although the commission is under the jurisdiction of the prime minister's office (Antimonopoly Law Art. 27(2)), it functions independently of the Cabinet including MITI and the other ministries.

Proceedings for cases involving violations of the Antimonopoly Law are based on evidence obtained by the commission's investigation bureau from those involved. The commission handles about five hundred complaints a year, other than such incidental complaints as unfair below-cost sales that are filed with local offices by small retailers.[34] Summary investigation procedures are generally used when a violation is not substantial or is limited in scope.[35] In formal investigations, if there is proof of a violation, the commission will generally take formal action, usually a formal recommendation under Article 48 of the statute. Where the evidence is insufficient to show a violation, the commission issues a warning to eliminate dubious activities; if there is no evidence of a violation, the commission dismisses the case. Summary investigations usually end with a warning to eliminate dubious activities or, if there is no proof of a violation, with dismissal.

A warning is not a formal public action. It is issued to a respondent when a violation is suspected but cannot be confirmed. Such warnings prohibit companies and trade associations from engaging in conduct that may be considered a violation. Thus the FTC uses warnings to eliminate activities that risk being violations.[36] The Antimonopoly Law provides for criminal penalties against illegal cartels (Art. 89). Only in exceptional cases, however, does the FTC file a criminal accusation with the public prosecutor. The most recent example was against the 1974 oil cartel.[37]

The Antimonopoly Law: A Comparative Overview

In Japan the Antitrust Law is supported by consumer organizations, legal scholars, economists, and small and medium enterprises. These groups have actively opposed any weakening of the law and have presented their views to a broad audience through newspapers and other media.

On the other hand, large enterprises and their related business circles have been strong antagonists in their opposition to antitrust policy despite that maintaining competition makes the private enterprise system possible with managerial and competitive freedom. However, they would not dispute the view that a market economy provides the best mechanism for allocating resources and assuring economic efficiency, or that the natural adjustment of interests among industries and consumers by the market is preferable to allocation by regulation. In Japan as in Western Europe and the United States, antitrust law provides the basis for economic order. There is an awareness that insistence on free international trade policies is inconsistent with support for restrictions on competition in domestic markets. Except for cartel-minded leaders in such major industries as iron and steel, there is no fundamental opposition to antitrust policy.[38] The desire of industry, particularly major industries, is to have the requirements for the approval of recession cartels eased.

For the most part, Japanese political parties take positions that reflect their supporters' views of antitrust policy. With the exception of the Communist party, each political party recognizes the principle of a market economy as the basis for Japan's economic system. The 1977 amendments strengthening the Antimonopoly Law, for example, were enacted with the support of all parties. Although the ruling Liberal Democratic party (LDP) generally defers to the industrial ministries in economic policy matters, it has been known to adopt disparate views in deference to supporters and as a matter of political necessity.

The following is a brief comparison of the provisions and practices of Japanese and United States antitrust law relating to cartels, private monopolization, and merger and shareholding control.

Cartels. With respect to the prohibition of cartels, Japanese antitrust law does not differ significantly from U.S. law except for complex exemption statutes. In Japan as in the United States, price and output cartels are deemed illegal per se and are also subject to criminal penalties. The principal evidentiary issue is generally whether or not there is a conspiracy.

In Japan Article 3 of the Antimonopoly Law proscribes cartels among entrepreneurs, and Article 8(1) prohibits trade association cartels. (Cartels are defined in Art. 2(6).) Price and output cartels are prohibited in principle and, as noted above, have been subject to a mandatory surcharge (*kachōkin*) since the 1977 amendments (Art. 7-2 and 8-3). Proof of "an agreement among entrepreneurs," which includes tacit agreements, has been the principal evidentiary issue in Japan. It is also necessary to show that the combined market share of the entrepreneurs involved is substantial because of the definitional requirement that the cartel in question has "substantially restrained competition in a particular field of trade" (Art. 2(6) and 8(1)). The smallest share under any FTC decision to date was the 20 percent share of the 1952 oil cartel.[39]

The prohibition against cartels under Japanese law differs from the American per se rule in which, in principle, market share is not considered. Except for this element, however, there is no significant difference between the two countries in practice concerning price cartels. American law is, of course, more stringent.

There have been quite a few Japanese FTC decisions relating to cartels; most have involved price and output cartels. A few formal adjudicated revisions (*seishiki shinketsu*) have dealt with other types of cartels (almost all of which involved rigged bidding arrangements). One reason is that Japanese antitrust policy has developed since 1960 in the context of anti-inflation and consumer protection policies. Concern for free competition as an ultimate objective and for diffusion of economic power has been rather weak in Japan, and thus opposition to concentrations of economic power, which underlies traditional American antitrust policy, has also been weak.

Such differences are especially relevant to the application of antitrust law to joint research and development projects. The antitrust approach in the United States has been articulated in the Department of Justice's 1980 guidelines,[40] under which a "rule of reason" standard is applied to such projects. Although there have been no formal adjudicated Japanese decisions concerning joint research and development, there is an unreported 1970 patent pooling case.[41]

Although the parameters of Japanese antitrust policy with respect to joint research and development projects are not clear, in view of past FTC decisions and accepted theory, such arrangements would not in principle violate the Article 3 prohibitions against unreasonable restraints of trade and private monopolization under the following conditions:

(1) Their objective is to promote technological development, and they do not in purpose or effect restrict technological development.

(2) They do not unfairly restrict either participation in or withdrawal from the project by third parties.

(3) The freedom of the participants to use or develop similar technology independently is not restricted.

(4) The results of such joint research are to be widely disseminated to nonparticipants.

(5) The arrangements do not include supplementary restraints on competition, such as division of territories and price restrictions.

(6) The project involves basic research related to new technology and no technology related to manufacturing or the production process.

Private Monopolization. After the 1945 Alcoa case,[42] a U.S. firm with a monopoly position could be deemed to have violated Section 2 of the Sherman

Act. In Japan, "control or exclusion of the business activities of another entre-preneur" is an element of private monopolization, prohibited under Article 3, as defined in Article 2(5). This element was construed by the Tokyo High Court in the 1957 Noda Shōyu case[43] to mean economic domination of a market. This covers a broad range of activities and is not significantly different from American law. However, there have only been four major private monopolization decisions.[44]

Under Japanese law, even if there is no "control or exclusion of the business activities of another entrepreneur," "monopolistic situations," as defined in Article 2(7), can be controlled under the provisions of Article 8-4, added in 1977, where there is fear of a concentration of economic power.

Merger and Shareholding Controls. Control over mergers and intercorporate shareholding in the United States has been gradually expanded pursuant to the 1950 amendment of the Clayton Act and subsequent judicial decisions. The Justice Department's 1968 and 1982 guidelines on mergers have further clarified the law. In Japan, to the extent the effect is a "substantial restraint of competition in a particular field of trade," the Antimonopoly Law prohibits intercorporate shareholding (Art. 10 and 14), mergers (Art. 15), and transfers of business (Art. 16). The criteria for determining whether these prohibitions apply are not as clear, however, as in the United States. Previously a market share of over 30 percent was considered to involve serious risk of a "substantial restraint of competition in a particular field of trade." However, the Japanese "Standards for Review of Corporate Mergers" issued by the FTC on July 25, 1980,[45] are somewhat more flexible than the American guidelines in that they provide for close scrutiny of mergers and acquisitions resulting in a market share of 25 percent or above or the highest market share for the relevant product line, and they set out separate criteria for horizontal, vertical, and conglomerate mergers.

To date there have been formal FTC decisions on merger and shareholding controls in only a few cases: the *Nippon Gakki-Kawai Gakki* case (under Art. 10);[46] the *Yawata-Fuji Merger* case (under Art. 15);[47] and the *Tōhō-Subaru* case (under Art. 16).[48] A number of other mergers have been blocked by the commission through informal consultation. Nevertheless, there have been fewer mergers between large-scale enterprises in Japan than in the United States.[49]

There is no counterpart in American law to the Japanese restrictions on intercorporate shareholding to prevent substantial restraint of competition in a given field of trade. These restrictions reflect special features of the Japanese economy. Intercorporate shareholding is prohibited in the following situations:

Holding Companies. Article 9 prohibits outright the establishment of holding companies, which are defined as "companies whose principal business is to control the business activities of a company or companies in Japan by means of holding stock." Because the controlling companies of the prewar *zaibatsu* concentrations were holding companies, this prohibition was intended to prevent the revival of similar industrial concentrations. And as a result of the holding company prohibition, contemporary enterprise groups lack a controlling organ and are accordingly less cohesive than their prewar counterparts.

Restriction of Aggregate Intercorporate Shareholding by Large-Scale Non-financial Enterprises. Article 9-2 restricts nonfinancial joint stock corporations from acquiring or holding stock in Japanese companies in excess of their own capital or net assets. The restriction applies to corporations whose capital is greater than 10 billion yen or to those with real assets exceeding 30 billion yen. Based on FTC reports on general trading companies completed in 1974 and 1975, this provision was added to the Antimonopoly Law in 1977 because of the rapid increase in intercorporate shareholding by general trading companies after about 1965.

Financial Company Intercorporate Shareholding Restrictions. Under Article 11 financial companies are not allowed to hold in excess of 5 percent of the total outstanding stock of any Japanese company. This restriction reflects a desire to prevent the concentration of economic power and any restraint on freedom of economic activities that could result from the strengthening of enterprise groups centered on financial companies. Since Japanese business enterprises depend largely upon banks for capital, they would become increasingly subject to control by financial institutions if such institutions were allowed to hold a significant proportion of their shares. The 1977 amendment to Article 11 reduced the permissible holding from 10 to 5 percent, based on the FTC's 1974 and 1975 reports on general trading companies.

Parallel Price Increase. The 1977 amendments also added a reporting system requiring firms in concentrated industries to report the reasons for their price increases. The provisions provide for a surveillance of concentration and monopoly lacking in U.S. antitrust legislation.

Influence of Administrative Guidance

Discussion of antitrust enforcement in Japan would be incomplete without touching on the influence of administrative guidance by industrial ministries, which is used for a variety of objectives and takes various forms. The problems posed can be roughly divided into four categories

The first consists of cases where the industrial ministries have used guidance to recommend output restrictions or price levels; and the target enterprises or trade associations have thereupon implemented such guidance by forming a cartel. As early as 1952 the FTC maintained that the formation of a cartel even in response to administrative guidance constituted an antitrust violation.[50] FTC decisions have involved both price fixing and output restrictions.[51]

A second form of administrative guidance is also given to enterprises through their representatives or through trade associations. Even if enterprises or trade associations enter into a formal cartel agreement based on such guidance, to act pursuant thereto is tantamount in substance to an agreement to form such a cartel. Because agreements by definition include tacit agreements, such a tacit agreement could be deemed to have been formed by virtue of the administrative guidance itself.

Furthermore, even if the guidance is directed to individual enterprises separately, if it consists of recommended levels of production or increases in prices, there is in the words of the Tokyo High Court, "a risk of concerted action by such enterprises since each would frequently follow [such guidance] on the assumption that the other enterprises would do likewise."[52] In other words, the enterprise would have entered into a tacit agreement in response to such administrative guidance. The FTC's 1981 statement on the Antimonopoly Law and Administrative Guidance was, as previously noted, issued principally to demand that the industrial ministries not engage in these forms of administrative guidance. Administrative guidance to an industry as a whole to restrict investment or capacity is subject to the same concerns as guidance related to prices and production, and should be treated similarly. In such cases the content of the guidance becomes the basis of a tacit agreement.

However, to the extent they are expressly authorized by the statute, measures based on a statute, such as setting standard prices or establishing plant capacity plans, are not in themselves antitrust violations, even if they result in tacit agreements related to prices or capacity. Nevertheless, actions taken by the enterprises concerned may violate the Antimonopoly Law if such agreements become express agreements and the statute then contains no provision for antitrust exemption.

The third pattern occurs when administrative guidance results in a restriction of competition without necessarily fostering a cartel. Illustrative of such guidance is that intended to aid large firms, encourage large-scale mergers, promote formation of joint sales companies, or restrict entry, as well as outright subsidies. Guidance of this sort is designed to increase market concentration and adjust profits among firms. Such guidance may not result in substantial restraint of competition in a given field of trade, but still the commission has jurisdiction over stockholding and mergers under the Antimonopoly Law. Even though this type of administrative guidance may not constitute a substantial restriction of competition, it may run counter to the principle of a free and competitive market. Hence, the objectives of such guidance should be carefully examined, and the FTC sometimes airs its views with the ministry responsible for such forms.

The industrial ministries also use administrative guidance through requests to businesses for monthly reports on production and turnover while providing them with data on short-term demand in return. This type of guidance falls into an intermediate category between the second and third, and the FTC has interceded with the ministries concerned to moderate its use.[53] Although employed in a different context, guidance to encourage export restraint also belongs in such an intermediate category.

A fourth type of administrative guidance consists of government requests prior to, or in lieu of, formal measures taken pursuant to a regulatory statute. Guidance in such cases presents no problems so long as it is not unreasonable, nor does it ordinarily involve any restriction of competition. All countries make use of guidance of this sort in the enforcement of regulatory statutes, although perhaps to differing degrees. Informal warnings by the FTC in enforcing the

Antimonopoly Law are an example of this. Nevertheless, cartels formed on the basis of either formal or informal measures pursuant to a statute constitute antitrust violations unless the statute contains an express provision for an antitrust exemption.

Avoiding the Pitfalls of Administrative Guidance: Policy Suggestions

The foregoing issues aside (except those associated with the fourth type of guidance), administrative guidance can harm certain enterprises and certain industries as well as consumers generally because it is often carried out without statutory authority (or outside the bounds of statutory requirements). Although compliance is technically voluntary, guidance often becomes compulsory because of the substantial power wielded by the administrative authorities behind it. As a result, administrative guidance can restrict the freedom of business activity and distort the open quality of a free market economy. It can disrupt the openness of the legal system as well by destroying the rule of law and the checks and balances built into the separation of legislative, executive, and judicial powers in the modern state. To prevent these consequences in areas where administrative guidance will have any substantial impact, it is important (1) to limit administrative pressure, (2) to open the process to the public to permit adequate opportunity for hearing the views of interested parties and consumers, (3) to limit the duration of such guidance, and (4) to set down in writing the rationales and content of such guidance for disclosure to the public.

CONCLUSION

Whether Japan's remarkably high rate of economic growth after World War II can be attributed to the maintenance of competition by means of antimonopoly policy or to skillful control and guidance through the use of industrial policy is subject to unending debate. Before attempting to resolve this question here, however, the relationship between industrial policy and antimonopoly policy should be reexamined.

Although Japan's postwar industrial policy involved a variety of actions taken to deal with specific problems, it had six basic features. (1) The industrial ministries collected information and data through public reports and private contacts with business circles. They analyzed such data and then disseminated what was considered important to the industries concerned. (2) The ministries selected industries, firms, and technology they considered essential to Japan's economic growth, taking into account the relevant industry's prospects, value added, demand for labor, and international competitiveness. (3) To protect and foster the industries, firms, and technology they had selected, the ministries resorted to a variety of measures, including import restrictions, tariffs, raw materials allocations, subsidies, special financing arrangements, preferential tax treatment, cartelization, and the promotion of mergers. (4) These ministries used similar measures to promote the protection and rationalization of depressed and failing industries, as well as small and medium enterprises. (5) They encouraged rationalization and standardization of production and distribution, and promoted research and development of technology to aid production. (6) Finally, they sought to reduce the social, economic, and international friction accompanying industrialization.

The measures noted in points (3) and (4) that were taken to promote and protect selected industries as well as other industries and firms, have been the core of industrial policy until now. Of these measures, the most problematical from the perspective of antimonopoly policy has been the promotion of cartels and mergers. The FTC has consistently opposed and criticized special legislation and administrative guidance directed toward these ends, and such anticompetitive measures have generally been rather limited and weak.

The postwar democratization of the Japanese economy, including the dissolution of the *zaibatsu*, the elimination of excessive concentrations of economic power, and termination of wartime control organizations, transformed the postwar economy into a competitive one. Also because, as noted, the conditions necessary for competition existed in Japan, Japanese enterprises have been fiercely competitive. On the other hand, the confrontations and adjustments between industrial policy and antimonopoly policy, both the competition fostered by the Antimonopoly Law and the necessary protection for infant industries promoted by industrial policy, existed side by side. Each independently stimulated enterprise activity, and the Japanese economy grew.[54] As can be seen in steel, automobiles, computers, semiconductors, and other industries, businessmen were willing to invest due to a sense of security fostered by protective industrial policy measures. Yet such measures did not stifle competition in these industries. Instead, competition functioned as an added catalyst for investment and in these industries was in fact far more intense in Japan than in the United States. Nonetheless, in some areas the industrial ministries did intervene too much with enactments of special legislation which allowed cartelization. Where competition was suppressed by cartelization, as in the textile, petroleum, and petrochemical industries, performance declined.[55]

By contrast, the automobile, motorcycle, camera, and electronics industries, where there was relatively little intervention by the industrial ministries, were able to achieve independent strength through competition and have enjoyed extremely high levels of performance. Thus, it can be said that although competition was a primary cause for industrial growth in postwar Japan, the development of infant industries was in a limited sense the result of protection by industrial policy. To the extent that industrial policy eliminated or suppressed competition, however, the ultimate consequence was economic failure. Japanese experience suggests that there is a certain boundary between the two—competition and protection—across which the one may not stray far into the other's territory without precipitating serious economic consequences. Moreover, although protection of infant industries is effective domestically, this does not mean that it is approved from the perspective of fair international competition, concern for which may lead to certain limitations imposed by General Agreement on Tariffs and Trade (GATT) or by other means, on the extent and duration of measures to protect infant industries and the types of industries eligible for such protection.

Japan's economic growth rate has recently declined. As Japan enters a period of low growth, there is concern that cooperation will increase, with a variety of attendant harms. In the past economic growth has helped prevent inefficient capital allocation, an inflexible industrial structure, and stagnation. Today, the need to preserve competition by means of the Antimonopoly Law has become all the more pressing.

Because Japan is a small country with a large population and few natural resources, sustained economic growth depends upon exports of manufactured goods. As a result, Japan benefits more than other countries from free international trade policies; indeed, Japan is a strong advocate of free trade. However, to advocate free trade abroad while supporting collusion at home exposes Japan to charges of unfair competition. Consequently, even from the international perspective, future industrial policy must provide greater support for competition, and in this context as well antitrust policy will continue to develop.

Today antitrust laws have been enacted and enforced as basic legislation in support of free market economies in all developed countries. Each country's antitrust policy reflects the particular characteristics of its cultural, social, and historical background. However, major enterprises from each of these nations engage in business throughout the world, and the economies of the advanced nations have become increasingly interdependent. It has become necessary, therefore, to design some means of international cooperation in the area of antitrust enforcement and to establish common rules of competition. To maintain fair competition among the business enterprises of the advanced countries, it is also necessary to establish common rules for governmental regulation and guidance that will influence a free and fair competitive international market order. The precarious balance that was struck between free competition and protective governmental guidance for three decades in Japan would merit replicating at the international level.

NOTES

1. *Shiteki dokusen no kinshi oyobi kōsei torihiki no kakuho ni kansuru horitsu* (Law concerning the prohibition of private monopoly and preservation of fair trade) (Law no. 54, 1947).

2. There are several different definitions for the term "industrial policy." It is used in this article to mean the policies carried out by the industrial ministries with respect to the industries under their jurisdiction.

3. For a more detailed treatment of this point, see Iyori Hiroshi and Uesugi Akinori, *The Antimonopoly Laws of Japan* (Federal Legal Publications, 1983), pp. 13–33, as well as Iyori Hiroshi, *Dokusen kinshi seisaku no kadai* (Topics in antitrust policy) *Nihon keizai seisaku gakkai nempō* 24 (Tokyo: Keisō Shobō, 1976): 54–60 and Kōsei Torihiki Iinkai (FTC), *Dokusen kinshi seisaku sanjūnen shi* (A thirty-year history of antitrust policy) (Kōsei Torihiki Kyōkai, 1977), pp. 77ff., 159ff.

A very detailed historical introduction to MITI's industrial policies may be found in Tsuruta

Toshimasa, *Sengō nihon no sangyō seisaku* (Industrial policy of postwar Japan) (Tokyo: Nihon Keizai Shimbunsha, 1982); Komiya Ryūtaro et al., *Nihon no sangyō seisaku* (Industrial policy of Japan) (Tokyo: University of Tokyo Press, 1984); and in Chalmers Johnson, *MITI and the Japanese Miracle* (Stanford, Calif.: Stanford University Press, 1982).

4. Tsūsanshō (MITI), *Sangyō gōrika hakusho* (White paper on industrial rationalization) (Tokyo: Nikkan Kogyo, 1957), pp. 42–43.

5. See Tsūsanshō (MITI), Sangyō Kōzō Chōsakai, *Nihon no sangyō kōzō I* (Japan's industrial structure I) (Tokyo: Tsūshōsangyō Kenkyūsha, 1964), pp. 213–14. For a survey of Japan's economic, industrial, and antitrust policies during this period, see William W. Lockwood, "Japan's New Capitalism," *The State and Economic Enterprise in Modern Japan* (Princeton, N.J.: Princeton University Press, 1965).

6. The Designated Industries Promotion Temporary Measures bill, *Tokutei sangyō shinkō rinji sochi hōan*, originally *Kokusai kyōsōryoku kyōka hōan*, was severely criticized for the extensive regulatory authority granted the government, but it should be emphasized that the bill failed to pass in the Diet because among other reasons, it weakened antitrust policy.

7. See Tsūsanshō, Sangyō Kōzō Chōsakai (MITI, Industrial Structure Investigation Committee), *Nanajū nendai no tsūshō-sangyō seisaku* (Trade and industry policies for the seventies) (1971), pp. 9, 19, and 70–72, and *Hachi-jū nendai no tsūshō-sangyō seisaku* (Trade and industry policies for the eighties) (1980), pp. 168ff.

8. *Tokutei fukyō sangyō antei rinji sochi hō* (Law no. 44, 1978), and *Tokutei sangyō kōzō kaizen rinji sochin hō*.

9. With the introduction of the cabinet system in 1875, the original industrial ministries—Finance, Agriculture, and Commerce and Communications—were established. At present the ministries with direct jurisdiction include International Trade and Industry, Finance, Transportation, Agriculture, Forestry and Fisheries, and Construction. Their jurisdiction is set out in their establishing legislation and under the general authority of the National Administrative Organization Law (*Kokka gyōsei soshiki hō*, Law no. 120, 1948). The ministries are subdivided into bureaus, sections, and smaller units, each with a specified responsibility. This system establishes the bureaucratic agency and particular agency subdivision responsible for any and all goods and services throughout the economy.

10. For an excellent discussion of the role of government in the Japanese economy, see Eleanor Hadley, *Antitrust in Japan* (Princeton, N.J.: Princeton University Press, 1970), chap. 16.

11. *Kuni* [Japan] v. *Sekiyu Renmei* et al. (Tokyo High Ct., Sept. 26, 1980). This case and its companion price-fixing case, *Kuni*, [Japan] v. *Idemitsu Kōsan K.K. et al.* (Tokyo High Ct., Sept. 26, 1980), are translated in part and analyzed along with related cases and developments in a symposium of articles in *Law in Japan: An Annual*, 15 (1982): 24–98.

12. Former FTC Chairman Hashiguchi has spoken before the Diet both on the restrictive effect that administrative guidance has on competition, insofar as it constitutes secret administrative action, and on the collusive effect such guidance has on the principle of the rule of law: "An administrative organ must act within the limits of the authority delegated to it by the highest organ of state power, that is to say, within the limits of enacted law. When administrative action is not subject to the rule of law, nor undertaken in accordance with written law, then inevitably it will be carried out informally by word of mouth. . . . And when administration is conducted in secret, behind closed doors, we find ourselves in a situation where responsibility cannot be adequately assigned should problems subsequently arise." *Shūgiin bukka mondai tō ni kansuru tokubetsu iinkai gijiroku* (Record of the proceedings of the House of Representatives Special Committee on Price and Other Problems), Nov. 6, 1980, p. 19.

For a translation of the FTC's March 1981 statement and MITI's official response, see the appendix to Lawrence Repeta, "The Limits of Administrative Authority in Japan: The Oil Cartel Criminal Cases and the Reaction of MITI and the FTC," *Law in Japan: An Annual*, 15 (1982): 53–56.

13. "Particularly under conditions of low economic growth it is necessary to maintain and stimulate the economy's vitality. For that reason government intervention and policies restrictive of competition which carry with them the danger of inducing economic rigidity and inefficiency must be vigorously avoided." FTC, Keizai Chōsa Kenkyūkai, *Teisei chō keizai ka no sangyō chōsei to kyōsō seisaku* (Industrial coordination and competition policy in a low-growth economy) (Tokyo: Kōsei Torihiki Kyōkai, 1982), p. 18.

14. See, for example, Edwin O. Reischauer, *The Japanese* (Cambridge: Harvard University Press, 1977), chap. 13.

15. The number of trade associations that had filed a "formation report" with the FTC pursuant to

Art. 8(2) of the Antimonopoly Law before 1982 exceeds 23,000. *Kōsei torihiki iinkai nenji hōkoku* (FTC annual report, 1981), p. 144. That figure does not include organizations under the purview of the various small business cooperative association statutes. There are thought to be about 77,000 such corporations (FTC, *Dokusen kinshi konwakai shiryōshū* [Antimonopoly materials] [Tokyo: Okurashō Insatsukyoku, 1979], 6: 189).

16. The Japan Chemical Industries Association (Nihon Kagaku Kōgyōkai), for example, comprises approximately 60 trade groups in addition to 170 individual affiliated companies. Among the latter are included almost all the major chemical companies, while the former include such groups as the Petrochemical Industries Association (Sekiyu Kagaku Kōgyō Kyōkai), the Petroleum Association (Sekiyu Renmei), the Japan Chemical Fiber Association (Nihon Kagaku Sen'i Kyōkai), the Japan Rubber Manufacturers Organization (Nihon Gomu Kōgyō Kai), and the Japan Federation of Pharmaceutical Trade Groups (Nihon Seiyaku Dantai Rengōkai), itself composed of 37 pharmaceutical-related trade groups. The Federation of Economic Organizations (Keizai Dantai Rengōkai, usually abbreviated as Keidanren) is composed of about 100 organizations such as the Japan Chemical Industries Association, and about 700 major corporations.

17. Of the 621 FTC decisions issued in connection with Antimonopoly Law violations during 1953 to 1983, 357 (55 percent) involved trade associations acting in violation of Art. 8(1) of the law. Additionally, many of the 215 decisions involving the cartel activities of entrepreneurs in violation of Art. 3 also implicated trade associations. *FTC Annual Report*, 1983, pp. 236ff.

18. Jigyōsha dantai no katsudō ni kansuru dokusen kinshi hō jō no shishin. Translated by James Sameth and John O. Haley in *Law in Japan: An Annual*, 12 (1979): 118–52.

19. Antimonopoly Law Art. 7–2. From 1977 through March 1984, surcharges amounting to ¥8.9 billion were imposed on 754 entrepreneurs in connection with 42 illegal cartel cases. *FTC Annual Report*, 1983.

20. A national system of decorations of honor was established by government Directive no. 54 (Taiseikan), in April 1875. Its operation was suspended for a time by a Cabinet decision of 1946. In 1963, however, it was reinstated with honors conferred upon those, usually aged seventy or more, who have rendered meritorious service to the state or the public at large and those who have contributed to the public welfare or have worked for the prosperity of the economy or of industry. At present, about four thousand people receive decorations of honor in the spring and in the fall each year. The honors range over eight classes of distinction within a number of categories.

21. In the United States each year there are over a thousand private antitrust actions. In Japan, in the thirty-five years from the Antimonopoly Law's inception through 1984 there have been only seven suits filed under the special compensatory damage claims provisions of Art. 25 of the Antimonopoly Law, and approximately thirty-five instances of compensatory damage suits under the general tort provisions of Art. 709 of the Civil Code. Since, however, a majority of those cases have been filed in the last ten years, their number has been increasing.

22. On the vague attitude of the Japanese toward contracts, see Noda Yoshiyuki, "Nihonjin no keiyakukan" (The Japanese mentality toward contracts) in Nichi-Futsu Hōgakkai, ed., *Nihon to Furansu no keiyakukan* (Japanese and French mentality toward contracts) (Tokyo: Yuhikaku, 1982), pp. 12–13. See also Kawashima Takenori, "The Legal Consciousness of Contracts in Japan," *Law in Japan: An Annual*, 7 (1974): 1–21, and Nakane Chie, *Japanese Society* (Berkeley and Los Angeles: University of California Press, 1970).

23. "If we disavow competitive policies at home, we shall not be able to stand for principles of free trade internationally. You see, for Japan, firm support of free trade principles is an even more urgent proposition than it is for the U.S. or Europe. That's something that even MITI realizes. So, if anything, Japanese industrial policy is shifting away from its past preoccupation with 'catching up,' to a concern for strengthening the vitality of the economy through policies supportive of competition." Tsujimura Kōtarō, "Gendai to keizaigaku to no taiwa dai nikai, shijō to keikaku I" (Another dialogue between modern times and economics: The market and planning, part 1) in *Ekonomisuto*, April 12, 1983.

24. Again, in periods of technological innovation and rapid growth, although on the surface static forces such as cartels may appear to be operating, they are not very significant. The true undercurrent during such times is competition. When a recession occurs in such a period, measures taken by the industrial ministries to restrict competition have the effect of allying the insecurities of managers who fear their enterprises might go bankrupt in a general recession. Such insecurities are palpable and widespread. There has always been a strong mood of pessimism in Japan regarding future economic prospects, particularly during the 1950s and 1960s, and today the Japanese economy is even hailed internationally for its soundness in this respect.

Restrictive measures taken in such periods thus act to check counterproductive economic activity and wasteful capital expenditure. In so doing they in fact promote competition in the next recovery period. Taken too far, however, such measures may contribute to unsound conditions in a given industry, as has occurred in the textile, petroleum refining, and petrochemical industries.

25. See Noda Minoru, *Ryūtsū keiretsuka to dokusen kinshi hō* (Vertical integration of distribution channeling and the Antimonopoly Law) (Tokyo: Ōkurashō Insatsukyoku, 1980) concerning this report and related materials.

26. See Uekusa Masu, *Sangyō soshiki ron* (Industrial organization) (Tokyo: Chikuma Shobō, 1982), pp. 12–22 and 25–26. The market concentration, among domestic makers, of the top four American automobile manufacturers, for instance, is 99 percent. The comparable figure for Japan is 83 percent. In the color television market, the figures are 66 percent in the United States and 58 percent in Japan. (American figures are for 1972, Japanese for 1980).

27. Each *zaibatsu* of prewar Japan was organized around a holding company. As noted in the text, holding companies are prohibited under Art. 9 of the Antimonopoly Law.

28. Kōsei Torihiki Iinkai (FTC), *Kigyō shūdan no jittai ni tsuite* (On the activities of enterprise groups) (Tokyo: Kōsei Torihiki Kyōkai, April 1983), pp. 5–8.

29. The proportion of purchases by nonfinancial firms in a group from nonfinancial firms in the same group to the total volume of purchases by nonfinancial firms in 1981 was 14.8 percent for former *zaibatsu* groups and 9.1 percent for non-*zaibatsu* groups. Intragroup sales to member nonfinancial firms amounted to 13.4 percent for former *zaibatsu* groups and 8.6 percent for non-*zaibatsu* groups. The proportion of purchases by manufacturers in a group from other manufacturers in the same group was 18.6 percent for former *zaibatsu* groups and 8.2 percent in the case of non-*zaibatsu* groups. As to manufacturer sales to group manufacturers, the proportions were 29.0 percent for former *zaibatsu* groups and 14.9 percent for non-*zaibatsu* groups. See ibid., pp. 39 and 42.

30. Hadley, *Antitrust in Japan*, p. 256.

31. See Appendix A on these exempted cartels.

32. *Tokutei sangyō kōzō kaizen rinji Sochi hō* (Law no. 53, 1983).

33. *Chūshō kigyō dantai no soshiki ni kansuru hōritsu* (Law no. 185, 1957).

34. As Japan does not have a federal system, these 500 cases include local cases. In 1982, investigations were conducted in 430 cases, of which 200 were carried over from the previous year and 230 represented new cases. Depending upon their importance, cases are divided into those subject to summary investigations and those subject to formal investigation procedures for which the commission authorizes staff to resort to the formal compulsory investigatory powers available under the Antimonopoly Law (Art. 46). See *FTC Annual Report*, 1982, p. 14.

35. In 1982, formal investigations were conducted in 50 cases and summary investigations were carried out in the remaining 380 cases.

36. In connection with a warning, the company or association may be required to agree to a broad resolution to discontinue engaging in the activities in question and to notify customers and company staff or association members that the conduct in question has ceased. If necessary, the contents of the warning may be made public.

Of the 430 cases investigated in 1982, 300 were concluded during this year. Ultimately, 19 of the 40 formal cases ended in recommendations, 19 in warnings, and the remaining were dismissed. Approximately 140 cases subject to summary investigation resulted in warnings and 120 were dismissed.

In each of the 19 cases that ended in recommendations in 1982, the respondent accepted the recommendation and the commission issued a formal recommendation decision. Of these 19, 11 involved price cartels (6 by individual firms and 5 by trade associations). A surcharge (Art. 48–2) also resulted in all but one of these cases, in which the products or industries involved were as follows: chemicals, 3; construction, 3; foodstuffs, 1; surveying, 1; bus sales, 1; motor vehicle repairs, 1; tools, 1. The remaining 8 cases included 4 resale price maintenance violations, 2 cases of unfair sales below cost, and 2 cases of illegal restriction of the economic activities of members by trade associations.

37. See Appendix B.

38. According to the questionnaire administered by *Nikkei Business*, 93.1 percent of the answers received from presidents of the companies listed in the Tokyo Stock Exchange were fundamentally that "antimonopoly law is necessary to the Japanese economy" and 54.3 percent answered that "it is indispensable for maintaining free competition" (*Nikkei Business*, Nov. 1, 1982, pp. 51–52).

39. See Iyori Hiroshi, "Ittei no torihiki bunya ni okeru kyōsō no jishitsu-teki seigen no kaishaku" (Construction of substantial restraints of competition in a given field of trade), *Kōhō to keizaihō no*

shomondai (Problems in public law and economic law), 2 (Tokyo: Yūhikaku, 1981): 197. I have had fundamental reservations over regarding market share as a major requirement in connection with price and output cartels.

40. U.S. Department of Justice, *Antitrust Guide Concerning Research Joint Ventures* (1980).

41. *FTC Annual Report*, 1970, p. 133. This involved a patent pool arising out of a contractual undertaking by two Japanese firms (A and B), an English company (C), a German company (D) and a Swiss company (E). The arrangement included an exchange of existing and future technology with respect to manufacturing machinery. Under the arrangement, the two Japanese firms agreed to refrain from sales to the United Kingdom, West Germany and Switzerland, and the three European firms agreed not to sell in Japan. In addition, they agreed that no party would license any patent in the pool to a third party without the consent of each of the other parties. Given the combined market position of the five companies, there was a significant risk that the arrangement would substantially restrain competition with respect to the product involved. Moreover, it was doubtful that such restraint could be considered an exercise of patent rights (exempted from antitrust regulation in Japan under Art. 23 of the Antimonopoly Law). As a result of FTC intervention, the parties agreed to eliminate the territorial restriction and modified the pooling agreement to permit any party to license third parties on terms not violating the Antimonopoly Law.

The standards applied to international patents provide some guidance, at least by analogy. See the FTC's 1968 Guidelines on International Licensing Agreements, translated into English by Iyori Hiroshi and Uesugi Akinori as *The Antimonopoly Law of Japan* (Federal Legal Publications, 1983), p. 271.

42. *United States* v. *Aluminum Company of America* (Alcoa), 148 F. 2d 416 (2nd Cir. Ct., 1945).

43. *Noda Shōyu K.K.* v. *Kōsei Torihiki Iinkai* [FTC], 10 Kōsai minshu 743 (Tokyo High Ct., Dec. 25, 1957). This case involved an appeal in re Noda Shōyu K.K., cited below in n. 45.

44. In re K.K. Saitama Ginkō [Saitama Bank], et al., 2 Shinketsushū 74 (FTC [Decision] no. 30, 1950, July 13, 1950); in re Noda Shōyu [Noda Soy Sauce] K.K., 7 Shinketsushū 108 (FTC [Decision] no. 2, 1955, Dec. 29, 1955); in re Yukijirushi Nyugyō [Snow Brand Dairy] K.K., et al., 8 Shinketsushū 12 (FTC Decision no. 4, 1954, July 23, 1956); in re Tōyō seikan [Tōyō can] K.K., 19 Shinketsushū (FTC [Decision] no. 11, 1972, Sept. 18, 1972).

45. *Kaisha no gappei to no shinsa ni kansuru jimu shori kijun* (Standards for review of corporate mergers) (FTC [Notification] no. 3, July 15, 1980). The English translation is seen in Iyori and Uesugi, *Antimonopoly Law*, p. 276.

46. In re Nippon Yakuhin Seizō K.K., 8 Shinketsushū 51 (FTC [Recommendation] no. 1, 1957, Jan. 30, 1957).

47. In re Yawata Seitetsu K.K., et al., 16 Shinketsushū 46 (FTC [Consent] no. 2, 1969, July 15, 1909).

48. In re Tōhō K.K., 2 Shinketsushū 146 (FTC [Decision] no. 10, 1950, Sept. 29, 1950), affirmed 8 Minshu 5 (Sup. Ct., May 25, 1954), 4 Kōsai minshu 497 (Tokyo High Ct., Sept. 19, 1951).

49. The legality of joint sales companies established by large-scale enterprises is determined by whether the motives for establishment, objective, and business activities together constitute a "substantial restraint of competition in a particular field of trade." In 1981, 17 polyvinyl chloride manufacturers established four joint sales corporations with market shares from 20 to 28 percent representing four groups (Mitsubishi, Mitsui, Kogyō Bank, and one other) (see Nikkei, Oct. 22, 1981); and in 1983 18 petrochemical companies similarly established four joint sales companies for polyethylene, with market shares of 44 to 27 percent, representing four groups (Mitsubishi, Shōwa Denkō, Sumitomo-Daiichi Kangyō Bank, and Mitsui) (See Nikkei Sangyō, Aug. 16–19, 1983). These were recognized by the FTC. Art. 8(2) of the 1983 Law for Temporary Measures for Structural Improvement in Designated Industries provides for industrial promotion by means of a structural improvement plan by two or more enterprises in a designated industry; Art. 9 provides for industry promotion but does not contain an Antimonopoly Law exemption. However, these four joint sales companies were approved by the Minister of International Trade and Industry under Art. 8(2) of this law.

50. In re Noda Shōyu K.K., et al., 4 Shinketsushū (FTC [Decision] no. 59, 1950, April 4, 1952).

51. In re Noda Shōyu K.K., et al., supra n. 50 (price-fixing); in re Tōyō Rayon K.K., et al., 4 Shinketsushū 17 (FTC [Decision] no. 2, 1952, Aug. 6, 1953) (output restriction).

52. *Kuni* v. *Sekiyu Renmei et al.* (Tokyo High Ct., Sept. 26, 1980), cited in n. 11.

53. See, for example, report on FTC action in 1979 with respect to the guidance following after the termination of the recession cartel in the synthetic fiber industry in *FTC Annual Report*, 1979, pp. 7–8.

54. For a similar view, see Tsujimura Kōtarō, "Sangyō seisaku to dokkinhō no kankei" (The relationship between industrial policy and antimonopoly law), *Nihon Keizai Shimbun*, Oct. 6, 1983.

55. On this point, see Kozo Yamamura, "Success that Soured: Administrative Guidance and Cartels in Japan" in Kozo Yamamura, ed., *Policies and Trade Issues of the Japanese Economy: American and Japanese Perspectives* (Seattle: University of Washington Press, 1982). Also note that even Amaya has admitted, "I don't think that industrial policy in Japan is successful in every respect. . . . To repeat trial and error is the only way to gain success. . . . The VLSI project, which is often referred to as a successful case of industry policy, is in fact a significant success but an exceptional one. There are such examples of failure as policies for coal, petroleum, and petrochemicals." Amaya Naohiro, "Sangyō seisaku hinan e no kaitō" (Reply to criticisms of industrial policy), *Voice*, Aug. 1983, p. 86.

APPENDIX A

RECESSION CARTELS

Exempted cartels numbered nearly a thousand between 1963 and 1972. After 1974 this figure declined, reaching 528 in 1977. It is also important to note that many cartels were regional, not national. Besides these, until about 1965 there were recommended production curtailments as set forth by administrative guidance.

There were no recession cartels exempted under Art. 24–3 of the Antimonopoly Law in March 1984. Of the 436 exempted cartels in existence in the same year, 5 were cartels exempted under the 1983 Designated Industries Structural Improvement Temporary Measures Law; 231, under the Medium and Small Business Association Law; 124, under the Law for Businesses Related to Environmental Health; and, 52 were export cartels exempted under the Export and Import Transactions Law. Most of the remaining 31 cartels were those of medium and small enterprise associations in fishing or transportation industries.

The Antimonopoly Law's Art. 24–3 exemption of recession cartels was modeled on the recession cartel exemption in the West German government's 1952 bill for the Law Against Restraint of Competition (*Regnierungsentwurf eines Gesetz gegen weltbewerbsbeschrukungen*). Under Japanese law the most important criteria for approving a recession cartel are that the price of the product in question has fallen below the average cost of production, and that a considerable number of the entrepreneurs in the relevant industry may be forced to discontinue production (Art. 24–2(1)(i)) because of extreme disequilibrium in the supply and demand for the product. The FTC thus requires that all participants in an exempted recession cartel file data on costs and prices. The FTC construes recession cartels as an emergency measure for recessionary periods and authorizes such cartels for only a short period of three to six months. Ordinarily, the purpose of the cartel exemption is to permit inventory adjustments. Since the commission also pays close attention to consumer opinion, there has not been any significant increase in prices as a result of recession cartels. Parties are free to remain "outsiders" and not participate in the cartel. (However, when recession cartels have been established in the past, the industrial ministries have pressured outsiders through "administrative guidance" to abide by the cartel restraints as an antirecession policy.)

A survey of the recession cartels exempted during recessionary periods pursuant to Art. 24–3 of the Antimonopoly Law reveals the following sets of exempted products (almost entirely those of large-scale industries): Eighteen products during the approximately two-year recession beginning in 1965, including automobile tires, cameras, sugar, cotton, staple fiber thread, cardboard, and steel bearings. Thirteen products during the 1971 recession, including unprocessed standard steel, stainless steel, vinyl chloride plastics, fiberboard, and ethylene. In the longer 1975 recession there were seventeen products, including cotton, staple fiber thread, cement, vinyl chloride plastics, aluminum sheeting, cardboard, and synthetic textiles, while in the latest recession since 1981 there have been ten items, including steel ships, vinyl chloride plastics, high-grade paper, and ethylene. Most of these have been cartels limiting production quantities. In 1977, a price cartel for steel rods, most of the producers of which are small or medium-sized enterprises, was recognized for a little less than two months.

Recently, recession cartel exemptions have been granted in principle for three-month periods with extensions. Of the twenty-two recession cartels, including all seventeen industries recognized during the 1975 recession, one continued for more than two years (shipbuilding), six for more than a year, six lasted between six months and a year, and nine less than six months.

In recession cartel arrangements permitted for fixed periods under Art. 24–2 of the Antimonopoly Law, activities of enterprises outside the cartels are completely free. However, in most cartels recognized by the responsible ministry or agency as coming under other applicable exemption statutes, the activities not only of cartel members but also of noncartel members are subject to regulation or guidance by that agency or ministry. This results in powerful restraint on competition.

Cartels under Art. 5 of the 1978 Temporary Measures for the Stabilization of Designated Depress Industries, *Tokutei fukyō sangyō antei rinji sochi hō*, Law no. 106, 1978) are for five-year periods and involve eight products in synthetic fibers, chemical fertilizer, cardboard, and other industries.

The 1983 Temporary Measures for the Structural Improvement of Designated Industries Law (as well as the 1978 Temporary Measures for the Stabilization of Designated Depressed Industries Law) provide for the designation by cabinet order (Art. 2) of "industries recognized as having a larger number of entrepreneurs whose business activities are especially unstable, which instability may continue for a long period of time" where "there is especially severe excess productive capacity." In the event the competent minister acknowledges that such entrepreneurs acting autonomously would not be able to adjust capacity under a "Basic Plan for Structural Adjustment" for the particular industry (Art. 3), the minister can require that the entrepreneurs in such industry take concerted action to restrict or prohibit improvement or expansion of facilities. Before so directing, the minister must get consent from the FTC (Art. 12), but concerted action based thereon is exempted from the Antimonopoly Law (Art. 11). Such a cartel will usually be effective for closure or termination of facilities for three to four years. If a basic plan is implemented without the need for a directed cartel, facilities can be closed or terminated by the industry as a whole under such a plan (see Art. 9).

As of March 1, 1984, twenty-one industries (such as aluminum, chemical fiber, chemical fertilizer, ferro alloys, machine-made paper, petrochemical, hard vinyl chloride tube, and sugar) were designated under the 1983 statute, and there were directed cartels under the same statute in five industries: chemical fertilizer, ethylene, polyorefin, and vinyl chloride resin, and machine-made paper.

The Medium and Small Business Association Law permits (Art. 17) the establishment of recession cartels by small and medium-sized business associations under much less stringent conditions than recession cartels under Art. 24–3 of the Antimonopoly Law. It also provides for compulsory measures to regulate nonparticipants ("outsiders") (Art. 55–58). There were 607 cartels under this statute in 1973. In conjunction with the strengthening of the FTC's enforcement program, the number dropped to 300 in 1977 and to 263 by the end of March 1984. Almost all were local cartels. These involved 18 industries, of which 14 were related to textiles. Of the restraint in the 18 industries, almost all involved capacity or output. There were only 2 cases of price restrictions. In 13 of the 18 industries (12 of the textile industries), "outsider" regulations were issued. Also in contrast to recession cartels under the Antimonopoly Law, Small and Medium Enterprise Association cartels tend to be of long duration. In March 1982, 123 cartels were exempted under the Law for Businesses Related to Environmental Health (*Kankyō eisei kankei eigyō no un'ei no tekiseika ni kansuru hōritsu*, Law no. 164, 1957), which covered 6 different fields, such as barbershops and beauticians.

The number of export cartels decreased under the Export and Import Transactions Law (*Yūshutsunyū torihiki hō*, Law no. 299, 1952) from a peak of 209 in March 1969 to 53 by March 1982. There were only 11 export cartels involving major manufacturers (Art. 5–3). Many of these export cartels reflected demands by other countries for voluntary export restaints. There were 2 import cartels under the same law in March 1983. (See Iyori and Uesugi, *Antimonopoly Law*, pp. 137–60, 172–83.)

APPENDIX B

SURCHARGES ON CARTELS

Though the 1977 amendments to the Antimonopoly Law added a surcharge to be imposed on price cartels (Arts. 7–2, 8–2), this is not a criminal penalty but more in the nature of an administrative fine. It has been applied quite effectively. Pursuant to the 1977 amendments to the Antimonopoly Law, the FTC is required to levy the surcharge against entrepreneurs who have participated in a price cartel or a cartel affecting prices by means of a restriction on output. The surcharge is paid to the national treasury and equals, for manufacturers, 2 percent (for retailers, 1 percent; wholesalers, 0.5 percent; and others, 1.5 percent) of the turnover of goods or services subject to the cartel for the period during which the cartel was in effect (Arts. 7–2, 8–3). From December 1977, the effective date of the amendments, through March 1978 (end of the 1977 reporting year), there were no cases. Surcharges from 1978 through 1982, with numbers of cases and entrepreneurs involved, are summarized in the accompanying table.

Year	Number of Cases	Number of Entrepreneurs	Amount of Surcharges (¥1,000)
1978	1	4	5,070
1979	5	134	1,571,740
1980	12	203	1,331,110
1981	6	148	3,730,200
1982	8	166	483,540
1983	10	42	1,466,109
Total (as of 1984)	42	747	8,587,769

The largest surcharge ordered in a single case was the ¥1,170,070,000 surcharge in a 1981 price cartel case involving Kraft liner wrapping paper (6 entrepreneurs). The highest amount paid by a single entrepreneur was ¥351,160,000 in the same case. The surcharge, temporary suspension of conferral of an imperial decoration on anyone who has participated in an antitrust violation, and the possibility of criminal sanctions cancel out the benefits of illegal activities.

The Evolution and Economic Consequences of Product Liability Rules in Japan

KOICHI HAMADA

HIDETOH ISHIDA

MASAHIRO MURAKAMI

The advancement of modern technology has created new types of social issues and conflicts to be handled by a variety of means. Striking examples of these new problems emerging in highly industrial societies are those caused by defective products. To cope with this type of problem, a society must be able to rely on private negotiations between the parties involved, legal sanctions and remedies, regulatory legislation, assistance provided by various governmental agencies, and so forth. In general, these measures should be so arranged as to most efficiently discourage the occurrence of product defects resulting in accidents. In this article, we shall survey legal and regulatory practices concerning defective products in Japan, assess the economic impact of these practices, and make some recommendations based on our assessment.

The number of incidents due to defective products has increased in postwar Japan. At one extreme are the very well known cases involving serious damage and injury to many people. The Kanemi Rice Oil, SMON (Subacute-Meylo-Optico-Neuropathy), Morinaga Powdered Milk, and thalidomide cases are among the most publicized and serious. With the exception, perhaps, of thalidomide cases in Europe, cases related to major airplane accidents caused by defects in airplanes, and to diethylstibestrol (DES) and asbestos in North America, these Japanese cases have involved more people than any others of this type. They are comparable to the severe pollution cases in Japan.

The opinions expressed in this essay are solely those of the authors and do not represent opinions of the Fair Trade Commission of Japan. We are much indebted to Professor Yukihiro Asami of Fukuoka University for his valuable suggestions in many stages of the preparation of this work. We also thank Mr. Naoto Yamauchi of the Fair Trade Commission for providing us useful information on product insurance.

At the other extreme are the many complaints, including minor ones, by consumers regarding defective automobiles, cosmetics, food, drugs, and other products. These complaints are handled on a daily basis by consumer institutions like the Kokumin Seikatsu Center (Japan Consumer Information Center) and Shōhi Seikatsu (local consumer) centers.[1] There are also special regulations to improve the quality of such consumer products as toys, electric appliances, and drugs.

Thus, legal procedures, public regulation, and governmental assistance are used to control and prevent damages caused by defective products in Japan. These objectives are realized through economic incentives that correspond to these rules and regulations, and particularly through raising the degree of care required of both producers and consumers. Although the economic aspects of legal practices have not been taken into consideration by many legal commentators, actual court decisions seem to have been affected by consideration of the benefits or costs of liability rules and the standard of care imposed on each party. Some economists and lawyers have begun to consider the economic impact of product liability rules in Japan.

In part one we describe alternative remedies for persons suffering from the results of defective products and various means of containing the costs arising therefrom in Japan. In part two we briefly survey the general characteristics of our legal system as a means of coping with the problems of defective products. Most decisions on product liability cases in Japanese courts are based on the tort provision (Art. 709) in the Civil Code. There the plaintiff who is injured or damaged by defective products can be compensated by the defendant, who is either a seller or a producer, if the plaintiff proves negligence on the part of the defendant. The strict liability rule (no-fault liability) quite common in the United States is not yet accepted in Japanese practice. In many product liability cases, however, courts have various techniques for modifying or reducing the burden of proof on those injured by defective products. In part three we sketch the significance of costs related to defective products by referring to statistical data.

With part four we proceed to an economic analysis of the Japanese liability rules for defective products. We summarize the deterrence effect of liability rules and public regulations and then explore the meaning of the Coase theorem as applied to this area. Here we see how Japanese legal procedures and public regulations have affected the incentives for producers as well as users, and how they have helped reduce the costs of defective products. We trace signs of the effects of economic analysis on the thinking of judges. In part five we briefly address the question of international and interjurisdictional aspects of product liability, referring to a few trans-Pacific lawsuits. The final section briefly compares Japanese practices, legal doctrines, and their economic impact with those of the United States.[2]

1. ALTERNATIVE REMEDIES IN JAPAN
FOR DAMAGES CAUSED BY DEFECTIVE PRODUCTS

In any modern society there are several ways to remedy damage due to defective products or services, and several ways to effect deterrence of accidents related to commodities. In Japan the following remedies and deterrence mechanisms are available:[3]

1. Consumers injured or damaged by defective products can, at least in principle, bargain directly with the sellers and producers of the defective products for compensation for damages.

2. Government institutions such as the Kokumin Seikatsu Center and the Shohi Seikatsu Center play the role of arbitrator or mediator for negotiations between buyer and seller, and between consumer and producer. Every year, innumerable cases are handled and mediated through these institutions. Consumer groups sometimes perform a similar function.

3. A few statutes have recently been enacted to cope with specific defective products. For example, the Consumer Daily Life Appliances Safety Law that provides safety standards and a compensation scheme for appliances was passed in 1973. The law establishing the Fund for Relief of Drug Side Effects, providing compensation for damages from medical products, was enacted in 1979.

4. Those harmed by defective products may bring suit. In postwar Japan courts have handed down a considerable number of decisions on various product liability cases. Academic lawyers have also compiled commentaries on these decisions.

5. Unlike cases involving pollution and environmental disruption, there is no specific legislation for criminal charges against producers and sellers of defective products. Article 211 of the Criminal Code, concerning the effects of violation of the care level required for professional trade, is applicable to producers of defective products that cause serious damages. Criminal charges were raised in the Morinaga Infant Powdered Milk case and in the Kanemi Cooking Oil case, two major cases we will explain later.

Here we shall discuss points one through three; four will be considered in the next section.

1. Consider first the direct bargaining process between seller and buyer and producer and consumer. This is in a sense a basic means of relief, and this process is used to explain the Coase theorem.[4] However, there is a great difference in information capacity and bargaining power between consumers, who are typically individual households, and producers, who are often large, incorporated businesses. Consumers are likely to bear the burden silently and reluctantly—they must, in effect, grin and bear it.

2. Many local Shōhi Seikatsu centers and Kokumin Seikatsu centers work actively to handle consumer complaints and to arbitrate defective product disputes. As indicated in table 1, for the two-year period fiscal 1978 and 1979 about 500 cases were reported to the national center directly or through local centers. The Economic Planning Agency carefully investigated 265 relatively serious

cases,[5] and was able to trace the final outcome of negotiations in 109 cases mediated or assisted by the consumer centers. The examples ranged from smoked *fugu* (globefish) poisoning, broken bottles of sparkling beverages, and fires caused by domestic electrical equipment, to injuries caused by the spike of the toy spaceship "Yamato." It is difficult to derive from these particular examples general principles regarding how cases are decided, but we can make the following observations.

It has not always been clear who was being asked to compensate for the damage. Consumers have usually just wanted to be compensated by somebody.

TABLE 1
Accidents Related to Consumer Products

	1978	1979
Household electric appliances	83	88
	(31.0)	(38.1)
Kitchen appliances	25	16
	(9.3)	(6.9)
Cooking and heating appliances	18	11
	(6.7)	(4.8)
Furnitures	19	22
	(7.0)	(9.5)
Vehicles	27	22
	(10.0)	(9.5)
Personal effects	12	14
	(4.5)	(6.1)
Health care products	4	. . .
	(1.5)	
Recreational equipment	24	14
	(9.0)	(6.1)
Infant supplies	32	30
	(12.0)	(12.9)
Textile products	4	12
	(1.5)	(5.2)
Others	20	2
	(7.5)	(0.9)
Total	268	231
	(100.0)	(100.0)

NOTE: These figures indicate the number of cases reported to consumer centers. Numbers in parentheses are percentages of all cases reported. Adapted from Masaru Etoh, "Shōhisha Higai to sono Kyūsai no Jittai" (Damages to consumers and Their Remedies), chap. 6 in Ken'ichi Miyazawa, ed., *Seizōbutsu Sekinin no Keizai Gaku* (Economics of Product Liability) (Tokyo: Sanrei Shobō, 1982).

Product manufacturers were usually the party making compensation. In most cases consumers were required only to demonstrate the existence of the products that created a hazard or were prone to create a hazard. In most cases, consumers did not demonstrate fault on the part of the producers.

Consumers centers were active in helping justify these claims in the negotiation process. The final outcomes of the 109 cases negotiated by consumer centers can be classified as follows (in some cases two or three actions were taken simultaneously by the centers, so the total is greater than 109): No action was taken in 17 cases, either because the claimant agreed to withdraw the action, because the product was not being used properly when the accident occurred, or because there was no direct relationship between the product and the damage. In 27 cases compensation for medical expenses, other costs, and lost earnings was awarded. The amount of compensation varied from small (several thousand yen) to considerable amounts (more than three million yen). *Solatia* (compensation for pain and suffering), again ranging from small to large awards, were paid in 34 cases. In 17 cases the defective products were replaced. In 16 cases refunds were given and the goods returned. In 7 cases warning statements to consumers, to be attached to the products, were introduced, or existing statements were improved. Apologies were made in two cases. In ten cases the products was ordered improved or redesigned. In four cases administrative guidance (*gyōsei shidō*) was provided by the centers or by related ministries.

One can see that these consumer centers serve a very important function for Japanese citizens, most of whom are reluctant to take these matters as far as lawsuits.

3. A few systems have been designed to promote faster and simpler recovery of damages. The ST (Safety Toy) seal system for toys was introduced through the efforts of toymakers, and the BL (Better Living) seal system for construction materials was introduced on the initiative of the Ministry of Construction. In the latter case, product liability insurance is combined with the BL emblem.

More important are the systems originated by special legislation. The SG (Safety Goods) seal system was introduced in 1973 by the Consumer Daily Life Appliance Safety Law. SG emblems are affixed to commodities exceeding safety standards. If a consumer is killed or injured by a defective product bearing the SG seal, compensation comes from a fund established under this law. The law formally requires that the producer be liable according to the Civil Code, but in actual practice the requirement of negligence on the part of the producer is not strictly examined. Thus, in a sense this system functions as a substitute for strict liability. According to the Economic Planning Agency (EPA), 54 products carry the SG seal. By September 1981, 141 cases had been filed, and compensation was paid in 98.[6]

In 1979, the Fund for Relief of Drug Side Effects was established. In the case of drugs, a delicate problem arises in the trade-off between technical progress and product safety. It has not always been possible for consumers to establish claims against producers, and recovery of damages has been a lengthy process. The new system provides faster and simpler relief for persons injured by drug side effects. Every producer who has a license to manufacture or import and sell drugs in a defined category makes annual contributions to the fund on the basis of annual gross sales of drugs. By March 1983, only 133 cases had been brought under this system; of these, payment was actually made in 66 cases.[7]

2. FEATURES OF THE JAPANESE LEGAL SYSTEM

It would take an entire article or even a book to describe the features of the Japanese legal system related to product liability.[8] Accordingly, we shall confine ourselves here to describing some features of the Japanese legal system important in understanding its economic impact.[9]

The Japanese legal system is based on the continental civil law system. The Civil Code of Japan (Mimpō) was introduced in 1876, following the model of the German Civil Code. Legal remedies in court have been basically provided by the application of articles in the Civil Code. This practice can be contrasted with that in common law countries like the United States and the United Kingdom.

When specific statutes are legislated in common law countries, however, the articles in the statutes tend to be interpreted and applied rather strictly. In those countries most court decisions are based on accumulated precedent. In Japan, on the other hand, the articles on tort and breach of contract pertinent to cases of defective products are rather simple. The courts have therefore supplemented and extended these articles by flexibly interpreting and applying them to meet the needs of our highly industrialized society.

Generally speaking, a plaintiff can bring legal action in two major ways to seek damages caused by defective products: remedy can be sought based on the articles concerning breach of contract or on the articles of tort. In recent years most cases have been based on the latter. We shall begin by discussing breach of contract.

According to Article 415 of the Civil Code, "if an obligor fails to effect performance in accordance with the tenor and purport of his obligation, the obligee may demand compensation for resulting loss." Further, according to Article 570, a purchaser of a product with a latent defect can rescind the contract or demand that the seller compensate him for damages. The number of cases in which plaintiffs have asked for compensation through contract provisions is limited. Since the obligor is expected to complete performance of a contract, the burden of proof that negligence is absent lies with the obligor. In this sense, the legal construction through breach of contract gives more protection to the plaintiff than the legal construction through tort. However, to obtain compensation by appealing to breach of contract, one must prove the existence of "privity" (direct contractual relationship) between the plaintiff and the defendant, which limits the effective range of the contractual approach. Of eighty-one court decisions analyzed by a team from the Economic Planning Agency directed by Akio Morishima,[10] in many cased the plaintiff sought remedy on grounds of breach of contract as well as tort. However, there were only four cases in which the court allowed remedies through the contractual approach. Only in the

Egg-Tōfu case did the court recognize the liability of the wholesaler without the privity requirement.

In the Egg-Tōfu case, 415 people were seriously poisoned by soybean curd contaminated by salmonella bacteria, and two girls died.[11] The heirs of the two victims sued the retailer, the wholesaler, and the manufacturer for resulting damages. The court not only recognized the claim for compensation against the manufacturer through tort provisions, but also the claim for compensation through breach of contract against the retailer and the wholesaler. The court held that even though formally the wholesaler was only liable through the privity requirement to the retailer, with whom he has a privity, nevertheless, the plaintiff, that is, the consumer, can claim damages directly from the wholesaler by subrogating the retailer's right against the wholesaler. This is an interesting legal construction.

The majority of claims concerning defective products, however, are based on tort provisions. The basic article on tort in the Civil Code, Article 709, states that "a person who violates the right of another intentionally or negligently is responsible to render compensation for harm arising therefrom." Most product liability cases are handled through the flexible application of this simple article, which has been so enriched by numerous court decisions and discussion by commentators that tort law is able to meet the needs of modern society.

Before analyzing the compensation mechanism by tort, it may be appropriate to explain four serious cases related to defective products in postwar Japan. First was the thalidomide case, a worldwide tragedy arising out of the side effects of this drug, which caused prenatal injuries in Japan as well as in Europe. The reported number of deformed babies was 309, although the actual number is estimated at up to 1,000. Legal action was brought against the Japanese manufacturer of the drug and the national government in 1963. The lawsuit did not, however, come to a court decision because the parties agreed to settle in 1974. Depending on the seriousness of damages, plaintiffs were given from nine to forty million yen, including three million yen for pain and suffering for each parent. Two-thirds of the settlement costs were borne by the manufacturing companies and one-third by the national government. The Ishizue (Cornerstone) Fund was established in 1974 for this purpose.

The second case was the Morinaga Powdered Milk case. A branch of the Morinaga Milk Company produced powdered milk for infants that contained arsenic, which had been erroneously mixed in a quality stabilizer. About 12,000 infants suffered ill effects, and 131 died. The parents of about 60 of the harmed infants brought a suit in the Osaka District court against the Morinaga Milk Company and the government. The case was settled by compromise. The Hikari-Kyōkai (Light for Children Fund) was founded under government auspices to supply annuities and medical care. In addition to this civil action, criminal charges were brought against members of the manufacturing company. The Tokushima District Court denied the charge against the factory chief as well as against the manufacturing section chief.[12] But the appellate court ordered a retrial, a decision supported by the Supreme Court.[13] In the retrial the Tokushima District Court held that the manufacturing section chief was guilty of neglecting the duty required in the food trade, but that the factory manager was not guilty because he was not directly in charge of the manufacturing process.[14]

The third serious case was the Kanemi Rice Oil case. The Kanemi Sōko (storage) Company manufactured and sold cooking oil contaminated by PCB (polychlorinated biphenyl). PCB was used as a heat medium, but it leaked into the rice oil. More than 10,000 people were injured and 51 died. About 40 patients filed a case before the central branch of the Fukuoka District Court against Kanemi Sōko and the PCB supplier, Kanegafuchi Chemical. About 700 people brought a suit in the Kokura Branch of the Fukuoka District Court, not only against the Kanemi and the Kanegafuchi companies but also against the national government and the city of Kita-Kyūshū. The claim against the national and local governments was based on their neglect of duty to keep food products safe. In the first case the Fukuoka District Court held the defendants liable.[15] A principle similar to *res ipsa loquitur* (the thing speaks for itself) was adopted for reducing the requirement of proof on the part of the plaintiffs.

On the other hand, the Kokura Branch maintained the traditional position that under the law the plaintiffs should bear the burden of proof of negligence.[16] However, citing the due-care standard required for food traders, the court held that the producers were liable but that the company president, the national government, and the city were not. Neither the national nor the local government was held liable because they had not been sufficiently negligent in exercising their discretionary power.

The fourth serious case concerned victims of SMON (Subacute-Myelo-Optico-Neuropathy). SMON is a neurological disease involving visual problems and serious pain in the feet. The cause had been unknown until the early 1970s when chinoform, a drug for diarrhea, was found to be the suspect. After 1971, about 6,000 victims brought legal actions in more than thirty courts all over the country. From Kanazawa to Maebashi, nine district courts handed down decisions recognizing the claim of the plaintiffs against pharmaceutical producers, importers, and the national government.[17] In many cases since 1977 plaintiffs and defendants have also agreed to settle in the judges' chambers. Settlements range from ten to forty-six million yen per victim. Most plaintiffs have eventually accepted settlements. It is worth noting that in many of the SMON decisions courts recognized epidemiological causation or statistical causation (the Tokyo District Court is a definite exception). There were also important cases concerning deafness as a side effect of streptomycin and the side effects of chloroquine, which is used for malaria.[18]

Let us turn to the requirements and effects of tort in Japan. The requirements of Article 709 may be analyzed and classified as follows: First, the palintiff suffers damages. Second, there is intent or negligence on the part of the defendant. Third, there is causation between the conduct (or nonfeasance) of the defendant and the plaintiff's damage. We shall comment on some important aspects of these requirements.

Let us begin with the requirement of negligence (*kashitsu*). *Kashitsu* is defined as the neglect of due care. According to the general interpretation of tort law in Japan, the burden of proof of negligence is with the plaintiff. However, in many cases concerning defective products, courts have tried to reduce the plaintiff's burden of proof. This is quite understandable because consumers do not usually have access to information within the producer's firm that is necessary to prove fault on the part of the producer. Thus, as in the case of Kanemi Oil,[19] a principle similar to *res ipsa loquitur* is adopted to ease the burden of proof on the part of the plaintiff.

Next, since fault is defined as neglect of the duty of care, the level of due care standard becomes a crucial problem. The standard of due care is determined by the dangerousness of possible damages. The required degree of due care differs from product to product because the degree of danger depends on the product. We should also mention the effect of the neglect of care on the part of consumers. The Civil Code adopts the rule of "setoff" (*kashitsu sōsai*)—the literal translation might be "blame sharing"—unlike contributory negligence but similar to comparative negligence in the United States. The Japanese Civil Code allows (but does not require) the court to take account of lack of care on the part of the injured party in determination of the amount of compensation (Art. 722). Under the rule of contributory negligence, courts are most likely to give all or nothing decisions on compensation. In Japan, the law and the courts take more flexible or adaptive attitudes by considering degrees of negligence on the part of the plaintiff, and they calculate the amount of compensation to be recovered by the plaintiff.

Let us turn to the problem of causation as one of the requirements of tort. In principle, it is necessary for a plaintiff to prove causation sufficient to justify the compensation between the defect in the product and the damages. It is not easy for injured consumers to prove this. Therefore, as in cases of pollution and environmental disruptions, many court decisions allow the use of epidemiological causation, or highly probably or statistical causation. In many of the SMON decisions, courts recognized the legitimacy of the epidemiological causation. (The Tokyo District Court explicitly stated, however, that it did not rely on the reasoning of statistical causation, but decided that there was a deterministic causation between the defect in the drug and the injury.) For economists, it seems quite natural and reasonable to recognize statistical causation. For many traditional lawyers, however, this might seem to be a substantial extension of the basic principle of the Civil Code.

Here we shall briefly sketch some characteristics of product liability with respect to different kinds of products. Examples of cases involving food are abundant, ranging from *fugu* (globefish) poisoning to *satsuma-age* (fish-cake fritters), from Egg-Tōfu to arsenic-contaminated milk. Because of the seriousness of possible injury that defects in food products can cause, courts require extremely high standards of care for producers and distributors. It is generally regarded as relatively easy to prove causation in food poisoning cases. In cases of *fugu* poisoning, the "setoff" rule has often been evoked. Because customers should know that *fugu* can be dangerous, the court held that assumption of risk on the part of the plaintiff should be taken into account.

In cases concerning medical drugs, the standard of care is also set at a high level. In this case there is an additional problem of how to establish causation. A delicate problem also exists concerning the predictability of side effects. Because many medical drugs are newly developed, it is frequently difficult or impossible for producers to foresee all possible side effects and related disturbances. Producers should be aware of all current scientific research in their field throughout the world.

Another common case is injury cased by defective automobiles. The Yokohama District Court stated that the care to be taken by an automobile company depends on the degree and probability of danger as well as the availability and cost of means of avoiding it.[20] This can be regarded as a slight move toward the application of a principle similar to the Learned Hand formula in the United States.

There have not been as many cases concerning machinery and equipment as one might expect. Although a great number of injuries and damages could be estimated from other survey data, only twelve decisions were relevant to this area among eighty-one court decisions analyzed by the EPA (see table 2). There are two possible reasons for the limited number of cases in this area. First, there is usually a seller-customer relationship between suppliers and users of appliances. They can negotiate with each other and settle without going to court. Second, compensation for employee accidents is covered under the workers' compensation scheme and tort action against their employers rather than against the producers of the equipment.[21]

Finally, we must examine injuries and damages caused by gas appliances and construction. Article 717 of the Civil Code says that "if any damage has been caused to another person by reason of any defect in the construction or maintenance of a structure on land, the person in possession of the structure shall be liable for compensation for harm to the injured party." Therefore, for example, in the case of propane gas containers, no-fault liability is sometimes imposed on the supplier.[22] This is an example in which the general principle of negligence system is modified in the direction of strict liability.

Thus, in general, Japanese court decisions have quite flexibly extended tort law in the Civil Code to meet the needs of modern society. However, because the Civil Code itself was product of the economic situation of the last century, the articles of the Civil Code are inadequate to protect the human rights of those who suffer damages caused by defective products. In light of this, a group of scholars organized by the late Professor Wagatsuma proposed a draft of a model product liability law to supplement the Civil Code.[23] Article 3 of this model law says, "The producers shall be responsible for compensating any natural person for injury to the life, to the person, or to property incurred as a result of a defect in a product." Thus, strict liability is imposed on producers of defective products. Even though Article 7 provides for relative negligence when there is fault on the part of the user, implementation of this model law would represent a radical change in the negligence principle in our tort law.

Another interesting aspect of the model law is that it declares, if not actually stipulating in concrete terms, the need for better procedures for consumer redress. On an additional note, it suggests the need for class actions whereby a specified party can represent the interests of several injured parties, or for other means of facilitating recovery of damages by consumers more quickly and in a more aggregate fashion than in current practice.

Despite the strong support of academics who proposed the model law, the Ministry of Justice does not seem inclined to promote the drafting of a special statute concerning product liability.[24] Ministry of Justice officials probably regard current practice in the application of the Civil Code to defective product issues as flexible enough. Naturally, there is resistance to such legislation for strict liability in the business community. (A survey by the EPA indicates that a majority of firms admit, though reluctantly, the necessity for such legislation.)[25] There seems to be some resistance on the part of attorneys to more categorized formats for product liability that might restrict their innovative activities or perhaps reduce the number of clients. The attitude of the ministry may perhaps reflect some of these feelings.

Possible disadvantageous effects on medium and small enterprises are sometimes pointed to as an argument against such legislation. We do not find this reasoning persuasive. Measures for the protection of small and medium enterprises, if needed, should be devised for their own sake, and not at the cost of future victims of defective products. As we shall discuss later, more explicit rules rather than the continued flexible, but sometimes uncertain, application of the Civil Code's tort provisions are desirable to preserve the resource allocation function of liability rules.

Indeed, we admire attorneys and judges who flexibly interpret tort law in the Civil Code. Their efforts have contributed much to generating public pressure against defective products as well as against pollution. From a historical perspective, we should recognize the positive side of the present system. At the same time, however, there must be many individuals who are compelled to accept hazards, either because of luck of information or because of the difficulty of taking legal recourse. We therefore would welcome the enactment of a new product liability statute to foster both justice and the more efficient functioning of our society.

3. EMPIRICAL ASSESSMENT
OF THE COSTS OF DEFECTIVE PRODUCTS

Here we shall attempt to estimate the costs incurred from defective products in Japan. Most of the data are too fragmentary to permit any definite conclusions, but it is useful to derive some basic magnitudes.

First, let us summarize the Economic Planning Agency's fiscal 1975 and 1976 survey on defective products covering housewives in 20,000 households consist-

TABLE 2

Number of Court Decisions on Product Liability Cases

	Food	Drugs	Automobiles	Appliances and Equipment	Gas	Buildings	Others	Total
–1944	1							1
1945–1949								
1950–1954								
1955–1959		1						1
1960–1964								
1965–1969		1			3		1	5
1970–1974	2		6	4(1)[a]	2(1)	3	3(1)	20(3)
1975–1979	6	10	11(2)	6(3)	4	5(1)	1	43(6)
1980–	1(1)	3(1)	1(1)	2	4(1)			11(4)
Total	10(1)	15(1)	18(3)	12(4)	13(2)	8(1)	5(1)	81(13)

[a]Numbers in parentheses refer to decisions by appellate courts.
SOURCE: Economic Planning Agency, *Shōhisha Higai no Kyūsai to Seizōbutsu Sekinin* (Remedies for Damages to Consumers and Product Liability) (Tokyo: Daiichi Hōki, 1982).

ing of more than two individuals.[26] The number of product liability cases by product type is shown in table 2. By the end of 1981, seventy-two cases had been brought to court, and eighty-one decisions (including appellate decisions) had been handed down, suggesting that the number of cases and decisions is rather small. (As indicated below, the number of claims in the United States in 1976 alone was estimated to be between sixty and seventy thousand.) Table 2 shows, however, that the number of cases has increased rapidly in recent years.

From this sample the agency distinguished four categories: damages due to imperfections of the product per se; extended injuries and damages deriving from product imperfection; damages due to unfair trading practices; and damages due to imperfect services. According to the survey, the annual average number of accidents related to goods and services amounted to about 1,800 in the sample. Damages due to imperfections of products per se occurred in 954 cases, and extended injuries and damages deriving from product imperfections occurred in 286 cases. Unfair trading practices were recognized in 304 cases, and damages due to imperfect services were reported in 247 cases.

Extrapolating from these sample figures, the EPA estimated the average annual number of accidents in the total population to be about 2.8 million, or one-tenth of the number of households. Of those, damages due to imperfections of products per se comes to 1.47 million, in 1.2 million cases of which sellers are consider responsible. Cases in which extended damages derived from product imperfections amounts to 440,000. Those due to unfair trading and imperfect services number 470,000 and 380,000, respectively. If we measure the costs of product hazards per se at their market values, they amount to 40 billion yen or almost 160 million dollars. Of this amount, 28 billion yen would be the cost of cases in which sellers were responsible.

More than 400,000 people were estimated to have been affected by extended injuries and damages deriving from defective products, about half in cases in which the sellers were responsible. In these cases damages including medical expenses and the purchase value of imperfect products causing damages, were estimated at 2 billion yen (14,000 yen per case). If we include cases involving reasons other than seller's responsibility (for example, misuse of products), estimated damages come to 11.4 billion yen (31,000 yen per case).

Compared, for example, with the GNP of about 170 trillion yen in fiscal 1976, these figures may not seem to be very large The incidents were primarily minor; serious cases such as thalidomide or SMON were not included in this survey.

The Committee for Improving Consumers' Lives (Kokumin Seikatsu Shingikai) provides an alternative set of figures in its estimates of damages directly or indirectly related to the use of commodities.[27] According to their estimates, calculated from such sources as premium payments to various insurance plans, total annual damages broadly related to commodities are 1,040 billion yen.[28] These figures include costs of automobile accidents, amounting to 483 billion yen for personal injury and 124 billion yen for property damage. If we subtract automobiles accident costs, remaining damages comes to 433 billion yen. These large figures contrast with the estimated derived from the questionnaire survey mentioned above, but they include not only the cost of accidents due to misuse of products, but also the tertiary costs of insurance and medical care.

In the United States, the National Electronic Injury Surveillance System (NEISS), developed by the Consumer Product Safety Commission, received 412,000 reports of dangerous products in 1976. It is estimated from this figure that about 8.7 million accidents due to defective products occurred that year. According to the 1977 Report of the Interagency Task Force, there were at most an estimated 60,000 to 70,000 claims related to product hazards, in more than 90 percent of which lawsuits were filed.[29] The proportion of product liability cases to the total number of civil cases was estimated at between 1 and 3 percent. The total damages to the American economy by defective products was estimated at more than 5.5 million dollars. Total insurance premiums paid for product liability insurance amount to 2.1 billion dollars, or about 0.3 percent of commodity value added that year.

These figures are the quantitative basis for the so-called product liability crisis, which refers to the escalation of insurance premiums after 1975. The figures for Japan may not be strictly comparable with those for the United States because of differences in statistical treatment. In general, the magnitude of product hazards in Japan may appear much smaller than that in the United States, but the seriousness of accidents and the importance of preventing damage in Japan should not be underestimated.

4. ECONOMIC EFFECT
OF PRODUCT LIABILITY RULES IN JAPAN

The issue of product liability emerges when someone is injured by a defective product. The question is, who should bear the burden of the cost? The classical rule of product liability is *caveat emptor*, that is, let the buyer beware. Because of the increasing need for consumer protection due to the development of modern technology, however, a principle of *caveat venditor*, or, let the seller beware, has recently been introduced under the name of strict liability. Between these two extremes are various degrees of care levels imposed on both buyers and sellers under which parties can be held liable. The content of the applicable liability rule affects not only the distribution of the burden of the accident, but also the quantity and quality of products. Naturally, product liability is an intrinsic economic problem.

The purpose of the economic analysis of legal practices and regulations with respect to defective products should be to assist us in designing a system of remedies that minimizes the costs of accidents without unduly discouraging efficiency in producing commodities. Economics therefore look at the trade-off between the deterrence of accidents and the costs of deterring them. Thus, economic analysis is primarily concerned with, and most effective at, the analysis of efficiency. We should also take into consideration equity and fairness in the distribution of burdens between the parties involved. Economic science, however, does not provide a final verdict on equity or the distributional problem.

Economic analysis may clarify the logical structure of value judgments, but it cannot decide unambiguously what is fair and just.

As a preliminary, let us begin by describing several features of product liability problems. First, many parties are involved. For example, consider the case of a beer bottle that explodes and injures a person. The victim may be the purchaser of the beer bottle or perhaps a third party—a bystander. The purchaser bought the bottle from a wholesale dealer, who in turn is supplied by a brewer. The brewer buys bottles from a bottle maker. Many layers of contracts and market relationships are involved, making the product liability relationships among the parties quite complex.

A second feature of product liability is that the parties involved are primarily limited to persons within the distribution chain (stream of commerce) or market relationships, except for bystanders. Therefore, it is relatively easy to specify both the group of people likely to be injured and that group likely to be the injurers.

Third, the injured and the injurers are directly or indirectly associated through price relationships. Therefore, when someone is held liable, the cost can be transmitted by the price mechanism to others. In the long run, producers are able to shift the cost of accidents to consumers or users by supplying safer but more expensive products. The existence of price relationships is crucial in the analysis of the economic effects of product liability.

Finally, the level of caution on the part of commodity users affects the incidence and seriousness of accidents. Improper use of a commodity may make damage more serious. Therefore, a suitable combination of care by both consumers and producers is necessary for the prevention of accidents.

In the following we shall present several observations on economic aspects of legal decisions in Japan and shall trace the general trend of discussion by commentators.

First, the necessity for an appropriate system designed for defective products in a highly industrialized society cannot be overemphasized. Particularly necessary are fixed, explicit rules of compensation.[30] There is a strong case for new legislation on product liability along the lines of the model law mentioned above, for example.

The present practice of modifying and adapting the articles on tort in the Civil Code has served with considerable success to cope with defective product issues. Court decisions have certainly affected producers' behavior, directly through incentives for increasing the level of care, and indirectly by making major social issues of product liability cases. We have not heard much recently about new occurrences of serious injuries and damages such as those in the SMON, Morinaga Milk, or Kanemi Oil cases. Incentives to deter accidents through liability rules have unquestionably been working even under the present rule. However, the current practice of adapting the general tort principle leaves more room for unpredictability in court decisions than would a special product liability statute. Establishing more concrete rules, such as strict liability of producers, appears preferable to the present situation.

This point, along with other implications, can be presented in economists' terms as follows: As indicated elsewhere,[31] a mechanism similar to the Coase theorem operates, even in the absence of a negotiating process, through the price relationship between the seller and the buyer of a product. Even though the seller and the buyer are usually unable to negotiate directly, social cost is minimized through the price mechanism. This is particularly true when the (marginal) effect of the exercise of care by one party does not depend on the level of care taken by the other party. If the buyer is liable, the demand price of a dangerous product will become lower. On the other hand, if the producer is liable, the supply price will increase by the amount of prevention costs. Both parties can shift the cost of accidents or prevention costs through the price relationship. Thus it can be shown that liability rules, whether *caveat emptor* or *caveat venditor*, do not affect the long-run equilibrium, provided that the care taken by both parties does not interact in preventing the danger. This is because neither the level of production nor the occurrence of accidents is affected, because the party liable for damages can shift its burden through the price mechanism. Income distribution in the long-run equilibrium position remains the same as well. This neutral result is an interesting theoretical proposition, but we must keep the following reservations in mind.

First of all, it is important to have some fixed rules of compensation or noncompensation known in advance to the relevant parties. Even in cases where the condition for the Coase theorem is satisfied and the content of liability rules does not matter, some well-defined rule is required. Otherwise the parties will not be given necessary incentives.[32] For this reason the establishment of some definite liability rules is to be welcomed. This reinforces our previous argument.

The second reservation is that the neutral effect on the long-run equilibrium occurs only when the parties foresee perfectly the degree of damages and the cost of preventing them. In particular, consumers are assumed to know the possibility of injury. If consumers are unaware of possible danger, and if the *caveat emptor* rule is adopted, then consumers do not bid down the demand price of the product. Under such circumstances, consumers are likely to be compelled to suffer damages without lowering the product's price.

Suppose, on the other hand, the strict liability rule is adopted. Once the producer is aware of possible danger, he will improve the product immediately. If it is true that the producer has more access to new information about the nature of a product, one can make a case for strict liability. By making the producer liable, we may be able to reduce the burden of economic loss imposed on consumers during the adjustment process in which consumers are not well informed.

The third reservation concerning this neutral outcome pertains to the protection of bystanders. The neutral result presupposes that victims of defective products or those who are likely to be victims can bid down the demand price. But bystanders cannot bid down the demand price. Therefore, producers' liability is required to protect the rights of bystanders.[33]

Finally, this theoretical result is based on the assumption that the levels of care taken by both parties do not interact; that is, if the effect of caution by one party is dependent on the level of care on the part of the other, then the court should impose some due care standard for each party, under which level of care a party is held to be liable.[34] In this case the kind of liability rule adopted matters a great deal, even in the long run. To determine the proper standard of care, one popular rule is the Learned Hand rule, which says that a party should be held liable if the expected value of the cost (the cost of an accident multiplied by the probability of the accident) exceeds the expected cost of preventing the accident.

This consideration is not explicitly reflected in court decisions in Japan. However, since the courts require different levels-of-care standards for different types of commodities—for example, a stricter standard of care for food products than for other products—a similar economic reasoning is in fact at work behind the court decisions. Hirai advocates a negligence rule similar to the Learned Hand rule in his commentary on Japanese tort law.[35] He maintains that three factors are crucial for determining whether a defendant should be judged negligent: first is the probability of the danger that might arise from the defendant's conduct; second, the seriousness of damages; and third, a comparison between the first two factors and the opportunity cost of avoiding the danger. He traces considerations of this type in a few past decisions in Japanese courts, although they are not decisions on product liability cases.

As mentioned above, it is interesting to note that the Yokohama District Court in an automobile accident case hinted, albeit indirectly, that the care standard is determined in relation to its prevention costs.[36]

Since shifting prevention costs is necessary and desirable for efficient resource allocation, the question arises of how much the strict liability rule will contribute to price increases. Yamauchi calculated possible price increases that would be caused by the adoption of strict liability.[37] First, he calculated the increase in cost due to everyday and minor accidents for various types of products and obtained an expected rate of cost increase ranging from 0.01 percent (e.g., food and infant supplies) to 1.5 percent (electric appliances) The average rate of increase for all items under consideration is about 0.08 percent. These estimates might be biased downward because serious and major damages were not taken into account; they might be biased upward, on the other hand, because all the costs were shifted to price. In the real world only a part of the costs can be shifted, as can be readily understood by drawing a supply and demand diagram.

To correct for these biases, Yamauchi calculated the cost of defective cars, inclusive of serious and major accidents. Costs due to everyday and minor accidents are estimated at 0.28 percent of total sales. When one takes account of serious and major damages, the cost climbs to 0.47 percent of total sales. However, when one incorporates elasticities of supply and demand, the estimated price rise comes to 0.17 percent of total price. As Yamauchi himself notes, the framework is rather simple, and this approach does not allow for the possibility of "me-too" price hikes—price increases just for the sake of keeping step with other producers, not motivated by increased costs. Nevertheless, his study is valuable because it gives quantitative estimates of the costs implied by introducing strict liability.

Another interesting area for the application of interdisciplinary methods to legal issues is the problem of epidemiological or statistical causation. In many court decisions on SMON cases, epidemiological causation is admitted as legitimate grounds for winning the case. Also, a principle similar to *res ipsa loquitor* is in effect adapted to suggest factual causation for defective products. These legal techniques have significantly helped plaintiffs, who generally find it difficult to collect materials on facts within large corporations. Japanese attorneys, as distinguished from public prosecutors, do not have rights of "discovery."[38]

Finally, the effect of product liability insurance should be considered. In general, the introduction of insurance would imply externalization rather than internalization of costs. It is indeed difficult to prevent all the elements of moral hazard in insurance. But for a society to secure safety and the assurance of compensation to victims, product liability insurance is necessary despite its externalization effect. A society must choose between efficiency and security in this case as well.

It is not easy to estimate the extent to which Japanese firms insure themselves against product liability claims; there are many different kinds of insurance. It is also difficult to identify the exact coverage. The EPA gives a rule-of-thumb estimate that 10 to 20 percent of firms above medium size are covered by some product insurance scheme.[39] At the same time, we might recall that, as mentioned, costs of product-related accidents were large when estimated from data on the payment of insurance premiums.[40] This indicates that insurance schemes play an important role in contemporary Japan, even though they may not be universal.

5. INTERNATIONAL ASPECTS OF PRODUCT LIABILITY

It seems appropriate, in a volume that focuses on legal and economic aspects of the U.S.-Japan relationship, to discuss some of the problems that arise from the transnational character of business activities. The conflict-of-law problem arises when it becomes necessary to determine which state's law should be applied when two different states' laws are involved. In Japan, however, no such problems arise in handling legal actions. All Japanese courts are required in each case to apply the same product liability rules provided by the Civil Code, though interpretation and application of those rules may vary to some extent, depending on the judges' opinions. Therefore, in Japan the problem of court jurisdiction has nothing to do with the conflict of laws. For domestic cases, the appropriate jurisdiction is determined on the basis of the plaintiff's and the defendant's convenience.

Recently, the Japanese courts have seen an increase in transnational legal cases, in which foreign consumers seek recovery of damages caused by defective Japanese products, a phenomenon that certainly reflects in large part the remarkable increase in Japanese exports of manufactured products to foreign countries. Such transnational cases sometimes raise conflict-of-law problems since they involve the different laws of two or more countries. Generally, an American consumer usually has little need to enforce a secured judgment in Japan or to bring an action before a Japanese court. Suppose an American consumer in a certain state suffers damages caused by a defective product manufactured and exported by a Japanese firm. He can sue the Japanese firm for compensation before the court of his state, which usually has jurisdiction over the case under the state's civil procedure code, particularly under the state's long-arm statute. Therefore, he can win the case based on that state's product liability rules and normally can subsequently enforce the judgment against a Japanese firm anywhere in the United States, as long as the Japanese firm owns property in the United States. And most Japanese firms now exporting manufactured products to the United States do in fact have branches or representatives there and usually own sufficient property in the United States.

Where a Japanese producer has insufficient property in the United States, however, an American consumer has to select one of two legal remedies. One option is to seek judgment in a Japanese court, under Japanese rules of product liability. The other is to secure an American judgment against the Japanese firm based on the product liability rules of a particular state, and then to seek approval before a Japanese court to enforce the judgment in Japan.

If the consumer selects the first option—bringing suit before a Japanese court—a Japanese court exercises jurisdiction over the case under Article 15 of the Code of Civil Procedure so long as the defective product is manufactured in Japan. The court decides the case by applying the Japanese product liability rules under Article 2(1) of Hōrei, which provides that a tort claim is determined by the law of the location of the wrongful event. Thus, American law may be applicable in theory. However, because Articles 2(2) and (3) of Hōrei restrict the applicability of foreign law, the Japanese court does not apply American law in practice.

If the consumer chooses the second remedy by bringing suit first before an American court, the American judgment has to win approval by a Japanese court through a suit for an execution judgment under Article 24 of the Civil Execution Law.[41] To secure an execution judgment in Japan, an American consumer has to show that his claim satisfies several requirements. The most critical problem for an American consumer who has secured an American judgment is that the judgment cannot be enforced when it does not meet the Japanese standard of "public order on good morals" (Art. 200 of the Code of Civil Procedure). Thus, an American judgment that follows a strict (no-fault) liability rule or admits a punitive damage rule may be denied enforcement because neither rule is recognized in Japan. An American judgment may also be denied enforcement in Japan if there has already been a Japanese judgment contradicting the American decision. This was exactly what happened in the *Marubeni-America* vs. *Kansai Iron Works* case.[42]

Marubeni-America, an American corporation, won final judgment against Kansai Iron Works, Ltd., a Japanese corporation, in the King County Superior

Court of the State of Washington on October 17, 1974, for indemnification of the damage caused by a defective power press manufactured by Kansai Iron Works. The court ordered Kansai Iron Works to pay $86,000 to Marubeni-America. Kansai Iron Works brought a countersuit against Marubeni-America in the Osaka District Court in Japan to seek a declaratory judgment that Kansai Iron Works owed no liability to Marubeni-America. Kansai Iron Works won its case on December 5, 1974,[43] presumably because of Marubeni-America's poor technique in legal proceedings. Marubeni-America was denied enforcement of the American judgment in Japan because it was decided that enforcement of a foreign judgment contradictory to an existing Japanese judgment on the same matter was repugnant to the "public order."

To an economist, jurisdictional issues present an interesting resource allocation problem. Suppose there is a difference in liability rules concerning defective products between the two countries involved. Each party tries, if possible, to bring an action before the court where the liability rule most advantageous to him has been adopted. Our conjecture is that such strategic interactions would lead to some distortion in resource allocation. Needless to say, this is a subject for economic research requiring careful analysis.

6. COMPARISON WITH THE AMERICAN CASE

In conclusion, let us comment on basic differences in the treatment of product liability in Japan and in the United States. As we have seen, Japan has a more unfortunate history of serious injury due to defective products than most other developed countries. The Japanese legal system has to some extent succeeded in coping with these serious challenges, not by enacting product liability rules, but by adapting the traditional tort provisions in the Civil Code.

In the United States there are at least four cases of action for damages due to defective products.[44] The first is negligence. The second is breach of an expressed or implied warranty, a rule stated in the Uniform Commercial Code that has now been adopted by almost all the states (UCC § 2-314-15). Third is strict liability developed by several court decisions in the 1960s and summarized in the Restatement (Second) of Tort § 402A. The fourth cause of action is misrepresentation by the seller to the consumer (cf. Restatement § 402B).

In contrast to American practice, the Japanese legal system gives no explicit recognition of a strict liability rule except for a few exceptions such as buildings and constructed objects, and thus still adheres to the traditional principle of compensation based on the negligence of the defendants. Hence, the first cause of action in the United States is prevalent in Japan, although a contractual approach somewhat similar to the second cause is taken in a few cases. The Japanese system requires the plaintiff to prove fault on the part of producers or sellers to win the case. Although various legal techniques can be used to considerably reduce the plaintiff's burden of proof, nevertheless, we need more systematic liability rules that prevent consumers from suffering damages without compensation. Hence the commendability of this draft model law prepared by the Product Liability Research Group.

In Japan negligence on the part of the plaintiff may be considered as cause for "setoff." This is in contrast to American practice, in which the principle of contributory negligence or comparative negligence has been adopted. The principle of setoff in Japan is similar to *partial* (not pure) comparative negligence, which requires greater fault on the part of the defendant to win the case. The Japanese system of setoff differs significantly from the principle of contributory negligence, which leads to a result of all-or-nothing compensation. This difference probably reflects the more adaptive, rather than discrete, character of Japanese thinking. More careful analysis would be required to determine how this principle of flexible distribution of burdens affects the deterrence of accidents. Our preliminary hypothesis is that this system may not be efficient when the desired care levels are known with certainty, but may be quite efficient when the desirable level of care is not absolutely known to the court.[45]

The number of product liability actions has been smaller in Japan, and the amount of compensation has also been relatively small. This has contributed to the absence of a product liability crisis in this country. Several reasons might explain both the small number of cases and the low amount of compensation. In Japan there is no practice of awarding punitive damages, and inflationary expectations are seldom counted as an adjustment for the plaintiff's loss of future income. There is no jury system in which citizen jurors may become more sympathetic to victims than are professional judges. Moreover, the contingency fee system for attorneys, apparently one of the main causes of "ambulance chasers" and the explosion of product liability suits in the United States, is hardly welcomed under present professional ethics in Japan. The class action has not yet been introduced, either. Finally, a tax (stamp duty) that depends on the value of the claim is imposed when one brings a legal action before a court.

The Japanese system may seem more favorable to producers than that of the United States because the principle of strict liability has not been generally introduced. In addition, the absence of explicit statutes for product liability leaves room for a failure to establish suitable economic incentives for preventing accidents. We contend, however, that the difference is not large. Although Japanese legal practice is formerly based on the Civil Code, actual practice as evidenced by the actions of lawyers, decisions by judges, and commentaries made by scholars has primarily followed American practice in product liability. Cases are quite similar in most developed countries, despite differences in basic legal construction, but practice in the United States, where product liability cases are numerous and doctrines highly developed, has provided the most reliable examples for Japanese lawyers.

With regard to other means of preventing hazards, in general the Japanese system has been less imposing on producers. There have been neither special statutes nor too many regulations. On the other hand, governmental persuasion might have worked to restrict business activities and prevent accidents through various informal means of checking the safety standard via *gyōsei shidō* (administrative guidance). Here again, the difference may not be as large as it appears. More empirical as well as theoretical research on practices related to defective products should be done to place the Japanese incentive structure in comparative perspective.

Finally, the attitude of the Japanese people toward legal action is quite different from that of Americans. Japanese people like to settle by compromise without going through formal legal proceedings, a fact reflected in the relative number of court appeals and lawyers in the two countries. There are 12,000 attorneys in Japan, compared to about half a million in the United States. This is one of the major reasons why there is no explosion of product liability cases in Japan.

Why legal attitudes of the Japanese differ from those of Americans is an interesting issue for dispute. It may reflect a more adaptive, group-oriented mode of thought and behavior on the part of the Japanese. A notion exists in Japan that both parties are to blame in a conflict—*kenka ryōseibai*, that is, in all disputes, both parties are presumed at fault. Kawashima, for one, has attributed this characteristic to the lack of consciousness of human rights among the Japanese.[46] He regards it as reflecting the remnants of feudalistic elements in Japanese society. In a recent monograph, Ohki[47] contends that the Japanese people have in the past possessed, and still do possess, a genuine legal consciousness that might assume different forms but is in principle based on the same universal rationality as is the legal consciousness in Western countries. According to him, the apparent paucity of legal actions can be regarded as the result of historical processes during which governments or rulers discouraged citizens from bringing suits at law. The intriguing questions remain as to whether one can discern a universal legal rationality among the Japanese and whether the lack of a legal consciousness merely reflects feudalistic elements or is idiosyncratic to the Japanese. Whatever the case, it is nonetheless true that an observable difference in attitudes toward legal actions does exist between the people of the two countries.

NOTES

1. The Kokumin Seikatsu Center is a *tokushu hōjin* (special legal entity) under the control of the Economic Planning Agency. Thus, consumer protection in Japan is integrated with the main governmental agency for monitoring the performance of the economy.

2. Zentaro Kitagawa, "The Japanese Experience with Product Liability: A Unique Development," in Andreas Heldrich et al., eds., *Konflikt und Ordnung*, Festschrift fur Murad Ferid Zum 70 (Munich: Beck, 1967), is an excellent article on a similar subject and quite complementary to our chapter.

3. Economic Planning Agency, Economic Welfare Bureau, First Consumer Affairs Division (Keizai Kikaku-chō, Kokumin Seikatsu Kyoku, Shōhisha Gyōsei Dai-ikka), ed., *Shōhisha higai no*

kyūsai to seizōbutsu sekinin (Remedies for damages to consumers, and product liability) (Tokyo: Daiichi Hōki, 1982).

4. The Coase theorem states that resource allocation is not affected by the liability rule because a negotiation mechanism operates between the parties in such a way as to achieve a Pareto-efficient outcome. Ronald H. Coase, "The Problem of Social Costs," *Journal of Law and Economics* 3 (1960): 1–44.

5. EPA, *Shōhisha higai no kyūsai to seizobutsu sekinin*.

6. Ibid.

7. Various other legislation contributes to controlling the quality of products and to promoting product safety. For a systematic discussion of these regulations, see Y. Asami, "Consumer Products Safety Regulations in Japan," *Japan Business Law Journal*, vol. 3, nos. 1, 2, and 3 (1982).

8. See, for example, Takeshi Kawai, *Seizōbutsu sekinin no kenkyū* (Studies in product liability) (Tokyo: Nihon Hyōronsha, 1979); and, for its economic implications, Koichi Hamada, *Songai baishō no keizai bunseki* (An economic analysis of compensation for damages) (University of Tokyo Press, 1977); and Economic Planning Agency, Shōhisha Gyōsei Dai-ikka (EPA), ed., *Zoku shōhisha higai no kyūsai to seizōbutsu sekinin* (An update: remedies for damages to consumers, and product liability) (Tokyo: Okurashō Insatsu Kyoku, 1978).

9. For a comprehensive survey in English of legal practices regarding product liability, readers are strongly recommended to consult the article by Adachi, Henderson, Miyatake, and Fujita in Hans-Ulrich Stucki and Peter R. Altenburger, eds., *Product Liability: A Manual of Practice in Selected Nations: Japan* (London: Oceana Publications, 1981). We owe much to their analysis as well as to their choice of English translations of legal terms.

10. Masaru Etoh, "Shōhisha higai to sono kyūsai no jittai" (Damages to consumers and their remedies) in Ken-ichi Miyazawa, ed., *Seizōbutsu sekinin no keizai gaku* (Economics of product liability) (Tokyo: Sanroi Shobō, 1982), p. 211ff.

11. Ogaki Branch of the Gifu District Court, Dec. 27, 1973, *Hanrei Jihō*, no. 725. See Adachi et al., *Product Liability*, p. 26.

12. Oct. 25, 1963, *Hanrei Jihō*, no. 356.

13. Takamatsu High Court, Mar. 31, 1966, *Hanrei Jihō*, no. 447, and the Supreme Court, Feb. 26, 1969, *Hanrei Jihō*, no. 547.

14. Nov. 28, 1973, *Hanrei Jihō*, no. 721.

15. Oct. 5, 1977, *Hanrei Jihō*, no. 866.

16. Mar. 10, 1978, *Hanrei Jihō*, no. 881.

17. For example, see *Hanrei Jihō*, no. 950, 1979.

18. For example, Tokyo District Court, Sept. 25, 1978; *Hanrei Times*, no. 387. Tokyo District Court, Feb. 1, 1982, *Hanrei Times*, no. 458.

19. Oct. 5, 1977, *Hanrei Jihō*, no. 866.

20. Yokohama District Court, Feb. 4, 1975, *Hanrei Times*, no. 321.

21. One of the reasons why many product liability cases concerning industrial equipment are brought to court in the United States seems to stem from compensation to workers usually being limited once they are covered by insurance schemes, and they cannot sue their employers any further. In Japan these limitations do not apply, however.

22. For example, the Matsumo Branch of the Nagano District Court, November 11, 1965, *Hanrei Jihō*, no. 427.

23. Product Liability Research Group, 1975. For the English translation, see Adachi et al., *Product Liability: Japan*, Appendix, pp. i–v. For a discussion of its significance, see Takeshi Kawai, *Seizōbutsu sekinin no kenkyū* (Studies in product liability) (Tokyo: Nihon Hyōronsha, 1970).

24. Adachi et al., *Product Liability*.

25. Economic Planning Agency, *Seizōbutsu sekinin to baishō futan* (Product liability and distribution of burdens) (Tokyo: Okurashō Insatsu Kyoku, 1980), pp. 17–21.

26. EPA, *Shōhisha higai no kyusai to seizōbutsu sekinin*.

27. See Kokumin Seikatsu Shingikai, Shōhisha Bukai (Hōkoku), *Shōhisha Seisaku no atarashii kadai* (New tasks for consumer policy) (Tokyo: Okurashō Insatsu Kyoku, 1979). See also Naoto Yamauchi, "Estimation of the Economic Effects of Product Liability," in Ken'ichi Miyazawa, ed., *Seizōbutsu sekinin no keizai gaku*.

28. These estimates are for costs around 1975–76.

29. Interagency Task Force, U.S. Department of Commerce, *On Product Liability, Final Report* (Washington, D.C.: U.S. Government Printing Office, 1977).

30. This is emphasized by Ken'ichi Miyazawa in "Seizōbutsu sekinin to gendai shakai" (Product liability and modern society), in Ken'ichi Miyazawa, ed., *Seizōbutsu sekinin no keizai gaku*.

31. See Koichi Hamada, "Liability Rules and Income Distribution in Product Liability," *American Economic Review* 66: 228–34. See also Richard A. Posner, *Economic Analysis of Law* (Boston: Little, Brown, 1972), chap. 4.

32. See Hamada, *"Liability Rules,"* for incentive mechanism.

33. If bystanders can sue buyers of a product, then the neutrality result still holds. We do not know, however, whether this is a reasonable solution.

34. John P. Brown, "Toward an Economic Theory of Liability," *Journal of Legal Studies* 2 (1973): 323–49. Also see Hamada, "Liability Rules."

35. Yoshio Hirai, *Songai baishōhō no riron* (The theory of compensation law) (Tokyo: University of Tokyo Press, 1971), and also Yoshio Hirai, *Gendai fuhōkōriron no ichitembō* (A survey of modern tort theory) (Tokyo: Ichiryūsha, 1980).

36. Yokohama District Court, Feb. 4, 1975, *Hanrei Times*, no. 324.

37. Yamauchi, "Estimation of Economic Effects," pp. 235–59.

38. Cf. Adachi et al., *Product Liability*, p. 26.

39. EPA, *Seizōbutsu sekinin to baishō futan*, p. 101.

40. According to another statistical source (ibid.), the estimated premium for product liability insurance in fiscal 1977 was around 6 billion yen.

41. Cf. Adachi et al., *Product Liability*, pp. 52ff.

42. Osaka District Court, Dec. 22, 1977, *Hanrei Times*, no. 366.

43. For reference, see Teruo Doi, *Amerika seihin sekinin hō* (American product liability law) (Tokyo: Sanrei Shobō, 1983).

44. See, for example, Teruo Doi, *Seizōbutsu sekinin* (Product liability) (Tokyo: Dōbunkan, 1978); and J. T. Elser in H. Stucki and P. R. Altenberger, eds., *Product Liability: A Manual of Practice in Selected Nations: United States of America* (London: Oceana Publications, 1981).

45. Cf. Brown, "Toward an Economic Theory."

46. Takeyoshi Kawashima, *Nihonjin no hōishiki* (Legal consciousness of the Japanese) (Tokyo: Iwanami, 1967).

47. Masao Ohki, *Nihonjin no hōkannen* (The Japanese people's concept of law) (Tokyo: University of Tokyo Press, 1983).

Administrative Guidance versus Formal Regulation: Resolving the Paradox of Industrial Policy

JOHN O. HALEY

Observers of Japan's postwar economy confront a paradox. Japan's recovery is ascribed by some to the promotional policies of a gifted and farsighted bureaucracy in large measure designed to suppress domestic competition.[1] For Japanese firms to become internationally competitive, government officials believed that, as former Prime Minister Kishi Nobusuke put it, the "bad habit" of fierce firm rivalry at home had to be restrained.[2] An industrial policy of protection, cartelization, and concentration has thus been viewed as a major ingredient in the Japanese recipe for economic growth. Others take issue with such assessments. They find the secret to economic success in the competitive freedom of the Japanese market.[3]

Advocates of both views eventually face the recognition that Japan's postwar experience includes both anticompetitive governmental policies and, at least in the most successful industries, a fiercely competitive environment. How the two relate and which deserves special emphasis are fundamental issues that must be resolved before Japanese economic success can be evaluated or the framework in which U.S.–Japanese trade relations function can be fully understood. Indeed, what is the Japanese "model"? Could government protectionist policies have achieved so much in the absence of competition? Or, conversely, how could competition have survived the onslaught of suppressive bureaucratic actions? What does the future hold for Japan?

To state my conclusion at the outset, the answers lie in part in the manner in which government policies generally, but economic policies in particular, were implemented. Administrative guidance (*gyōsei shidō*), that ubiquitous process for enforcing administrative policy in Japan, provides one a key to unlock the paradox of industrial policy, of regulation with competition. Although administrative guidance is quite accurately described as the means by which the Ministry of International Trade and Industry (MITI), the Ministry of Finance, and other economic ministries in Japan used to restrict competition and to circumvent Japan's antitrust law, reliance upon guidance rather than formal regulation as a process of governing insured that ultimately the competitive forces of the market place, not bureaucratic aims, determined economic policy in postwar Japan. This does not mean that government intervention had no impact or that all sectors of the economy were effectively governed by market forces or firm rivalry, or that there has been no resort to formal regulation. However, as exemplified in a recently published study of industrial targeting in Japan by the United States International Trade Commission,[4] there has been a misplaced emphasis on administrative guidance as a means used by the government "to encourage private firms to take actions that [the government] deems useful or necessary."[5] A more accurate description would stress the extent to which government policies reflected the needs and demands of those being "guided." Japanese industrial policy—if the various economic measures of the Japanese government can be properly so labeled—comprised more of a series of responses to immediate economic conditions and events than a carefully designed plan implemented by effective governmental persuasion.

My purpose in this essay is to examine the function and consequences of administrative guidance as the predominant process of governance in Japan and to show that as a species of informal law—or policy—enforcement it helped to preserve a competitive market economy in contrast to formal regulation, that, intended or not, more effectively suppresses competition. The choice between administrative guidance and formal regulation involves not only the selection of a means of implementing policy that is flexible and responsive to market forces, but also one that as a consequence precludes the successful or full implementation of policy. In other words, the predominance of administrative guidance as a regulatory form for government intervention in the economy—that is, the process itself as distinguished from the content of any particular policy—has helped to preserve a competitive market economy by maximizing the freedom of individual firms over economic decisions although behind the veil of pervasive governmental direction. Japanese postwar economic achievement can thus be credited in part to administrative guidance because it ensured the failure of a bureaucratically set agenda.

ADMINISTRATIVE GUIDANCE AS INFORMAL LAW ENFORCEMENT

The economist and the lawyer tend to use the term administrative guidance differently. For the economist administrative guidance refers primarily to the content or substance of Japanese postwar economic policies. The main features of these policies are well summarized in the paper by Iyori Hiroshi in this volume. Those usually discussed under the rubric of "administrative guidance" relate to particular measures designed either to suppress competition or to achieve the perceived gains of concentration. With increasing frequency during the 1950s and 1960s, the economic ministries, particularly MITI, resorted to informal, often extralegal direction or requests to the private business sector to enter a variety of cartel or cartellike arrangements, to coordinate investment, production, and prices as a means of reducing or eliminating competition or to consolidate or merge to achieve greater economies of scale.[6] Administrative guidance has thus become a frequently used label for these policies.

For the lawyer, however, administrative guidance is descriptive of a process for implementing public policy as distinguished from the policy itself. With few, if any, exceptions it is defined quite simply as advice or direction by government officials carried out voluntarily by the respondents. By definition it involves neither formal legal action nor direct legal coercion. Compliance is thus voluntary in the narrow legal sense. Moreover, as explained below in greater detail, resort to guidance instead of formal regulation was a political and legal necessity.

As a recent and impressive Japanese study[7] notes, administrative guidance is not a technical legal term, but rather an academic concept. As such it has been the subject of considerable scholarly analysis and discussion in Japan, the United States, and, more recently, Germany.[8] As illustrated by Professor Narita Yoriaki's now classic study published in 1966 in *Gendaiho*,[9] Japanese legal scholars tend to treat administrative guidance, as one might expect, in relation to basic administrative law issues, ranging from direct judicial review or other forms of legal redress by private parties to the ultimate if more abstract question of the legality of particular instances of administrative guidance.

These are, of course, critical questions for those concerned with the legal issues administrative guidance poses within the Japanese legal system. For instance, the restrictive approach adopted by Japanese courts in defining administrative measures subject to judicial review has insured that neither the recipients nor third parties adversely affected by administrative guidance have had access to the courts except in a few instances through damage actions.[10] Moreover, as a closed process of continuous interaction between government officials and a limited number of private parties, official resort to administrative guidance is also excoriated for exclusion of public participation and political review.[11]

At least in part because Japanese perceive the administrative process in the West to be a formal and more clearly defined procedural process, Japanese observers think of administrative guidance as a uniquely Japanese phenomenon. It is commonly regarded as the product of Japan's particular historical and social context and thus endemic as an aspect of the "Japanese climate."[12] Many western observers similarly emphasize the uniqueness of administrative guidance to Japan. Although all major studies in English and German recognize that practices analogous to administrative guidance can be found in the West, most emphasize the cultural factors that seem to explain administrative guidance as a peculiar Japanese institution. They find the underpinnings for administrative guidance in a neo-Confucian deference to authority and related desire to maintain harmony and cooperation and to avoid adversarial posturing, in other words, in the special social psychology of the Japanese. Paul Davis, for example, lists the persistence of patron-client relations, the continuity of traditional attitudes toward officials, a strongly held desire to avoid confrontation, and a weak "legal consciousness" as the main cultural props.[13] Elaborating upon these points, Wolfgang Pape is more sweeping:

> [T]he vertical structure of Japanese society allows open intercourse between those "above and below" and demarcates only in perpendicular fashion the interests of each group. This prevents formation of class consciousness and leads to a high degree of permeability in the traditional hierarchy from the Emperor to the common people (*shimojimo*). The structure of the smallest community of interest is transmitted to all other social units. Consequently, corresponding patterns of conduct are manifested between teacher and pupil, employer and employee, large firm and sub-contractor and in like manner between public administrators and private enterprises, without regard to any identity of interest on a horizontal level.[14]

Pape adds the "average man's longing for *amae*" and "the reciprocal obligatory effect (*giri*) of all kinds of favors or acts of benevolence (*on*)"[15] to his list.

Such explanations cannot be dismissed out of hand. Some explanation is necessary to explain what appears to be an extraordinary feature of the Japanese system of governance—that informal requests to produce compliance—for Japanese and Western commentators alike assert or seem to presume that administrative guidance is an effective means of implementing policy. "Compliance," Jeffrey Lepron claims, "is the typical Japanese corporate response to administrative guidance."[16] Chalmers Johnson essentially makes a similar claim, coining the term "developmental" as a new rubric under which administrative guidance as a cooperative process for implementing economic policy is viewed as a cornerstone of Japan's postwar recovery.[17] Although many duly note the role of private business in formulating economic policy and a Japanese stress on consensus, they appear uniformly to believe that what officials want, officials get by voluntary compliance. Were this true, Japan would indeed be a unique case.

The mist clears and an array of fundamental misconceptions disappear, however, when administrative guidance is viewed simply as a Japanese species of informal enforcement. As such, administrative guidance is not peculiarly Japanese, except perhaps for its ubiquity. Informal enforcement by official suggestion, advice, recommendation, or pointed direction is not only common to all legal systems, it is indeed the most common form of law enforcement.[18] All legal systems depend upon voluntary compliance with the law from the payment of taxes to regulatory control. No regime except perhaps one of absolute terror relies principally upon direct coercion, and even then compliance is usually not involuntary in the narrow sense of a response to legally binding orders backed by immediate and direct threats of compulsion. Fear is a formidable means of coercion.

Informal enforcement by United States antitrust authorities may contrast starkly in policy but not as process with MITI practice. As described by William G. Shepherd of the University of Michigan: "[T]he real influence of antitrust reaches much farther than the classic federal cases filed and litigated. Most of it occurs unseen through negotiations and threats that deter mergers and other actions. The antitrust agencies often intervene in regulatory cases through informal persuasion, by threatening to go to court or through testimony at formal public hearings. Such antitrust pressure was important in pushing forward every one of the seven major instances of deregulation in the 1970s, from airlines to stockbrokers' fees."[19] Much the same could be said for Japanese antitrust enforcement. The vast majority of all antitrust violations investigated by Japan's Fair Trade Commission (FTC) are resolved informally and without publicity either through negotiated settlement or at most the issuance of a warning.[20] Whether labeled administrative guidance or informal enforcement, and whether carried out by the Japanese FTC, MITI, or United States Federal Trade Commission and Justice Department officials, the process is the same.

What distinguishes Japan is the persuasive resort to informal enforcement in contexts that seem to require formal regulation in other industrial states. In Japan informal enforcement is not *a* process of governing, but has become *the* process of governing. It is used to implement nearly all bureaucratic policy, whether or not expressed in statute or regulation, at all levels of government and all administrative offices. Japanese officials use informal enforcement to implement policy in every conceivable situation from antitrust violations and price controls to regulation of financial institutions and bowling alley business hours to reduce juvenile crime.[21]

This emphasis on informal enforcement, as Japanese scholars have emphasized, leads to two separate concerns. First, informal enforcement appears to permit Japanese officials significant autonomy in determining the policies to be enforced. Administrative guidance is law enforcement therefore only in the sense that law is equated with whatever policies the officials choose to implement. A series of antitrust decisions from the 1950 Hokkaido Butter case through the 1980 Oil Cartel cases,[22] illustrate MITI's use of informal enforcement to encourage business enterprises to engage in prohibited anticompetitive conduct for which MITI had little or no statutory authority. Second, the resort to informal enforcement appears at least superficially to be effective. If compliance were not forthcoming would not, one asks, government officials turn to more coercive forms of law enforcement? Thus the persuasive use of administrative guidance itself suggests the effectiveness of informal enforcement in Japan to implement bureaucratic aims.

Analysis of the nature and consequences of informal enforcement in general raises doubt, however, as to the extent of official autonomy and the effectiveness of informal enforcement in Japan. Again to state my conclusion, the persuasive resort to informal enforcement in Japan is best explained by two factors: the predominance of promotional as opposed to regulatory policies and the weakness of formal law enforcement. These two factors not only force reliance on administrative guidance as an informal means of implementing policy, but by the same token significantly curtail the autonomy of the bureaucracy in formulating policy. Both the aim of assisting industry and a lack of strong legal sanctions or other forms of formal legal coercion in effect compel officials in Japan to negotiate and compromise with respect to the policies they seek to implement. As a result in many instances—expecially in economic policy—private parties possess more leverage in dealing with officials in Japan than in the United States. The lack of procedural controls over discretion can thus be explained in that private interests with political influence do not gain by the introduction of formal procedures designed to limit official discretion. Moreover, the increasing political influence of business interests relative to the economic ministries and the ruling political party in the legislature ensures that the bureaucracy has been unable to acquire the legal powers necessary to overcome their reliance on informal persuasion. This is not to say, I hasten to emphasize, that informal enforcement is necessarily ineffective or weak from the perspective of the enforcer. My argument is only that unless backed by formal legal powers it becomes a weaker and less effective means of enforcement than formal regulation.

THE NATURE AND CONSEQUENCES OF INFORMAL ENFORCEMENT

For a lawyer to delve into the causal factors of social behavior is a necessarily speculative venture. However, there is at least a certain common-sense reasonableness in an initial assertion that individuals or other decision-making units of society will ordinarily do what they perceive to be in their self-interest to do. The economist's assumption of rational behavior is surely a reasonable point of departure for all facets of social behavior so long as self-interest is defined broadly to include more than economic gain (or avoidance of economic loss) and "perception" of self-interest is acknowledged to be influenced by values and other nonrational impulses. With this set of caveats, use of informal means of law enforcement, such as administrative guidance, can be explained as a rational choice by officials in implementing policy. Their decision involves the balancing of gains against costs. Informal enforcement is preferred to the extent it results in the desired conduct without the costs of formal procedures. Conversely, officials will resort instead to formal enforcement wherever the anticipated gains outweigh the costs of enforcement.

Many of the gains relate to the policies being implemented. Some laws or policies may not be particularly important to the enforcement authorities and thus are not enforced diligently or at all. In such instances, the costs of any enforcement are perceived to outweigh the gains. In addition, the importance of a particular policy is not left solely to the subjective judgment of the officials. The primary enforcement officials may not give a hoot about the policy itself but still be diligent law enforcers if they perceive they personally or institutionally have something to gain or lose by their conduct.[23] If, for example, the policies affect strongly held legislative views or the desires of supporters, and the law enforcer fears legislative or bureaucratic wrath if the policies are not enforced, then the gains of enforcement may be considerable.

The costs of enforcement also include a variety of factors. All law enforcement involves the immediate costs of time, effort, and personnel. There are also political costs, as evidenced by the United States Federal Trade Commission's attempts to regulate used car sales and funeral home operations.

Compliance with formal law enforcement involves a similar balancing of gains and costs by the respondents. In deciding whether to comply with an informal, nonbinding request by government officials, the respondent balances the advantages against the disadvantages. Informal enforcement is most effective therefore to the extent that what is requested is viewed as ultimately beneficial or relatively more beneficial to the respondent or that failure to comply is perceived to be likely to result in greater disadvantage than would compliance. For example, taxpayers in the United States routinely comply with tax officials' nonbinding requests for audits. To refuse is viewed as a futile and possibly more costly gesture. (As noted below, the Japanese taxpayer's response may be quite different.)

Cultural factors are not irrelevant to these decisions. A community or individual sense of the legitimacy of government actions and policies may determine in particular instances whether a party will comply or not. Tax evasion, for instance, increases as taxpayers question the fairness of the tax system. Similarly, what is considered to be an illegitimate request by officials will be likely to produce greater efforts to avoid compliance. Consequently, the Japanese may be more tolerant of informal enforcement than Americans or Europeans, as both Japanese and non-Japanese observers suggest, because of traditional attitudes, or simply habit. Ultimately, however, such cultural factors cannot be considered determinative except in situations where the official or the private party or both would have acted differently out of self-interest but for a cultural imperative. Only if, for instance, the respondent of an official request complies even though doing so runs counter to economic or other gain, can cultural considerations be viewed as crucial.

Because officials are more likely to resort to informal enforcement whenever it is more or equally effective in implementing policy—and it tends to be effective to the extent that the respondents perceive that they will gain by the policies or are likely to suffer greater disadvantage by failing to comply—the determining factors cluster around the nature of the policies being enforced and the certainty and severity of any penalties for noncompliance.

The sanctions for noncompliance may be extralegal. Informal enforcement is used in all systems where it is backed by the threat of formal sanctions or extralegal difficulties. American taxpayers submit to tax audits, as noted, in part because of the authority of the Internal Revenue Service to assess taxes unilaterally but also in part to avoid a closer scrutiny than a routine audit. Of course, the greater the officials' scope of permissible discretionary action, the greater the availability of informal sanctions.

The choice between informal and formal enforcement also involves a comparative calculation of which means is the *more* effective, not which is effective in any absolute sense. Law enforcement authorities must rely on informal means of implementing policy in circumstances where formal enforcement would be *less* or *no more* effective. In such cases, enforcement becomes a process of negotiation and compromise. Officials are forced to bargain and strike the best deal they can get. In this context official policy requires consensus and acceptance by those being regulated, and any demand by officials that is too costly to the respondent will not be implemented. That by virtue of tradition or cultural concerns the officials may put their best face forward, treating as official policy what has been produced by such negotiated consensus, does not alter the basic fact that the policymaker or policy enforcer has little if any real discretion to determine the ultimate conduct of those subject to regulation. Consequently, the discretionary powers of officialdom will not be a matter of any significant concern. Indeed, if anything, private parties gain by the lack of formal procedural restrictions in the decision-making process because they may be able to dominate in an informal bargaining.

The availability and certainty of sanctions for failure to comply with government policies is therefore the single most important factor in determining the outcome of informal law enforcement. If sanctions against noncompliance are available and certain, informal enforcement will be used extensively as the most efficient and effective means for implementing policy. If not, informal means of enforcement also will be used, but the outcome will be a product of negotiation and compromise.

Why then, one might ask, would formal enforcement ever be used? The answer is quite simple. First, to be credible as a threat, formal sanctions must both be available and actually used. Unions, for example, will strike to preserve the efficacy of the threat of a strike for future contract negotiations. So too will formal sanctions be tested and applied. Second, as formal regulatory controls by government increase, demand for control over discretionary powers exercised by regulatory authorities also increases. Such demand tends to be satisfied in responsive political systems. In authoritarian political regimes, government officials have both broad legal enforcement powers and discretion. In more democratic or responsive political systems, there is usually less extensive formal governmental enforcement powers or more controls over official discretion. However, legal controls over discretion in fact reduce the certainty of sanctions and thus arguably produce greater resort to formal enforcement.

ADMINISTRATIVE GUIDANCE RECONSIDERED

The prevalence of administrative guidance can be explained by two basic features of postwar Japan: the essentially promotional thrust of Japanese economic and social policies and the intrinsic weakness of formal law enforcement in Japan. These factors are themselves influenced if not produced by the particular configurations of Japanese political and economic reality. The tapestry of postwar Japan is too rich and intricate to be explained by looking at a single thread, whether it be law, economics, or politics. But for each, however, the system would unravel.

Promotion versus Regulation

It is axiomatic to characterize as pervasive the role of government in the economic life of all industrial societies. There has been a tendency, however, to stress that role for modern Japan as if the Japanese government played an exceptional part compared with the United States and Western Europe. Many appear to ignore, for example, the extent of government participation in the United States during the heyday of laissez-faire sentiment. Whether in the form of subsidies, as in the case of the railroads, or legal restrictions, as in the trade union movement, governments at all levels, acting through legislatures and the courts, were involved directly and positively in the economy. During the mid- to late-nineteenth century, it is difficult to say the Meiji government intervened any more actively than its counterparts in the West.

What changed in the West, particularly the United States, was not intervention but the policies being implemented and the form or process of that intervention. Whereas the Japanese continued through the 1970s to pursue the goal of economic growth by promoting the private industrial sector, by the late nineteenth century the United States had begun to regulate the economy extensively in the public or consumer interest. While the Meiji government was selling off the vestiges of productive property owned by its Tokugawa predecessors, the United States was creating the Interstate Commerce Commission (1887) and enacting the Sherman Act (1890). As Kenneth Culp David reminds us,[24] nearly a third of all federal administrative agencies (unrelated to wartime needs) were established prior to 1900. Yet, the type of restrictive public controls that had become familiar to American enterprise even before World War I were unknown in Japan until after World War II. Even today restrictive economic regulation is relatively exceptional in Japan. Promotional intervention to assist industry remains the usual pattern.

The Interstate Commerce Act and the Sherman Act also exemplify the inconsistencies of regulation in the United States. Both statutes were enacted ostensibly to protect the consumer and the public interest, yet in practice they have been used for cross purposes. Antitrust legislation—the Sherman, Clayton, and Federal Trade Commission Acts—was designed to police the economy to prevent private restrictions on competition and other forms of anticompetitive conduct, but procompetition legislation did not keep pace with regulatory legislation, like the Interstate Commerce Act, which in practice created major legal barriers to entry and competition. As evident in current charges that deregulation leads to "destructive competition,"[25] regulation intended to protect the public rapidly became a means to protect industry from competition.

Since World War II many seem to misconceive Japan as a more highly concentrated and cartelized economy than the United States or other industrial countries.[26] As I have argued elsewhere,[27] during the 1920s and 1930s Japan was not a player but the principal national victim of the international cartel movement. Among the great ironies of the Allied occupation was the imposition of stringent antitrust legislation, since at no time in Japanese history before or since has its economy been so thoroughly controlled by public authorities than under the Supreme Commander for the Allied Powers (SCAP). Nearly all of postwar Japan's major regulatory statutes were sponsored and most actually drafted by occupation authorities. The Foreign Exchange and Foreign Trade Control Law,[28] for example, was drafted by Jan V. Mladek of the International Monetary Fund at SCAP invitation. The broad discretionary powers over foreign trade and foreign exchange controls that statute provided enabled MITI and the Ministry of Finance especially in the 1950s and 1960s not only to restrict access by Japanese firms to imported resources and to export markets, but also to prevent foreign competitors from penetrating Japanese markets. Control over the allocation of foreign exchange and import and export licenses provided the coercive force to administrative guidance to firms to enter or abide by cartel agreements or to merge. Firms that refused to comply with official or MITI-approved trade association requests to curtail production or stabilize prices could be denied foreign exchange or allocations of raw materials.[29]

Regulation without Sanctions

The formal regulatory controls that do exist in Japan are remarkably weaker than those in the United States.[30] Regulatory statutes drafted by SCAP authorities, such as the Antimonopoly and Fair Trade Law, almost invariably contain extensive enforcement provisions reflecting American practice and administrative powers. The lack of contempt power by the courts or an analogue to it, however, precludes effective formal legal enforcement. The investigatory powers of Japanese government agencies are nowhere near as extensive as administrative agencies in the United States. The Japanese FTC, for example, relies almost exclusively on voluntary submissions or surprise searches. Japanese tax auditors rarely confront fully compliant taxpayers.[31] Indeed, Japanese businessmen and lawyers express shock at the Internal Revenue Service practice of assigning tax auditors permanently to major firms, which provide office space in their corporate headquarters. Without significant civil or administrative sanctions, the primary formal legal means in Japan for compelling conduct in conformity with regulatory prescription is the criminal penalty. Even in the United States criminal sanctions are difficult to apply against corporate executives.[32] In Japan it is inconceivable that criminal penalties could be applied with the certainty and regularity necessary for them to provide a meaningful deterrent. A dearth of procurators makes resort to criminal sanction all the more difficult.

As a result of the weakness of formal sanctions, Japanese government officials are forced to rely in most instances on extralegal sanctions for what coercion is required. The potential denial of a foreign exchange approval or an import license for failure to abide by some unrelated regulation—the typical sanctions used by the economic ministries during much of the postwar period—was the fear that gave administrative guidance coercive effect in the 1950s. Yet resort to these indirect sanctions were always subject to both formal legal as well as political challenge as an illegitimate governmental response. Extralegal sanctions are not a fully effective substitute for legal means of compulsion.

Because of the promotional thrust of Japanese economic policies, however, the inherent inadequacy of formal legal sanctions has not been readily apparent. Most government actions benefit those subject to official direction, and thus the issue of how to compel compliance only rarely surfaces. Even where the immediate impact of an official request for action may have adverse consequences, in most instances Japanese firms have been able to expect protection from major losses and have thus been willing to accommodate official policy. The necessity of formal enforcement and regulation by negotiation and compromise is evidenced, however, in those cases where the adverse consequences of governmental policies are too great to be bargained away.

Just as during extreme wartime circumstances the military was unable to assert full government control over private industry,[34] during the postwar period the economic ministries failed in most attempts to strengthen their statutory authority to provide greater direct legal powers for coercion. As indicated above, the principal sources of regulatory power, such as foreign exchange and foreign trade controls, were authored and directed by SCAP, not the Japanese bureaucracy. The repeated efforts to have the Diet enact legislation to weaken antitrust enforcement in the late 1950s and the Designated Industries Promotion Special Measures bill[35] in the early 1960s illustrate the inability of the economic bureaucracies to override industry opposition to any increase in bureaucratic power.[36]

Informal enforcement through administrative guidance may free the bureaucracy from direct accountability to the public through either the Diet or the courts, as most critics of administrative guidance point out, but it also has denied officials formal legitimacy and authority to act. Moreover, in many instances, only by closed private settlement has administrative guidance been able to operate. Although of little solace to third parties without any say in the policies being negotiated, the necessity to minimize public disclosure and the possibility of embarrassing political controversy, including interrogation in the Diet, often provides the recipients significant leverage. For the recipient of governmental requests to protest publicly can cause officials acute political embarrassment.

Although exceptional and usually cited for the compelling effect of administrative guidance, the 1965 Sumitomo Metals Mining Company incident illustrates the effect of public disclosure of official guidance without direct statutory authority. MITI demanded that the steel industry reduce production of blister steel. When Sumitomo refused to agree to the production quotas because it felt its share did not fairly correspond to its competitive position, MITI reduced Sumitomo's access to import coal. By making the entire episode public, Sumitomo was able to force MITI to retract this action and increase its share of production.[37] In other words, the bureaucracy's hold on political power has been far less secure than many believe. Without industry support and willingness to cooperate, the economic bureaucracies have not been able to act effectively.

The Politics of Administrative Discretion

Both Japanese and Western lawyers correctly regard administrative guidance in Japan as the product of broad administrative discretion. As a review of almost any legislation relating to the economy reveals, the Diet almost invariably delegates broad authority to the bureaucracy to formulate policy and to enforce it by means of recommendations, suggestions, directions, and other forms of nonbinding requests. Why, one should ask, has the Diet not limited the powers of the bureaucracy or at least placed greater controls over discretion as in the United States, or, conversely, if the ultimate sanctions are weak, why hasn't the bureaucracy pressed for stronger, more effective enforcement powers? The explanation in answer to these questions can be found in the realities of Japanese politics.

Although the Japanese bureaucracy during the postwar era has exerted a remarkable influence within the ruling Liberal Democratic party (LDP), its position has been fragile. The political influence of MITI and the other economic ministries has depended perhaps foremost upon a national consensus giving overriding priority to economic growth as well as on the delicate balance within the LDP between party politicians and former bureaucrats, conflicting claims by rival ministries, and the support of various economic interests—the "client" industries of each economic ministry. The influence of the national bureaucracy as a whole has never translated into sufficient political power to gain whatever it desired. Only the Ministry of Agriculture, Forestry, and Fisheries, which is protected by the dependency of party politicians within the LDP on its "client" interests, has had the political influence within the Diet to insure legal authority. Japan's rice-support system, for instance, is implemented by effective formal controls, not administrative guidance. Nor is it surprising that the most intractable trade issues between the United States and Japan have involved agricultural products.[38]

The consequence has been the incapacity of MITI or any other ministry to extract significant enforcement powers from the Diet. Moreover, Japanese bureaucrats like their American counterparts expend considerable effort to avoid the embarrassment of legislators' criticism because they too are subject to legislative control. Moreover, as illustrated by the defeat of the Designated Industries Promotion Special Measures bill, noted above, industry opposition has been sufficient to kill any attempt by MITI or other ministries to gain formal legal powers to enforce policies they have been unable to persuade industry to accept. The history of antitrust legislation in Japan exemplifies the gradual erosion of MITI's ability to establish its industrial policy as the centerpiece of Japanese economic law.

MITI's capacity to implement an industrial policy effectively is also exemplified in its failure to prevent new entry. Both the political need for consensus to make administrative guidance a workable process as well as the anticompetitive and proconcentration basis of MITI's policies dictated limiting new industrial entrants to the extent possible. Attempts were thus made to prevent Sony,

Honda, and Kawasaki and Kobe Steel, to name a few of the best known examples, from entering or expanding in targeted industries. Yet enter or expand they did. Without effective formal regulatory controls, MITI was essentially powerless to prevent new firms who could acquire capital to enter. Thus postwar Japan witnessed the growth of eight postwar entrants in the automobile industry, the proliferation of electronics firms, the expansion of petroleum and integrated steel producers,[39] and the spectacular growth of "super" store retailers, all despite informal and extralegal bureaucratic controls.

Where formal legal controls limiting new entrants through approvals or licenses by the central authorities did exist, administrative guidance as a means of effective policy implementation fared much better. As a consequence of the formal barriers to entry in banking and the securities industries, the Ministry of Finance has thus outdistanced MITI considerably in its capacity to govern financial institutions by administrative guidance. The resistance by the Ministry of Finance to a free capital market relates directly therefore to an appreciation of its fundamental sources of power.

The underlying weakness of MITI and most other economic bureaucracies also explains the lack of legal controls over bureaucratic discretion. Major business interests have had little to gain by insisting on procedural safeguards in the administrative process since the necessity for business acquiescence itself precluded most arbitrary exercises of power. On the other hand, notwithstanding inherent "cultural" patterns, the revival of antitrust enforcement and the legislative strengthening of the FTC's formal enforcement powers, especially the addition in 1977 of a mandatory cartel profits surcharge, led to reinforcement of procedural controls over administrative discretion by the FTC. The additions included new provisions requiring the commission to explain in decisions the reasons for not adopting evidence presented by respondents or hearing examiners,[40] expanding the opportunity for direct hearings before the commission,[41] limiting the commission to findings based on evidence introduced at hearings,[42] giving respondents greater opportunity to introduce new evidence or appeal,[43] and prohibiting any persons involved in the investigation of a case from serving as hearing examiners.[44] Several of these provisions, including the last, restated in statutory form existing commission regulation.[45] It was not coincidental, therefore, that the one administrative agency with regulatory functions that most closely resembles the American pattern should also become increasingly subject to legal controls over discretionary enforcement, or judicialized decisional processes that are equally typical of American administrative law.

To be sure, there are instances where the government does not lack formal or informal means of coercion. Compliance with administrative guidance in three instances is compelled. Japanese protectionist policies of the 1950s and 1960s illustrate the effectiveness of coercive administrative guidance vis-à-vis foreign enterprises. Foreign enterprises faced a bureaucracy with formidable extralegal power. Foreign equity investment for the establishment of subsidiaries and technology transfers required approval under the Foreign Investment Law[46] and there was a reporting requirement for branch establishment under the Foreign

Exchange and Foreign Trade Control Law. By administrative manipulation of the reporting requirement, no foreign company was permitted in effect to operate without approval. Policies formulated within the bureaucracy without legislative sanction were enforced by the effective control of the authorities over foreign exchange, foreign trade, and Japan's tightly knit system of commercial banks. Although there were instances of evasion, to be in "contempt of MITI" was powerful enough a threat to ensure that foreign firms acquiesced in what was demanded of them, in terms of royalty rates and the conduct of business in Japan. There is not even a known case of an application for approval of foreign invest-ment being denied formally. MITI or other ministry officials merely had to request withdrawal of the application, and the foreign firm withdrew it.[47] It is no wonder then that American lawyers and businessmen who confronted these barriers to entry into the Japanese market in the 1950s and 1960s view adminis-trative guidance as an effective and essentially coercive means of enforcing policy, exercised by a seemingly monolithic bureaucracy.[48]

Yet even for the foreign enterprise there was some room for negotiation. There was never a formal blanket denial of foreign investment but rather the require-ment for case by case review and approval. Those who had the will to drive hard bargains—and had the bargaining chips—could gain entry. Such cases, as Japanese officials would quickly point out to others seeking equal treatment, were exceptions and not precedents for similar investment by others.

As the beneficiaries of Japanese protectionism, Japanese industrial firms and privileged foreign enterprises had little cause to challenge the economic minis-tries' resort to extralegal actions or the informality of enforcement in the regula-tion of foreign trade and investment. There was therefore little if any domestic political pressure to institute formal procedural protections from administrative discretion against foreign firms seeking access to the Japanese market.

THE CONSEQUENCES: THE DETERMINATIVE ROLE
OF MARKET FORCES AND COMPETITION

Administrative guidance, as other forms of informal law enforcement, is a flexible and adaptable process. Once in place, as the proponents of deregulation in the United States have discovered, formal regulation like statutes require equal if not greater effort to change. Moreover, the legal restraints on official discretion to formulate policy apply with equal force to their discretion to repeal or modify previous policies.

On the other hand, almost exclusive reliance on administrative guidance to implement postwar economic policy in Japan has lessened the capacity of the government to affect market forces significantly, except perhaps for very brief periods. Without strong formal enforcement powers MITI's administrative guid-ance to domestic industries thus necessarily involved negotiation and comprom-ise and a flexible response to industry needs as determined by changing market conditions. The consequence was an unintended responsiveness to market forces. Unlike regulated industries in the United States, government-sponsored cartels in Japan have not been significantly stronger than purely private cartels. Only in highly concentrated industries with substantial barriers to entry, not subject to significant competitive pressures, do guidance cartels seem to have been effective, at least in the long run. As illustrated by Japan's electronics, automobile, retail, and even steel industries, government policies designed to control domestic entry, achieve concentration or coordination as to prices and production, were not as successful as they would have been with formal enforcement. As noted, Honda, Sony, Matsushita, Kawasaki, and Kobe Steel successfully challenged existing firms with strong government ties, despite initial (and often continued) efforts by government officials to prevent their entry.

The paradox of a highly competitive economy subject to pervasive anticompetitive government policies is thus explained by administrative guidance when viewed as a process of compromise and negotiation that forces the government ultimately to defer to and meet the demands of the market. There might be industrywide consensus in periods of excess supply or low demand that cartellike arrangements were necessary but allocation of production quotas or establishment of proper price levels required accommodation of disparate interests. As market conditions changed and some firms no longer gained by the arrangement, administrative guidance permitted continuing modification. Moreover, cheating was seldom legally proscribed, and, as suggested by the prevalence of rebating and discounting, appears to have been widespread. Even when formal controls were instituted as evidenced by the "check-price" system, they were often equally easily evaded.[49] As Yamawaki Hideki's study of the effect of industrial policy on prices and capacity in Japan's steel industry confirms,[50] administrative guidance is too pliable an instrument of enforcement to compel industry cooperation.

The determinative force of the market is perhaps best illustrated by the Japanese experience with price controls in the 1970s. Thanks to the study by Malcolm D. H. Smith,[51] Japanese reliance on informal guidance to restrain prices has been amply described. However, Smith does not deal with the results—the actual effect of administrative guidance on prices.

The following conclusions are drawn from comparisons between the United States and Japan of consumer or wholesale price changes between 1971 and 1976 for selected commodities subject to either formal or informal price controls in Japan.[52] Rice, electricity, and gas were selected to illustrate the effect of formal price controls. The commodities subject to informal price controls were sugar, cooking oil, instant ramen, beef, pharmaceutical drugs, gasoline, building materials, and textiles.

For each product subject to formal regulation, as one would expect, a "staircase" pattern of regulated prices prevailed. Periods of constant price levels without change were followed in each instance by brief but steep rises to higher plateaus with relatively long periods of constant prices at the higher levels. There was a marked difference between the predominately market-determined, fluctuating movement in the price of rice in the United States during this period in contrast to the rigid pattern of change under Japan's formal price support system. Similarly the formal approval system for gas and electricity supply services under the Electricity and Gas Enterprise Laws[53] was equally effective in controlling prices. Gas and electricity prices in the United States do not indicate market-determined price fluctuations. Their more gradual rise without a staircase pattern is probably the result of reliance on state and local regulation and thus the greater diversity of regulated rates.

Administrative guidance was apparently the primary means for controlling the price of sugar, cooking oil, instant ramen, beef, pharmaceuticals, and gasoline, especially between February 1973 and February 1974. As the preceding analysis of the effect of administrative guidance suggests, there is little evidence of any significant difference between predominantly market-dictated U.S. prices and "guided" price changes in Japan. Further, as illustrated in broader comparisons of price changes during this period, there is no evidence that administrative guidance had any substantial effect on price levels.

The stability of prices in certain industries, such as pharmaceuticals in both Japan and the United States, may be explained by an array of factors other than administrative guidance and formal regulation that limit competition and the full play of market forces. Such factors, ranging from the patent to monopoly to the structure of the industry and levels of concentration may effectively shield particular industries from competition. Price fixing and output restrictions in certain industries, even those subject to significant firm rivalry, may have stabilized prices for various periods.[54] Nonetheless, the culprit is not a guided industrial policy.

CONCLUSION

In sum, administrative guidance should be treated as a generally weak means of enforcing government policy, one which absent formal controls and sanctions leaves room for maneuver and manipulation by those being regulated. As a result, bureaucratic efforts to suppress or restrain firm rivalry by administrative guidance were not likely to have significant impact in industries that were otherwise competitive. MITI thus could not by guidance force client industries to withstand the pressures of the market. New entrants could not be shut out, technology licenses could not be denied, and price controls could not work.

As the predominant process of implementing administrative policy, administrative guidance therefore freed Japanese firms from the more restrictive consequences of formal controls and in turn subjected them more fully to the discipline of market forces. The unintended benefits of informal enforcement were evidenced by the growth and international competitiveness of those industries that experienced sustained competition within the Japanese market during the postwar peiod. Where, however, formal statutory authority and extralegal sanctions have permitted more effective implementation of government policies, either through administrative guidance or mandatory controls, the consequences appear to have been less positive. In agriculture and financial services restrictive government policies have not achieved the benefits claimed. The

Japanese experience is thus a telling reminder that the ultimate role of law is to prevent nonconforming conduct not to stimulate innovation. Law, as Donald Black reminds us, is conservative.[55]

NOTES

1. See, e.g., E. Vogel, *Japan as Number One: Lessons for America* (Cambridge: Harvard University Press, 1979). Vogel's assertion (p. 72) that "MITI's aim is not to reduce competition among Japanese companies . . . " is belied by the array of anticompetitive actions MITI has taken. For a remarkable essay in support of such actions by one of their principal architects, see Amaya Naohiro, "Harmony and the Antimonopoly Law," *Japan Echo*, no. 1 (1981), pp. 85–102.

2. From Kishi's address to the opening meeting of the special commission to study antimonopoly law reforms in October 1957, quoted in Kōsei Torihiki Iinkai [FTC], *Dokusen kinshi seisaku nijūnenshi* (Twenty-year history of antimonopoly policy) (Tokyo: Okurasho Insatsukyoku, 1968), p. 152.

3. See, e.g., M. Friedman, *Freedom to Choose* (New York: Harcourt, Brace, Jovanovich, 1980). For a more moderate view, but one that exposes without resolving the paradox of persistent competition despite anticompetitive government policies, see H. Patrick, and H. Rosovsky, *Asia's New Giant* (Washington, D.C.: Brookings Institution, 1976), p. 50.

4. U.S. International Trade Commission, Foreign Industrial Targeting and Its Effects on U.S. Industries: Japan (USITC Publication 1437, Washington, D.C., 1983).

5. Ibid., p. 71.

6. These actions are detailed in English in K. Yamamura, *Economic Policy in Postwar Japan* (Berkeley and Los Angeles: University of California Press, 1967) and C. Johnson, *MITI and the Japanese Miracle* (Stanford, Calif.: Stanford University Press, 1982).

7. *Gyōsei shidō ni kansuru chōsa kenkyū hōkokusho* (Report on investigative study of administrative guidance) (Tokyo: Gyōsei Kanri Kenkyū Sentā, 1981) (hereafter *Administrative Guidance Research Report*). The report was prepared for the Administrative Management Agency (Gyōsei Kanri Chō) by a committee of Japan's leading legal scholars in administrative law and select businessmen and government officials.

8. The principal studies are listed in the appended bibliography.

9. Narita Yoriaki, "Gyōsei shidō," in *Gendaihō* (Contemporary law) (Tokyo: Iwanami shoten, 1966), 4: 131–68, translated ("Administrative Guidance") in *Law in Japan: An Annual* 2 (1968): 45–79.

10. See, for example, the summary of Japanese requirements for standing in Ogawa Ichiro, "Judicial Review of Administrative Actions in Japan," *Washington Law Review* 43 (1968): 1075–94. For a study of judicial review by means of damage actions, see M. Young, "Judicial Review of Administrative Guidance: Governmentally Encouraged Consensual Dispute Resolution in Japan," *Columbia Law Review* 84 (1984): 923-83, abstracted in "Administrative Guidance in the Courts: A Case Study in Doctrinal Adaptation," *Law in Japan: An Annual*, 17 (1984): 120–52.

11. See, for example, Yamanouchi Kazuo, "Administrative Guidance and the Rule of Law," *Law in Japan*, 7 (1974): 22, 31–33. See also Watanabe Yoshifusa, "Gyōsei shidō o meguru shomondai" (Problems with administrative guidance), *Jurisuto*, no. 342 (1966), pp. 46, 48-49.

12. *Administrative Guidance Research Report*, pp. ii–iii.

13. P. Davis, *Administrative Guidance, Sophia University Socio-Economic Institute Bulletin*, 41 (1972), pp. 7–11.

14. W. Pape, "Gyōsei shidō and the Antimonopoly Law," *Law in Japan: An Annual* 15 (1982): 15. See also W. Pape, *Gyosei shido und das Anti-Monopol-Gesetz in Japan* (Cologne: Heymanns, 1980), pp. 41–50.

15. Pape, "Gyōsei shidō," p. 16.

16. J. Lepron, "Administrative Guidance in Japan," *Fletcher Law Forum* 2 (1978): 143.

17. Johnson, *MITI and the Japanese Miracle*.

18. Kenneth Culp Davis estimates that in the United States "more than 90 percent of all administrative action is formal." K. C. Davis, *Administrative Law Treatise* 1, § 1.4 (2nd ed. 1978): 14.

As in Japan most informal action escapes judicial review. Moreover, ties outside of legislation govern administrative procedures. See G. Robinson, E. Gellhorn, and H. Bruff, *The Administrative Process* (St. Paul, Minn.: West Publishing Co., 2nd ed. 1980), p. 33. See also H. Austern, "Sanctions in Silhouette: An Inquiry into the Enforcement of the Federal Food, Drug and Cosmetic Act," *California Law Review* 51 (1963): 38–50, especially p. 41.

19. Letter to editor, *Regulation* (May/June 1983), p. 2.

20. As Iyori Hiroshi notes in this volume, approximately a third of all cases investigated end with a warning. Less than a tenth result in any formal action.

21. The *Administrative Guidance Research Report* includes detailed studies of administrative guidance by each of the economic ministries in transportation, petroleum, agriculture, forestry, fisheries, pharmaceuticals, labor, and construction.

22. See in re Hokkaido Batā K. K., et al., Shinketsushū 103 (FTC Decision no. 28, Sept. 18, 1950); in re Noda Shoyu, 4 Shinketsushū 1 (FTC Decision no. 59, April 4, 1952); in re Tōyō Rēyon et al., Shinketsushū 17 (FTC Decision no. 2, Aug. 6, 1953); *Kuni [Japan]* v. *Sekiyu Renmei, et al., Hanrei jihō*, no. 983, 22 (Tokyo High Court, Sept. 26, 1980); *Kuni [Japan]* v. *Idemitsu Kōsan K. K., et al., Hanrei jihō*, no. 985, 3 (Tokyo High Ct., Sept. 26, 1980). For full discussion of these and related cases, see the symposium on the oil cartel cases in *Law in Japan: An Annual*, 15 (1982): 1–98.

23. See, for example, A. Sajo, "Why Do Public Bureaucracies Follow Legal Rules," *International Journal of the Sociology of Law* (1981), pp. 69–84.

24. K. C. Davis, *Administrative Law Treatise* (2nd ed., 1982), 1: 17.

25. See, e.g., R. Noll, and B. Owen, eds., *The Political Economy of Deregulation: Interest Groups and the Regulatory Process* (Washington, D.C.: American Enterprise Institute, 1983).

26. Richard Cover and Mesu Uekusa perceive a similar misconception, Cover and Uekusa, "Industrial Organization" in H. Patrick, and H. Rosovsky, eds. *Asia's New Giant: How the Japanese Economy Works* (Washington, D.C.: Brookings Institution, 1976), p. 470.

27. J. Haley, "Antitrust Policy in Postwar Germany and Japan," paper prepared for Conference on the Political Management of the Postwar Economy in Germany and Japan, Ita, Japan, 1982.

28. *Gaikoku kawase oyobi gaikoku boeki kanri hō* (Law no. 228, 1949).

29. See, for example, cases cited in Imai Ken'ichi, "Dokusen kinshi seisaku to gyōsei shidō" (Antimonopoly policy and administrative guidance), *Jurisuto*, no. 566 (1974), pp. 36–40.

30. See J. Haley, "Sheathing the Sword of Justice in Japan: An Essay on Law Without Sanctions," *Journal of Japanese Studies* 8, no. 2 (1982): 265–81.

31. Ibid., p. 267.

32. See, e.g., K. Elzinga, and W. Breit, *The Antitrust Penalties* (New Haven: Yale University Press, 1976), pp. 30–43. Also H. Packer, *The Limits of the Criminal Sanction* (Stanford, Calif.: Stanford University Press, 1968), especially pp. 354–63.

33. There are only about two thousand procurators in Japan. Haley, "Sheathing the Sword," p. 274.

34. See J. Cohen, *Japan's Economy in War and Reconstruction* (Minneapolis: University of Minnesota Press, 1949), pp. 28, 76.

35. *Tokutei Sangyō shinkō rinji sochi hōan*.

36. See J. Haley, "The Oil Cartel Cases: The End of An Era," *Law in Japan: An Annual*, 15 (1982): 9.

37. See Narita, "Administrative Guidance," p. 58; also H. Kawasaki, "Gyōsei shidō no jihai" (Reality of administrative guidance), *Jurisuto*, no. 342 (1966), pp. 51–56.

38. As of 1981, for example, Japan had import quotas on twenty-seven products, of which twenty-two were agricultural.

39. On the role of Idemitsu as a maverick in the petroleum industry, see Kawasaki, *Gyōsei shidō*, and M. A. Caldwell, "Petroleum Policies in Japan: State and Industry in a Changing Industry Context" (Ph.D. diss., University of Wisconsin, 1980). Comparative research on the Japanese and U.S. steel industries by Patricia A. O'Brien, a doctoral candidate in the Graduate School of Business Administration of Harvard University, confirms the inability of MITI to prevent new entry in integrated steel production.

40. Antimonopoly Law, Art. 52-2.

41. Ibid., Art. 53-2-2.

42. Ibid., Art. 54-3.

43. Ibid., Art. 81.

44. Ibid., Art. 51-2.

45. *Kōsei Torihiki Iinkai no shinsa oyobi shimpan ni kansuru kisoku* (Fair Trade Commission

regulations on investigations and hearings) (FTC Regulation no. 5, Oct. 10, 1953, as amended) § 26[2].

46. *Gaishi in kansuru hōritsu* (Law no. 163, 1950; repealed by Law no. 65, 1979). For a lucid description of the purpose and operation of the Foreign Investment Law, see D. Henderson, *Foreign Enterprise in Japan* (Chapel Hill: University of North Carolina, 1973), pp. 195–236. Henderson only notes in passing the parallel restrictions on branch operations (p. 235).

47. There is at least some cause to speculate whether foreign firms acquiesced too readily and failed to take advantage of available forms of judicial review. All Japanese concerned profited by the uncontested view of the inherent power of MITI and other economic ministries.

48. See, e.g., Henderson, *Foreign Enterprise*, p. 200.

49. The check-price system involved the taxing of minimum export prices by MITI ostensibly as a means to prevent dumping, but more realistically as a mechanism for enforcing export cartels. The system was actually initiated but later discontinued by SCAP. The practice was apparently reinstituted by MITI during the summer of 1951 to aid the textile industry although publicly justified as a means to prevent dumping. See R. Takahashi, "Trade Policies of the New Japan," *Foreign Affairs* 30 (1952): 289–97, especially p. 292. See contracts in violation of the check price are enforceable. See *Domex International Co.* v. *Yokohama Tsusho K.K.*, 16 Kakyū minshū 1342 (Tokyo Dist. Ct., Aug. 28, 1965). As evidenced in television exports during the 1960s, Japanese firms have been able to disregard such price controls with relative impunity. See Reply Brief of Appellants, Zenith Radio Corporation and National Union Electric Corporation, at Ke-22, *Zenith Radio Corporation* v. *Matsushita Electric Industrial Co., Ltd.*, 723 F.2d 238 (3rd Cir. 1983).

50. Yamawaki Hideki, "Tekkōgyō" (Steel industry), in Komiya Ryūtarō, Okuno Masahiro, and Suzumura Kotarō, *Nihon no sangyō seisaku* (Japan's industrial policy) (Tokyo: University of Tokyo Press, 1984), p. 270.

51. M. Smith, "Prices and Petroleum in Japan: 1973–74—A Study of Administrative Guidance," *Law in Japan: An Annual*, 10 (1977): 81–100.

52. The sources for the statistics on prices were as follows: *Historical Statistics 1900–1980* (OECD Economic Outlook, 1982); *International Energy Annual* (Aug. 1980 U.S. Dept. of Energy Information Adm.); *International Financial Statistics. Supplement on Price Statistics, no. 2.* (International Monetary Fund, 1981); *International Financial Statistics – Yearbook*, (International Monetary Fund, 1982); Statistical Yearbook, 31st Issue (UN: Dept. of International Economic and Social Affairs – Statistical Office, 1980). Complete sets of graphs are on file with the editors.

53. *Denki jigyō hō* (Electricity enterprise law), Law no. 170, 1964; *Gasu jigyō hō* (Gas enterprise law), Law no. 51, 1954).

54. A recent unpublished study by Professor Sanekata Kenji of Hokkaido University raises serious doubts about the ability of even private cartel arrangements to affect prices. Professor Sanekata traced price movements for commodities subject to cartels that were later investigated and held to be illegal by the FTC—covering eight commodities—motor vehicle tires, cellophane, plated glass, methanol, synthetic dyestuffs, acrylic, nylon, and polyester. Except in the cases of cellophane and synthetic dyestuff there was no perceptible change in price after the cartel agreement was concluded. Sanekata Kenji, "Antitrust in Japan: Recent Trends and its Social and Political Background," paper presented to the conference on Japanese law held at the University of Washington Lake Wilderness Conference Center in August 1983.

55. D. Black, *The Behavior of Law* (New York: Academic Press, 1976).

BIBLIOGRAPHY OF MATERIALS
ON LEGAL ASPECTS OF ADMINISTRATIVE GUIDANCE

Western

Davis, Paul A. *Administrative Guidance in Japan—Legal Considerations* Tokyo: Sophia University Socio-Economic Institute Bulletin no. 41, Tokyo, 1972.

Gellhorn, Walter. "Settling Disagreements with Officials in Japan." *Harvard Law Review* 79 (1966): 685–732.

Haley, John O. "The Oil Cartel Cases: The End of an Era." *Law in Japan: An Annual* 15 (1982): 1–11.

Kaplan, Eugene J. *Japan, The Government-Business Relationship* Washington, D.C.: U.S. Department of Commerce, 1972.

Lepron, Jeffrey M. "Administrative Guidance in Japan." *The Fletcher Forum* 2, no. 2 (1978): 139–57.

Pape, Wolfgang. *Gyoseishido und das Anti-Monopol-Gesetz in Japan* Cologne: Heymanns, 1980.

———. "Gyōsei shidō and the Antimonopoly Law." *Law in Japan: An Annual*, 15 (1982): 12–23.

Young, Michael K. "Judicial Review of Administrative Guidance: Governmentally Encouraged Counsensual Dispute Resolution in Japan." *Columbia Law Review* 84 (1984): 923–83. Abstracted in "Administrative Guidance in the Courts: A Case Study in Doctrinal Adaptation." *Law in Japan: An Annual*, 17 (1984): 120–52.

Upham, Frank K. (with J. Mark Ramseyer). "Administrative Guidance in Japan: In Decline or Evolution?." In *U.S.-Japan Relations in the 1980s: Toward Burden Sharing* pp. 121–28. Annual Report, Harvard University U.S.-Japan Relations Program, 1981–82.

Japanese

Arai Ryuichi, "Tsūtatsu gyōsei no konnichi-teki shikaku" (Current state of administration by circulars). *Hōritsu no hiroba* 17, no. 10 (1964): 30–35.

Atsuya Shōji. "Gyōsei sochi ni yoru kyōsō seigen" (Restraints on competition by administrative measures). *Horitsu jiho* 39 (1967): 43–47.

———. "Dokusen kinshi hō to gyōsei shidō" (Antimonopoly law and administrative guidance). *Jurisuto*, no. 741 (1981), pp. 53–61.

Chiba Isao. "Gyōsei keikaku oyobi gyōsei shidō" (Administrative planning and administrative guidance). In Sugimura, ed., *Gyōsei hō gaisetsu* (Overview of administrative law), pp. 139–46. Tokyo: Yuhikaku, 1969.

———. "Gyōsei shidō no hōteki shomondai" (Various legal problems with administrative guidance). *Ōsaka keidai ronshū* 99 (1974): 28–55; 101 (1974): 19–42.

Gyōsei shidō ni kansuru chōsa kenkyū hōkokusho (Report on investigative study of administrative guidance). Tokyo: Gyōsei Kanri Kenkyū Senta, 1981.

Horie Takashi. "Gyōsei shidō" (Administrative guidance). *Shōji hōmu*, no. 863 (1974), pp. 44–46.

Imai, Ken'ichi. "Dokusen kinshi seisaku to gyōsei shidō" (Antimonopoly policy and administrative guidance). *Jurisuto*, no. 566 (1974), pp. 36–40.

Itoda Shōgo. "Dokusen kinshi hō to gyōsei shidō" (Antimonopoly law and administrative guidance). *Jurisuto*, no. 566 (1974), pp. 20–25.

Iyori Hiroshi. "Dokusen kinshi hō to gyōsei shidō" (Antimonopoly law and adminstrative guidance). *Jurisuto*, no. 342 (1966), pp. 59–63.

Kanazawa Yoshio. "Dokkin hō to gōseichō no kankoku" (Antimonopoly law and recommendations by administrative agencies). *Kōsei torihiki*, no. 136 (1962), pp. 10–14.

———. "Dokusen kinshi hō to gyōsei shidō" (Antimonopoly law and administrative guidance). *NBL*, no. 65 (1974), pp. 8–12.

Kaneko Shōhei. "Gyōsei shidō no hōteki shomondai" (Legal problems with administrative guidance). *Komazawa daigaku hogaku ronshu* 16 (1977): 121–43.

Karashima Shuro. "Gyōsei shidō to dokkinhō ni tsuite no ichi shiken" (Personal views on administrative guidance and antimonopoly law). *Jurisuto*, no. 566 (1974), pp. 26–35.

Kawagoe Kenji. "Saikō kakaku no kyōtei to gyōsei shidō" (Agreements to raise prices and administrative guidance). *Jurisuto bessatsu*, no. 26 (1970), pp. 36–39.

Kawasaki Hirotaro. "Gyōsei shidō no jittai" (Reality of administrative guidance). *Jurisuto*, no. 342 (1966), pp. 51–56.

Matsushita Mitsuo. "Kankoku sōtan to jigyōsha dantai ni yoru seisan seigen tō" (Production and other restrictions resulting from government recommendations to trade associations). *Jurisuto bessatsu*, no. 26 (1970), pp. 42–44.

Mizuno Hajime. "Iryō gyōsei to gyōsei shidō" (Medical regulation and administrative guidance). *Jurisuto*, no. 741 (1981), pp. 69–72.

Murakami Yoshihiro. "Gyōsei shidō to hōritsu no konkyo" (Administrative guidance and statutory authority). *Ōsaka furitsu daigaku keizai kenkyū* 16, no. 2 (1971): 15–43.

Narita Yoriaki. "Gyōsei shidō" (Administrative guidance). In *Gendaihō* 4 (1966): 131–68, translated into English (Anderson transl.), as "Administrative Guidance," *Law in Japan: An Annual* 2 (1968): 45–79.

―――. "Gyōsei shidō no kinō to kōzai" (Function and value of administrative guidance). *Jurisuto*, no. 741 (1981), pp. 39–44.

―――. "Hikenryoku gyōsei no hōritsu mondai" (Legal problems with unauthorized administrative actions). *Kōhō kenkyū* 28 (1966): 137–65.

―――. "Kigyō to gyōsei shidō" (Enterprises and administrative guidance). *Jurisuto bessatsu "Kiso hōgaku shirizu I"* (1969), pp. 87–93.

Negishi Akira. "Gyōsei shidō to kakaku karuteru" (Administrative guidance and price cartels). *Jurisuto bessatsu*, no. 53 (1977), pp. 85–86.

―――. "Sangyō gyōsei to gyōsei shidō" (Industrial administrative policy and administrative guidance). *Jurisuto*, no. 628 (1977), pp. 145–49.

Omori Yukio. "Hosō gyōsei to gyōsei shidō" (Broadcasting and administrative guidance). *Jurisuto*, no. 741 (1981), pp. 64–68.

Sanekata Kenji. "Gyōsei shidō to dokusen kinshi hō" (Administrative guidance and the antimonopoly law). In Takeuchi, ed., *Gendai shōhōgaku no kadai: Suzuki Takeo sensei koki kinen* (Problems in contemporary commercial law: In celebration of Professor Takeo Suzuki's 70th birthday), pp. 1379–99. Tokyo: Yuhikaku, 1975. Translated into English as "Administrative Guidance and the Antimonopoly Law." *Law in Japan: An Annual*, 10 (1977): 65–80.

Sato Hidetake. "Gyōsei shidō to dokkinhō" (Administrative guidance and antimonopoly law). *Hōritsu jihō* 46, no. 7 (1974). 53–58.

Shinono Hiroshi. "Gyōsei shidō" (Administrative guidance). In Tanaka, ed., *Gyōsei koza* 6: 13–31. Tokyo: Yuhikaku, 1965.

Shōda Akira. *Saikō kakaku no kyōtei to gyōsei shidō*" (Agreements to raise prices and administrative guidance). *Jurisuto bessatsu*, no. 53 (1977), pp. 28–29.

Suzuki Tsuneo. "Gyōsei shidō o meguru hanrei no dōkō" (The trend of cases on administrative guidance). *Jurisuto*, no. 741 (1981), pp. 45–52.

Takada Bin. "Gyōsei shidō to 'hōritsu ni yoru gyōsei' no genri" (Administrative guidance and the principle of administration under law). *Jurisuto bessatsu, "hōgaku kyōshitsu II,"* no. 5 (1974), pp. 84–90.

Takase Masao. "Kyōsō seigenteki gyōsei shidō to dokusen kinshi hō" (Administrative guidance and the antimonopoly law). *Hōritsu jihō* 49, no. 11 (1977): 38–43.

Tanka Jirō. "Gyōsei shidō to hō no shihai" (Administrative guidance and rule of law). In Takeuchi, ed., *Gendai shōhōgaku no kadai: Suzuki Takeo sensei koki kinen* (Problems in contemporary commercial law: In celebration of Professor Takeo Suzuki's 70th birthday) 2: 1427–58. Tokyo: Yuhikaku, 1975.

Tōdō Hiroshi. "Gyōsei shidō ni tsuite omonkoto" (Thoughts on administrative guidance). *Jurisuto*, no. 741 (1981), pp. 62–63.

Yamanouchi Kazuo. "Gyōsei shidō to hōchishugi" (Administrative guidance and the rule of law). *Jurisuto*, no. 566 (1974), pp. 14–19. Translated into English (Figdor transl.) as

"Administrative Guidance and the Rule of Law." *Law in Japan: An Annual,* 7 (1974): 22–33.

Zadankai. "Gyōsei shidō" (Symposium, administrative guidance). *Jurisuto,* no. 342 (1966), pp. 21–45. Translated into English in John O. Haley, ed., *The Public Law System of Japan* (unpublished University of Washington Asian Law course materials).

————. "Gyōsei shidō—Dokkin seisaku to sangyō seisaku" (Symposium, administrative guidance—antimonopoly policy and industrial policy). *Jurisuto,* no. 741 (1981), pp. 15–38.

Part 2

JAPAN'S LEGAL FRAMEWORK
AND FOREIGN ACCESS TO THE JAPANESE MARKET

Access to the Japanese Market:

Some Aspects of

Foreign Exchange Controls and Banking Law

DAN F. HENDERSON

The interplay of "law and economics"[1] in U.S.–Japanese relations involves many areas of law. But among them, none has had more persistent influence on American interests than Japan's Foreign Exchange and Foreign Trade Control Law (FECL).[2] Its control of the yen has been influential on interest rate differentials, related capital movements, exchange rates, and balance of payments, but it has also functioned specifically and directly by entry restrictions to block foreign access to those Japanese markets where Americans might have a competitive edge. During thirty years of growing U.S.–Japanese interdependence (1950–80), the statute remained unchanged as the key instrument of Japanese protectionism.[3] During that time, supplemented by the recently repealed Foreign Investment Law (FIL), the FECL guarded Japanese businesses from competitive imports and kept the entry of businesses controlled by foreigners to a minimum;[4] it also screened technology licensed by foreigners to build Japan's whole complex of modern industries.[5]

This discussion of the FECL is therefore necessarily about Japanese protection. It must inevitably neglect, except as mentioned here for perspective, other parts of U.S.–Japanese economic relations, such as competitiveness and Japanese suggestions that in Japan the foreigners "do not try hard enough." It neglects also domestic policy on both sides related to quality of merchandise and comparative performance of our respective industries. Nor does it treat American protection. Probably today official barriers (FECL) provide less protection than the Japanese domestic law and business environment, which also can only be mentioned in passing. All of the foregoing issues are important in the overall context, but not the subject of this study.

Our topic, the negative legal impact of the FECL, is well known and has been much criticized[6] as unfair and inconsistent with free trade theory, treaty obligations, and recent Japanese affluence ever since Japan became an "advanced nation" by joining OECD in 1964. But by the 1970s, lack of access to Japanese markets, though still real and irritating to many, began to be a secondary problem as the impact of Japanese exports here drew ever more attention. What is easy to overlook in this shift of focus, however, is that the blocking of imports and then the targeting of exports were linked: throughout the post-World War II period, Japanese could (1) acquire foreign technology; (2) make products for the huge Japanese market protected for the Japanese makers; then (3) know when up to speed in the exclusive Japanese enclave, launch an export drive targeting a narrow product line (usually inexpensive, high-volume items), priced to break into our market. With the combined U.S. and Japanese markets (denied our makers), the Japanese exporters could overwhelm producers here with the cash flow generated by such tactics. Also important to success, of course, was a quality product and lower wages. But the FECL was an essential legal adjunct to these export strategies; it preserved exclusively for Japanese their huge domestic market, second in size only to ours. The FECL was also influential in credit, interest, and exchange-rate management for national advantage.

This second point—control of outward (and inward) capital flows[7]—is under-emphasized. Such controls are necessary to exclude and restrict foreign banking and to shield from international market forces Japan's high savings managed by a controlled banking system,[8] fixed interest rates, and preferential credit allocations (discriminating against small producers and consumers) essential to the large export firms. Nothing but a fully internationalized yen[9] will address these effects, which handicap foreigners and run counter to U.S. policies of freer capital movement. So the FECL may function in blocking foreign ingress to Japan, but this protection at the same time promotes targeting of export drives, which are now taking most of the heat of foreign criticism, along with the suspicions of a controlled yen. Many aspects of this system of insular internationalism have long been criticized, as inevitably evoking a "quasi-state-trading regime."[10]

What do the legalities of protectionism mean in economic terms? Under the old regime to 1980, restrictions had long been useful to protect Japanese producers from foreign comparative advantage, especially technological and financial advantage. And the free world economy to which all of us pay lip service is based presumably on free (not restricted) comparative advantage. Our most important comparative advantage has always been higher technology—now software, space, computers, new ceramics, nuclear, genetic engineering, aircraft, pharmaceuticals, and the like. Are technological innovations to be exempted forever by infant industry analyses? Up to a point within free trade theory, Japan could invoke "infant industry" exceptions for its new industries. But by 1983 the "infant" exception itself raises problems of critical importance that invite American re-analysis: (1) When does the infant grow up? (2) How long does it take to nurture a domestic industry? (3) How much exclusion and subsidy by either side can be tolerated now in the "free" bilateral economic process? (4) In the new high-tech areas it seems the "infants" can only be nurtured by nationalistic competitions, not between enterprises but governments themselves; how can free trade theory accommodate such industrial policy, or targeting? (5) What in the long run is the economic measure of this kind of contrived comparative national advantage that will enlighten bilateral interests? (6) During periods of indeterminancy and contrived advantage, are there measures better than responsive quotas and other reactive counterprotections for trading partners whose markets are relatively open initially? Is a kind of quasi-state trading not likely to result wherein government to government haggling ceases to preserve a free-trade system but replaces it?

For free-trade economists, these are presumably formidable questions raised by Japan's recent history of entry by subsidy into industries created by American technology,[11] especially when the entry is buttressed by exchange controls and a restricted yen. Some of these problems could be alleviated perhaps by Japan's giving up the restrictions of the FECL. Indeed, the first major revision in over thirty years has been widely heralded as such a move, undertaken in large part to dampen yet another round of strident foreign criticism. Surely then, this latest "liberalization" of the FECL deserves our attention if it contributes to a freer Japanese environment for competitive foreign business. Does it?

What we may find is that purely domestic regulatory law and the business culture in Japan will provide equally effective barriers to frustrate free trade theorists, even if threshold legal barriers of the FECL are relaxed. To anticipate a bit, my guess is that Japanese exports and technology exchanges will have to be addressed by our own political measures,[12] both domestic and bilateral, simply because the FECL relaxation (if that really does happen at the bureaucratic level where it matters) will be offset by domestic regulations and business practices uncongenial to foreigners trying to do business in Tokyo. Japanese may continue to feel that they can not accommodate foreigners and remain as productive as they now are in their homogeneous insular enclave. There are interesting arguments to be made for that stance, quite apart from Japan's advantages inherent in its insular internationalism.

Our effort to open the Japanese markets thus should not blur over the cultural and political nature of the problem, as if tinkering with free trade economics[13] is all that is involved. The cherished American goal of a combined binational market, free to both Japanese and Americans, equally, on both sides of the Pacific is not, judged by past official performance, shared by Japan. Yet our unilateral espousal of it has even given rise to naïve American suggestions that the distribution and employment systems of Japan, even the language, are species of nontariff barriers. In reverse, the Taft-Hartley Act may be a barrier to Japanese enterprise on our side.[14]

Our topic, the FECL, though a direct official obstacle confronting foreigners at the threshold, is thus only a part of the problem of access to Japanese markets. Above all, most Japanese domestic markets are fiercely competitive, and a tough place to do business, even for Japanese. Japanese collusion abroad[15] and cartels at home are seen as a part of the context, but cannot be dealt with tangentially here in a discussion of the new FECL. Finally, an argument frequently made by Japan is that American business does not try hard enough to adapt its products and make or sell them in Japan. Sometimes there is truth in the suggestion, too, but it does not address the real difficulty and discrimination also encountered by the foreigner.

Even the entire access problem itself is but a small part of the overall trade problem today. As noted, most of the American criticism has shifted to the effect of Japanese exports here. This has raised a whole new set of issues, simply because the volume of exports in steel, cars, and electronics threatens basic manufacturing of importance to our national interest. We must ask why we are so uncompetitive on our own turf? U.S. as well as Japanese policies, heretofore regarded as purely domestic concerns, become part of the trade debate over the "level playing field." Targeting and industrial policy are the new rhetoric, but do we not have equally serious problems of productivity right here at home wholly unrelated to Japanese effectiveness?

Quite apart from the happy consumers, anguished enterprises, and unemployed Americans, the integration and growing interdependence have required reassessments of our productivity and performance. The reappraisal goes beyond Japanese tariffs to nontariff barriers and subsidies and then comes back to a deeper analysis of our own profligate internal policy-mixes, of subsidized consumers, of ossified management practices, of monopoly-union labor overpriced even on the American wage scale. Even life styles may be questioned as cost factors in attempts to reduce expense and remain competitive.[16] No doubt this whole reappraisal forced upon us by consumer alternatives in the form of better products and prices from Japan will have some positive pay-off for us.

One aspect of this deeper probing in the name of trade or industrial policy involves again the effect of interest and yen-dollar exchange rates. Here the FECL in Japanese export strategy must not be overlooked. Probably discretionary controls on capital movements (in conjunction with controlled domestic interest rates and banking channels) will be the most important use of the FECL in the near term. This aspect, as well as our deficit and high interest rates, requires separate study to determine the effect on the overpriced dollar. Until the yen is truly internationalized, perhaps the playing field cannot be leveled.

So the entire trade context is of course much broader and more complex than the problem of Japanese protectionism and foreign access to Japanese markets. But in this limited review of the new FECL, the concern is narrowed to Japanese protectionism as one cause of friction, and here the FECL is still important. It embodies bureaucratic and insular attitudes and habits toward Japanese business as well as toward foreigners, which in an affluent and powerful new Japan have outlived their time. Since, as we shall see, the statute still allows for discretionary restrictions, we must look for fairer trade in changed bureaucratic practices in future transactions.

RELEVANCE OF 1980 CHANGES IN THE FECL

In discussing the specifics of the access problem, we can start with an anecdote about anecdotes. Early in 1983, Japan specialists from government and academics assembled[17] in Washington along with others recently attracted to the Japan problem. The purpose was yet another discussion on whether the Japanese markets are open. Position papers were presented.[18] There was support for the Japanese line that Japanese markets were reasonably accessible, if the foreigners would only try a little harder.[19] A major question was, however, what to make of all these anecdotes (horror stories) one continually hears about individual businesses being stiff-armed either at the Japanese entry window, or in the domestic labyrinth of regulations, business associations, and cartels in a wide variety of transactions and complex distribution channels. In entry cases, whether imports or investments, the practice seemed to differ from the law and policy. How seriously do we take these anecdotes?

To this lawyer sitting there mostly listening, it was somewhat disconcerting to have everyday businessmen's problems of the past thirty years of my experience treated as aberrational oddities. Those horror stories have been too common[20] and important to handle simply by shrinking them down to the status of anecdotal trash to be swept under the rug. Rather, I should have thought that cumulatively they state in a more meaningful way the operative Japanese policy of the past thirty years toward foreigners in Japan. The anecdotes *are* Japanese policy; Japan is restrictive; it is a difficult place for foreigners to do business. Fact though it is, the difficulty is not simply a Japanese fault. True, there are deep problems of cultural interaction exposed by growing interdependence, and they cannot be solved by recreating Japan in our own image; nor are these problems susceptible to any other quick fix. But to recognize the cultural problems does not change the fact that Japan is not "open."

The anecdotes explain the awkward gap between Japanese enunciations about liberalization and the continued practice of restricting competitive foreigners, especially where they have the technological edge. Japanese bureaucratic policy (concerning both imports of foreign goods and entries of foreign enterprises into Japan) has consistently been and still is to protect Japanese business from foreigners who happen to have a better product or price—especially in high technology. When specific Japanese businesses or products become fully competitive (i.e., no longer need protection), liberalization has indeed occurred. This is spurious liberalization; real liberality would allow entry even if the competitive foreigner might get some business.

Today most of Japanese manufacturing needs little *official* protection within Japan addressed specifically to foreigners. In a gross statistical sense, most industries are therefore liberalized. Acquisitions of viable, established firms are, however, blocked; takeovers are covered by blanket restrictions, and the few acquisitions by agreement usually involve only weak and minor fiems (see p. 144). Japanese imports are also quite liberal in gross percentages or in terms of items by tariff classification, counting within the total all of those raw materials not found in Japan and which must be imported anyway. Important barriers do, however, still exist where they matter (i.e., products in which foreigners are competing effectively with Japanese). In products of the Pacific Northwest, for example, they include plywood, lumber, seafood, apples, and others.

The contrast between public relations pronouncements and bureaucratic practice has brought Japanese official credibility in the United States to an all time low. And our press and other media still present Japanese statistical generalizations[21] about free trade, as if they were reflected in bureaucratic reality.

In 1983, high technology products and financial services at one end of the spectrum and agriculture at the other are the areas where Americans may still have some competitive advantages to redress our trade imbalances. In neither of these areas have Americans been allowed to freely deal in Japan based on their only strengths. As an aside, Japan is also notoriously protective against light manufacturers from Taiwan and Korea, which have become competitive with Japanese.

Liberalization has been effected only in the broad middle ground of manufacturing where Japan has learned to excel, often with aid of our markets and technology. This way of looking at Japanese liberalization, I suggest, bridges the awkward gap of liberal rhetoric and actual tactics[22] told only by the anecdotes. The anecdotes tell us how competitive foreign business is treated, and without some familiarity with trade and investment at the level of the transactions, operative Japanese policy is apparently still indiscernible to many of us.

As noted, the 1980 amendment to the FECL was the first major statutory revision since its enactment in 1949. Through the years, administrative practices under the statute changed gradually to approve routine transactions. These administrative changes are what has been called liberalization in the press during the past twenty years. Basically, the restrictive statutory framework remained: all transactions with foreign investors and nonresidents were prohibited, until approved by the government. It is in this context that the 1980 amendments as they relate to specific transactions deserve attention. Do they make any difference to the foreign competitor selling or manufacturing in Japan? We will answer that question by reviewing the coverage and major features of the new FECL[23] and then examining the effect of the law on some typical transactions (see Appendix).

COVERAGE OF THE NEW FECL

Important definitions and provisions for control of exchange rates are set out in chapter one (Art. 1-9). Several new concepts and definitions are added to the new FECL by these provisions, which are highly technical but essential to an understanding of the law in practice.

1. Foreign transaction (*taigai torihiki*)[24] covers, besides resident/nonresident dealings, business in foreign exchange between residents, or business in yen between nonresidents.

2. "Adjustments" (*chōsei*) is used in addition to the traditional "control" (*kanri*) in stating the purpose of the law.[25] Where prior approval (*kyōka*) is not now required, adjustment contemplates other measures, where needed, such as: prohibiting interest payments on nonresident deposit accounts; limiting

foreign exchange holdings of "authorized foreign exchange banks"[26]; placing other conditions on the operations of authorized foreign exchange banks; or recommendations (*kankoku*) and orders to change the content (or to suspend) transactions reported. Such "adjustments" are all authorized for certain capital transactions,[27] direct investments,[28] and technological transfers.[29]

Besides fourteen other technical definitions, including residents (*kyojūsha*) and nonresidents (*hikyojūsha*) provided in the general provisions,[30] the definition of inward direct investment (*tainai chokusetsu tōshi*) is to be found among the later provisions.[31] It includes portfolio purchases (in listed companies) of 10 percent or more of the stock.[32] Also consent (by two thirds or more of the shares) for change in the business purpose of an existing company is an "inward direct investment" when foreign investors are involved.[33] And, as a major change in handling branches (*shiten*) of foreign companies, the law now treats them too as inward direct investments.[34] Certain loans for one year or more (and exceeding certain amounts) are direct investments. And, finally, technological assistance contracts (*gijutsu dōnyū keiyaku*), though not specifically defined as inward direct investments, are treated like them and must be reported before the contract is signed or made effective.[35]

Outward direct investment (*taigai chokusetsu tōshi*) is classified as a capital transaction (*shihon torihiki*),[36] instead of testing it by analogy by subjecting it to the tighter controls for inward direct investment. Outward direct investments were not covered specifically as a separate category by the old FECL, and the provisions for it in the new FECL are an important clarification.[37] But the different treatment of inward and outward direct investment certainly enables Japan to exploit American liberality without reciprocating.

The past system of authorized foreign exchange banks (*gaikoku kawase kōnin ginkō*) was continued; it, in effect, makes the authorized banks enforcement agencies of the government. Banks are required to obtain an authorization (*ninka*) from MOF and a license (*shōnin*)[38] to deal in foreign exchange. A condition of the license is that the banks obey the MOF controls. These controls may include possible limits on each bank's foreign exchange position and prohibitions against paying interest on certain deposit accounts.[39] Banks are required to assure themselves that their clients have complied with the new FECL.[40] The same applies to licensed moneychangers (*ryōgae- shō*), and both banks and moneychangers must report as provided by cabinet order. Designated securities firms are used in somewhat the same fashion as enforcement devices in stock exchange transactions, as we shall see below. The framework of the FECL was enlarged to cover the following major categories of transactions, including those previously contained in the FIL (repealed):

Payments (*shiharai*)—chapter 3 (Arts. 16–19).
Capital transactions (*shihon torihiki*)—chapter 4 (Arts. 20–25).[41]
Inward direct investment (*tainai chokusetsu tōshi*)—chapter 5 (Arts. 20–46).[42]
Foreign trade (*gaikoku bōeki*)—chapter 6 (Arts. 47–55).

The remaining chapters (6 [2]-9) establish the new Council on Foreign Exchange (*Gaikoku Kawase tō Shingikai*) and provide procedures for administrative complaints (*fufuku mōshitate*), as well as penalties for violations. Notable also is a specific provision[43] to the effect that the new FECL is not to be construed to affect the application of the Antimonopoly Law (AML) or its enforcement by the Japanese FTC.

THE MAJOR FEATURES OF THE REVISION

Approval-in-Principle

The rhetoric has been changed to approval-in-principle. Much is made of "liberality-in-principle"; it has replaced the old "prohibition-in-principle." This is not the first time such rhetoric has been used in Japanese controls over foreigners. Let there be no mistake: the Japanese bureaucracy has no background of liberalism toward foreigners, foreign business, or foreign products in any situation where foreigners have the competitive edge. Discrimination has long been the rule.[44] After being burned before, foreigners should look only to liberal practice in competitive transactions for a reading on Japanese policy.

As early as 1964, when Japan became an "advanced nation" (by joining OECD and by accepting an Article 8 status in the IMF), it was announced that under FIL Article 8(1), the "positive" criteria would not be required of an investment application and that it would be denied approval only if it ran afoul of the "negative" criteria of Article 8(2). In retrospect, this "liberal" pronouncement, widely publicized at the time, was little more than a placebo for the critics. In fact, the simultaneous abolition of the "yen company" in 1963 was a tightening of controls[45] of some importance to those of us in practice and to a few business friends.

Until Japan became an advanced nation, protectionism in the name of infant industries was obviously prevalent and understandable. But after the infants grew up, protectionism has not gone away, as it should if the policy of both the United States and Japan is to support a combined free market for enterprises from both countries. Anyway, few foreigners found the effect of the "positive" formula of any real importance in the continuing restrictive bureaucratic practice.

Likewise, in the 1967–73 era of "liberalization," the "automatic" validations under the FIL were widely heralded in Japan's official public relations abroad. Yet automatic approvals were conferred only after stringent conditions were met and then only to investments in firms to be newly established by foreigners; acquisitions of established firms and takeovers (as in the past) were still subject to approval under the liberalization measures, as they still are now. All the while Japanese are free to buy here, even banks.[46] And all will remember the opposition of Japanese competitors to Dow Chemical getting an "automatic" approval to build a plant otherwise entitled to automatic approval in a liberalized industry.[47] My advice would be to assume that all investments proffered by foreigners of any consequence to Japanese competitors will encounter much the same pervasive protectionism under the new FECL. Certainly the discretion to do so is there.

If liberality-in-principle is anything more than yet another round of window dressing, it will have to be demonstrated henceforth in the bureaucratic practices in Tokyo. But we must remember that the access problem is a rather narrow focus. I have my own doubts about the efficacy of Washington's efforts to pry open the Japanese market as a solution to U.S.–Japanese economic problems. There are probably more fruitful avenues of redress for the United States. Too many of our problems (deficits, entitlements, low savings, and low productivity, etc.) are caused by a poor domestic policy mix unrelated completely to external affairs.

Repeal of FIL

The most striking feature for practitioners in this area of law for the past thirty years is the outright repeal of the FIL. Foreigners will find, however, that most of its controls have been modified and moved to the new FECL,[48] although the FIL definition of foreign investors included resident non-Japanese but the new FECL treats them as residents.[49]

Regulation Simplification

The entire system of regulations has been simplified. Besides inclusion of FIL concerns in the new FECL, the whole tangle of subsidiary cabinet orders (seirei; hereafter CO) and ministerial orders (shōrei; hereafter MO) detailing the administration of the foreign controls, has been integrated under this one new law. The frequently changing, multilayered regulations had been cross-referenced almost beyond comprehension. So confusing to Japanese and foreigners alike were they that often only the bureaucrats in charge could understand their effect on specific transactions, even when the law, as opposed to bureaucratic discretion, was dispositive. Those of us who made our living by thumbing those regulations must now undertake a retooling fully as onerous as that of General Motors in scaling down for small cars.

Codification of Practice

The purpose of the law is to preserve the balance of payments, stabilize the currency, and develop the national economy with a minimum of controls and adjustments (chōsei).[50] Though not explicit in the law, the commentaries[51] mention that the revision was an attempt, once again, to quell foreign criticism of the Japanese controls supposedly long since liberalized.

Actually, the revision seems to codify, in a sense, much of the recent practice under the old FECL and FIL, whereby many routine and petty transactions, which still were prohibited by the law until approved, had been in fact routinely approved by delegation to the Bank of Japan and authorized banks under regulations issued for that purpose. Most of this bramble of regulations has been repealed or rewritten and now prohibitions are more selective or discretionary where useful to Japanese protectionism.

New Licensing Standards

The new substantive standards for licensing of competitive transactions have been recast into an elaborate hierarchy of controls ranging from requiring little more than the normal commercial paper work (e.g., in routine banking or portfolio investments) to requiring the old restrictive device of prior approval, presumably because some Japanese business complains or because of some foreign competitive advantage. The whole range may be charted as follows (from least restrictive to most restrictive):

(a) Routine share purchases through the designated securities firms[52] or standardized trade payments and money transactions through the authorized banks[53] are excepted from the comprehensive reporting requirement normally imposed upon one or both of the parties as a minimal control. This is in effect a reporting system but the records and reports are done by the banks and other firms.

(b) All capital (including technology) transactions, not excepted above, are subject at least to advanced reporting to MOF (or MITI)[54] before the transaction is executed.[55]

(c) Next, certain categories of transactions must be reported by the parties in advance and are then subjected to a waiting period (usually twenty to thirty days) while the ministries review the transaction.[56]

(d) If the review turns up a problem (e.g., adverse effect on the international money market, capital market, *Japanese business activities*, or treaty obligations), then MOF may recommend (*kankoku*) alterations,[57] and if the parties accept the recommendations, the transaction may proceed, as amended. If not accepted, the bureaucrats may order alteration or suspension.[58]

(e) Still, certain capital transactions are subjected to the prior approval of MOF similar to the old regime for all transactions.[59] The transactions that get this unwelcomed advanced scrutiny are: deposit (or trust) contracts between residents and nonresidents; sales of claims to foreign-means-of-payment between residents and nonresidents; deposits, trusts, and loans in foreign currency between residents and nonresidents; and issuing securities in yen by a nonresident (Art. 21(1)).

Emergency Powers

Very general emergency powers are granted[60] to the competent ministers to suspend all FECL transactions deemed necessary in case of drastic economic changes. Suspension is to be spelled out by cabinet order. In addition, other emergency powers are granted, specific to the several types of transaction:

Concerning Payments (Shiharai). Emergency powers are reserved for use at the discretion of the ministers and as provided by cabinet order. This permits broadening of the area covered by the prior approval system, if deemed necessary for the following reasons: (a) To maintain "the equilibrium" of the balance of international payments; (b) "to secure the effective enforcement" of the new FECL and subsidiary orders; or (c) as deemed "necessary for faithful performance of Japanese treaties or other international agreements."[61]

These discretionary powers to require a prior license (to be exercised in accordance with a cabinet order) may be applied (a) to all payments between residents and nonresidents by means "other than standard methods" (e.g., debiting or crediting accounts)[62] (b) imports or exports of "means of payment or securities";[63] (c) exports or imports of precious metals;[64] (d) waivers of claims by residents against nonresidents.[65]

Over Capital Transactions. Discretion is delegated to MOF to require a prior approval of any transaction deemed to adversely affect: balance of payments; currency stability; capital markets, by "transfer of funds in a large volume" to or from Japan.[66]

Over Certain Capital Transactions. MITI is given discretion subject to cabinet order (similar to that of MOF above) to require prior approval for loans in connection with export of goods or technological transfers on similar conditions.[67]

Over Service Transactions (yakumu torihiki). The competent ministers have power to require prior approval of service transactions concerning the processing of minerals (including oil) or transfer of mining rights or others, as prescribed by cabinet order.[68]

Over Inward Direct Investments.[69] Discretion to alter or suspend resides in MOF and the competent minister in charge of the industry involved, but is exercised only after getting the opinion of the Council on Foreign Exchange[70] and the review period may be extended up to four[71] or five[72] months; the purpose[73] is to determine whether the direct investment might adversely affect national security, or *Japanese business activity*, or whether there is no reciprocity from the investor's country, or might be subject to prior approval as a capital transaction because it endangers the balance of payment, stability of the currency, and the like, under Article 21(2).

Over Imports of Technology. MOF and the minister in charge of the industry involved must again seek the opinion of the Council on Foreign Exchange before suspending or altering the agreement and may delay the transaction four (or five) months for review on the same conditions as for direct investment.[74]

Once the foregoing hierarchy of review procedures is grasped overall, past experience tells us that it is designed to sift out the large volume of foreign payments, trade, and investment in areas of little competitive consequence and to process the paper through controlled banks and securities firms. It is not as if they are, however, purely private matters; the banks are required to keep meticulous records and report to MOF. Careful scrutiny can be focused on foreign transactions that affect Japanese business competitively.

This sifting was being done by delegation before the revision, but the old prohibitions remained formally more comprehensive than Japanese protectionism required under recent conditions; also the controls had become an incomprehensible thicket of cross-referenced regulations. What also seems clear enough from this listing of the important discretionary and emergency powers is that the law still provides ample opportunity for official intervention. To delay, alter, frustrate, and prevent foreign transactions is surely as possible as it always was in the past, whenever there was substantial Japanese business opposition to a better foreign product or price.

Import and Export Controls

The new import and export controls[75] over shipments of goods into (or out of) Japan are handled somewhat differently and in general entrusted to MITI.[76] Licensing (shōnin) of exports and imports may be handled by MITI or delegated to the customs chief.[77] Methods of payment and evidence of payment[78] may be specified by cabinet order. However, export and import regulation is another special problem, and will be paraphrased below.

Council for Foreign Exchange

The final feature to be noted here is the establishment of the new Council for Foreign Exchange (Gaikoku Kawase tō Shingikai) of fifteen members appointed by MOF.[79] At the same time the old Foreign Investment Council (Gaishi Shingikai) was abolished with the FIL. Procedure for hearing complaints (fufuku mōshitate) against administrative dispositions are provided,[80] and are still a prerequisite to filing a suit in the courts to redress actions under the new FECL.[81] These procedures have been little more than formality because as noted in the early 1970s:

> The criterion for handling applications is a matter of bureaucratic discretion, much as the procedures for shaping useful foreign inputs by renegotiating contracts are largely left to official "guidance." The applicant is seeking a privilege; screening is a simple administrative process, unencumbered by a foreign rule-of-law ideology, because there is no practicable way to judicially review the substance of restrictive decisions nor to challenge in a due process sense the procedures by which decisions are reached.[82]

It is well to remember that, in the real world, the management of foreigners is pure administration in Japan. There is little justiciable law in the new FECL any more than there was in the old version or in the old FIL. It is the same in this respect. No suit was ever brought by a foreign investor until Mr. Wang, a thwarted Hong Kong trader, sued in 1981 under the new FECL, charging unfair "designation" of Katakura Kōgyō K. K. He got a lot of publicity, but no satisfaction in the courts so far.[83]

Whatever its merits, the new FECL has not significantly reduced the discretion available to Japanese officialdom to enable them to sift out and obstruct all truly competitive foreign high-tech entries. Nor does the law address two other perennial problems experienced in dealing with the Japanese bureaucracy. First is the use of guidance to induce concessions on the pretext that compliance is thus voluntary and wholly outside the purview of law (or administration); second, the habit at the bureaucratic desks of not "receiving" an application or report until it has been changed to comply with official requirements. This converts a reporting requirement into an equivalent of the "prior approval" (kyōka) in many cases, as practitioners soon learned in handling foreign branch regulations.

There are, however, improvements in the revision, even if it is not per se liberal. Controls over all foreign transactions are found in one comprehensive law. The implementing cabinet and ministerial orders are simplified, if not yet simple. Most important, perhaps, is the strict time limits imposed on bureaucratic action; the ministries must now act in twenty days (for example, to propose altering loans) or in thirty days for direct investments. Reviews by the ministers and Council for Foreign Exchange of direct investments and technological transfers must be concluded in four (or five) months at most. This is progress compared to the old days when applications might lie in the same ministries for months on end. But applicants who want to start the clock running would do well to assure that the application is "received," which differs from "filing." It is received only when stamped with a case number and date; it is received and stamped only if found acceptable to the clerk at the window.

THE IMPACT OF THE FECL REVISION

For those who wish to simulate the future battle in the trenches under the new FECL, it is imperative to read the Appendix. The cases there are the best clues to the operation of the new law as it applies to inward transactions. Reading only the statute in English is as unenlightening as translations of legal conceptualisms usually are. Reading the Japanese version, though coherent, requires uncommon tenacity, even before one gets to the cabinet and ministerial orders. Press coverage cannot be relied on; it has been downright misleading for twenty years at least about "liberalization"; liberalization there has been, but not to open competitive opportunities where it made real differences to inward transactions in significant Japanese markets, such as the markets that Japanese have come to share in the United States. In sum, then, the anecdotes and the transactions alone speak meaningfully about the liberality of Japanese bureaucratic practice[84] explained in the Appendix.

One type of transaction must not, however, be relegated, out of courtesy to lay readers, to the Appendix. I refer to acquisitions (or takeovers) of established Japanese companies. Despite the attractiveness of acquisitions and takeovers as entry devices in this country, with rare exceptions, they simply are not an effective device for Americans to enter the Japanese market for several reasons.[85]

First, a takeover of a Japanese company without its agreement is in Japanese eyes very bad form at best, and gangster tactics at worst. It is not done; whatever exceptions may be found are the kind that prove the rule. Such acquisition as there is in Japan is almost always by agreement and usually means that the acquired company needs to be rescued from financial difficulty by merger with an affiliated company in its family of companies (*keiretsu*).

Nothing better illustrates the foreigner's problem in entering Japan because an acquisition is the easiest way to establish a beachhead, given the Japanese site problems, rental costs, and hiring and employment practice. Whether he tries for control by stock exchange purchases or by negotiating for acquisition, the foreigner is usually thwarted from entering Japan by an acquisition. He is thus deprived of a running start that might insure some success in an otherwise difficult environment.

In the United States, Japanese acquisitions of our companies have become routine.[86] Companies often invite Japanese bids. Indeed, state after state, by unseemly processions of our politicians, troop through Japan inviting Japanese enterprise to come over here to "create jobs," as they like to put it for the ears of the folks back home, or in justification of their expense accounts.[87] The contrast is striking on this issue of acquisitions. And it is an important matter—not just another incident, like for example the baseball bat dispute. Are both countries really liberal? Is the trans-pacific entrepreneurial game being played on a level field? Though the answer is "no" in simple terms, the acquisition issue is not simple.[88]

The acquisition issue poses sharply the deeper questions about fair trade that we now realize means integrating our economy further with that of Japan, or, as an alternative, tooling up for the national rather than enterprise competition. For example, there are good Japanese reasons for resisting foreign acquisitions of their firms—reasons we can understand if we understand the Japanese firm and the way it is managed and staffed. To exaggerate[89] only a little to make the point: the typical Japanese export-oriented firm desirable for such an American acquisition has been built and managed largely for lifetime members, both blue- and white-collar in the plants and offices,[90] not the shareholders in our sense. This means that a foreigner's purchase and control of blocks of the stock would be like buying a community (or a "second village"),[91] not just corporate shares.

Also, to interpret the transaction in Japanese terms, we need to extrapolate on some matters of finance as they affect the picture. Typically, for example, the past debt-equity ratio in major Japanese manufacturers has been in the range of 85 percent to 90 percent bank debt (not bonds) to 10 percent-15 percent equity, though now debt is being drastically reduced in a few companies. Thus, highly leveraged, the acquisition of controlling shares could involve relatively little money in terms of the scale of business. Also the shareholding pattern affects the nature of the acquisition, and it is unusual by American standards. The leading shareholders are likely to be the several financial institutions that provide the 85 percent of debt capital alluded to above. Sister companies from the same family of companies[92] (*keiretsu*) also have major shareholdings in each other, thus further reducing the truly "outside" equity. So the acquisition is not only a purchase of a community but a sale of a sister as well. Would a foreign acquirer understand and respect these Japanese differences in the business entity? If properly briefed, he would probably wonder whether it was a business or responsibility he was buying. Normally Japanese corporate dividend practices are no incentive to buy a corporation there.

By reflecting, we can see in this sketchy glimpse of acquisitions in Japan why they are resisted. We can see also that solutions to the foreigner's access problems are elusive.

Certainly Japan is in important ways closed; it is an uncommonly difficult place for foreigners to do business. Only part (and increasingly a small part) of the difficulty comes from official barriers such as the FECL. Social and cultural barriers are much more important. Besides the firm itself, the comprehensive network of business organizations (associations and cartels) are usually uncongenial, even frightening, to American enterprises reared on antitrust psychology. Entering foreigners inevitably have a low rank in a confining pecking order perpetrated by long association and by market shares. Other business groupings (e.g., *keiretsu*) are important and closed to outsiders. The distribution system has been rigid, complex, and inefficient, especially difficult and costly for foreigners to use as it is, or to find a way around. And then there are the language, educational system, hiring and employment patterns, and other subtleties. In a foreigner's eyes, these latter features are well-nigh insurmountable barriers, but they are hardly nontariff barriers to be removed for the convenience of foreign business guests.[93]

From the Japanese perspective, the whole integrated system of government-business organization, the dual economy with its exploitable lower tier of subcontractors, and the social patterns are arguably quite as essential to the productivity achieved by Japanese export firms as they are difficult for foreigners to fathom. Quite understandably, the awkward foreigner is often excluded as a potential irritant. Like the oyster confronting a grain of sand, it is better to keep it out than try to convert it to a pearl.

Thus perceived, some more adequate framework for American policy may be required other than prying the Japanese market open to achieve a single, combined, free, U.S.–Japanese market in which business from both sides can compete equally. That view has been more romantic than real and needs to be forthrightly recognized as such. The invisible hand that in the name of fairness requires Japan to reorganize its firms, policies, even culture to become like ours is not only failing but is also a bit naïve, if not arrogant.

Back to the FECL: the basic restrictive potential of the old FECL remains. True, the bulk of transactions will flow unobstructed through the Bank of Japan, the authorized banks, and designated securities firms. The time schedule for handling applications is improved and definite. But liberal in spirit the law is not. Its comprehensive and detailed coverage stifles any such pretensions. It runs all foreigners through closely watched wickets; some of its controls inward are more stringent than those outward (e.g., land purchase and direct investment); but all are monitored carefully. Japan branches of foreign corporations are treated by the potentially stricter procedures for inward direct investment, whereas before they were formally subject only to reporting and payment control. As noted, the anti-takeover regulations against foreigners purchasing more than 25 percent of designated corporations listed on the stock exchanges are not administered in a straightforward way. Their rationale is stated in terms of protecting the national security, or public safety or smooth management of the economy. Yet all of the designated companies have only one thing in common: high foreign shareholding. Foreign takeovers in the Japanese context are not necessarily a good thing, but neither is confusing euphemism in the law.

As law, the new statute is still pure administration. Its hallmark is unchallengeable discretion in practically every provision. Even the substantive standards in the statute are but generalizations to justify discretionary actions. And then there are always the emergency powers conferred generally (Art. 9) and *seriatim* for every category of transaction. This is not a policy statement that believes in comparative advantage, free market forces, or a free market bigger than Japan, except for Japanese. The policy of the past can survive within this law and without judicial relief. Only liberal practice can signal a change in the bureaucratic handling of foreigners.

In sum, Japanese protectionism is a potential factor in capital and technology at the FECL level in areas that matter. Barriers of culture and business channels are even more formidable, and Japanese competitors are tough. Also, Americans have often not adapted their products to Japanese needs; they have often "not tried hard enough." All this says to me that opening the Japanese market should happen in all fairness, but it is not the major answer to the overall trade problem. The real problem comes from our record of productivity largely caused by a consumer orientation and hostile labor-management-government stance. In the cliché of Pogo: "We have met the enemy and he is us." Recognition of these basics in Congress is a first step toward raising our performance, and toward reducing U.S.–Japanese trade frictions. On the government to government level, it would help to recognize that "insular internationalism," "contrived competitiveness," and "quasi-state trading" are political problems, not economic maladjustments. In the national competition and bargaining, we must get some quid pro quo for our free market.

NOTES

1. "Law-and-Economics" is a recent buzz-word among lawyers. It has a more generalized meaning, I suspect, for economists. In legal scholarship it signifies a very definite and recent movement, largely of the past decade, producing a distinct body of work written by legal scholars and influenced by the methodology of microeconomics. As such it has apparently had relatively little impact on economics scholars. See Henry Hansmann, "The Current State of Law and Economics Scholarship," *Journal of Legal Education* 33:217.

It is interesting to note that the law and economics movement in recent years has signified, among other things, a shift in emphasis by its adherents in law schools away from the prior heavy weight given to public law and toward a renewed interest in private law and transactions. See Edmund W. Kitch, "The Intellectual Foundations of Law and Economics," *Journal of Legal Education* 33 (1983): 184.

2. *Gaikoku kawase oyobi gaikoku bōeki kanri-hō no ichibu o kaisei suru hōritsu* (Law to revise a part of the foreign exchange and foreign trade control law), Law no. 65, Dec. 18, 1979. The new FECL became effective a year later on Dec. 1, 1980.

3. This is my fifth discussion of Japanese liberalization in the last decade: *Foreign Enterprise in Japan*, (Chapel Hill: North Carolina Press, 1973) pp. 195–290; "Japan's Administration of Foreign Direct Investment" in *Private Investment and International Transactions in Asian and South Pacific Countries*, ed. Virginia Cameron (New York: Matthew Bender, 1974), pp. 321–71; *Joint Ventures and Investments in Japan* (Melbourne: Japanese Studies Centre, 1981), pp. 1–7; and "New Foreign Exchange Law" (paper presented to Parker School, in Columbia University, 1982). Portions of the last paper have been incorporated in this discussion, though the focus is broader here.

4. Japanese business investment in the United States in 1983 stood at $8.7 billion compared to $6.8 billion for the United States in Japan, though Japan's economy is only half the size of ours. See U.S. Dept. of Commerce, *Survey of Current Business*, vol. 12 (Aug. 1983).

5. See Dan Henderson, *Foreign Enterprise in Japan*, chap. 6. Also see generally, Moritani Masanori, *Japanese Technology: Getting the Best for the Least* (Beaverton, Ore.: ISBS, 1982), p. 12.

6. For example, OECD, *Liberalization of International Capital Movements: Japan* (Paris: OECD, 1968).

7. James Horne, *National, International and Sectional Interests in Policy Making: The Evolution of the Yen Bond Market 1970–1982* (Canberra: Australia-Japan Research Centre; Pacific Economic Papers, no. 90, 1982), p. 56.

8. *Ginkō-hō* (Banking Law), Law no. 59, June 1, 1981, effective April 1, 1982. This extensive revision replaced the Banking Law, Law no. 21 of 1927 in its entirety. See Shimojō Masahirō, "Japan's New Banking Law: Securities Business by Banks," *UCLA Pacific Basin Law Journal* 1 (1982): 83–116; and see generally Suzuki Yoshio, *Money and Banking in Contemporary Japan* (New Haven: Yale University Press, 1980), pp. 26, 29, and 37.

9. See, for example, Eric W. Hayden, *Internationalizing Japan's Financial System* (Stanford, Calif.: Stanford University Press, 1980), p. 29.

10. These are my own terms of a decade ago. Henderson, *Foreign Enterprise in Japan*, p. 3.

11. Still Japan cartelizes, protects, and/or subsidizes software, data transmission, and telecommunications, to name a few. See *Wall Street Journal*, Feb. 8, 1984, p. 8. These are not minor restrictions still lingering (despite massive trade imbalance). They are precisely the areas where Americans can compete. The same goes for space. See Japanese refusals to buy much cheaper satellites from the United States. *Nikkei sangyo*, Oct. 14, 1983, p. 5.

12. Already the United States has taken such political measures in the form of the trigger prices and various quotas, besides dumping, countervailing duty, and antitrust suits. These might be seen as a policy themselves, but I view them as more of a response to competitive Japanese practices, which are perceived in Washington to be unfair given our initially relatively free market. My discussion of the FECL restriction does not overlook these U.S. restrictions, nor deal with them. In passing, I should say that I did not approve of the trigger price for steel and did participate actively in attempts to defeat it in court. See *Davis Walker Corp. v. Blumenthal et al.*, 460 F. Supp. 283 (1978). Some commitment from uncompetitive industry to modernize (or trim down) should be required for limited protection. Otherwise, trigger prices and the like are indefensible subsidies by our consumers.

13. Since the United States has been the leading proponent of postwar free trade, Japanese restrictions are generally seen here as illegitimate on the assumption that both Japan and the United States are, or should be, equally free parts of the binational combined free market. Other than GATT and economic free trade theory and its adjustment mechanism, the "invisible hand," the U.S. free-trade policy has lacked specific content. It only becomes specific in terms of quotas and protective meaures; in other words, its maximum clarity is found in the exception to it. Recently, however, U.S. efforts have been made to bring nontariff barriers as well as tariffs, and services as well as goods, within the concept of free trade and within the purview of GATT. Such moves call into question respective domestic industrial policies that previously could not have been included in the topic of "trade" as such.

14. In the GM-Toyota discussion about a joint auto plant in California, surely Toyota could view

the UAW as a cultural barrier, not simply because of the high wages it exacts but because the intermediation between the company and the worker of American-type unions is adversarial and not conducive to the Japanese style of production. See Henderson, *Foreign Enterprise in Japan*, chap. 4.

15. The TV import issue had several facets, but see the report on the Zenith case, *BNA Antitrust and Trade Regulation Report* 45:982 (Dec. 15, 1983). See also last chapter of this volume.

16. See Kamata Satoshi, *Japan in the Passing Lane* (New York: Pantheon, 1982) p. 195, for the cost in terms of life style of Toyota's productivity.

17. The meeting was on February 16, 1983, at the Institute for International Economics and the topic was, "How Closed is the Japanese Market?"

18. Among these were: Gary Saxonhouse, "The Micro and Macroeconomics of Foreign Sales to Japan"; Office of U.S. Trade Representative, "Japanese Barriers to U.S. Trade and Recent Japanese Government Trade Initiatives"; and also a paper by William Kline.

19. Jon Woronoff, "World Trade War," *PHP*, Vol. 50 (July 1983) gives a cogent answer to those who claim that American problems in Japan are simply because our businessmen do not try hard enough. That some indeed do not try hard enough can also be documented.

20. One of the more recent ones was occurring at the same time (April 1983) Prime Minister Nakasone was proclaiming once again that barriers were being removed. It involved the Ministry of Agriculture's refusal to grant a Japan Agricultural Seal for soy isolate to Archer-Daniels-Midland of Illinois. See *Far Eastern Economic Review*, April 1983. Specific examples of restrictions can be found weekly in the *Nihon keizai shimbun* (hereafter, NKS) and in its English version, *Japan Economic Journal*. Knowledgeable Japanese treat them forthrightly. See editorial, "Shin-gaitamehō to nottori," *Shōji homū kenkyū*, no. 894, p. 100 (1981); NKS, Mar. 3, 1981, p. 2. For example, *The Japan Law Letter* (June 1983), pp. 41, 42, 43, 53, 57, 61; id. (Sept.-Oct., 1983), p. 8 (computer sales); p. 22 (aircraft); p. 28 (Japanese acquisition of U.S. bank but not American acquisition in Japan); p. 29 (yen bond restrictions); p. 30 (expensive duplicative foreign stock listing requirements), p. 58 (foreign phones resisted by NTT); NKS (Aug. 22, 1983), p. 3 (computer subsidy).

Other examples gleaned in recent reading: *Newsweek* (Oct. 17, 1983), p. 7 (no purchase of U.S. satellites though Japan's are three or four times as expensive); *Nikkei sangyō* (Aug. 17, 1983), p. 1 (MITI's drive to stop import from United States of nuclear fuel insulation tubes and organizing a consortium of government, insurance, and finance to push nuclear export); *Japan Times* (Aug. 14, 1983), p. 8 (U.S. Embassy urges Japanese department stores to buy American merchandise directly because Japanese middlemen make retail prices two or three times as high as U.S. prices); NKS, July 30, 1983, p. 1 (MITI worried about further tariff cuts, because 1983 cuts exhausted areas where Japanese were "super-competitive" already); *Sekai nippō*, Sept. 2, 1983, p. 7 (MOF orders twenty-three life insurance companies not to buy foreign securities); *Asian Wall Street Journal*, Sept. 23, 1983, p. 3 (Citibank finally allowed in underwriting like Japanese banks); *Japan Times*, July 31, 1983, p. 2 (special labeling of food additives from United States); NKS, Sept. 23, 1983, p. 1 (delay and inequity in NTT procurement); *Business Week* (Int'l. ed.), Dec. 5, 1983, p. 33 (contrasting NEC success in United States); NKS Sept. 20, 1983, p. 9 (IBM fears discriminatory new legislation on supplying VAN); *Nihon kōgyō shimbun*, Sept. 7, 1983, p. 13 (plywood protection); *Sekai nippō*, Sept. 23, 1983, p. 7 (tariffs lowered on items, after confirming no Japanese supply); *Japan Times*, Oct. 6, 1983, p. 5 (government involvement in machine tool subsidy); NKS, Sept. 15, 1983, p. 1 (agricultural protection). Further examples of Japanese official restrictions and subsidies appear almost daily in one or another of the publications cited above. Convenient, monthly summaries of legal news containing similar examples is available in *The Japan Law Letter*, ed. Rod Seeman (Tokyo: Eagle Enterprise).

21. The Japanese press, too, has often been quite witty and cynical about this "numbers game"; see Henderson, *Foreign Enterprise in Japan*, chap. 7.

22. My "war" terminology is used, with tongue in cheek, in emulation of the pervasive military rhetoric of the Japanese language press in dealing with foreigners and overseas business strategies. The ultimate "battle tactic" might be joining the USSR. See coverage by NKS of that suggestion by MITI official, Wakasugi, Nov. 31, 1982. Japanese sometime assume that the language barrier will insulate their battle plans from foreign scrutiny better than it in fact does. See, for example, Sony's Morita Akio's embarrassing candor intended only for the Japanese press. Urban C. Lehner, "Japanese View U.S. as Ungrateful Ally," *Asian Wall Street Journal* (Mar. 24, 1982), p. 2.

23. Convenient commentaries on the new FECL may be found in: Fukui Hiro, *Shōkai gaikoku kawase kanri-hō* (Detailed commentary on the foreign exchange control law) (1981); and Fukui Hiro, *Atarashii gaikoku kawase kanri-hō* (The new foreign exchange control law) (1980).

24. FECL, Art. 1 (hereafter citations to articles alone indicate the new FECL).

25. Art. 1.
26. Art. 11-2.
27. Art. 23, 24.
28. Art. 27.
29. Art. 30.
30. Art. 6(1).
31. Art. 26(2).
32. Art. 26(2)(3).
33. Art. 26(2)(4).
34. Art. 26(2)(5).
35. Art. 29.
36. Art. 22(2).
37. Art. 22(1) and (4); COFE Art. (6).
38. Arts. 10 and 11.
39. Art. 11-2.
40. Art. 12.
41. Note that outward direct investment is specifically covered as a capital transaction, Arts. 22(1) and (4).
42. As under the old FECL, "Technological induction contracts" are still treated in a way similar to inward direct investment (Arts. 29 and 30), and also establishment of a branch office in Japan is now an inward direct investment, whereas they had been FECL (not FIL) matters before. Note that the Notice of Designated Technology (n. 68 infra) uses the term "technological assistance contract" (gijutsu enjo keiyaku).
43. Art. 65.
44. See the long list of discriminatory practices listed by the American Chamber of Commerce in Japan. Japan Times, Mar. 22, 1982. They have existed for decades, amidst the PR for at least fifteen years from JETRO, MITI, and other agencies about liberalization, automatic approvals, and long detailed (and largely meaningless) lists of liberalized imports and industries.
45. The yen company was popular with some foreigners then because with it they could renounce any requirement of guarantees for repatriation of their investments and thereby begin operating in Japan without the delay of having the bureaucrats rewrite their contracts in the name of administrative guidance (gyōsei shidō).
46. See, for example, Japan Economics Journal May 10, 1983, for a report of Fuji Bank's purchase of a Walter Heller subsidiary here, at the same time describing the two-year delay in getting an approval from MOF for a Solomon Brothers branch in Tokyo. Japan Times (Aug. 25, 1983) p. 6, for Mitsubishi Bank purchase of Bank of California.
47. The trumpeting of the 1967–73 "liberalization" went on for several years in response to foreign criticism of the unfair treatment in Tokyo. Again, the liberal press here, also most of its "experts" (academics, big-government bureaucrats, etc.), played it straight with the Japanese, even deploring the "Nixon shock" (actually a long overdue exchange rate adjustment) as unfair to Japan. Although my comments explained at length (05 pages) how illiberal the "liberalization" was by American standards, my position in 1972, at the end of it, was overly optimistic. See Henderson, Foreign Enterprise, pp. 237–44.
48. See particularly Arts. 24 to 30.
49. Art. 6(5).
50. Art. 1.
51. Fukui, Atarashii gaikoku kawase kanri-hō.
52. Art. 22(1).
53. Art. 21(1).
54. Art. 24.
55. Arts. 22(1) and 26(3).
56. E.g., Arts. 23(1), 26(1), 29(3).
57. E.g., Arts. 23(2), 27(7), 30(1).
58. E.g., Art. 23(7), concerning payments.
59. Art. 21(1).
60. Art. 9.
61. Art. 16(1).
62. Art. 16(2).
63. Art. 18(1).

64. Art. 18(2).
65. Art. 19.
66. Art. 21(2); also see 21(3).
67. Art. 24(1).
68. Art. 25.
69. Art. 26(1) gives a detailed list of transactions deemed to be "inward direct investment."
70. Art. 27(2).
71. Art. 27(1).
72. Art. 27(3).
73. Art. 27(1).
74. Art. 30(4).
75. Arts. 47–55.
76. Art. 48.
77. Art. 54.
78. Art. 49.
79. Art. 55-3.
80. Art. 56.
81. Art. 57.
82. Henderson, *Foreign Enterprise*, p. 227.
83. The case is well presented in Paul Wilson, "Can MOF foil this gaijin's fight to invest in Japan?," *Asian Banking*, pp. 36–42, April 1981; see also Michiko Itō Crampe and Nicholas Benes, "Majority Ownership Strategies for Japan," *UCLA Pacific Basin Law Journal* 1:41 at 54 (1982).
84. See Appendix but note that business organizational patterns and purely domestic practices as well are major barriers to acquisitions.
85. In the past thirty years (1955–1985) Japan has become the second largest national market in the world, and foreigners have been able to acquire control of only a couple of dozen established firms. Small in scale, these acquired firms have all had a small share in their respective markets and have all been financially weak, including *Banyu Seiyaku* (acquired by Merck, 1983), the only listed Japanese firm among them. More detail may be found in Walter Ames, "Entering the Japanese Market via Acquisitions," *East Asian Executive Reports*, p. 9 (Feb., 1985).
86. While practicing in California, I remember a bank acquisition for Japanese more than twenty years ago and that bank now has a ranking that dwarfs anything American banking has in Japan. In 1983 Mitsubishi Bank was allowed to acquire the Bank of California (with tri-state banking licenses). Such a thing is simply unthinkable in Japan; finally we are beginning to see the one-sidedness of "insular internationalism." See *Wall Street Journal*, Jan. 8, 1982, for Japanese acquisition of a defense-related company.
87. See "Angling for Capital," *Wall Street Journal*, July 11, 1975. Also in the August recess (1983), Japanese are apparently hosting a visit of California congressmen to Tokyo, and five Washington congressmen are being sponsored by the Japan-American Society of the State of Washington, rather than wholly Japanese hosts.
88. Appreciation of the subtlety of this issue is growing in the United States. See Urban C. Lehner, "Japan's Ultimate Barrier to U.S. Trade," *Asian Wall Street Journal* (July 19, 1982), p. 2.
89. The nuances and qualifications required to deal with this subject are not possible here. But we should note changes in the permanent employment system, the debt/equity ratios, and bank funding of Japan business. None of these is static, nor is their prevalance uniform throughout Japan.
90. There is variation industry to industry and company to company depending on size and profitability and the like. See Robert E. Cole, *Japanese Blue Collar Worker* (Berkeley and Los Angeles: University of California Press, 1971); Thomas P. Rohlen, *For Harmony and Strength* (Berkeley and Los Angeles: University of California Press, 1974); Rodney Clark, *The Japanese Company* (New Haven: Yale University Press, 1979).
91. This is a common reference in Japan to the similarity of role of the present-day company and the traditional village (*mura*) in which at least 85 percent of Japanese spent their entire lives, confined, socialized, and nutured within its boundaries.
92. See Henderson, *Foreign Enterprise in Japan*, chap. 9.
93. There was still much talk of this sort at the Institute of International Economics conference in Feb. 8, 1983, in Washington D.C. See also *Washington Post*, Nov. 31, 1982, for Commerce Secretary Baldridge's demand for Japan's cultural change.

APPENDIX

Only the broad outlines of the 1980 reforms are contained in the statute described in the text. Everywhere working details are to be supplied by cabinet and ministerial orders. To show the effect of some of these regulations issued under the new FECL, let us take the experience of a hypothetical American businessman in a series of transactions in Japan. They are probably the most typical dealings affecting foreign investors. As can be seen from the outline of the FECL (in the text), payments, outward investment, and two-way trade in goods are equally important subjects also covered by the FECL, but for brevity excluded in the illustrations below. The discussion is based on the major CO's and MO's[1] as of January 1982, and intended to lend them concrete meaning.

Transaction 1. A man from Seattle, John Doe, is a computer engineer with important technology concerned with computer manufacturing. Through Nomura Securities Co., he decides to buy 50,000 shares in Ringo K.K., a Japanese corporation (*kabushiki kaisha*; K.K.) and home computer manufacturer listed on the Tokyo stock exchange. Although this purchase is a capital transaction[2] normally requiring a prior report, none is required here because shares purchased through a designated securities firm such as Nomura are excepted.[3]

If he had purchased 50,000 shares directly from a Japanese shareholder, Doe would have had to report (*todokeide*) to MOF ten days[4] in advance;[5] or if the shares purchased had constituted 10 percent or more of the shares outstanding in a listed company, the purchase would have come within the definition[6] of an inward direct investment (*tainai chokusetsu tōshi*) subject to different controls to be discussed below. But since Doe's purchase runs afoul of neither of these restrictions, the paper work done by Nomura will suffice.

Transaction 2. Next Doe decides to buy, again through Nomura Securities, another 600,000 shares, bringing his holding in Ringo K.K. to more than 10 percent of shares outstanding.

Now he must make a prior report through BOJ to both MOF and the ministry in charge of the industry involved because he is an individual nonresident, and as such is a foreign investor[7] as defined in the new FECL. His stock-exchange purchases in a listed company, if they amount to more than 10 percent, fall within the definition of an inward direct investment,[8] which starts at 10 percent by cabinet order.[9] His report must be filed three months before the investment is made[10] on a form designated.[11]

To report and process his proposed inward direct investment in a listed Japanese corporation, Doe must appoint a resident agent.[12] This requirement is quite general throughout the new FECL where reporting is imposed on the foreign investor. The content of the report includes essentials concerning both the foreigner and the corporation invested in.[13]

After the report, the authorities may review it and recommend alterations based on opinion of the Council on Foreign Exchange.[14] A delay of four months may be ordered to determine whether the transaction might (1) imperil national security, (2) adversely and seriously affect activities of business . . . or smooth management of our national economy, (3) emanate from a country without treaties or reciprocity for Japanese investments, or (4) require an approval under FECL Art. 21(2) because it affects the balance of payments, currency stability, or capital markets.[15] If the council finds it necessary, the delay may be extended to five months.[16] In response to a recommendation for alterations, Doe must comply or reject within ten days.[17] If he makes no response or rejects the recommendations, the bureaucrats may then order alteration or suspend the transaction.[18]

Though the regulations give no helpful guidance for applying the broad standards for review of an inward direct investment, a joint notification[19] of 1980 lists sensitive areas of technology including computer technology. Mr. Doe may therefore expect a time-consuming scrutiny of his acquisition of a 10 percent interest in Ringo K.K.

Note that if Doe were to agree with Ringo K.K. to establish a new fifty-fifty joint venture for computer development in Japan using his technology, he would confront roughly the same procedure during review of his acquisition in such a closely held corporation. But in an unlisted new corporation, the percentage of foreign shares is not important. Any foreign holding, up to 100 percent is an inward direct investment, whereas in listed publicly held companies the minimum qualifying as a direct investment is ten percent and should the foreign holdings approach 25 percent, the issuing company may be "designated" and controls imposed requiring prior validation (*ninka*)[20] of further acquisitions to prevent a foreign takeover.

Transaction 3. How does the law treat technology transfers?

Suppose Doe sets up with Ringo K.K. a fifty-fifty joint venture, incorporated in Japan as Doerin K.K., and gets his 50 percent share acquisition approved (se transaction 2 above). Doerin K.K. is to work in the area of computer design. Part of Doe's joint venture commitment to Ringo K.K. was that he would license his inventions in the computer field to Doerin K.K., when incorporated.

Such a license contract, between a nonresident licensor and resident licensee involving designated technology is subject to the new FECL provisions governing the conclusion (*teiketsu*) of a "contract for induction of technology" (*gijutsu do'nyū keiyaku*).[21]

Both Doe and Ringo K.K. must report to MOF (and the ministry in charge of the industry) thirty days before conclusion of the contract for induction of technology. The contents of the report are specified by cabinet order.[22] Doe must appoint a resident agent in Japan to make the report and receive any recommendations.[23] After filing, the parties must not conclude the contract for thirty days,[24] unless the period is shortened at the discretion of the officials. If it is shortened, the waiting period after filing the report depends on (1) whether the technology is "designated" (as it is in our problem) and (2) the amount of compensation to the nonresident licensor (Doe). In the case of a shortened period, involving undesignated technology, a contract may be concluded on the date of filing. Also, even if the technology is designated technology, the contract may be concluded on the date of filing if the nonresident's compensation is less than ¥100,000,000 (between $400,000 to $500,000 by today's fluctuating rates). If the period is shortened, for contracts involving designated technology and compensation of ¥100,000,000 or more, the parties must wait until the day following lapse of two weeks from filing.[25]

If the screening office (initially BOJ) declines to shorten the period for conclusion of the contract on the grounds that the contract requires further review, then the new FECL requires[26] an initial thirty days before the contract can be concluded. In this review, if the ministries find that (1) the contract might imperil national security or (2) adversely and seriously affect *business activity* or smooth management of the national economy, they may extend the review to four (or even five) months. The parties may be asked to alter the contract in compliance with the opinion sought from the new Council on Foreign Exchange.[27] If they choose not to do so, an order to alter may be given or the transaction may be suspended. In other words, the procedure follows closely that for inward direct investment.[28]

All of the foregoing is concerned only with handling of the prior report, but in the case of designated technology, the ministerial order requires further reports (within thirty days after conclusion of the contract) concerning the final agreement and sublicensing.[29]

Transaction 4. But let us say Doe succeeds, and next he wishes to diversify his Japanese interests and agrees to buy from several Japanese shareholders 25 percent of a listed spinning company, Kanto K.K.

It turns out that it is a designated corporation as defined in the new FECL provisions, designed to require approvals and prevent foreign acquisitions and takeovers by stock exchange purchases. These restrictions authorize MOF with the concerned ministry in charge of the industry to jointly designate any company, if holding by nonresidents of more than the amount of its shares fixed by cabinet order (25 percent) is deemed to "imperil national security . . . or adversely and seriously affect the smooth management of our national economy."[30] Unfortunately, Doe's proposed purchase involves a designated company in the magic amount (25 percent).

These restrictions apply only when foreigners, in the aggregate, push their collective holdings in a listed company to at least 25 percent . The restriction applies to that last purchase, which on top of all others reaches 25 percent or the percentage fixed by notice.[31] No single foreigner need possess the 10 percent necessary to amount to an inward direct investment. In our problem, of course, the application is clear because Doe's purchase alone qualifies for official scrutiny. So Doe must file a report as in the case of an inward direct investment.[32]

If a buyer does not know whether his purchase will bring the total held by foreigners up to the 25 percent limit, he must obtain a confirmation from MOF that other foreign holdings added to his would be less than the 25 percent limit.[33]

Transactions 5. Next suppose Doe decides to buy land in Japan and rent it to Doerin K.K. for a plant site. This is a capital transaction[34] and requires a prior report filed by Doe through BOJ to MOF.[35] Here the land purchase in Japan by a nonresident is handled differently from a Japanese purchase of land abroad, which requires no such report. Doe not only must report, but he must also appoint an agent to file the report and receive recommendations, if any, from MOF.[36]

Also land purchases by foreigners are among the specified capital transactions for which the new FECL provides a twenty-day waiting period after filing the report[37] and possibly a review. If MOF finds that the purchase will cause any of the following difficulties, it may recommend that Doe alter or cancel the land purchase: 1. Adverse effect on balance of payments or Japan's credit. 2. Adverse effects on the money or capital markets. 3. Adverse influence on the business activity or the management of the national economy. 4. Preventing the maintenance of international peace, order, and treaties.

If a recommendation is made and is not accepted by Doe within ten days, then MOF may order (within twenty days) that he cancel the land purchase.[38] Doerin K.K. is not required to report (or obtain approval) for its lease from Doe.

Transaction 6. Next Doe proposes to loan ¥150,000,000 to Doerin K.K. for six years to build the plant (above).

All such loans are treated as simple capital transactions, except those that qualify as inward direct investments.[39] The loans that qualify as inward direct investments are those with specified periods and amounts[40] as fixed by cabinet and ministerial orders.[41] The result and these combined regulations limit loans that qualify as inward direct investments to the following: (a) Loans for terms from one to five years in amounts of at least ¥200,000,000; and (b) Loans for more than five years in amounts of at least ¥100,000,000.

Since Doe's proposed loan is for ¥150,000,000 for six years, it will be treated as an inward direct investment. As such, the loan must be reported by Doe. Also, it may be subject, at the discretion of the officials, to the waiting periods, recommendations, and possible alterations or suspension outlined in transaction 2 above.

Note, though, that the waiting period of the new FECL[42] has been shortened to the day after the lapse of two weeks, unless the officials in their discretion require the thirty days of the new FECL and its other review procedures.[43]

Transaction 7. If Doe limits his loan to one year or less than ¥100,000,000 then it is treated as a mere capital transaction.[44] Doerin K.K. (not Doe) must file a report with MOF.[45] The waiting period of twenty days and the review then follows the procedures explained in transaction 5.

Transaction 8. If instead of lending to Doerin K.K., Doe has Doerin borrow locally from Ginko Bank, and guarantees Doerin's borrowing of, say, ¥10,000,000 no report is required.

Although such a guaranty contract is defined as a capital transaction,[46] prior reports are required only when a resident of Japan guarantees a nonresident corporation's issuance of securities.[47] Such is not the case here so Doe's guaranty requires no report by either party.

NOTES TO APPENDIX

1. The following new cabinet orders (*seirei*) and ministerial orders (*shōrei*) are cited hereafter by their respective abbreviations listed below.

COFE: *Gaikoku kawase kanri-rei* (Cabinet Order on Foreign Exchange Controls), Cab. Order no. 260, Oct. 11, 1980.

MOFE: *Gaikoku kawase tō kanri ni kansuru shō rei* (Ministerial Order Concerning Foreign Exchange Controls), MOF Ministerial Order no. 44, Nov. 15, 1980, effective Jan. 1, 1982.

COIDI: *Tainai chokusetsu tōshi tō ni kansuru seirei* (Cabinet Order Concerning Inward Direct Investment) Cab. Order no. 261, Oct. 11, 1980.

MOIDI: *Tainai chokusetsu tōshi tō ni kansuru meirei* (Joint Order Concerning Inward Direct Investment), Order no. 1, Nov. 11, 1980.

Notice of Designated Technology: *Kokuji dai-san-gō (tainai chokusetsu tōshi tō ni kansuru meirei dai-go-jo, dai-ni-ko dai-ichi-go no kitei ni motozuku shitei gijutsu)* (On designated technology under MOIDI art. 5[2][1]), Notice no. 3, Nov. 27, 1980.

Notice of Designated Listed Companies: *Kokuji dai-ichi-gō (gaikoku kawase oyobi gaikoku boeki kanri-hō fusoku dai-ni-jō, dai-ikkō narabi ni tainai chokusetsu tōshi to ni kansuru seirei dai-shichi-jō dai-ni-kō oyobi dai-go-kō no kitei ni motozuku shinsa no taisho to subeki kaisha oyobi tokutei no kaisha in tsuite toku ni hitsuyō ga aru to mitomete sadameru ritsu)* (on the ratio fixed as necessary in designated companies and companies to be examined under FECL Supp. Art. 2[1] and COIDI Art. 7[2]), Notice no. 1 (Jt. MOF, MITI, et al.), Jan. 26, 1980.

2. Art. 20(5).
3. Art. 22(1) (proviso).
4. MOFE Art. 9.
5. COFE Art. 12 and MOFE art. 7.
6. Art. 26(2).
7. Art. 26(1).
8. Art. 26(2)(3).
9. COIDI Art. 2(50).
10. COIDI Art. 2(10).
11. MOIDI Art. 2(3)(1). See also MOIDI, Appended form 1.
12. COIDI Art. 2(11).
13. COIDI Art. 2(12).
14. Art. 27(2).
15. Art. 27(1).
16. Art. 27(3).
17. Art. 27(4).
18. Art. 27(7).
19. MOIDI Art. 5(2)(1); Notice of Designated Technology, item 6 (1980).
20. See Notice of Designated Listed Companies (See n. 68 supra).
21. Art. 29(1).
22. COIDI Art. 4(3); see also MOIDI, Appended form 9.
23. COIDI Art. 4(2).
24. Art. 29(3).
25. MOIDI Art. 6(2)(3).
26. Art. 29(3).
27. Art. 30(2).
28. Art. 30(4); cf. Art. 27(7).
29. MOIDI, Appended forms 17 and 18.
30. FECL Suppl. Provision Art. 2(1).

31. Notice of Designated Listed Companies. (See n. 68 supra).
32. Suppl. Art. 3(8).
33. Supp. Art. 3(3).
34. Art. 20(8).
35. Art. 22(1)(7).
36. COFE Art. 12(2).
37. Art. 23(1).
38. Art. 23(7).
39. Art. 20(2).
40. Art. 26(2)(6).
41. COIDI Art. 2(7); MOIDI Art. 2(1).
42. Art. 26(4).
43. MOIDI art. 6(1).
44. Art. 20(2).
45. Art. 22(1)(1).
46. Art. 20(2).
47. Art. 22(1)(1).

The Role of Intellectual Property Law in Bilateral Licensing Transactions between Japan and the United States

TERUO DOI

Rapid technological advance in both the United States and Japan and increasing mutual dependence between the two countries have greatly enhanced bilateral trade in intellectual property. This trend will undoubtedly make the role of intellectual property lawyers and specialists in various sectors increasingly important.

Today, when a comparative study is made of the intellectual property laws of Japan and the United States, one comes to realize that both countries share many similar problems despite the Japanese legal system being based on civil law, whereas the United States retains a common law tradition. Indeed, in the field of intellectual property law, Japan has learned much from the United States in the past, and must learn more in the future, as in the case of intellectual creations. At the same time, Japan is certainly one of the most attractive markets for the United States and an increased understanding of Japan's intellectual property law is indispensable for the full exploitation of American intellectual property in Japan.

The purpose of this chapter, therefore, is to discuss the legal aspects of bilateral licensing transactions involving intellectual property between Japan and the United States and some of the problems arising under such transactions. The term "intellectual property," *chitekishoyūken* in Japanese, is defined by Article 2 (viii) of the Convention Establishing the World Intellectual Property Organization, signed in Stockholm on July 14, 1967, as including "the rights relating to literary, artistic and scientific works; performances of performing artists, phonograms, and broadcasts; inventions in all fields of human endeavor; scientific discoveries; industrial designs; trademarks, service marks, and commercial names and designations; protection against unfair competition; and all other rights resulting from intellectual activity in the industrial, scientific, literary or artistic fields."

Transactions involving intellectual property are quite extensive and only a representative sample can be given here. They include patent and know-how licensing and technical assistance, which are broadly called "technology transfer"; distributorship contracts under certain trademarks; franchise agreements involving trademarks, service marks, and trade names; and various kinds of licensing agreements involving copyright. Copyright licensing transactions include book publishing agreements, motion picture distribution agreements, mechanical license agreements or license agreements for the manufacture and sale of phonograph records, character merchandising agreements, and catalogue agreements of musical works.

In the field of intellectual property, there are two basic multilateral conventions aimed at securing international protection among member states: the Paris Convention of March 20, 1883, for the Protection of Industrial Property, and the Berne Convention of September 9, 1886, for the Protection of Literary and Artistic Works. Member states of these conventions respectively form unions. As of May 1, 1985, the Paris Union had ninety-seven member states, including Japan and the United States, and the Berne Union had seventy-six states as members. The fundamental principle of international protection under both conventions is the principle of national treatment among member states. Since the United States is not a member of the Berne Union, national treatment between the United States and the Berne Union countries, including Japan, is secured by the Universal Copyright Convention signed in 1952, and revised in Paris in 1971.

Under these conventions, protection given by, or exclusive rights granted under, the laws of each member state are territorial in principle and do not extend beyond the boundaries of that state. In the various forms of licensing transactions listed above, the object of licenses is always the granting of exclusive rights in designated countries, particularly the licensees' countries. Therefore, in this chapter I will discuss the domestic laws of both Japan and the United States with a focus on Japanese law, due in part to the Japanese parties being licensees in a majority of cases. Despite the rapid technical advance of Japanese companies, there is still a great trade imbalance in favor of the United States in intellectual property transactions. Certainly, Japan is one of the biggest overseas markets for American intellectual products.

For American businessmen, Japanese intellectual property law is as important as the corresponding body of law in their own country. Members of the legal profession in both countries can easily communicate on subjects of common interest, such as patent application, copyright protection, and unfair competition, but understanding one another's intellectual property law is not as easily accomplished. It must be emphasized that comparative study is a necessity for success in intellectual property transactions.

There are five main topics for discussion in this chapter: the patent system and its role in the transfer of technology; protection of technical know-how as a basis for transfer of technology; legal protection of computer software; character merchandising; and franchising businesses. With the limited space available for discussion of these rather broad topics, readers are recommended to consult with various reference materials for detail.[1]

THE PATENT SYSTEM AND ITS ROLE
IN THE TRANSFER OF TECHNOLOGY

The technological advance of Japan today depends heavily on the reception of foreign technology. The Science and Technology Agency of the Japanese government reported that in 1981, 2,076 new technology introduction agreements were concluded with foreign technology suppliers and the amount of consideration paid to them reached $537,000,000.[2]

The largest supplier of technology to Japan is the United States. Out of 2,076 technology introduction agreements, 977 (47 percent) were concluded with the United States, 244 (10.8 percent) with France, 219 (10.5 percent) with the Federal Republic of Germany, 175 (8.4 percent) with the United Kingdom, and 119 (5.7 percent) with Italy.[3] Of these agreements, 603 involved the licensing of patents, including inventions under pending applications. Such statistics show the important role the patent system plays in Japan in the reception of foreign technology.

The patent system in Japan is based on the Patent Law (Law no. 121, 1959) and supplemented by the Utility Model Law (Law no. 123, 1959). The utility model system or petty patent system adopted in 1905 when Japan was still a technologically backward country, was designed to protect small inventions made by Japanese. The utility model system is somewhat contradictory to the basic policy of the patent law, as the latter is designed to protect inventions that meet the higher standard of inventive step or nonobviousness. However, the utility model system is still retained despite Japan's remarkable technological development. Not only small individual inventors but also large manufacturing companies with advanced research and development facilities benefit from utility model registrations by filing numerous applications annually.[4]

In 1982, the Japanese Patent Office received approximately 440,000 patent and utility model applications, which represented 40 percent of the total number of patent and utility model applications filed throughout the world.[5] Of those, the Japanese Patent Office received 235,324 patent applications and issued 50,601 patents, and it received 202,702 utility model applications and granted 55,304 registrations. In the same year, the United States Patent and Trademark Office received 109,625 patent applications and issued 57,889 patents. These figures are far greater than corresponding figures of other industrialized countries.[6]

Among the 235,324 patent applications filed with the Japanese Patent Office in 1982, 24,427 applications were filed by nonresidents, including 10,050 applications filed from the United States. And, of the 50,601 patents issued by the Japanese Patent Office, 8,378 were issued to nonresident applicants, 4,101 of those to U.S. applicants. Of 109,625 patent applications filed in the United States in 1982, 46,309 were filed by nonresidents, including 16,068 from Japan. And, among the 57,889 U.S. patents issued, 23,993 were to nonresident applicants including 8,149 to Japanese inventors.[7]

These statistics show the inventive activities in both Japan and the United States to be quite extensive in comparison to other industrialized countries, and the patent systems of both seem to encourage new inventions and improvements. On the other hand, the ever-increasing number of patent applications creates a backlog of pending applications in the patent offices in both countries and results in an increased length of the pendency of applications. This problem is more acute in Japan for reasons to be discussed.

The history of the Japanese patent system is interesting but cannot be explored in detail here.[8] The patent system established in Japan in 1885 by the Patent Monopoly Ordinance (Senbaitokkyo Jōrei) incorporated some elements of French and U.S. patent laws. The Patent Monopoly Ordinance was replaced by the Patent Ordinance (Tokkyo Jōrei) of 1888. This ordinance was the product of a thorough investigation and study of the patent systems of advanced countries conducted by Takahashi Korekiyo (1854–1936), who was then director general of the Patent Office.[9] In 1899 Japan acceded to the Paris Convention for the Protection of Industrial Property, and enacted the Patent Law, the Design Law, and the Trademark Law under which the rights of aliens were recognized for the first time.[10]

The Patent Law describes its objective in Article 1 as: "To encourage inventions by promoting their protection and utilization and thereby to contribute to the development of industry." Article 1 of the Utility Model Law similarly sets forth its objective as: "To promote the protection and utilization of devices relating to the configuration or structure, or combination of both, of goods, with a view to encouraging creation of such devices, and thereby to contribute to the development of industry."

The word "invention" (hatsumei) is defined by Article 2 (1) of the Patent Law as "the highly advanced creation of technical ideas utilizing natural laws." On the other hand, the Utility Model Law Article 2 (1) defines "device" (kōan) as "the creation of technical ideas utilizing natural laws." These definitions differ in that patentable inventions must be highly advanced, whereas technical ideas are not required to meet such a high standard to qualify for utility model registration. This difference is also reflected in the Patent Office's examination of the inventive step.

Patentable inventions include both new and useful products and processes. This is clear from the definition of "working" (jisshi) in Article 2 (3) of the Patent Law with respect to "the invention of a thing," "the invention of a process," and "the invention of a process of manufacturing a thing." Article 32 of the Patent Law excludes the following from patentable subject matter: the invention of a substance to be manufactured by a method of transformation of atomic nuclei; or any invention likely to harm public order, good morals, or public hygiene. The 1975 amendment of the Patent Law removed food and beverages, pharmaceutical products, and chemical compounds from the list of excluded inventions. They had originally been excluded because the granting of patents for these products was historically considered to restrict their supply in the domestic market through the exercise of patent monopolies, and thereby forced consumers to suffer from an inadequate supply. In addition, the weak competitive power of Japanese companies in the food, pharmaceutical, and chemical industries made special protection necessary against domination by foreign enterprises through their patent powers. In drafting the 1975 revision it was felt that these fears had virtually disappeared and that the granting of patents to chemical compounds and pharmaceutical products would keep the Japanese patent system up to date with the systems of advanced countries where these products were not excluded from patent.

For an invention to be patentable, it must meet the requirements of novelty, utility, and inventive step or nonobviousness under Article 29 of the Patent Law:

> Any person who has made an invention which can be utilized in industry may obtain a patent for such invention, with the exception of the following inventions: (i) An invention which was publicly known in Japan prior to the filing of the patent application; (ii) An invention which was publicly worked in Japan prior to the filing of the patent application; and (iii) An invention which was described in a publication distributed in Japan or in any foreign country prior to the filing of the patent application.
>
> When an invention is such that it could have easily been made, prior to the filing of the patent application, on the basis of the invention mentioned in any of the items of the preceding paragraph, by a person having an ordinary knowledge in the technical field to which such invention pertains, it shall not, notwithstanding the provision of the same paragraph, be entitled to a patent.

Article 3 of the Utility Model Law provides similar requirements of novelty, utility, and inventive step for utility model registration. Note that Article 3 (2) sets forth a less strict requirement of inventive step "when a device is such that it could have *quite easily been made*, prior to the filing of the application for utility model registration, on the basis of the device mentioned in any of the items of the preceding paragraph, by a person having an ordinary knowledge in the technical field to which such device pertains" (emphasis added).

Examination of applications is carried out by an examiner in accordance with standards compiled by the Patent Office,[11] which include the examination standard for computer program-related inventions adopted in 1975,[12] and the examination guideline for inventions using microcomputers adopted in 1982.[13]

Any person who has made an invention may apply for a patent. Although the inventor must be a natural person, the right to obtain a patent is assignable and an invention made by an employee is assignable to the employer. Such an assignee or employer may file an application in his own name. Joint owners of an invention must file an application jointly. An alien who has a domicile or residence, or a business establishment in the case of a corporation, in Japan may apply for a patent. An alien who has neither a domicile nor a residence in Japan is not entitled to a patent, unless the country of his nationality extends patent protection to Japanese nationals on the basis of reciprocity, or protection is otherwise provided by treaty. The provisions of the Patent Law on these matters are applicable *mutatis mutandis* to applications for utility model registration under the Utility Model Law.

Japan has treaty relationships under the Paris Convention for the Protection of Industrial Property and/or treaties of friendship, commerce, and navigation with a majority of the nations of the world, and national treatment in the enjoyment of industrial property rights is assured under these treaties. Japan ratified the Patent Cooperation Treaty in 1978 and, therefore, international applications under this treaty are acceptable by the Japanese Patent Office. The Patent Office uses the International Patent Classification (IPC) under the Strassbourg Agreement, of March 24, 1971, concerning International Patent Classification ratified by Japan in 1976.

To cope with the ever increasing number of applications, the revisions to the Patent Law and Utility Model Law in 1970 adopted the early disclosure and examination-on-demand systems. However, the trend toward increasing applications still continues, especially in such fields of technology as electronics, communications, optics, automobiles, medical care, terminal printers, and nuclear power. The increase of applications in these fields represents 65.7 percent of the total increase in applications in all fields of technology.[14] The electronics and communications fields concern technology relating to information storage, semiconductors, facsimile, television, and computers.

The trend of increasing applications is in part attributable to the encouragement given by Japanese companies to their employee-inventors. In fact, many companies reward an employee when his invention results in the filing of an application for a patent or utility model registration, or when a patent or utility model registration is granted to his invention.[15] Such a practice tends to lower the quality of inventions for which patent or utility model applications are filed. The Patent Office attributes the high rate of refusal of patents of nearly 50 percent to the lower quality of applications prepared after insufficient search of prior art or inventions lacking novelty or inventive step. To remedy this situation, the Patent Office has reviewed the examination standards and has asked for the cooperation of industry in improving the quality of applications.[16]

Japanese is the only official language used by the Patent Office. This practice may make foreigners who submit applications skeptical as to whether they are being fairly treated by the Patent Office. The results of a statistical study conducted recently by an American expert did "not appear to substantiate any discriminatory attitudes on the part of the Japanese Patent Office against foreigners, especially U.S. applicants."[17]

The grant of a patent confers upon the patentee an exclusive right to work the patented invention as a business for a limited period of fifteen years from the date of the publication of the application, but no longer than twenty years from the date of filing. On the other hand, utility model registration confers upon the registrant an exclusive right to work the registered device as a business for ten years from the date of the publication of the application, but no longer than fifteen years from the date of filing.

Both patents and utility model rights, having the attributes of personal property, can be assigned in whole or in part, or licensed on either exclusive or nonexclusive bases. These transactions can be effected by a contract between the parties concerned, but a record of the transaction is necessary with the Patent Office in order to assert the effect of the transaction against a third party. Since these transactions are an important means for technology transfer to Japan, a full explanation of the statutory provisions is appropriate. Provisions for assignment and licenses under the Patent Law are applicable *mutatis mutandis* to utility model rights by the Utility Model Law.

Both transfer of a patent right and establishment or transfer of an exclusive right to work (*senyō jisshiken*) must be recorded with the Patent Office to make them effective against third parties under Article 98 of the Patent Law.[18] Thus, when an exclusive license is granted to a patent and this license is recorded as *senyō jisshiken* on the Patent Office registry, the licensee, as the holder of a kind of real right, can bring an infringement action in his own name. It is therefore recommended that a recordation clause be inserted in a license agreement for the license to take the benefit of recording.[19] When a patent is licensed on a nonexclusive basis, the license can be recorded on the Patent Office registry as *tsūjō jisshiken* (lit., an ordinary right to work). The effect of such recordation is more limited. The licensee can only assert his nonexclusive right to work the licensed patent against a subsequent assignee or exclusive licensee (*senyō jisshikensha*) of the licensed patent.[20]

Since patents are assets that can be entered upon a balance sheet, they can also be transferred to a company in exchange for shares of stock. Such a contribution in kind must follow the requirements and procedures provided in the Commercial Code. In organizing a company, only the promoters can make contributions in kind under Article 168 (2) of the Commercial Code. A contribution in kind does not take effect unless the name of the person making the contribution, the property to be contributed, its value, and the number of shares to be issued in exchange for the contribution are stated in the articles of incorporation under Article 168 (1). Contributions in kind are subject to inspection by an inspector appointed by the competent court under Article 173. These provisions are also applicable when a patent license (either in the form of *senyō jisshiken* or *tsūjō jisshiken*) or unpatented know-how is contributed in exchange for shares.

The validity of a patent can only be challenged before the Patent Office by filing a demand for a hearing for invalidation on any ground provided in Article 123 (1) of the Patent Law. When the defendant in a patent infringement action files such a demand with the Patent Office, the court may suspend the litigation and halt proceedings until the Patent Office renders a final decision in the invalidation trial as provided in Article 168 (2). These provisions are also applicable to registered utility models.

The technical scope of a patented invention must be determined in accordance with the description of "the scope of claim for patent" in the specification. The parties in an infringement action may demand that the Patent Office give an interpretation of the technical scope of the patented invention concerned. In an infringement action, the court can rely on the doctrine of equivalents to avoid a result harsh to the patentee under a literal interpretation of the technical scope of the patented invention concerned.[21] The opposite doctrine of file wrapper estoppel is also recognized by the courts in appropriate circumstances.[22] The same rules are also applicable to registered utility models.

The exclusive right of a patentee to work his patented invention is granted on an earlier application under Article 72. The exclusive right is also subject to the right of a prior user of the invention. Under Article 79, a person who made the same invention independently of the patentee and who has been engaged in the business of exploiting it is entitled to continue his business on a nonexclusive basis after the grant of a patent to the patentee. Article 79 is also applicable to registered utility models.

The exclusive right of a patentee is subject to a compulsory license to be granted on the grounds of the nonworking of the patented invention by the patentee under Article 83, and public interest under Article 93.

First, under Article 83, if a patented invention has not been worked properly in Japan continuously for more than three years, any person interested in the patented invention may negotiate with the patentee or his exclusive licensee for a grant of nonexclusive license (*tsūjō jisshiken no kyodaku*) of said patented invention. If no agreement is reached or no negotiation can be held with the patentee or his exclusive licensee, the interested party may demand arbitration by the Patent Office. There has been no reported case of a compulsory license granted under Article 83. It should be noted that the 1964 report of the Secretary General of the United Nations pointed out that in every country surveyed, although compulsory license for the nonworking of a patented invention has rarely or never been sought, it certainly stimulates licensing activities of foreign patentees.[23]

Second, compulsory license is likewise available when there is a strong need for exploiting a patented invention for public interest under Article 93. Although the importance of the role of compulsory license for public interest is well recognized, this provision has never been invoked. The Utility Model Law similarly provides compulsory licenses under the above circumstances in Articles 21 and 23, respectively.

The parties to a license agreement are fairly free in providing the terms and conditions of the license in their agreement, however, they must observe the prohibition of restrictive clauses under the Antimonopoly Law. Licensing agreements with foreign parties must also be reported to the Fair Trade Commission within thirty days of their conclusion. The Antimonopoly Act Guidelines for International Licensing Agreements published by the Fair Trade Commission in 1968 is useful to parties in an international licensing agreement.[24]

PROTECTION OF TECHNICAL KNOW-HOW AS THE BASIS
FOR THE TRANSFER OF TECHNOLOGY

While the licensing of a patent does not require disclosure of the patented invention to the licensee because it was already made public when the patent was granted, the licensing of technical know-how requires disclosure of the know-how by way of supplying specifications, blueprints, drawings, and other documents to the licensee and allowing the licensee to visit and inspect the licensor's facilities. In addition, it is often necessary for the licensor to train the licensee's technical personnel at the licensor's facilities and to send the licensor's technical specialists to the licensee's factory plants and other facilities to teach the licensee's technical personnel the actual working of the know-how. Such technical assistance is particularly important when the licensee's technical level, in both facilities and personnel, is not high enough to work the disclosed know-how on a commercial basis.

The transfer of technology by means of know-how licensing and technical assistance depends primarily on contractual arrangements including secrecy agreements, but the legal protection of unpatented technical know-how as trade secrets in the technology recipient's country serves as the basis for such contractual arrangements, in much the same way the patent system serves as the basis for the licensing of patented inventions. Due to the legacy of over two decades foreign technology reception, the English word "know-how" has become a common term in Japanese society, but the trade secrets law has not yet been developed to assure the owner of valuable technical know-how, customer lists, or other kinds of trade secrets satisfactory remedies against their misappropriation.[25]

The often-quoted description of this state of the Japanese law is the holding of the Tokyo High Court in *Deutsche Werft Aktiengesellschaft* v. *Chūetsu-Waukesha Yūgen Kaisha.*[26] This is the only case in Japan that mentions the legal status of know-how by using the Latin term *expressio verbis*. In this case, the claimant, Deutsche Werft, a German company based in Hamburg, concluded an agreement with Waukesha Bearings Corporation, a Wisconsin corporation, by which the claimant granted an exclusive license to manufacture and sell, in the United States and Canada, oil-lubricated stern tube sealings for the propellor shafts of ships, using the claimant's know-how. Waukesha agreed to keep the process secret. Waukesha, for manufacturing and selling the stern tube sealings in Japan, signed a joint-venture agreement with Chūetsu Metal Works, a Japanese corporation, and organized the respondent corporation, Chūetsu-Waukesha Yūgen Kaisha, each party contributing 45 percent, and another Japanese company contributing 10 percent, of the capital. The respondent started operations, and the claimant filed a petition for a temporary injunction against the respondent, contending that the latter's act of manufacturing and selling the stern tube sealings constituted violation of the contract between the claimant and Waukesha, and that, therefore, the claimant was entitled to an injunction against both the respondent and Waukesha. The Tokyo District Court denied the injunction, and the claimant appealed. The Tokyo High Court, in dismissing the appeal, held as follows:

> No matter how know-how is to be considered under the law, it has property value and yet it has not been recognized as a legal right. Under the know-how contract (technological assistance contract), the other contracting party, the licensee (as to the know-how), owes the duty of not disclosing the know-how that it obtains under the contract outside the scope limited by the contract, and such a duty is a contractual obligation. The obligor (not the respondent in this petition) which has revealed the know-how to outsiders in violation of the contract is clearly liable to pay damages under contract law.
>
> But if a third person who is not the contracting party is informed of the said know-how by the obligor or obtains the knowledge of it accidentally and engages in manufacturing by using the know-how, it is proper to construe that the claimant is not entitled to an injunction, since there is no specific provision under the present statutes.
>
> Although know-how has property value, it cannot be considered, at the present moment, that the law recognizes the effect of a right (whether it is an incorporeal right or a right of obligation) which is enforceable against a third party. Protection of know-how can only be achieved by the effort of the owner to maintain it as an industrial secret and prevent disclosure to others. The respondent Chūetsu-Waukesha Yūgen Kaisha has the obligor as one of its members, and the latter is a party to the aforementioned contract (contributing 45 percent of the capital), and two of the directors were appointed by the obligor company.
>
> But the respondent is a third person in a legal sense with regard to the said contract, as admitted by the appellant. Hence, even if it is admissible that the respondent has committed an illegal act by assisting the obligor company in the nonperformance of the latter's duty, the cause for a temporary injunction in the instant petition is not clearly stated.

The Tokyo High Court's statement that "know-how has property value and yet it has not been recognized as a legal right" is true, but requires some further explanation. The court intends that know-how is not an exclusive right established by law like a patent, and, therefore, there is no legal basis to enjoin the joint venture company from the working of the know-how, so long as it was not a party to the know-how license agreement and it was "informed of said know-how" by the licensee or obtained "the knowledge of it accidentally." The question left unanswered by the court is what kinds of remedies are available to the owner of know-how when his know-how is misappropriated or obtained by unlawful means by a third party.

Civil remedies against unauthorized disclosure or misappropriation of trade secrets must be sought under the general tort provisions of the Civil Code. The basic tort principle is set out in Article 709 of the Civil Code as follows: "A person who, willfully or negligently, has injured the right of another is bound to compensate him for the damage which has arisen therefrom." If Article 709 is strictly interpreted, the injured party can recover damages from the wrongdoer only where he can prove that he has a right, and that this right was injured. But by a liberal interpretation, if the injured party can prove that he has an inviolable interest and this was injured by an illegal act, he can recover damages. The liberal theory suggests that "injury of right" should be interpreted to mean the existence of "illegality" in the defendant's act.[27] Thus, according to this theory, the owner of trade secrets can recover damages under Article 709 from a person who has misappropriated his trade secrets. However, there has been no court decision supporting this contention.

In certain types of torts, such as misappropriation of trade secrets, injunctive relief is more important than the recovery of damages, but there is no express provision in the tort chapter of the Civil Code to grant such remedy. One must look at Article 198 of the Civil Code, which provides that "If a possessor is disturbed in his possession, he may, in an action for maintenance of possession, demand discontinuance of the disturbance as well as reparation of damages." As a proper extension of this provision, an injunctive remedy may be granted when the claim is based on ownership or other exclusive rights. The basis for the remedy is considered to be the inviolability of the right in question, and thus the remedy is extendable to certain exclusive rights other than real rights.[28] Therefore, the probability of the courts applying Article 198 to cases involving trade secrets is low.

The holding of the Tokyo District Court and the foregoing discussion on the availability of the general tort principles to cases involving misappropriation of trade secrets lead us to conclude that the principal means for the protection of trade secrets is a contractual restriction on the use and disclosure of the trade secrets to apply to persons given access to them. The next question, then, is to what extent are such contractual restrictions enforceable. Stated simply, a contractual restriction is valid and enforceable unless it is contrary to public order, good morals, or a mandatory provision of the law, such as the Anti monopoly Law.

Only one case has touched upon the validity of a restrictive clause in an employment contract. Japanese companies in general adhere to the practice of lifetime employment and there is not much mobility of engineers and techni cians from one company to another. Under these conditions, trade secret litigations between companies and their former employees are less likely to occur. The validity or enforceability of a postemployment restriction had never been contested in the courts until *Yūgen Kaisha Forseco Japan, Ltd.* v. *Okuno and Daimatsu.*[29]

In this case, the claimant employer, Forseco Japan, is a joint-venture company established by Forseco International of Great Britain and Itō-chū, and other Japanese companies. The respondents, Okuno and Daimatsu, were employed by the claimant's predecessor, Yūgen Kaisha Foundry Services Japan Company in 1958. The claimant, to preserve the secrecy of various technical information concerning metal casting, asked the respondents to sign an agreement that contained the following provisions: (1) The respondents shall not disclose secret information they acquire in the course of their employment, during employment as well as after its termination; and (2) the respondents shall not, directly or indirectly, engage in any business in competition with the claimant for two years after the termination of the employment contract. The claimant paid a special secret duty allowance to all nonmanagerial employees in its research and development department including the respondents. In June 1969, the respondents left the claimant's employ almost simultaneously and became directors of a newly organized company. The claimant filed a petition for a temporary injunction against the respondents with the Nara District Court. The court found that the restriction was reasonable and did not violate public order and good morals and granted a temporary injunction. The court held as follows:

> The respondents contend that the special agreement in this case is exceedingly detrimental to them and threatens their livelihood and is therefore invalid as against public order and good morals. If the convenant not to compete exceeds its reasonable scope and unduly restrains the respondents' freedom of choosing an occupation and thereby threatens their livelihood, it is against public order and good morals, and therefore invalid.
>
> In order to determine the reasonableness of the restrictive convenant, the claimant's interest (protection of industrial secrets), the respondents' suffering (restriction on the freedom of changing occupation or employment), and the social interest (likelihood of monopoly and concentration and injury to the consuming public) must be weighed as to the period of restriction, the place of restriction, the field of business subject to restriction, compensation, etc.
>
> The period of restriction in the instant case is two years, which is relatively short. The field of business subject to restriction is the manufacture and sale of metal casting materials in which the claimant is engaged. Since the claimant's business is in the special area of the chemical and metalwork industry, the field of restriction is comparatively narrow. The place of restriction is unlimited. This may be considered necessary in view of the technical character of the claimant's trade secrets. Although the claimant does not pay compensation after employees under the covenant leave the claimant, the claimant pays special allowance for the secrecy obligation. Under such circumstances, the restriction on competition under the agreement in the instant case cannot be said to exceed its reasonable scope, and therefore the agreement is not invalid.

A number of statutes impose a confidential obligation upon certain persons according to their position or profession. Article 644 of the Civil Code provides the duty of diligence of a mandate as follows: "A mandatary is bound to manage the affairs entrusted to him with care of a good manager in accordance with the tenor of the mandate." The duty of diligence of a mandate should naturally include the confidential duty, but there has been no reported case. Article 254-3 of the Commercial Code provides for the duty of loyalty of corporate directors. This duty should also include the confidential duty. In addition, Article 264 of the Commercial Code provides the duty of corporate directors not to compete with their corporations. Article 134 of the Criminal Code punishes persons in certain professions who disclose their clients' or customers' secrets. These persons include doctors, pharmacists, druggists, midwives, lawyers, defense counsels, and notaries. Laws that regulate various professions contain similar provisions. For example, Article 23 of the Lawyers Law provides the confidential duty of attorneys.

For parties to technology transfer agreements, it is important to know whether or not a confidential duty can be imposed even in the absence of express statutory provisions. In *Toyota Concrete K.K.* v. *Director-General of the Patent Office*, the court, as a dictum, indicated the possibility of protecting trade secrets under the general principle of good faith.[30]

In this case, the plaintiff, Toyota Concrete, filed a patent application for a structural device for a prefabricated building. Before filing, the plaintiff entered into a research and development contract with the Japanese Public Housing Corporation under which the plaintiff agreed to construct an apartment house using the structural device under patent application. The plaintiff duly constructed a house, had this house tested by the research institute of the Ministry of Construction, furnished the data, and delivered the house, together with the title, to the Public Housing Corporation. The house had been occupied and used by the corporation's employees at the time of the plaintiff's filing.

However, the Patent Office refused the patent application on the grounds that the testing and experiment conducted by the plaintiff under the above contract constituted a public working of the invention before the patent application was filed, and that, even if this was not so, the use of the house after completion of testing amounted to a public working of the invention and, therefore, the plaintiff's invention had lost its novelty. The Tokyo High Court upheld the Patent Office's decision, holding that the Public Housing Corporation was under a secrecy obligation but that this obligation terminated when the apartment house was delivered by the plaintiff to the corporation. The court, *obiter*, indicated the possibility of protecting trade secrets under the general principle of good faith:

> In order to find that the plaintiff's invention was publicly known or publicly worked before a patent application was filed with the Patent Office, the corporation must have been under no obligation to maintain the secrecy of the plaintiff's invention.
>
> As the plaintiff asserts, the acquisition of knowledge of the invention by joint researchers, research assistants, or persons engaged in the testing after completion of the invention does not itself render the invention publicly known or publicly worked. This is because such *joint researchers are under an obligation, either based on a contract or on the principle of good faith deriving from their legal relationship with an assignee of the right to apply for a patent from the inventor, to maintain the secrecy of the invention.* [emphasis added] Such an obligation of secrecy is not forever, and it may terminate when a change occurs in the legal relationship between the joint researchers and the inventor.
>
> Under the principle of good faith, the plaintiff and the corporation are under a duty of mutual cooperation in order to achieve the purpose of the contract, even in the absence of a special agreement to that effect. Since there is no proof that the plaintiff has no intention to keep the invention secret, the corporation was under an obligation based on the principle of good faith to maintain the secrecy of the invention.
>
> In the instant case, the purpose of the contract was fulfilled when the plaintiff furnished all the data it obtained from the experiment and testing, and delivered the house together with title to it to the corporation, and thereupon the duty of

cooperation under the principle of good faith between the corporation and the plaintiff was terminated.

In a civil litigation, a witness is excused from testifying on matters involving trade secrets under Article 281 (1) of the Code of Civil Procedure, which provides that "a witness may refuse to testify in the following circumstances: . . . (iii) when he is asked to testify on matters of technical or professional secrecy." In *United States* v. *Matsumura*,[31] the Osaka High Court, under Article 281 (1) of the Code of Civil Procedure, upheld the decision of the Osaka District Court, which dismissed a petition filed by the United States to take testimony from an employee of a Japanese company that owed a duty of secrecy to its American licensor. In this case, the respondent was a director and the manager in charge of electronic tubes of Matsushita Electronic Industries K.K., a joint-venture company organized by Matsushita Electric Industries K.K. and Phillips. The United States petitioned the Osaka District Court to take testimony of the respondent concerning the labor and sales costs of certain electronic tubes for receiving sets for a case pending before the United States Customs Court, *Mitsui & Company* v. *United States*.

The Tokyo High Court's recognition of the property value of know-how in the Deutsche Werft case is in accord with the courts' acceptance of know-how as property and a proper subject of a contribution in kind in exchange for shares of stock when a corporation is organized.[32] As mentioned with respect to patents, transfer of know-how to a newly organized corporation as a contribution in kind can be made only by promoters and the particulars must be stated in the articles of incorporation under Article 168 of the Commercial Code. A court-appointed inspector will examine the transfer of know-how and report to the court in accordance with Article 173 of the Commercial Code.

In licensing transactions, know-how can be assimilated to patents in many respects. Know-how is licensed either on an exclusive or nonexclusive basis and the consideration for it usually stipulated in terms of royalty. Therefore, know-how licenses are treated like patent licenses under the application of the Antimonopoly Law. The Antimonopoly Act Guidelines for International Licensing Agreements published by the Fair Trade Commission in 1968 states in item 2 that "the aforementioned guidelines shall apply to international know-how licensing agreements." It should be borne in mind, however, that the guidelines concerning patent licensing agreements are not always applicable to know-how licenses because of their different legal nature. Indeed, some fundamental questions regarding know-how licenses are left unanswered by the guidelines.

LEGAL PROTECTION OF COMPUTER SOFTWARE: A REVIEW OF RECENT DEVELOPMENTS

One of the hotly debated topics in the area of intellectual property law at present is the legal protection of computer software. While possibilities of various forms of protection had been discussed quite extensively in the past,[33] it is only recently that copyright protection has become a serious concern and the possibility of such protection has been confirmed by the courts in Japan, the United States, and other countries. Copyright protection has recently become the basis for the licensing of computer programs, however, licensing practices have not been firmly established in Japan in the software industry. It is, therefore, more appropriate to review the recent development in the direction of copyright protection rather than focusing our attention on transactions.

The World Intellectual Property Organization (WIPO) convened, from June 13 to 17, 1983, the second session of the Committee of Experts of the Paris Union on the Legal Protection of Computer Software at its headquarters in Geneva. Thirty nations including Japan and the United States were represented at the conference. The Committee of Experts discussed the substantive provisions of the Draft Treaty for the Protection of Computer Software prepared and presented to the Committee by the International Bureau.[34]

After lengthy deliberation, the committee considered that it was "premature to take, for the time being, a stand on the question of the best form for the international protection of computer software," and recommended that "the consideration of the conclusion of a special treaty as presented to it should not be pursued for the time being." In reaching this conclusion, the committee recorded that

The Committee took note of the information given at the meeting on *the increasing trend at the national level in a certain number of countries of granting protection under copyright law to computer software*. It noted that this situation could have—thanks to the national treatment—the consequence that the need for international protection may, between such countries, be satisfied to a considerable extent by means of the international copyright conventions. The Committee also noted that WIPO, jointly with UNESCO, suggests undertaking a study and convening a committee of governmental experts on the protection available for computer software under existing copyright laws and treaties.[35] [emphasis added]

Both Japan and the United States are among a "certain number of countries granting protection under copyright law to computer software." The Japanese delegation presented information on two committees set up by the Japanese government, one in the Ministry of International Trade and Industry and another in the Copyright Council of the Cultural Affairs Agency, to study the problem; in addition, the delegation stated that "two court decisions were rendered concerning the protection of software under copyright law." The U.S. delegation concluded that the program "was not considered to be patentable, but could only be protected under the copyright law" and that a "recent amendment of the United States Copyright Act had removed any possible remaining doubt in that respect."[36]

Before discussing the recent development in Japan, it may be appropriate to explain briefly the substantive provisions of the draft treaty. The term "computer software" is used to include "computer program," "program description," and "supporting material," all of which are defined in Article 1. Article 3 sets forth the principle of national treatment. The fundamental principles of protection are provided under Article 4(1) (Protection Against Unlawful Acts) providing that

> the Contracting States undertake to grant protection to computer software against the following acts:
>
> (i) disclosing the computer software or facilitating its disclosure to any person before it is made accessible to the public with the consent of the proprietor;
>
> (ii) allowing or facilitating access by any person to any object storing or reproducing the computer software, before the computer software is made accessible to the public with the consent of the proprietor;
>
> (iii) copying by any means or in any form the computer software;
>
> (iv) using the computer program to produce the same or a substantially similar computer program or a program description of the computer program or of a substantially similar computer program;
>
> (v) using the program description to produce the same or a substantially similar program description or to produce a corresponding computer program;
>
> (vi) using the computer program or a computer program produced as described in (iii), (iv) or (v) to control the operation of a machine having information-processing capabilities, or storing it in such a machine;
>
> (vii) offering or stocking for the purpose of sale, hire or license, selling, importing, exporting, leasing or licensing the computer software or computer software produced as described in (iii), (iv) or (v);
>
> (viii) doing any of the acts described in (vii) in respect of objects storing or reproducing the computer software or computer software produced as described in (iii), (iv) or (v).

It should be noted that the Draft Treaty Article 4 (iii) and (iv) grant protection against unauthorized copying and, therefore, these provisions take a copyright approach. Article 4 (i) and (ii) grant protection against unauthorized disclosure, that is, trade secret protection.

In the United States, the 1980 amendment to the Copyright Act of 1976 (17 U.S.C. § 101 et seq.) added a broad definition of "computer programs" to § 101[37] and, thus, it was made clear by legislation that "computer programs" were eligible for copyright under § 102 (a), which provided that "copyright protection subsists, in accordance with this title, in original works of authorship fixed in any tangible medium of expression, now known or later developed, from which they can be perceived, reproduced, or otherwise communicated, either directly or with the aid of a machine or device."

One question raised regarding the Copyright Act of the United States is whether or not an object code program stored in a ROM (read-only memory) is a "copy" of the original program as the term is used in § 106 of the Copyright Act, which provides that the copyright owner's exclusive right extends to the reproduction of the copyrighted work in "copies."[38] However, this question has been answered in a series of consistent court decisions,[39] including the appellate decision that reversed the district court decision that first brought it into question.[40]

In many countries, of which Japan is no exception, manufacturers of amusement machines and personal computers are vigorously fighting the unauthorized copying of computer programs. Several cases are pending before the courts; three have been decided. To illustrate the status of computer programs and the extent of their protection under the Japanese Copyright Law (Law no. 48, 1970), we will examine each case in more detail below.

The first case is *Taitō K.K.* v. *K.K. ING Enterprises*,[41] in which the Tokyo District Court expressly held that the computer program of a video game was a work of authorship under the Copyright Law and the object code program stored in ROM was its reproduction, and, therefore, the copying of the object code program into another ROM was an act of reproduction. In this case, the defendant converted its customers' video game machines into the plaintiff's Space Invader Part II machines. In the conversion, the defendant first removed the printed circuit board from each machine, and then stored the plaintiff's object code program into the ROMs attached to or newly added to the printed circuit board. The plaintiff brought an action in the court for damages against the defendant, alleging that the computer program of the video game was a work of authorship and that the object code program, which was a conversion of the program's assembly language version into a machine-readable language version, was a reproduction of the program, and that the defendant's act of storing the plaintiff's object code program into the ROMs attached to the defendant's customers' video game machines constituted a reproduction of the original program and, therefore, the defendant infringed upon the plaintiff's right of protection against unlawful reproduction.

The court first recognized that the plaintiff's program was a work of authorship under the Copyright Law. It observed that

> The plaintiff's program is designed to display the contents of the game on the cathode ray tube of the plaintiff's machine. It was made after analyzing diversified problems and finding their solutions to accomplish the above purpose, and is based upon the flow chart prepared in accordance with the solutions thus discovered. It is an expression of a series of instructions in combination with other information in the assembly language that can be communicated to third parties having expertise.
>
> The discovery of solutions and combination of instructions naturally requires logical thinking by the creator, and, therefore, the program as finally completed reflects the creator's individual characteristics, which are different from other programmers'. The plaintiff's program is a creative expression of the scientific thoughts of the creator. It is a work of authorship that is entitled to protection under the Copyright Law.

The court then ruled that

> "the plaintiff's object code program is a reproduction of the original program, and the act of Denshō Services K.K., not a party to this litigation, of storing the plaintiff's object code program into other ROMs constitutes creation of another reproduction of the plaintiff's program, and is therefore a reproduction in a tangible form of the plaintiff's program, which is a work of authorship."

Article 2 (1) of the Copyright Law defines "works of authorship" as "production in which thoughts or emotions are expressed in a creative way and which fall in the literary, scientific, artistic or musical domain." The word "*fukusei*" (meaning reproduction) is defined in Article 2 (1)(xv) as "to reproduce [*saisei*] in a tangible form by means of printing, photography, copying [*fukusha*], sound recording, visual recording or other method." Under this broad definition of "reproduction," one can easily conclude, as the Tokyo District Court did in the Taitō case, that when a computer program is embodied in a ROM, the ROM is a reproduction of the program and copying of the ROM into another ROM is another reproduction. The same is true when a computer program is embodied on a magnetic tape or floppy disk.

The second case, *Taitō K.K.* v. *Makoto Denshikōgyō K.K.*,[42] was decided by the Yokohama District Court. In this case the plaintiff's video game was Space Invader. The defendant manufactured and sold a counterfeit video game called Super Invader. The plaintiff brought an action for damages against the defendant claiming that the defendant's manufacture and sale of a counterfeit video game constituted an act of unfair competition as well as infringement of the plaintiff's copyright in the original drawings of the images, as works of art, and in the software program of the game. The court granted damages on the ground of copyright infringement of the plaintiff's software program.

The court ruling applied only to the plaintiff's claim of copyright infringement in its computer software. The court first determined that the plaintiff's program was a creative expression of the programmer's thoughts that fell under the scientific domain and was a work of authorship entitled to protection under the Copyright Law. The court, in discussing how the plaintiff's program was made, found that the object code program was a copy of the original program. Therefore, the defendant's act of storing the plaintiff's object code program in ROMs, after changing the names of both the game and manufacturer, was reproduction, in a tangible form, of the plaintiff's original program.

In the third case, *Konami Kōgyō K.K.* v. *K.K. Daiwa*,[43] the plaintiff's video game, Strategy X, was counterfeited by the defendant who manufactured and sold printed circuit boards of a video game called Strong X. The plaintiff brought an action for an injunction and damages against the defendant on the grounds of copyright infringement and unfair competition. The plaintiff asserted its right of copyright in both the computer program of its video game and in the images of the game as a cinematographic work. The court granted an injunction and damages on the basis of copyright infringement of the computer program of the plaintiff's video game. The court held that the plaintiff's computer program was a work of authorship in the scientific domain and the object code program stored in the ROM attached to the printed circuit board of the plaintiff's game was its reproduction, and that the defendant's act of copying the object code program from the plaintiff's ROMs into other ROMs with the aid of an ROM writer was a reproduction that infringed upon the copyright of the plaintiff's computer program.

As demonstrated in the Konami Kōgyō case above, in a copyright infringement action involving a counterfeit video game, the plaintiff may also assert copyright in his video game as a cinematographic work. Article 2 (3) of the Copyright Law provides that "cinematographic works" (*eiga no chosakubutsu*) include "works expressed by a process of producing visual or audiovisual effects analogous to those of cinematography and fixed in a tangible form." The Copyright Law adopted this broad definition to include any new works that could be assimilated to motion pictures. When a video game is played, it produces a series of moving images on the picture tube. These images come out of a prefixed program. In every moment of game playing, the player is simply selecting one of the limited number of prefixed images.

In the recent case of *K.K. Namco v. Suishinkōgyō et al.*,[44] the court held, for the first time, that the video game Pacman was a cinematographic work under Article 2 (3) of the Copyright Law. The defendants who placed counterfeit Pacman video game machines in their coffeeshops for customers' use, therefore, were liable for infringing upon the plaintiff's right to publicly present a cinematographic work under Article 26.

As can be seen in the above case, when a video game is regarded as a cinematographic work, a broader protection can be sought. For example, the manufacturer of an arcade game can claim copyright infringement against the manufacturer of a hand-held game based on the original arcade game. On May 24, 1982, K.K. Namco filed suit at the Tokyo District Court claiming copyright infringement against K.K. Bandai who manufactured and sold a hand-held game, Pakkuri Monster, alleging that Bandai infringed upon Namco's reproduction right in its Pacman game.[45]

When a video game designed for professional use becomes very popular, the manufacturer may find that a home or personal use version is being manufactured and sold by a third party, as in the above case. Such a version will be regarded as a reproduction of the cinematographic work of the original game if there exists substantial similarity in the form of expression in the display between the two. But it may also be regarded as a derivative work, transformation, or adaptation of the original game under Article 27 of the Copyright Law. Article 27 provides that "the author shall exclusively have the right to translate [*honyaku*], arrange musically [*henkyoku*], transform [*henkei*], dramatize [*kyakushoku*], cinematize [*eigaka*], or otherwise adapt [*hon'an*] his work."

Furthermore, when a video game becomes very popular and is expected to be in use for a much longer than expected period, the proprietors of game parlors may wish to make the game more attractive and challenging by attaching a small printed circuit board called an "enhancement kit" or "speed-up kit" to the original printed circuit board. Such an enhancement kit can be regarded as a derivative work. An unauthorized manufacture of an enhancement kit can be enjoined as infringing upon the right to create a derivative work. But it can also be enjoined as infringing upon the author's moral right, because it distorts the original cinematographic work. The author of the original game may claim that his moral right, that is, the right to the integrity of his work, has been infringed.

Article 21 (1) of the Copyright Law provides that "the author shall have the right to preserve the integrity of his work and its title against any distortion, mutilation, or other modification against his will."

The subcommittee on computer problems of the Copyright Council, an advisory committee to the Cultural Affairs Agency, concluded in a report in 1973 that computer programs were works of authorship entitled to copyright protection.[46] No actions had been brought before courts, however, until video game manufacturers first filed suits against manufacturers of counterfeit games. The video game industry, in a sense, represents the entire software industry in their efforts to secure legal protection for their intellectual creations.

The Copyright Law seems to assure sufficient protection against unauthorized reproduction of a computer program, whether embodied in a ROM or a floppy disk. Nonetheless, MITI disclosed its plan to submit a bill entitled the Program Right Law to the Diet, in accordance with the recommendation made by the Information Industry Committee of the Industrial Structure Council. In an interim report on the legal protection of computer software submitted on December 9, 1983, the committee recommended enactment of a special statute tentatively called the Program Right Law, under which the proprietors of computer programs are to be granted exclusive right to use, reproduce, and lend computer programs for a limited period of fifteen years and a compulsory license to reproduce a computer program is to be granted by arbitration when it is necessary for public interest or when it is not properly worked.[47]

On the other hand, subcommittee 6 of the Copyright Council submitted an interim report to the council on computer software on January 19, 1984. This report recommended a revision of the Copyright Law to make it more suitable for the protection of computer programs, including a definition of what a computer program constitutes. The Cultural Affairs Agency also planned to submit a bill for revision of the Copyright Law along with this recommendation.

Due to the conflict between these two plans, a settlement must be reached between MITI and the Cultural Affairs Agency before any bill is submitted to the Diet for enactment. This did not take place during the past session of the Diet ending in June 1984. In addition, the proposed Program Right Law had to be reexamined in light of existing copyright conventions, to avoid any conflicts with the latter.

However, in March 1985, an agreement was reached between MITI and the Cultural Affairs Agency under which MITI would withdraw its plan to enact the Program Right Law and support copyright protection of computer programs instead. It seems that MITI was influenced by the world trend for copyright protection as confirmed by the group of experts on the Copyright Aspects of the Protection of Computer Software convened at the WIPO Headquarters, Geneva, from February 25 to March 1, 1985.[48] Accordingly, the Cultural Affairs Agency presented a bill for the partial amendment of the Copyright Law to the 102nd Session of the Diet and the bill was passed by the Houses of Representatives and Councillors on May 23 and June 7, 1985, respectively. The amendment will become effective from January 1, 1986. The gist of the amendment is as follows:

First, the word *puroguramu* (computer program) is defined as "an expression of combined instructions given to a computer so as to make it function and obtain a certain result" (Art. 1 (1)(xbis)). Second, *puroguramu no chosakubutsu* (program work) is added to the list of works of authorship (Art. 10 (1)(ix)). Third, a new provision is added to Article 10 as para. (3) which provides

> The protection granted by this Law to works mentioned in para. (1), item (ix) shall not extend to any programming language, rule or algorithm used for making such works. In this case, the following terms shall have the meaning hereby assigned to them respectively:
>
> (i) 'programming language' (*puroguramu gengo*) means letters and other symbols as well as their systems for use as means of expressing a program;
>
> (ii) 'rule' (*kiyaku*) means a special rule on how to use in a given program a programming language mentioned in the preceding item;
>
> (iii) 'algorithm' (*kaihō*) means methods of combining, in a program, instructions given to a computer.

Fourth, a new provision is added to Article 15 as para. (2), which provides that "The authorship of a program work that, at the initiative of a legal person, etc., is made by its employee in the course of his duties, shall be attributed to that legal persons, etc., unless otherwise stipulated in a contract, work regulation or the like in force at the time of the making of the work."

Fifth, the following provision is added as item (iii) to Article 20 (2) that provides for exceptions to an author's right to the integrity of his work under Article 20 (1): "Modifications necessary for enabling the use in a given computer of a program work that is otherwise unusable in that computer, or to make more effective the use of the program work in a computer."

Sixth, the following provision is newly inserted as Article 47-2 to provide exceptions to an author's exclusive right of reproduction or adaptation: "The owner of a copy of a program work may reproduce or adapt (including reproduction of a derivative work created by adaptation) of that work to the extent deemed necessary for using that work in a computer by himself."

Seventh, Article 76-2 is newly added to register the date of creation of computer programs. When the date of creation of a given computer program is registered, the registration creates only a presumption that the program was created on that date.

Eighth, a new paragraph is added to Article 113 to provide that "An act of using in a computer, in the conduct of business, of a copy made in infringement of the copyright in a program work . . . is deemed to be an act of infringement of that copyright only where the actor was in bad faith when he acquired the title to use the copy."

Because of the establishment of a public lending right by the 1984 amendment of the copyright,[49] the copyright owners of computer programs are now able to control unauthorized public lending of computer programs.

It must be added that the 102nd Session of the Diet enacted in May 1985 a law submitted by MITI concerning circuit layouts of semiconductor integrated circuits. This law is designed to protect circuit layouts of semiconductor integrated circuits against unauthorized production, assignment, lending, displaying for the purpose of assignment or lending, or importation of objects to be used for copying the circuit layouts. A circuit layout right is established upon registration for a period of ten years. The enactment of this law has made an important question moot. This question is whether or not the proprietor of a semiconductor chip product in Japan is entitled to protection under the newly enacted Semiconductor Chip Protection Act of the United States availing himself of either the national treatment of the Universal Copyright Convention or the broad protection against unfair competition under Article 10bis of the Paris Convention.[50]

CHARACTER MERCHANDISING: ITS LEGAL BASIS

Fictional characters acquire good will and a power to attract customers when publicized in newspapers, magazines, radio, television, and other media. Hence, well-known fictional characters are extensively licensed to the manufacturers of various consumer goods such as books, toys, greeting cards, underwear, shoes, school utensils, cakes, and candies. In this case, manufacturers intend primarily to use the good will of the licensed characters rather than their ornamental value.

Fictional characters, particularly those of American origin, are licensed to such manufacturers in Japan directly or through local representatives. In addition to fictional characters, the names and likenesses of world-famous designers, actors, singers, and other figures are licensed to various manufacturers for the same purpose. The names, acronyms, and symbols of foreign sports teams and nonprofit organizations are likewise licensed, even though the legal basis is not entirely clear. It is apparent that Japan is a great market for American licensors.

Since extensive merchandising activities began in Japan in the mid-1960s, there have been interesting developments in cases involving fictional characters, including cases that present a conflict between copyright and trademark protections. A recent case awarded damages to a well-known actor against a company who used his name and likeness in a television advertising film. These cases are very important to the merchandising industry because they help clarify the legal basis for merchandising activities and develop preventive measures against counterfeit goods in an industry.[51]

The legal basis for the licensing of merchandising rights in fictional characters is found in the Copyright Law. Fictional characters of comic strips are regarded as works of art under Article 10 (1),[52] which lists various types of works of authorship entitled to copyright protection. The exclusive right of the copyright owner of fictional characters includes the right of reproduction under Article 21, as well as the right to create derivative works under Article 27. Article 21 provides that "the author shall exclusively have the right to reproduce his work," and Article 27 provides that "the author shall exclusively have the right to translate, arrange musically, transform, dramatize, cinematize, or otherwise adapt his work."

The practice of licensing merchandising rights preceded the court's recognition of its legal basis. The first leading case in *Machiko Hasegawa* v. *Tachikawa Bus K.K.*[53] In this case, the court properly found that the defendant, who reproduced the plaintiff's comic characters on the bodies of sightseeing coaches it operated, infringed upon the plaintiff's copyright. The court calculated damages on the basis of the plaintiff's loss of profit, which was determined as 3 percent of the revenue accruing from the operation of the defendant's sightseeing coaches, a rate considered by the court to be in wide use in merchandising rights licensing. Although the defendant used the plaintiff's comic characters as a service mark to identify the defendant's business, the court did not distinguish such use from ordinary ornamental uses on goods for sale.

When a fictional character originally drawn on a piece of paper is used for three-dimensional goods such as toys, the use may not be regarded as a reproduction of the original work. In such a case, Article 27 of the Copyright Law mentioned above should be applied. In *K.K. Fuji Television* v. *K.K. Sapporo Dolls*,[54] the plaintiff was the owner of copyright by assignment in the drawing of a *taiyaki* cake in a human form created by an artist. This drawing was widely shown on the plaintiff's television broadcast. The defendant manufactured and sold dolls based on this drawing. In an action for copyright infringement, the court found that the defendant's dolls were transformations of the plaintiff's drawing under Article 27 and, therefore, these dolls infringed upon the plaintiff's copyright in the drawing.

The Copyright Law provides for civil remedies as well as penal sanctions against copyright infringement.[55] When the amount of damages is very small, which is often the case, criminal prosecution serves as a more effective deterrent against possible copyright infringement. The first reported case in the character merchandising field applying the penal provisions of the Copyright Law was *State* v. *Gen Kondō*.[56] In this case, the defendant manufactured and sold children's T-shirts on which the comic character of "Candy" was reproduced from the television animation film "Candy-Candy," the copyright of which was owned jointly by the film producer, Tōei Animation Company, and the artist who created it. The Tōei Animation Company filed a complaint with the district prosecutor's office and the defendant was prosecuted and tried before the Osaka District Court. The court sentenced the defendant to two years of penal servitude with hard labor, which was suspended for three years. For the first time, the court recognized the status of the producer of an animation film to be the author of a derivative work, as distinguished from the author of the original comic strip.

Character licensors often require licensees to attach seals of approval to the goods manufactured under the license to distinguish these goods from non-licensed goods. Although it is not unusual for licensors to find infringing goods bearing counterfeit seals, counterfeit seals can be suppressed on the grounds of trademark infringement or unfair competition. In addition, the manufacturer of a counterfeit seal can be prosecuted for document forgery under the Criminal Code, if the seal bears a certain statement of facts—for example, a statement to the effect that "this is a certificate of the grant of a license." Licensors may even find that genuine seals of approval are sold by their licensees to third parties. Such conduct must be strictly forbidden through licensing agreements.

Since the Trademark Law of Japan (Law no. 127, 1959) does not require actual use of a trademark for its registration, but rather, is granted to the first applicant, the copyright owner of a fictional character and his licensees may encounter a situation in which a third party obtains a trademark registration for the character and sues the licensees on the basis of trademark infringement. As a result, the copyright owner should make every effort to watch applications for trademark registration and take necessary measures to prevent trademark registration by an unauthorized third party.

Article 4 of the Trademark Law lists various circumstances under which trademarks will not qualify for registration even though they meet the requirement of distinctiveness under Article 3.[57] Under Article 4, public interest, private interest, or the interest of the consuming public may be invoked as grounds for preventing registration of a particular trademark. Unfortunately, Article 4 does not extend to the situation where a trademark under application will infringe upon the copyright of another, when it is used on goods.

In *In re Walt Disney Productions*,[58] the Patent Office dismissed a petition filed by Walt Disney Productions to invalidate the registration of a trademark consisting of a combination of the words "Micky Mouse" (the "e" is lacking) and a drawing of a black mouse. The petitioner stated the grounds for its petition as follows: "An unauthorized use of a trademark of a work of another which is entitled to copyright protection under Japanese law not only constitutes copyright infringement or tort but also an act which is subject to criminal punishment. If the trademark registration were to be held valid, the antisocial criminal conduct and tortious act of the registrant would fully enjoy an exclusive right, and thereby violate public order and good morals."

The petitioner relied on Article 2 (1)(iv) of the old Trademark Law, similar to Article 4 (1)(vii) of the present Trademark Law,[59] which made a trademark contrary to public order or good morals unregisterable. The Patent Office dismissed the petition on the grounds that "even though the use of the registered trademark conflicts with the copyright owned by the petitioner, there is no likelihood that it will disturb public order or good morals to the extent that necessitates invalidation of its registration, although its use may be restricted."

The Patent Office should have interpreted the public order provision more broadly to prevent the registration of trademarks that misappropriated fictional characters. The trademark examination standards compiled by the Patent Office[60] suggest such a possibility. The examination standards interpret Article 4 (1)(vii) of the Trademark Law to disqualify for registration "a trademark the use of which is prohibited by other laws, a trademark which is defamatory to a specific country or its nationals, and *a trademark which is contrary to international good faith*" (emphasis added).[61]

Mickey Mouse was not the only victim of the trademark registration system. Osaka Sankei K.K. registered a trademark that consisted of an English word, "Popeye," and Popeye's standing figure in a sailor's outfit, for clothing, handkerchiefs, buttons, and pins. In *Osaka Sankei K.K.* v. *Ox K.K.*,[62] the registrant brought a trademark infringement action against the manufacturer of children's undershirts that bore, under a license from the copyright owner, the word "Popeye" and Popeye's character in sailor's uniform as well as the copyright notice "© King Features Syndicate." The defendant asserted noninfringement on two grounds.

First, the defendant contended that its use of Popeye's comic figure together with its name on the undershirts was simply an ornamental use and not use as a trademark, and that the defendant's own trademark was indicated on a tag attached to the neck portion of each shirt. Second, the defendant asserted that its shirts were made of cloth manufactured under a license granted by the copyright owner and hence the defendant's act was an exercise of copyright that superseded the plaintiff's registered trademark under Article 29 of the Trademark Law. Article 29 provides that "the owner of a registered trademark or his exclusive or nonexclusive licensee cannot use his trademark when it conflicts with a design of another person registered under an application filed before the filing of an application by the trademark owner, or when it conflicts with the copyright of another person created before the filing of an application by the trademark owner." The court dismissed the action on the first ground, and did not rule on the second defense. It was rather a disappointment to copyright defenders.

In a recent case, *Osaka Sankei K.K.* v. *Kawamura Shōji K.K.*,[63] however, the court recognized the defendant's defense of prior copyright in Popeye's character under Article 29 and dismissed the same plaintiff's claim of trademark infringement.

The names and likenesses of well-known public figures play the same function of attracting customers as fictional characters do when they are displayed on consumer goods or used in advertising. The licensing of the name and likeness of a well-known personality for merchandising purposes is based on the assumption that such a person has an exclusive right to use his name and likeness for economic gain and can legally enjoin unauthorized use of his name or likeness by a second party.

In the United States, this right of well-known personalities is recognized under common law. It is called the "right of publicity" as opposed to the "right of privacy" of ordinary citizens.[64] Although the commercial practice of licensing the names and likenesses of well-known personalities long preceded the court's recognition of its legal basis in Japan, the landmark case that first recognized the right of publicity was *Mark Lester et al.* v. *Tokyo Daiichi Film K.K.*,[65] decided in 1976.

In the Mark Lester case, the defendant took a still picture from a film entitled *Eyewitness* and used it for a combined television advertisement of the film and the sponsor's candy. Mark Lester was then a well-known British child film actor.

The still picture showed Mark Lester's face and the upper half of his body. Mark Lester brought an action for damages against the defendant under the general tort provision of the Civil Code, Article 709. The court held that the plaintiff, as an actor, had an economic interest in his name and portrait independent of a moral interest and, therefore, the plaintiff was entitled to damages for his lost earnings as well as for his mental suffering. The damages were calculated on the basis of the remuneration Mark Lester usually received when he performed for an advertising film.

This case is an important contribution to the development of Japanese intellectual property law, because the court recognized the right of publicity for the first time, although it did not use this term. The court's reasoning seems to have been influenced by American common law. Previously, in *Arita* v. *Yukio Mishima*,[66] the same court recognized the right of privacy and added this English term (*puraibashi-ken*) to the Japanese legal glossary. The term *paburishiti-ken* (right of publicity) should likewise be added to the Japanese legal glossary.

In a more recent case, *Steve McQueen* v. *Tōhōtōwa K.K.*,[67] Steve McQueen sued the makers of a television commercial advertising both a film entitled *LeMans* and the products of the sponsor simultaneously. In this case, the court found that such a joint advertising scheme was within the permissible scope of the film distribution contract and dismissed the plaintiff's action.

The name, acronym, or symbol mark of a sports team or nonprofit organization such as a university can be licensed for ornamental use on consumer goods such as shirts, although copyright protection does not extend to it, nor is it registered as a trademark or design. A problem arises when someone without a license uses the name, acronym, or mark on his goods to appropriate the good will associated with it. One possibility of enjoining such an unauthorized use is to invoke Article 1 (1)(i) or (ii) of the Unfair Competition Prevention Law (Law no. 14, 1934). Article 1 (1) lists six types of unfair competition and provides that a person whose business interest is likely to be injured by any one of these acts may sue for an injunction. The list includes: one, use of a name, symbol, and so forth, which is similar to a well-known name, symbol, and so forth, of another and likely to cause confusion as to the source of goods; and two, use of a name, symbol, and so forth, that is similar to a well-known name, symbol, and so forth, and likely to cause confusion as to business establishment or activities. Article 1-2 provides for the recovery of damages.

In *National Football League Properties and Sony Kigyō K.K.* v. *Marutake Shōji K.K.*,[68] the court granted an injunction and damges under Article 1 (1)(i) and (ii) and Article 1-2 of the Unfair Competition Prevention Law. The claimant in this case, National Football League Properties, Inc. (NFLP), is a California corporation engaged in licensing the merchandising rights of the symbol marks of each member football team (club) of the National Football League (NFL) to various manufacturers. NFLP granted an exclusive license to the other claimant, Sony Kigyō, to operate a business merchandising the NFL's symbol and to grant sublicenses to various manufacturers in Japan. NFLP and Sony Kigyō jointly filed a petition with the Osaka District Court for a temporary injunction against the respondent, who had been using the NFL's symbol on its portable wardrobes. The court, in granting the remedies sought by the claimants, broadly interpreted Article 1 (1)(i) and (ii) to cover a situation where the NFL's symbol had become well known as indicating the goods of these manufacturers and their business of merchandising. In a formal action for an injunction and damages brought jointly by NFLP and Sony Kigyō against Marutake Shōji, the same court rendered a judgment for the plaintiffs on the same ground.[69]

This case should be compared with *K.K. Poppy* v. *K.K. Nakai Shōten*[70] in which the Tokyo District Court held that the characters embodied in the plaintiff's goods were not indications well known in Japan as identifying the plaintiff's goods because the characters in question were licensed by the copyright owner to a number of manufacturers.

THE FRANCHISING BUSINESS: ITS LEGAL BASIS AND STRUCTURE

Franchising involves a licensing of the franchisor's trademarks, service marks, or other trade symbols. In view of the expansion of American franchisors' activities into the Japanese market, it is appropriate to discuss the legal basis and structure of the franchising business in Japan.[71] According to a survey conducted by the Department of Commerce, Japan ranks second behind Canada in the number of franchising outlets established by American franchisors.[72] The Department of Commerce points out that "Japan continues to be the second-largest market for U.S. franchisors with a total of 3,999 units of which 73 percent represent various food categories such as restaurants, doughnut shops, ice cream stores, and convenience food stores."[73]

The United States Department of Commerce, in its survey of franchising businesses, reported that "Expansion into foreign markets by U.S. franchisors continues as these markets exhibit an active and persistent demand for a variety of consumer goods and services. The growth of modern communication networks and improved transportation networks have helped to narrow the gap in consumer tastes around the world and have made distant neighbors more aware of American-style franchising."[74] American franchisors who wish to engage in franchising in foreign markets must comply with the laws and regulations of the host countries. The Department of Commerce stated that "Franchisors must comply with the same local requirements as domestic businesses and the franchise agreements must comply with local contract laws, antitrust laws, and trademark licensing laws. There are no national laws restricting franchising per se. However, other laws and regulations governing international business transactions apply which could inhibit franchising activities."[75]

The forms of entry of foreign franchisors into Japan vary greatly,[76] but the essential element remains the same: the licensing of trademarks, service marks, or other trade symbols and the accompanying control of the quality of goods or services offered to the public by franchisees.[77] When a franchise contract accompanies a license of the franchisor's registered trademark, the relevant provisions of the Trademark Law are applicable. These include provisions concerning recordation of licenses and cancellation of a trademark registration for lack of proper control over licensees.

It must be noted that service marks do not qualify for registration as such under the Trademark Law. The word "trademark" (shōhyō) is defined by Article 2 (1) as "characters, letters, figures, or signs, or any combination of these and colors which a person who, as a business, produces, processes, certifies, or assigns goods, uses on such goods." Hence, "trademark" under the Trademark Law does not include service marks, trade names, configurations of goods, or sounds. Service marks, trade names, configurations of goods, or other symbols may be protected under the Unfair Competition Prevention Law when requirements are met, however, even though they are not registered as trademarks.

The definition of trademark must be read with Article 3 (1), which provides that "trademark registration may be obtained for any trademark to be used for goods relating to one's own business." Under Article 3 (1), proof of use is not necessary for an applicant to register a trademark. Thus, anything that qualifies as "a distinctive quality" can be a trademark even though it has not been actually used. However, a trademark must be used after its registration to avoid cancellation of the registration for nonuse[78] or to secure a renewal of the registration.[79]

Exclusive right to use a trademark is established when it is registered under Article 18 (1), which provides that a trademark right (shōhyōken) comes into existence by registration of its establishment. The duration of a trademark right is ten years from the date of the registration of its establishment under Article 19 (1).

To discuss the legal aspect of franchising, it is necessary to explain the provisions of the Trademark Law concerning licenses in more detail. Under the Trademark Law, trademarks are regarded as property distinct from the business or good will associated with them. Trademarks can be assigned without involving the transfer of any business associated with the mark, and can be subject to an exclusive or nonexclusive license. Trademarks can be co-owned or pledged.

Trademarks can be licensed on either an exclusive or nonexclusive basis. Under the Trademark Law, an exclusive license is called senyōshiyōken and a nonexclusive license is called tsūjōshiyōken. These literally mean "an exclusive right to use" and "an ordinary right to use," respectively. The grant of an exclusive license is called senyōshiyōken no settei (establishment of an exclusive right to use), whereas a grant of nonexclusive license is called tsūjōshiyōken no kyodaku (grant of an ordinary right to use).

Article 30 of the Trademark Law provides that "a trademark right owner can establish senyōshiyōken with respect to his trademark right," and makes Article 98 (1)(ii)[80] of the Patent Law applicable mutatis mutandis to an exclusive license of a trademark. Article 31 provides that "a trademark right owner can grant tsūjōshiyōken to other persons with respect to his trademark right," and makes Article 99[81] of the Patent Law applicable mutatis mutandis to a nonexclusive license of a trademark.

These provisions of the Patent Law deal with the effect of the recordation of licenses on the Patent Office registry and have been discussed above. Recordation of an exclusive license enables the licensee to assert his exclusive right to use the licensed trademark against third parties, whereas recordation of a nonexclusive right to use the licensed trademark against subsequent assignee or exclusive licensee of the licensed trademark.

In a franchise system, it is essential for the franchisor to supervise and control the quality of goods and services offered to the public by his franchisees to assure that a trademark or service mark used by his franchisees consistently represents the standard of quality set by him. For this purpose, it is necessary for the franchisor to insert a proper provision in each franchise agreement to enable him to exercise such supervision and control. Lack of control will lead a franchise system to collapse, although the legal sanction against failure to exercise quality control is not severe.

Under the Trademark Law, lack of quality control in a trademark license creates only the risk of registration cancellation. Article 53 of the Trademark Law provides in effect that if an exclusive or nonexclusive licensee uses the licensed registered trademark and thereby misleads the public as to the quality of the goods or causes confusion with the goods of another, any person may demand of the Patent Office a trial hearing to cancel the registration. So far as reported cases are concerned, a lack of quality control in a trademark license has never been made a defense in actions involving trademark infringement.

The legal nature of a franchise system was adequately analyzed and clarified by two unfair competition cases. In *Hokkoku Shōji K.K. v. Eikō Shōji K.K.*,[82] the franchisor, Hokkoku Shōji, adopted "Sapporo Rāmen Dosanko" as its service mark, and displayed the mark on its signboards, curtains, and lanterns in a very distinctive way. The Tokyo District Court enjoined the defendant from imitating the plaintiff's franchised restaurant under Article 1 (1)(ii) of the Unfair Competition Prevention Law.[83] As discussed above, Article 1 (1)(ii) prohibits a person from using a well-known mark of another and thereby causing confusion as to business establishment or activities.

The court held as follows:

The signboards, curtains, lanterns, and so on, which bear the plaintiff's mark "Sapporo Rāmen Dosanko" are "marks . . . well-known in the territory where this Law is in force" within the meaning of Article 1 (1)(ii) of the Unfair Competition Prevention Law, and are "indications of the business" of the plaintiff. Franchisees themselves are independent business proprietors, and the use of such signboards, curtains, lanterns, and so on, by such business proprietors cannot be said to be the use of an indication which represents the plaintiff's business alone.

But those who sell Sapporo rāmen under such signboards, curtains, lanterns, etc., are regarded to be persons who sell such products as integral parts of the organization of a single business enterprise. In fact, the plaintiff, acting as the franchisor, exercises a certain degree of control over these independent proprietors and maintains the unity of a business organization under the mark. Thus, the plaintiff franchisor and his franchisees form a kind of an organized body, which functions as a single business enterprise under the plaintiff's control. Therefore, such signboards, curtains, lanterns, etc., used by these franchisees must be regarded as indications of the plaintiff's business within the meaning of Article 1 (1)(ii) of the Unfair Competition Prevention Law.

In *Gotō, Sasakawa and Takeshita* v. *Shioya*,[84] the franchisor and two of his franchisees, as coplaintiffs, brought an action to enjoin the defendant from using the trade name "Hachiban rāmen," and for the cancellation of the registration of the defendant's trade name under Article 1 (1)(ii) of the Unfair Competition Prevention Law. In granting the remedies sought by the plaintiffs, the court discussed the relationships between the franchisor and his franchisees as follows:

> Although the plaintiffs Sasakawa and Takeshita are merely owners of one store each in Takaoka City of Toyama, each franchised store, which is selling Hachiban rāmen under a uniform trade name and business form under Gotō's headquarters, is an integral part of a single enterprise. The plaintiff Gotō acts as the headquarters in order to exercise control and supervision over each independent business enterprise under the franchise system and maintains the unity of a business organization under the trade name. To this extent, the plaintiff Gotō as the franchisor and his franchisees constitute a kind of organization and this organization functions as a single independent business enterprise under Gotō.

This case differs from the first case in that two franchisees were joined as coplaintiffs, although it was not necessary. Under a franchise system, franchisees' use of the franchisor's trademark, trade name, or other symbol inures to the benefit of the franchisor, thus the franchisor alone can sue the defendant.

As can be seen from these cases, service marks, trade names, and other symbols of franchise systems can be protected under the Unfair Competition Prevention Law even though they are not registered as trademarks. But, in an action under this law, the plaintiff must establish that his mark is well known and the defendant's use of the same or similar mark causes a likelihood of confusion as to the goods, business establishment, or activities.

Franchisors in Japan must carefully watch trade name registrations under the Commercial Code, because their well-known trademarks or service marks are often registered as trade names by unauthorized third parties. This is because the Commercial Code does not prevent registration of a trade name that appropriates a trademark or service mark of another. The only restriction is the prohibition of registration of a conflicting trade name with the same city, town, or village.[85] The only remedy against such unauthorized trade name registration is to seek cancellation of the trade name registration under Article 1 (1) of the Unfair Competition Prevention Law. Registration (*tōki*) under the Commercial Code is different from registration (*tōroku*) under the Trademark, Design, and Utility Model laws, and is administered by the justice minister in accordance with the Commercial Registration Law (Law no. 125, 1963).

Since franchised outlets are usually small, family-owned enterprises, they can avail themselves of the benefits under the Medium and Small Retail Business Promotion Law (Law no. 101, 1973). This law was enacted to assist individuals and companies who engage in medium and small retail businesses with a capitalization of less than 10,000,000 yen and not more than fifty employees. Article 11 of this law imposes certain disclosure requirements upon persons operating a chain-store business by licensing their trademarks and trade names to prospective members and collecting fees, guarantee deposits, and other charges from them. This provision is applicable to franchisors.

Under Article 11, the operator of a franchise business is required to furnish to prospective franchisees a written statement of the following matters and explain them in accordance with an ordinance of the Ministry of International Trade and Industry: (1) fees, guarantee deposits, and other charges to be collected at the time of joining; (2) conditions of sale of commodities to the member; (3) guidance in the operation of the business; (4) the trademark, trade name, and other indications to be licensed; (5) the term of contract, its renewal and termination; and (6) other matters required by an ordinance of the Ministry of International Trade and Industry.

Of course, franchise agreements, like license agreements involving patents, know-how, and trademarks, are subject to the Antimonopoly Law and, therefore, franchisors must pay due attention to the regulation of restrictive business practices under the law.

CONCLUSION

Comparative studies of intellectual property law between Japan and the United States should not be limited to the substantive and procedural aspects of protection. Rather, the study should be extended to various related areas such as tariff, antitrust tax, and business corporation laws. The foregoing study will serve as an introduction to an exploration into these more specialized areas, in which the role or treatment of intellectual property must be carefully examined.

NOTES

1. For further discussion on this subject, readers are referred to the following works I have published to date in English: *The Intellectual Property Law of Japan* (Alphen aan dem Rijn, The Netherlands: Sijthoff and Noordhoff International Publishers, 1980); *Trademark and Unfair Competition Law of Japan: Digest of Court Decisions*, vol. 1 (Tokyo: AIPPI Japan, 1980); *Digest of Court Decisions in Trademarks and Unfair Competition Cases* (Tokyo: American Chamber of Commerce in Japan, 1971); "Industrial Property Law," in Akira Kawamura, ed., *Law and Business in Japan* (Tokyo: Japan-Australia Business Cooperation Committee, 1982), pp. 170–95; Doi and Shattuck, eds., *Patent and Know-How Licensing in Japan and the United States* (Seattle: University of Washington Press, 1977). See also Heinz Dawid, ed., *Pinner's World Unfair Competition Law: An Encyclopedia* (Alphen aan dem Rijn, The Netherlands: Sijthoff and Noordhoff International Publishers, 1978). The following periodicals contain reports of Japanese court decisions and other information relating to the intellectual property law: *Patents and Licensing* (bimonthly; Japan Engineering News, Tokyo); *Journal of the Japanese Group of* AIPPI (quarterly; AIPPI Japan); and *European Intellectual Property Review* (monthly; ESC Publishing, Oxford, England).

2. Kagaku Gijutsuchō (Science and Technology Agency), ed., *Gaikokugijutsudōnyū nenjihōkoku Shōwa 56 nendo* (Annual report on foreign technology introduction for 1981), pp. 8–9.

3. Ibid., p. 9.

4. A detailed study of the role of the utility model system in the development of technology was made by a committee set up jointly by Sangyōkenkyushō (Industry Institute) and Hatsumeikyōkai (Association of Inventions and Innovations) and chaired by the author. The committee's report was published by the two sponsoring organizations: *Shingijutsu Kaihatsu ni Okeru Jitsuyōshinan Seido no Yakuwari* (The role of the utility model system in the development of new technology) (Tokyo: Hatsumeikyōkai, 1981).

5. Japanese Patent Office, *Obtaining Patent Rights in Japan 2* (Tokyo: Japanese Patent Office, 1982).

6. See World Intellectual Property Organization, *Industrial Property Statistics 1982*, Publication B (Geneva: WIPO, 1982), Patents Chart Ia and Utility Models Chart Ia.

7. Ibid., Patents Chart Ib.

8. For details, see Doi, *The Intellectual Property Law of Japan*, pp. 1–9.

9. Takahashi, as the director of the Patent Office, visited Washington, D.C. for two months to study the patent system of the United States. See Tsukasa Kamitsuka, ed., *Takahashi Korekiyo Jiden* (Autobiography of Korekiyo Takashi), 1 (Tokyo: Chūōkōron-sha, 1976): 220–26. When Takahashi visited the United States Patent Office, he remarked that "We have looked about us to see what nations are the greatest, so that we can be like them. . . . We said, 'What is it that makes the United States such a great nation?' and we investigated and found that it was patents, and we will have patents." U.S. Department of Commerce, *The Story of the United States Patent Office* (Washington, D.C.: Department of Commerce, 1972), p. 20.

10. Before Japan's accession to the Paris Convention, Takahashi strongly urged that aliens' rights should be recognized in Japan in "Summary of Opinion Concerning Future Policy of the Patent Office," submitted to the Minister of Agriculture and Commerce in 1890. Tsūshōsangyōshō (Ministry of International Trade and Industry), ed., *Shōkō seisakushi* (History of commerce and industry), 14 *Tokkyo* (Patents) (Tokyo: MITI, 1964): 646.

In the Summary of Opinion, the arguments of the patent abolitionists and the evils of the patent system were carefully studied. Responding to those people who believed that if patent protection was accorded to foreigners, they would acquire most of the patents and thereby obstruct the development of domestic industry, the Patent Office stated if such a cowardly attitude were taken, inventive activities would not be promoted in this country.

11. See Tokkyochō (Patent Office), ed., *Shinsakijun no Tebiki* (Guidelines for examination standards) (revised 14th ed.) (Tokyo: Patent Office, 1980).

12. For the English translation, see David S. Guttman, "Japanese Patent Office Examination Standard for Computer Program Related Inventions," *Patents and Licensing* 8, no. 3 (1983): 15.

13. See the English translation by David S. Guttman, "Japanese Patent Office Examination Guideline for Inventions Using Microcomputers," *Patents and Licensing* 8, no. 5 (1983): 11, and 8, no. 6 (1983): 9.

14. See Reikichi Shirane, ed., *Sentangijutsu ni Miru Maikon no Ōyōgijutsu Senryaku* (Tactics of applying microcomputer technology as seen in high technology) (Tokyo: Hatsumeikyōkai, 1982), pp. 3–4.

15. For details, see Teruo Doi, "Employees' Inventions: The Law and Practice in Japan," in Jeremy Phillips, ed., *Employees' Inventions: A Comparative Study* (Sunderland, Tyne, and Wear, England: Fernsway Publications, 1981).

16. Tokkyochō, *Tokkyochō kōhō* (Patent office gazette), *Tokkyochō nenpō* (Patent office annual report) 35 (1982): 2–3.

17. See Samson Helfgott, "Statistical Study of the Japanese Patent Office's Handling of Foreign Patent Applications," *Patents and Licensing* 13, no. 2 (1983): 7, 14.

18. Article 98 of the Patent Law provides:

The following matters shall not take effect unless they are registered: (1) Transfer (other than by inheritance or by any other general succession), extinction by abandonment or restriction on disposition of a patent right; (2) Establishment, transfer (other than by inheritance or by any other general succession), alteration, extinction (other than by merger or extinction of the patent right) or restriction on disposition of an exclusive license (*senyōjisshiken*); and (3) Establishment, transfer (other than by inheritance or other general succession), alteration, extinction (other than by merger or extinction of the obligation to be secured) or restriction on disposition of a pledge upon a patent right or an exclusive license.

19. See William Woodward and Kazuko Matsuo, "Drafting License Agreements in Japan and in

the United States," in Doi and Shattuck, eds., *Patent and Know-How Licensing in Japan and the United States*, pp. 124, 126.

20. Art. 99 (1) of the Patent Law provides that "a nonexclusive license (*tsūjōjisshiken*), if it is registered, takes effect against a person who subsequently acquired the patent right or exclusive license (*senyōjisshiken*) or an exclusive license (*senyōjisshiken*) with respect to the patent."

21. The doctrine of equivalents was clarified for the first time by the Osaka District Court in *Badische Anilin und Soda Fabrik A.G. v. Sekisui Kagaku Kōgyō K.K.*, 12 Kakyu minshu 937 (Osaka Dist. Ct., May 4, 1961).

22. See *Muranaka v. K.K. Daiwa Gomu Seisakusho, Hanrei Taimuzu* (No. 247) 263 (Tokyo Dist. Ct., Mar. 25, 1970).

23. United Nations Department of Economic and Social Affairs, *The Role of Patents in the Transfer of Technology to Developing Countries*, Report of the Secretary General (New York: United Nations, 1964), pp. 24–25.

24. For more details of the regulation of licensing agreements under the Antimonopoly Law, see Michiko Ariga, "Regulation of International Licensing Agreements under the Japanese Antimonopoly Law," in Doi and Shattuck, eds., *Patent and Know-How Licensing in Japan and the United States*, pp. 278–319. See also Doi, *The Intellectual Property Law of Japan*, pp. 258–79.

25. For a general discussion of the law of trade secrets in Japan, see Teruo Doi, "Protection of Know-How in Japan," in Herman Cohen Jehoram, ed., *The Protection of Know-How in Thirteen Countries* (Deventer, The Netherlands: Kluwer B.V., 1972), pp. 57–67; John Lyon and Teruo Doi, "The Protection of Unpatented Know-How and Trade Secrets in the United States and Japan," in Doi and Shattuck, eds., *Patent and Know-How Licensing*, pp. 30–74.

26. 17 Kakyu minshu 769 (Tokyo High Ct., Sept. 5, 1966).

27. See Ichirō Katō, *Fuhokōi* (Torts) (Tokyo: Yuhikaku, 1957), pp. 30–38. Kenichirō Ōsumi, former justice of the Supreme Court, discussed the availability of protection for know-how under Article 700 of the Civil Code as follows:

We should recognize the creation of a tort (unlawful act) for infringements of know-how. As already stated, know-how itself possesses an independent property value, but it is not something that is the subject of specific rights; moreover, Civil Code Art. 709 makes an "infringement of right" the requisite for tortious conduct. However, this so-called infringement of rights is nothing more than a symbol for illegality, and if we rely on the modern theories that consider a tort to have been created in the case where one has inflicted damages upon another by an illegal act regardless of whether or not a specific right has been infringed, the unlawful infringement of know-how must be recognized as constituting a tort. If one insists on making a problem out of the infringement of right, let us say that people have the right not to be hindered in the pursuance of their business by another as a "right of pesonality" and that infringement of know-how is an infringement of this right of personality, but I do not feel that it is worthwhile to stretch the argument that far.

The above quotation is from Kenichirō Ōsumi, "Know-How and Its Investment," *Law in Japan: An Annual*, 1 (1967): 92 and 102.

28. Justice Ōsumi, in the article cited in n. 27, discusses further that

Consequently, for the protection of know-how there is really no alternative in cases where there has been an infringement but to look for a remedy in the general provision of the Civil Code. Yet, even in those instances where there has been a theft of know-how by someone else or some other such unlawful infringement, the right to petition for an injunction is not recognized on this point, since the right to petition for an injunction is not recognized (where a patent has been applied for), even though after the publication of the patent application the right to receive a patent constitutes the same kind of right of exclusive use as a patent (Patent Law Art. 52), this situation probably must be accepted. [P. 101–2]

29. *Hanrei Jihō* (no. 264), p. 78 (Nara Dist. Ct., Oct. 23, 1970).

30. 6 *Mutaizaisan reishū* 170 (Tokyo High Ct., June 18, 1974).

31. *Hanrei Jihō* (no. 737), p. 49 (Osaka High Ct., July 12, 1973).

32. For courts' practice, see Kenji Koseki, *Tokyo chisai ni okeru nōhau no toriatsukai jisseki* (Treatment of know-how in the Tokyo District Court), *Shōjihōmukenkyū* (no. 191), p. 7 (1960).

33. In Japan, two government committees were established in the early 1970s. The Ministry of

International Trade and Industry (MITI) established the Committee to Study Legal Protection of Software in June 1971. This committee published an "Interim Report on the Legal Protection of Software" in May 1972. The Copyright Council of the Cultural Affairs Agency established a subcommittee on computer problems in 1972, which submitted its report to the Council on June 1, 1973. See Teruo Doi, "Legal Protection of Computer Programs: Reports of Two Government Committees," *Patents and Licensing* 3, no. 6 (1973): 3.

34. WIPO document LPCS/II/3.

35. WIPO document LPCS/II/6, Annex I, p. 1.

36. Ibid., p. 3.

37. The definition reads as follows: "A 'computer program' is a set of statements or instructions to be used directly or indirectly in a computer in order to bring about a certain result."

38. This doubt was cast by the United States District for the Eastern District of Pennsylvania in *Apple Computer, Inc.* v. *Franklin Computer Corp.*, 545 F.Supp. 812 (E.D. Penn. 1982).

39. *Tandy Corp.* v. *Personal Micro Computers, Inc.*, 524 F.Supp. 171 (N.D. Cal. 1981); *Williams Electronics, Inc.* v. *Arctic International, Inc.* 685 F2d 870 (3d Cir. 1982); *Apple Computer, Inc.* v. *Franklin Computer Corp.*, 562 F.Supp. 775 (C.D. Cal. 1983); *Hubco Data Products Corp.* v. *Management Assistance, Inc.*, CCH Copyright Law Decisions, 219 U.S.P.Q. 450 (D. Ida. 1983).

40. *Apple Computer, Inc.* v. *Franklin Computer Corp.*, 714 F. 2d 1240 (3d Cir. 1983).

41. *Hanrei Jihō* (no. 1060), p. 18 (Tokyo Dist. Ct., Dec. 6, 1982).

42. *Hanrei Jihō* (no. 1081), p. 125 (Yokohama Dist. Ct., Mar. 30, 1983).

43. *Hanrei Jihō* (no. 1106), p. 134 (Osaka Dist. Ct., Jan. 26, 1984).

44. *Hanrei Jihō* (no. 1129), p. 120 (Tokyo Dist. Ct., Sept. 28, 1984).

45. *Nihon keizai shimbun*, June 3, 1982.

46. See Teruo Doi, "Legal Protection of Computer Programs: Reports of Two Government Committees," *Patents and Licensing* 3, no. 2 (1973): 6.

47. See the Program Right Law proposed by the Information Industry Committee of the Industrial Structure Council in its Interim Report.

48. See report of the Group of Experts, UNESCO/WIPO/GE/CCS/3.

49. The Copyright Law was amended by Law no. 46, enacted on May 24, 1984, and became effective Jan. 1, 1985.

50. Art. 10bis of the Paris Convention for the Protection of Industrial Property provides as follows: "Article 10bis (Unfair Competition). (1) The countries of the Union are bound to assure to nationals of such countries effective protection against unfair competition. (2) Any act of competition contrary to honest practices in industrial or commercial matters constitutes an act of unfair competition. . . ."

51. For a detailed discussion of the legal basis for merchandising rights licensing and analysis of cases, see Teruo Doi, "Character Merchandising in Japan: Protection of Fictional Characters and Well-Known Personalities as the Basis for Merchandising Activities," *Annual of Industrial Property Law* (London: European Law Center, 1978), pp. 283–306.

52. Art. 10 (1) of the Copyright Law lists, as examples, various works of authorship: novels, dramas, theses, lectures, and other literary works; musical works; choreographic works and pantomimes; paintings, woodcut prints, engravings, sculptures, and other works of art; architectural works; maps as well as plans, charts, models, and other figurative works of scientific nature; cinematographic works; and, photographic works.

53. *Hanrei Jihō* (no. 815), p. 28, *Chosakuken Hanreishū* 721 (Tokyo Dist. Ct., May 26, 1976).

54. *Chosakuken Hanreishū* 713 (Tokyo Dist. Ct., Mar. 30, 1977).

55. The Copyright Law, chap. 6, "Infringement of Rights" (Arts. 112 to 118), provides for civil remedies against infringement of moral right, copyright, publication right, and neighboring rights, and chap. 7, "Penal Provisions" (Arts. 119 to 124), provides for criminal sanctions against infringers.

56. *Hanrei Taimuzu* (no. 396) 64 (Osaka Dist. Ct., Aug. 14, 1979).

57. Art. 3 (1) of the Trademark Law provides that "trademark registration may be obtained for any trademark which is to be used for goods relating to one's own business, with the exception of the following trademarks," and then lists trademarks that are unregisterable as lacking distinctive quality. Art. 3 (2) permits registration of a trademark which is originally descriptive when it has obtained a secondary meaning.

58. *Shinketsu kōhō* (no. 226), p. 23 (Pat. Off., Apr. 25, 1960).

59. See the Trademark Law, Art. 4 (1).

60. Tokkyochō, ed., *Shōhyō Shinsakijun* (Trademark examination standards) (Tokyo: Patent Office, 1971).

61. The trademark examination standards explain Art. 4 (1)(vii) as follows:

1. "A trademark contrary to public order or good morals" should be interpreted to include situations where a trademark consists of extreme or obscene letters or designs as well as where a trademark that does not consist of such letters or designs but may harm the interest of the society or the public or contravene the general moral standard of the society.

2. A trademark the use of which is prohibited by other laws, a trademark defamatory to a specific country or its nationals, and a trademark contrary to international good faith come under the provision of this item.

62. 8 Mutaizaisan reishū 102, *Chosakuken Hanreishū* 889 (Osaka Dist. Ct., Feb. 24, 1976).

63. Tokkyo to kigyō, April 1984, p. 79 (Osaka Dist. Ct., Feb. 28, 1984).

64. See M. B. Nimmer, "The Right of Publicity," *Law and Contemporary Problems* 19 (1954): 203; D. R. Ginsburg, "Transfer of the Right of Publicity: Dracula's Progeny and Privacy's Stepchild," *UCLA Law Review* 22 (1975): 1104.

65. *Hanrei Jihō* (no. 817), p. 23, *Chosakuken Hanreishū* 771 (Tokyo Dist. Ct., June 29, 1976).

66. 15 *Kakyū minshū* 2317 (Tokyo Dist. Ct., Sept. 28, 1964).

67. *Merchandising Rights Report*, January 1981, p. 19 (Tokyo Dist. Ct., Nov. 10, 1980).

68. 8 Mutaizaisan reishū 441 (Osaka Dist. Ct., Oct. 5, 1976).

69. 12 Mutaizaisan reishū 321 (Osaka Dist. Ct., July 15, 1980).

70. 8 Mutaizaisan reishū 145, *Chosakuken Henreishū* 872 (Tokyo Dist. Ct., Apr. 28, 1976).

71. The following book contains the code of ethics of the Japan Franchise Association, the association's guidelines for franchise contracts, various laws and regulations, and court decisions concerning franchising: Nihon Furanchaizuchen Kyōkai (Japan franchise association), ed., *Furanchaizu Handobuku* (Franchise handbook) (1982).

72. Ibid., p. 6. The following table is based on the chart prepared by the department:

International Franchising in 1981

(Franchising companies, 288; Number of franchising outlets, 21, 416)

Canada	7,068	Caribbean	541
Japan	3,999	Africa	515
Continental Europe	3,393	Mexico	403
United Kingdom	2,113	South America	318
Australia	1,693	Near East	184
Asia	746	Central America	140

73. Ibid., p. 7.

74. U.S. Department of Commerce, Bureau of Industrial Economics, *Franchising in the Economy 1981–1983*, p. 5.

75. Ibid., p. 5.

76. The U.S. Department of Commerce notes that "The form of entry into foreign markets varies considerably, with many firms using more than one method in conducting foreign operations. Of the 288 franchisors doing business in foreign countries in 1981, 274 sold their outlets to franchisees either directly or through a master licensee who received the right to develop the franchisor's system in a specific country or region, 21 operated joint ventures, and 30 had some company operated units. Twenty-two of these companies derived 10 percent or more of their income from foreign operations, 20 firms received between 5 and 9 percent, 94 between 1 and 4 percent, and 152 received less than 1 percent. Ibid., p. 7.

77. The following statement of Judge Dawson in *Susser* v. *Carvel Corp.* is often quoted in the literature on franchising as adequately describing the essential feature of a franchise system: "the cornerstone of a franchise system must be the trademark or trade name of a product. It is this uniformity of product and control of its quality and distribution which causes the public to turn to franchise stores for the product." *Susser* v. *Carvel Corp.*, 206 F. Supp. 636 (S.D.N.Y. 1962).

78. Art. 50 (1) of the Trademark Law provides that when a registered trademark has not been used in Japan for more than three consecutive years for the designated goods by the owner or any of its exclusive or nonexclusive licensees, a trial hearing may be demanded of the Patent Office for the cancellation of the registration of such trademark, unless there is a justifiable reason for the nonuse. In such a trial hearing, the owner of the registered trademark has the burden of establishing the use of his trademark to avoid cancellation under Art. 50 (2).

79. Under Art. 19 (2) of the Trademark Law, the duration of a trademark right is not renewable

when neither the trademark owner, his exclusive licensee nor his nonexclusive licensee has been using the registered trademark within three years before the filing of a renewal application.

80. See n. 18, above.

81. See n. 20, above.

82. *Hanrei Jihō* (no. 710), p. 76 (Tokyo Dist. Ct., Nov. 27, 1972).

83. See n. 64, above.

84. *Hanrei Jihō* (no. 734), p. 91 (Kanazawa Dist. Ct., Oct. 30, 1973).

85. Art. 19 of the Commercial Code provides that "a trade name registered by another cannot be registered in the same city, town, or village for the same business."

Part 3

THE AMERICAN LEGAL FRAMEWORK

AND BILATERAL ISSUES

Escape Clause Relief and Recessions:
an Economic and Legal Look at Section 201

PAULA STERN
ANDREW WECHSLER

In the United States import relief, industrial policy, and foreign economic relations have come under the increasing scrutiny of a public battered by recent economic problems and a Congress ever more skeptical about the ability of the United States to prosper without basic changes in the "way we do things." Proposals run the gamut from the narrow to the grand, from an increased reliance on the market to a significantly greater role for government leadership, from a focus on the internal problems of U.S. labor and management to one on the practices of our major international competitors, particularly Japan. Recent general import relief cases[1] at the U.S. International Trade Commission (USITC) and congressional proposals for revision of section 201 of the Trade Act of 1974 (under which those investigations were conducted) have made the statute a watershed for discussion about how U.S. industries function, what import relief is and ought to be, and how the United States and Japan ought to resolve economic conflicts tied in part to the recent misfortunes of certain U.S. industries. Temporal and long-run concerns often merge in the discussion of how the statutes should function and whether they need revision.

This debate proceeds simultaneously on three levels. The first level boils down to what role trade protection should have in any program to revitalize U.S. industry. With historically high real interest rates, a strong dollar, and record import penetrations accompanying the deep malaise of some of America's largest industries, the first and most wide-ranging level of discussion is on what role imports have had in reducing these once-proud industries to their present state and what kind of corrective policies are necessary. The stakes are high because the role of cyclical industries in U.S. trade is large, particularly with Japan.

Although the authors have both been associated with the U.S. International Trade Commission, the judgments expressed in this essay do not necessarily reflect the views of the USITC.

There is a growing perception in the United States that our most successful trading partners have consciously formulated coherent industrial policies to deal with structural change. For instance, Japan's Ministry of International Trade and Industry coordinates the development of limited-life recession cartels of firms wishing to cooperate.[2] Participants are exempted from certain antitrust provisions and encouraged to coordinate their capacity and share of the domestic market. Prices are sustained in excess of average costs, and imports are discouraged. The objective is to facilitate more orderly adjustment to tough economic conditions. The United States has no such general approach. Import relief is often the only alternative that is institutionally available.

On a second level, the adequacy of U.S. import relief statutes is hotly contested. Since these statutes are a central part of the U.S. commitment to the postwar, open, international trading system represented by the General Agreement on Tariffs and Trade (GATT), the stakes here are also high. Finally, on a third level, the administration of those statutes, particularly section 201, which is aimed at structural adjustment, has been on the front burner since the USITC turned down the relief requested by the hard-pressed automobile industry in 1980. In the American context, section 201 serves as a springboard for much of the discussion on trade policy and industrial problems. This essay therefore concentrates on examining exactly how section 201 as presently written operates at the USITC.

It is our contention that much of the discussion of section 201 has been based on an incorrent impression of what the commission did in *Automobiles*[3] and an unjustified conclusion that general import relief is not available to cyclical industries when they may need it most—during the depths of a recession. This essay examines the application of section 201 to industries simultaneously confronting both strong cyclical downturns and severe import competition. We trace the progress in developing an adequate methodology to carry out the present law. But this process takes us to the edge of more general issues: problems in the structure and administration of general import relief, and what positive role the USITC (referred to also as the "ITC," or "commission") may play in the adjustment of U.S. industry to international competition.

First, the statute and the USITC are briefly reviewed. The treatment of cyclical industries is surveyed. Then the salient points of the investigations of the U.S. automobile, motorcycle, and specialty steel industries are analyzed. An analytic framework for assessing the effect of imports on cyclical industries is proposed. Finally, some issues in the administration of section 201 are briefly evaluated.

THE GENERAL IMPORT RELIEF STATUTE

The United States has had a general import relief statute in its law since the Trade Agreements Expansion Act of 1951.[4] Following two decades of virtually no trade, it was adopted as a concession to domestic interests that perceived the executive's authority to reduce tariffs and the postwar restoration of trade as a threat.[5] The law established standards and procedures for securing import relief in the form of quotas and/or tariffs in cases where injury was pronounced, but not necessarily related to any potentially unfair activity such as foreign dumping or subsidization of imports into the U.S. market. Its principles became embodied in Article 19 of GATT,[6] the "escape clause" by which a signatory nation may, under appropriate circumstances, escape from its other GATT commitments and raise protective barriers for an injured industry. Section 201 of the Trade Act of 1974[7] is the latest version of the U.S. law that reflects Article 19. Congress was quite explicit on the rationale underlying the escape clause and the reasons for replacing its previous formulation in the Trade Expansion Act of 1962[8] with section 201. General import relief was "aimed at providing temporary relief for an industry so that the industry will have sufficient time to adjust to the freer international competition."[9] The 1962 formulation had required that increased imports result "in a major part" from trade concessions and be the "major cause"—greater than any other—of a U.S. industry's serious injury. Congress concluded that the 1962 Act was consequently an "inadequate mechanism for providing relief to domestic industries suffering from import competition." Interestingly enough, the Senate Finance Committee noted that one result was the development of "voluntary" agreements, and commented: it is better to provide a fair and reasonable test . . . —a determination made by an independent fact-finding body such as the International Trade Commission—than to rely on ad hoc agreements for a few select industries."[10] It was hoped that section 201 would guarantee a rule of law rather than an ad hoc approach where only industries with the requisite political clout could obtain relief. Because this statute underlines this entire essay, a brief summary of its salient provisions may be useful.[11]

Any entity representative of industry—for example, trade association, firms, certified union, group of workers—may petition the ITC for relief to assist in adjusting to new competition by methods that may even include at one extreme an orderly exit from the industry. Commission investigations under section 201 may also be initiated by the president, the U.S. trade representative, the Committee on Ways and Means of the House, the Senate Finance Committee, or the ITC itself.

Three conditions must be fulfilled before the commission can make an affirmative finding and recommend a remedy to the president: (1) There must be increased imports—either actual or relative to domestic production—of an article into the United States; (2) the domestic industry producing an article like or directly competitive with the imported one must be seriously injured or threatened with serious injury; (3) the increased imports must be a substantial cause of the serious injury, or the threat thereof, to the domestic industry making the article in question. "Substantial cause" is defined by Congress to mean "a cause which is 'important' and not less than any other cause."[12]

The commission is required to complete its investigation "at the earliest practicable time" but no later than six months after initiation. If the commission recommends a remedy,[13] the president has sixty days to proclaim a remedy or deny relief.[14] Relief may consist of any combination of tariff increases and quotas, or negotiated orderly marketing agreements (OMAs) with the relevant foreign nations. There are constraints on this relief: the maximum tariff increase is 50 percent ad valorem above existing tariffs; the maximum period of relief is five years but relief in excess of three years is, to the extent possible, to be phased down. Relief may be further extended for an additional three-year period on advice of the commission. Two years must elapse between relief and a new investigation of the same industry. Finally, if the president's recommendation differs from that of the majority of the commission, section 203(c)[15] provides for a legislative override by a simple majority of both houses of Congress, which would result in the commission's remedy taking effect.[16]

This essay concentrates on the role of the commission in the section 201 import relief process. Because of its unique institutional character, a brief examination of the USITC will be useful.

THE U.S. INTERNATIONAL TRADE COMMISSION

The USITC is an independent, fact-finding, and advisory panel responsible for providing the president and Congress with as objective an analysis as possible of international trade issues. It also has quasi-judicial functions that require its commissioners, within a strict legal framework established by Congress, to make decisions in import relief investigations. The commission administers trade laws rather than formulating trade policy.[17]

The USITC is governed by U.S. legislation dating back to 1916, but its name and powers come from the Tariff Act of 1930, the Trade Act of 1974, and most recently, the Trade Agreements Act of 1979, the U.S. law that implemented the GATT codes produced by the Tokyo Round of the Multilateral Trade Negotiations.[18]

There is a common structure to all ITC investigations. If the petition is legally adequate, public notice is given that a case has begun. Then a staff of 300 investigators, lawyers, economists, accountants, and commodity experts gathers data and prepares a report on each investigation. Public hearings give all interested parties a chance to present their views. The commissioners act as judges. Decisions are reached by public votes on the basis of the established facts and strictly defined standards. After the commissioners vote, a final report is issued containing a factual record and the views of the commissioners that support their findings.

ITC decisions are made by this presidentially appointed panel of six members, no more than three of whom can come from any one party, and who serve terms up to nine years. It is unlikely that any one president will have the opportunity to appoint the entire commission. It is expected that commissioners from one political party will often be appointed by a president from the other party. These presidential appointees must be approved by the Senate before they take effect. Senate approval, even when the president and the Senate majority are from the same party, is not automatic.

Thus, Congress has designed the ITC to keep it clear of political pressure from both the executive and the legislature. The commission has been referred to as a "shield of Congress"—an instrument that allows a nonpolitical approach to trade issues that would be difficult for elected congressmen, senators, and the president to adopt.

Not all trade and commercial disputes come to the independent ITC and even those which do are sometimes settled elsewhere. The U.S. trade representative, the Commerce Department, and the State Department—all under the direction of the president—play a role in either bilateral or multilateral negotiations. With those agencies, politics—domestic and international—have a legitimate standing. Thus, while the overall system of trade regulation is basically rule-oriented, there may be certain forums where political implications are considered and one forum—the ITC—where those implications are prohibited.

SECTION 201 AND RECESSIONS

The injury and causation tests are two essential elements of any 201 investigation. Has the industry been seriously injured? If so, have imports been a substantial cause?

Industries characterized by strong cyclical behavior intimately related to the overall pattern of boom and recession in the national economy present special problems when answering these legally required questions. Should the effects of a "normal" business cycle on the decline in demand for a specific industry's output be factored into or out of the picture? Should only injury beyond that reasonably expected in a downturn be assessed when determining serious injury and causation? Should a recession and its direct effects be weighed as a unitary cause other than imports, or fractured among many causes? Or should it be ignored as the background environment to an industry's performance?

The questions can cut many ways. By factoring out normal declines, it becomes *more* difficult for a cyclical industry to demonstrate serious injury; yet it becomes *less* difficult to show that imports are a substantial cause because an important nonimport source of injury has been removed from the picture. And, of course, some may straddle the fence by counting regular cyclical influences in the injury test but ignoring them as a separate explanation in the causation tests. The issue is not merely a technical one because the way in which it is resolved dictates the circumstances under which such industries can obtain relief under the present law.

The legislative history provides little direct guidance on the subject. Section 201(b)(2) directs the commission to "take into account all economic factors which it considers relevant." This would tend to support the argument that the commission may analyze the impact of business cycles in any way it deems appropriate, including isolating their effects. However, section 201(b)(2)(A) states that "with respect to serious injury, the significant idling of productive facilities in the industry, the inability of a significant number of firms to operate at a reasonable level of profit, and significant unemployment and underemployment within the industry" are among the factors that the commission must consider. These appear to be the types of negative indexes apparent in business cycle downturns. Thus, it can be argued that section 201(b)(2)(A) envisions no elimination of injury of one sort (i.e., that caused by normal business cycle downturn) from an analysis of whether the industry in question is seriously injured. And it is unlikely that Congress intended to make relief *more* difficult to obtain for industries beset by repetitive cyclical downturns.

Our review of past commission decisions reveals that this important conceptual question was never directly addressed prior to the 1980 investigation of imported automobiles.[19] Commission practice confirms only its discretion to analyze industry performance in any way it deems best.[20]

To the best of our knowledge, the lack of a consistent approach to the analysis of recession-beset cyclical industries generated no serious doubts about the import relief process before *Automobiles*. But the stakes were not as big then. Faith in the U.S. economy remained largely intact. Problems in specific industries were yet not perceived as endemic to the whole economy. And while Japan drew increasing attention through the 1970s, no serious challenges had yet emerged to the U.S. commitment to the international trading order of which the United States had been a prime beneficiary. With *Automobiles*, the trade world changed radically. In a negative environment of declining output, staggering unemployment, and growing import penetrations facing basic industries in their once-secure home markets, confidence in the United States was seriously shaken. The automobile industry, facing imports that had captured almost 30 percent of the U.S. market, was denied relief.

The ITC was perceived—incorrectly as we shall see—to have resolved the recession issue in a manner that would make it virtually impossible for cyclical industries to get relief in downturns. Whatever the cause, activity under section 201 fell off dramatically after *Automobiles*. In the three years following the commission's automobile decision,[21] only four general import relief investigations were initiated. In two, the ITC recommended and the president accorded relief. By comparison, in the three years prior to the institution of *Automobiles*, seventeen investigations were conducted under section 201. Of these, twelve resulted in relief recommendations from the ITC.[22] In these instances, the president accorded relief to six industries, though in one case the relief consisted of adjustment assistance rather than any action against imports.[23]

There are many factors underlying this record. Some industries were large, others small; some highly cyclical, others not; some had special political clout; and certainly the overall economic and political situation was not a constant. But the current debate on protection, free trade, and industrial policy was off and running, with Japan the prime foreign focus. A look back at the investigations of the automobile, motorcycle, and specialty steel industries, all conducted during the recessionary period 1980–83,[24] demonstrates that some elements of this debate were improperly formulated.

AUTOMOBILES (DECEMBER 1980)

The precipitous decline of the U.S. automobile industry in 1979–80 caused severe tension in U.S.–Japanese relations. Despite moves by Honda to open a U.S. plant and measures to promote Japanese imports of U.S. automobile parts, the United Automobile Workers—self-proclaimed as "The International Union"—reluctantly turned 180 degrees from its traditional free trade posture and initiated in May 1980 the largest investigation in the history of the commission. By August, the Ford Motor Company, makers of the "world car," joined the UAW as petitioners. Hearings were held in October and the commission announced its decision in November. The subject of considerable attention in an election year, the case contributed more to the present scrutiny of import relief than any other single event.

There was little issue whether the industry passed the serious injury test. But, *Automobiles* was decided by a split commission, with Chairman Alberger, Vice-Chairman Calhoun, and Commissioner Stern in the majority. And there was by no means a uniform methodology even among the majority, though few if any observers seemed to have made note of this point. Alberger and Calhoun chose to count fully a recession-related decline in demand as an alternative cause of injury. In reaching his negative finding, Chairman Alberger stated, "I have found the decline in demand for new automobiles and light trucks owing to the *general* recessionary conditions in the United States economy to be a far greater cause of the domestic industries' plight than the increase in imports."[25] Consistent with this choice, he then relied on shift-share analysis, an arithmetical exercise based on alternate scenarios for the behavior of the market share held by imports over a time period, to weigh the two alternative causes: recession and imports.

Vice-Chairman Calhoun appears on this matter to have shared Chairman Alberger's views. After noting that "decline in demand, in this investigation, is the result of the recessionary pressures on the economy," he concluded, "the decline in demand was and is a more important cause of serious injury than increased imports."[26] Vice-Chairman Calhoun, with reservations, also applied a shift-share analysis.[27]

Though Stern too found in the negative, her methodology was clearly distinguishable. Having concluded that proper application of section 201 requires adjustments for cyclical industries, there remained the problem of where these adjustments should be considered—during the examination of serious injury, in the analysis of substantial cause, or with some combination of the two. Stern made no attempt to adjust the injury indicia for expected downturns in the industry.[28] Realizing that any such adjustments would be inherently subjective, the relatively objective injury data were left undisturbed and all adjustments were made in conducting the inevitably more qualitative examination of causation.[29]

Stern's treatment of cyclicality could be confined to causal considerations in

Automobiles in part because the question of serious injury was so clearly established. It was a rather sterile semantic problem to debate whether a cyclical industry in a normal downturn should be denied relief because it is not legally injured (the fall-off in performance being a regular and expected phenomenon), or because the cyclical injury reflected in its weakened performance is not related to imports. Thus, the convention adopted of taking into account such considerations when examining causation rather than injury was a matter of presentation, not substance.

By analyzing the *elements* of the decline in demand that the industry was experiencing, Stern separated out normal cyclical fluctuations from the departure from the trend in the industry's performance. At least two causes (and perhaps a third) were found to be more important than imports as a substantial cause of serious injury. Stern's statement of the cause she found most important demonstrates the salient methodological point separating her from her colleagues in the majority, Alberger and Calhoun: "(1) A general decline in demand due to rapidly increasing costs of car ownership and operation (added to normal—if not precisely predictable—recessionary effects on consumer income and confidence)."[30] Stern went on to specify the relative importance of all the important causes of injury:

> (2) A seemingly permanent shift in consumer tastes to relatively smaller, more fuel-efficient autos;
> (3) A substantially negative accounting impact on profits resulting from huge investments to transform the industry; and
> (4) Success of imports in head-to-head competition.
> The decline in demand and shift in demand are more important causes of injury to the auto industry than increasing imports, *per se*. I have not been able to evaluate fully the relative significance of the massive capital costs of transforming the industry; however, I believe that their impact on domestic industry performance is at least of the same magnitude as that of imports. It is doubtful that in the absence of the first three causes the remaining injury attributable to imports would be serious.

Shift-share analysis was of little assistance in moving beyond the simple imports-versus-recession framework employed by Alberger and Calhoun.

The affirmative minority in *Automobiles* distinguished its causal analysis from that of the majority on the basis of the number of causes to be weighed against imports. Commissioners Moore and Bedell summarized their findings on causation as follows:

> Section 201(b)(2) does not limit us to consideration of only certain economic factors in determining whether increased imports are a substantial cause of serious injury. We are to take into account "all" relevant economic factors. We believe that there are a number of other individual causes of injury, such as increased costs of passenger automobiles, the shift in consumer preferences from large to small cars, high interest rates, a shortage of consumer credit, increased gasoline prices, shortages of gasoline (in 1979), the failure of domestic corporate management to anticipate current conditions, and costly Government regulations. We find that none of these other

causes, even if considered an important cause of injury, are a more important cause of serious injury to the domestic industry than increased imports.[31]

Strongly believing that the automobile industry merited 201 relief, the minority noted that if one aggregated "the negative economic factors in comparing them with increased imports, there would be 'few, if any,' Commission decisions favorable to a domestic industry during economic downturns." Drawing no distinction between the differing methodologies of the majority, they spoke directly to the issue of how to deal with cyclical industries:

> We reject the notion that the statute permits the Commission to aggregate a number of economic factors which in combination are to be weighed against increased imports to find the substantial cause of serious injury. Further, we believe that economic downturns represent the concurrence of a number of adverse factors. We do not believe that Congress envisioned that the Commission would consider an economic downturn per se to be a single economic factor in determining injury in section 201 investigations. Instead, we believe that Congress intended the Commission to examine imports and their impact on the domestic industry over the course of the business cycle—during both good and bad years—in order to ascertain whether import penetration is increasing and, if so, whether the increasing penetration is seriously injuring the domestic industry. This is the approach we have followed in past section 201 cases.[32]

While quite explicit on the level of causal aggregation they felt inappropriate, Moore and Bedell were less clear on exactly how to evaluate the performance of an industry over the course of a business cycle.

Automobiles saw the commission treating recessions in three distinct fashions. Though obviously not resolved, the recession issue had been posed more clearly than ever before. No developments of any significance on the analytical issue of recessions took place until the motorcycle industry came before the commission in 1983. However, outside the ITC, heated debate on the law continued during the intervening period. Much of it was based on a misreading of what had happened in automobiles: the majority was perceived as having chosen a methodology (recession a single, greater cause) and as a result relief henceforth would not be available to cyclical industries in a downturn. Congressional intervention seemed likely.

Despite the ITC's negative vote, Japan announced a "voluntary restraints agreement" (VRA) in May 1981 in an atmosphere of increasing congressional support for automobile import quotas, domestic content legislation, and sectoral reciprocity in conducting trade relations. The treatment of the recession by some commissioners had been responsible in part for the negative finding. Now the VRA exhibited the effects of the recession on the trading system itself, rather than just the auto industry: a new ad hoc bilateral arrangement outside the GATT framework. Discontent with the causal standards of section 201 grew. In 1983, two very visible investigations served as additional focal points in a debate that had raged since 1980.

MOTORCYCLES (FEBRUARY 1982)[33]

When the heavyweight motorcycles 201 investigation came to the ITC for consideration in September 1982, it faced a commission with an entirely different complexion than that which had decided *Automobiles* two years earlier. In fact, with three seats vacant, two-thirds of the commission consisted of relatively new Reagan administration Republican appointees who had participated in few previous 201 investigations.[34] Clearly, the new commission had the potential to put a fresh stamp on a statute whose conceptual framework had only first been bared to the bones in the 1980 *Automobiles* case. The commission reached this potential with some anomalous results.

In *Motorcycles*, all the statutory criteria were seriously contested among the interested parties.[35] In sorting out the claims and counterclaims, a good deal was learned. A split commission recommended strong tariff relief. In a virtually unique response to a commission remedy recommendation, the president adopted intact the rather draconian 45 percent tariff increase proposed by the majority.[36]

Harley-Davidson also wanted imported subassemblies included. But since they are merely captively consumed components of finished motorcycles, there was no direct competition between them and domestically produced subassemblies. Chairman Eckes joined Stern and constituted a majority on this point. Thus, no relief could be accorded by quotas or tariffs on imported subassemblies.

The most vexing question was who should be counted among the ranks of domestic producers. Harley, the producer of the famed "Hog," said only itself. Kawasaki and Honda wanted to be included as well. As production in virtually all industries becomes more internationally integrated, the concept of who is a domestic company is increasingly difficult. Obviously when facing potential restrictions on imports, the advantage of the domestic label rises dramatically. In *Motorcycles*, the decision of what properly constituted the domestic industry became the result of a sophisticated analytical process. Five tests to be considered together were enunciated by Stern: substantial change, domestic content, major component, commitment to the United States, and degree of control.[37]

The commission found that three companies, Harley-Davidson, Honda of America, and Kawasaki U.S.A., qualified as domestic manufacturers. In this respect, *Motorcycles* was a significant advance because for the first time a set of criteria was elaborated for dealing with the natural contradiction between import relief granted at a national level to industries increasingly multinational in character.

The parties' differences over who constituted the U.S. industry dictated differing positions on whether it was seriously injured. Although two of the three U.S. firms were doing quite well, on the basis of individual and aggregate data the entire commission agreed that the industry as a whole was seriously injured.

Honda began its Marysville, Ohio, production in 1979 but achieved full production only in 1981. Partial year data for 1982 showed continued improvement over 1981 in all its financial indicators. Kawasaki, producing part of its stock in the United States since 1975, voluntarily withdrew from most U.S. production except police cycles, a minor market segment, so an analysis of its data added little. Finally, Harley's performance first began to sour in 1981 and continued to do so in 1982, as its market share and employment both declined. A great deal of the decline in Harley's operating profit reflected a decrease in total net sales; but another significant factor was the accounting impact of unusual one-time expenses associated with its change of ownership. Net profitability was further damaged by the substantial interest expenses related to the purchase of the company from American Machine and Foundry. Since Harley accounted for about three-fourths of the productive resources of the U.S. industry, and was in real financial straits, the commission unanimously found the U.S. industry to be seriously injured. But each commissioner issued separate views.

The split findings came to rest on what factors accounted for the industries' problems, with the recession at issue.

Chairman Eckes—in contrast to Alberger and Calhoun in *Automobiles*—apparently chose to factor out all recession-related effects, both normal and unusual, in reaching his affirmative findings:

> In reaching this conclusion I have considered the significance of the present recession in my analysis. Without a doubt the unusual length and severity of the present recession has created unique problems for the domestic motorcycle industry. Without a doubt the rise in joblessness, particularly among blue-collar workers, who constitute the prime market for heavyweight motorcycles, has had a severe impact on the domestic industry. Nonetheless, if the Commission were to analyze the causation question in this way, it would be impossible in many cases for a cyclical industry experiencing serious injury to obtain relief under section 201 during a recession. In my opinion Congress could not have intended for the Commission to interpret the law this way.[38]

Commissioner Haggart commented, "In reaching this conclusion, I have considered other causes of the threat of serious injury, such as high interest rates and the decline in demand for heavyweight motorcycles caused by unemployment. However, I have concluded that the increase in imports of heavyweight motorcycles is a far more important cause of a threat of serious injury."[39] Although silent on the issue of recession, some of the alternate causes cited by Haggart could be regarded as disaggregated recessionary effects.

Stern found that declining demand for heavy motorcycles in 1980 and 1982 and Honda's rapid entry as a U.S. producer after 1980 were more important than imports as a cause of injury. Therefore, the *substantial* criterion that requires imports to be as important as any other cause was not met. In *Motorcycles*, the difficult and subjective process of concentrating on the peculiar aspects of a recession's effects on a cyclical industry was a little easier, because—pardon the expression—there was no evidence to show that demand for motorcycles was particularly cyclical.[40] But there were peculiar problems for Harley in 1981 and 1982, which had little or nothing to do with imports. 1981 was no normal recession year for this industry. The largest single group of purchasers of heavy cycles are blue-collar workers who make 50 percent of the purchases. Blue-collar unemployment rose from 10.3 percent in 1981 to 15.9 percent in October 1982, while overall unemployment rose from 7.6 to 10.4 percent. Harley had earlier faced a decline in demand in 1980 that, due to inventory buffers, did not show up on its books until 1981. Harley's losses in 1981 and 1982 thus reflect a decline in demand and, in part, a loss of domestic market share to Honda, as Honda of America's share rose dramatically from 1981 to 1982.

Interestingly, the market share of imports fell in 1982, as foreign sales plummeted twice as quickly as domestic sales (compared to 1981). There lies the story of how the commission majority arrived at an affirmative finding, for two members found imports to *threaten* serious injury.[41]

SPECIALTY STEEL (MAY 1983)

In May 1983, the commission returned to the 201 arena shortly after the smoke had begun to clear from the president's sharp action on imported heavyweight motorcycles. Tariff-free quotas effectively exempted lower volume imports from Europe. Thus, as had *Automobiles* before it, *Motorcycles* concentrated on Japan. In *Specialty Steel*,[42] a general import relief case would prove to be truly general, though Japan was a principal party. The affirmative determinations and remedies for four separate specialty steel industries and the unanimous "Views" created the general perception that the commission was unanimous. True, one commissioner (Stern), did not find that imports had been a "substantial" cause of serious problems of the U.S. stainless steel plate producers. But imports were an important cause even in that industry, and she was able to join in an across-the-board recommendation for relief. True, another commissioner (Eckes) issued a separate remedy recommendation. But it was based on technical differences with the majority about the base years to be used as a "most representative" recent period. Some basic points, however, united the commission: the industry was ailing and quota relief was recommended for all product areas for a period of three years. Examination beneath this surface unanimity, however, reveals a much greater lack of uniformity in methodology.

The issue of cyclicality was now squarely before the commission. Although this question had arisen in *Automobiles*, the issue was even more clearly set as the menu of serious alternative causes to rising imports was now much simpler. In *Specialty Steel*, the only contenders were declining domestic demand and faltering exports by the domestic industry. The factors behind these phenomena were indeed complex; only three causes of injury clearly emerged. The "Views of the Commission" were unanimous with some relatively minor exceptions. Little explicit attention was devoted in those views to specifying the alternative causes, no less explicitly weighing them against each other. Only one alternative cause was specifically mentioned: "decline in consumption." In fact causation—the crucial issue on which the entire investigation turned—occupied but a small part of the views. Some comments in the views did indicate the overall framework of the commission. In discussing why one form of quantitative analysis did not decide this case, the commission noted: "It has been argued that a decline in consumption should be considered as a single indivisible cause. We do not believe this approach is appropriate in the context of this case. Many potentially independent, fundamental causes, such as technological change or product substitution, or interest rates, may be partially responsible for a decline in demand. Shift-share analysis does not answer the question of whether and how a decline in demand should be allocated to such causes. Thus, its results should not be considered dispositive."[43]

The commission then noted that "the causal relationship between imports and serious injury to domestic producers can be seen most clearly in the different indicia for each industry." All subsequent discussion in the views concentrated on the economic trends. Stern did attempt in additional views to analyze in detail recessionary issues.[44] We now discuss the approach applied by Stern in *Specialty Steel* because it provides a fully articulated methodology that is compatible both with the statute and reasonable economic analysis. Furthermore, it delineates the range of other available choices.

Framework for Analysis

Some have oversimplified the choice facing the commission when it analyzes cyclical industries during recessions. One extreme would treat all recession-related effects as a single cause to be weighed against imports; another would eliminate recession as a possible alternate cause. The law is silent on a direct resolution of this issue, but it does intend that all industries, whether heavily cyclical or not, be on an equal footing when applying for section 201 relief. To count blindly all recession-related effects as one single cause weighed against imports could effectively thwart cyclical industries, like steel, from getting relief when they may need it most. On the other hand, eliminating from consideration all recession-related effects could give highly cyclical industries special advantages in obtaining relief during a downturn.

Fortunately, there is a path between these two extremes: considering only the unusual or abnormal effects on an industry in a downturn as causes of injury. This gives any kind of industry *equal access* to import relief.[45]

A solution to the question of how to analyze causation in a cyclical industry may be approached by considering the regular[46] pattern of that industry. Any mature industry in healthy condition must be able to replenish depleted capital and survive to the next period. In addition, a growth industry must be able to attract net new investment. Both of these activities are inherently "pro-cyclical." Investment does occur during downturns, but it is far more intense during upswings. Clearly, the exigencies of capacity limitations that stimulate the desire to replace and expand the capital of a firm are most palpable during upswings. Increased profits in boom times make it possible for firms to finance internally a greater portion of investment, thus diminishing less desirable exposure to debt financing or raising equity on a stock market subsequently depressed by bad business expectations. Compared to relatively more stable branches of the economy, heavily cyclical industries must generate heavier profits during the upswings to make it through the downturns. Injury (from imports or other sources) *can* occur during either part of the cycle if those profits are squeezed or losses magnified. But it is obvious that heavily cyclical industries (e.g., steel, automobiles, housing) can more easily demonstrate injury during downturns.[47] It is also clear that no remedial action is necessary for industries experiencing normal or expected downturns because the cycle itself will replace such temporarily difficult times of below-average profits with the above-average profits of the upswings.

The conceptual foundation of the process of adjusting for normal cycles can be made clear by the following approximation. Cyclical industries are moving targets and hence it is more difficult to focus on them. Amidst the peaks and troughs of their cycles, one can draw an imaginary trend line that smoothes out the cycles. This puts cyclical industries on the same conceptual basis as those not so exposed to the effects of recessions and booms. The criteria of section 201 may then be applied to any departure from this imaginary trend line to answer how large the departure is (the question of serious injury) and what factors are responsible (the question of substantial cause).

Moving to either of the extremes set forth at the outset—fully counting recession-induced downturns as a cause other than imports or fully eliminating such downturns—would subject cyclical industries either to special advantage or disadvantage in obtaining import relief. In *Automobiles*, as noted earlier, a major concern had been to avoid any methodology that would make relief relatively more difficult for cyclical industries in downturns.[48] In *Motorcycles*, the other side of the coin had proved to be of equal importance because the law shows no indication whatsoever that Congress intended to make it easier for cyclical industries to obtain relief *simply because they are cyclical*.

The balanced approach to examining cyclical industries rests on three factors:

First, in the total absence of any indication otherwise, the congressional intent is that all industries—heavily cyclical or stable—have equal access to protection under the import relief statutes.

Second, when a statute is subject to a number of different interpretations, the commission should choose the interpretation most in accord with the intent of Congress when the statute was passed.[49]

Third, the difficult process of factoring out the "usual" aspects of a recessionary downturn is the approach that best upholds congressional intent and gives economic meaning to the 201 import relief process. The terms "abnormal," "peculiar," "unexpected," or "unusual" may be subjective but they reflect the only practical approach to sorting out what factors may be responsible for lowering a cyclical industry's performance below the trend line discussed above.

Congress was well aware that 201 analysis was inevitably subject to individual judgment and not a direct function of quantitative calculations. The Senate Finance Committee explicitly recognized this situation when it stated:

> The Committee recognized that "weighing" causes in a dynamic economy is not

always possible. It is not intended that a mathematical test be applied by the Commission. The Commissioners will have to assure themselves that imports represent a substantial cause or threat of injury, and not just one of a multitude of equal causes or threats of injury. It is not intended that the escape clause criteria go from one extreme of excessive rigidity to complete laxity. An industry must be seriously injured or threatened by an absolute increase in imports, and the imports must be deemed to be a substantial cause of the injury before an affirmative determination should be made.[50]

Analytical tools such as shift-share analysis and econometric modeling can provide insights, but—as shall shortly be seen—they rarely are capable of matching one-for-one the considerations required of the commission by Congress and suggested by sound legal and economic reasoning. To limit one's choice to either of the two extremes mentioned above simply because the numbers are more straightforward would be foolish. Attempts at analysis should not be abandoned simply because economic theory has not yet been able to quantify fully certain considerations. That would be bad policy indeed. Both quantitative and qualitative elements are indispensable to carry out congressional intent in any meaningful manner.

Problems of the Specialty Steel Industries

The exercise of weighing among the causes to determine whether imports are as important as any other cause of injury in the specialty steel investigation is much more reliably done and understood when the nonimport problems confronting the industry are explicitly described and their relative importance is assessed. A look beyond the microdata on each specialty steel product group given in the unanimous Views of the Commission allows us to see the forest from the trees by concentrating on the most important phenomena. Finally, briefly reviewing Stern's causal analysis in *Specialty Steel* demonstrates how the statute can be applied to a cyclical industry. We first summarize the causes and then examine them to see the interplay of the underlying factors.

Imports, benefiting from an array of factors, including a significantly overvalued dollar,[51] were the most important cause of the serious injury experienced by all the U.S. specialty steel industries[52] except stainless steel plate.[53] An unusual decline in demand due to the domestic effects of the extraordinarily high (real and nominal) interest rates was the second most important cause of injury except in plate, where it was a more important cause of injury than imports. These historically unprecedented interest rates[54] brought on, deepened, and lengthened the current recession. They constituted an unusual factor (beyond any normal cyclical decline in demand) in the current downturn in specialty steel. Except in plate, a third cause of injury, the decline in U.S. exports, was clearly less important than both imports and the unusual decline in demand. With respect to plate, declining exports vied with the unusual decline in demand as a substantial cause—but both factors were more important than imports as causes of injury.

Other possible causes of injury were considered. Some of these, while playing significant roles in the plight of other larger cyclical industries such as carbon steel and automobiles, were far less important in the problems of specialty steel producers. Interest expenses of the specialty steel producers increased significantly over the five years for which we have collected data, but had small overall significance in explaining the fate of U.S. producers.[55] Transportation costs can be a significant factor in the final cost of a product in the United States. However, this factor was considerably more important in the case of lower-valued products such as carbon steel than in the case of specialty steel. The high value to weight ratio of specialty steel (coupled with transportation costs based primarily on weight) reduced the relative importance of transportation costs. Locational factors also served to diminish the importance of transportation costs for specialty steel. Most specialty steel products are both produced and consumed in the Northeast and the North Central regions of the United States. (By comparison, carbon steel also is primarily produced in this industrial belt, but its customers are much more widely distributed and thus affected by changing transport costs.) Technological change can also cause injury to U.S. producers if U.S. producers fail to adopt useful technology or the user industries switch to new alternatives. Neither was the case in specialty steel.

Independent modeling of recessionary influences on large industries may be impossible. Many of the factors important to an understanding of any industry operate simultaneously. Time-series data often are limited because investigations usually cover only five years. The law dictates that imports be treated as a separate cause. Yet, particularly with the large industries that 201 investigations often cover, imports are not truly independent of domestic causal factors. Thus, weighing among various causes may necessarily become a more qualitative than econometric effort. The causes of the problems of the specialty steel producers we have discussed demonstrate all these considerations.

The law specifically requires that increased imports be treated as a unitary cause. Therefore, the law requires at a minimum that the effects of interest rates on imports be considered separately from their nonimport effects. The appropriate level of aggregation of various factors into causes that are weighed against each other must be done on a case-by-case basis. For instance, in *Specialty Steel*, the U.S. interest rates of the last two years were perhaps the single largest factor in the recent story of U.S. specialty steel's performance. But interest rates could not legally be treated as a unitary nonimport cause. Rather, their effect on exchange rates (along with other factors) explained (along with other factors) two separate causes of injury: increasing imports and declining U.S. exports. The domestic effects of interest rates—through an extraordinary impact on inventory policies and demand by user industries—explain yet another cause of injury: a decline in demand above any expected recessionary fluctuation. Interest rates also directly accounted, in part, for the worsened financial picture of domestic producers. In short, high interest rates spun a web around the industry. But the effects of this single factor were best analyzed by dividing them among a number of causes, each with independent standing in the weighing process of this 201.

OVERVIEW

Section 201, in its present form, has been a very visible part of the import relief framework of the United States since 1974. The statute survived almost a decade without a clear delineation of how it should be applied to cyclical industries, which may seem surprising in retrospect, but it's telling. First, the trade act itself left significant latitude. Second, to some extent the solution of the problem was elusive. And third—at least until recently—the recessions were sufficiently mild, the nation's trade problems sufficiently tractable, and the condition of basic U.S. industries apparently resilient enough to allow the issue to remain unresolved.

This breathing space for the statute began to vanish with the onset of the 1980–83 recession years. Industries sensitive to interest rates led the decline— most notably automobiles and housing. But the ailing carbon steel industry was not far behind. And as the dollar soared along with real interest rates and unemployment, other sensitive manufacturing industries—like the modern specialty steel producers—went into tailspins as well. These three significant import relief cases discussed here afford an appreciation of the evaluation of the specific methodology we have proposed to handle the problem of applying section 201 to cyclical industries during recessions (or booms).

Still, much concern remains about the viability of the import relief scheme and the vitality of the basic U.S. industries that have suffered unprecedented problems. Based on our examination, a few comments are in order:

(1) A correct reading of *Automobiles*, in conjunction with *Motorcycles* and *Specialty Steel*, demonstrates that there is no barrier in the present statute to offering relief to cyclical industries beset by recessionary problems. Escape clause import relief is most definitely available.

(2) A majority of the commission has never endorsed the view that a decline in demand due to a general recession is to be treated as a unitary cause to be weighed against imports in applying section 201. In fact, the commission has never adopted any uniform methodology. The one proposed here has economic and legal merit. But additional congressional guidance on the subject would be useful to the commission.

(3) Some have argued that the "substantial cause" criterion is too demanding and should be replaced by an easier standard. Much of this discussion is based on the negative commission finding in *Automobiles* and the firm belief that the need for import relief was obvious. While the commission can only apply the criteria as legislated by Congress,[56] the "substantial cause" criterion was not a problem in *Motorcycles* and *Specialty Steel*.

The scrutiny given the auto industry by the commission in the section 201 investigation demonstrated that there were other significant problems that import relief could never touch. The performance of this industry since the imposition of the VRAs confirms the validity of the industry assessment shared by the majority. As we have seen in the three case studies, when the commission wrestles with an import relief investigation, it develops most of the ingredients necessary for a detailed assessment of an industry's problems. This is particularly true when the weighing process of section 201 is explicitly applied. More use can be made of the commission's valuable experience as an industry assessor in the formation of an overall economic policy toward problem industries that goes beyond just a reaction to imports.[57]

NOTES

1. Throughout we adopt the convention of using "general import relief" to mean relief from imports not tied to any specific unfair practice.

2. "Recession" cartels in Japan are a tool for structural rather than cyclical adjustment. Japanese industrial policy, including recession cartels, has been discussed in depth in *Foreign Industrial Targeting and Its Effects on U.S. Industries, Phase I: Japan*, USITC Pub. no. 1437, October 1983, Other U.S. government sources include U.S. General Accounting Office, *Industrial Policy: Case Studies in the Japanese Experience*, GAO/ID-83-11, 1982, and *Industrial Policy: Japan's Flexible Approach*, the Controller General of the United States, GAO/ID-82-32, 1982. Kozo Yamamura has treated the subject in "Success that Soured: Administrative Guidance and Cartels in Japan" in *Policy and Trade Issues of the Japanese Economy*, ed. Kozo Yamamura (Seattle: University of Washington Press, 1982). Finally, Iyori Hiroshi discusses the subject in his chapter in this volume. There is no general agreement that Japanese industrial policy has been or continues to be critical to Japan's success. However, public perception is an undeniable factor in the widespread doubts on the adequacy of U.S. import relief law.

3. *Certain Motor Vehicles and Certain Chassis and Bodies Therefor*, Report to the President in Inv. TA-201-44 under sec. 201 of the Trade Act of 1974, USITC Pub. 1110 (1980). Referred to hereafter as *Automobiles*.

4. Trade Agreements Expansion Act of 1951, § 7, 65 Stat. 73. The first escape clause procedure was established by President Truman's executive order that an escape clause be inserted in future trade agreements. Exec. Order 9832, 3 C.F.R. 624 (1943–45 Comp.)

5. Dean Acheson, *Present at the Creation* (New York: Norton, 1969), pp. 200–201. Subsidized and less-than-fair-value imports are covered by Title VII of the Tariff Act of 1930.

6. GATT Art. 19.1(a) states: "If, as a result of unforeseen developments and of the effect of the obligations incurred by a contracting party under this Agreement, including tariff concessions, any product is being imported into the territory of that contracting party in such increased quantities and under such conditions as to cause or threaten serious injury to domestic producers in that territory of like or directly competitive products, the contracting party shall be free, in respect of such product, and to the extent and for such time as may be necessary to prevent or remedy such injury, to suspend the obligation in whole or in part or to withdraw or modify the concession."

7. 19 USC 2251–53. The provisions mentioned below actually appear in secs. 201, 202, 203; for convenience sake, they will be referred to as they are in common parlance, sec. 201. We mention only those provisions of interest to our theme. The act provides for trade adjustment assistance and other items of interest in contexts other than the present one.

8. 19 USC 1801 et seq.

9. See legislative history in *Trade Reform Act of 1974, Report of the Committee on Finance*, U.S. Senate (93d Cong., 2d Sess., 1974), Rept. no. 93–1298, p. 119. Referred to as "S. Rept. no. 93–1298."

10. Ibid.

11. S. Rept. no. 93–1298, pp. 27, 119–24.

12. The commission is required under sec. 201(d)(1) when making an affirmative recommendation to choose increased duties and/or import restrictions (quotas) which "prevent or remedy such injury" or recommend adjustment assistance when it is deemed an effective alternative.

13. In determining whether and how to provide relief, the president is directed by sec. 202 to consider certain factors including the national economic interest of the United States. Sec. 202(c) specifies such factors as the likely effectiveness of import relief as means to promote adjustment, the effect on consumers, the effect on U.S. international economic interests, the impact of any expected

demands for compensation by trade partners, the extent to which the U.S. market is a focus for imports due to restrictions elsewhere, and the economic and social costs of denying relief. The listing of presidential considerations is not exhaustive as the president is permitted to take into account other considerations "as he may deem relevant." The Senate Finance Committee cautioned, however, that it felt "no U.S. industry which has suffered serious injury should be cut off from relief for foreign policy reasons" (S. Rept. 93–1298, p. 124).

14. 19 U.S.C. 2253(3).

15. On June 23, 1983, the Supreme Court in *Immigration and Naturalization Service* v. *Chadha*, Slip Op. no. 80–1832, ruled that a one-house legislative veto in another act was unconstitutional. On July 6, 1983, in a second related case, the court affirmed in *Process Gas Consumers Group* v. *U.S.*, without opinion the decision of the Federal Circuit Court of Appeals for the District of Columbia in *Consumers Union of U.S.* v. *F.T.C.* that the two-house legislative veto in the F.T.C. Improvements Act was also unconstitutional. It, therefore, appears that the veto provisions of the Trade Act have been nullified by these decisions. Congress has not yet solved the looming problem of how best to retain legislative control over authority delegated to the executive. The current unclear post-Chadha status of the legislative veto is documented in Louis Fisher, "Developments after the Supreme Court's Decision in the Legislative Veto Case," Congressional Research Service, Library of Congress, Washington, D.C., September 20, 1983.

16. The Trade Act does not expressly provide for judicial review of sec. 201 actions, and the commission has taken the position, when the question of review has been raised, that sec. 201 actions are not reviewable. However, the courts in two instances have concluded that at least some aspects of commission decisions are reviewable. In *Sneaker Circus, Inc.* v. *Carter*, 457 F. Supp. 771 (E.D.N.Y. 1978), in which the plaintiff sought invalidation of certain orderly marketing agreements on imports of footwear, the court held, among other things, that a commission decision that there was good cause to reinvestigate the same subject matter within one year of a previous determination, was reviewable. In *Maple Leaf Fish Co.* v. *United States*, which is pending before the U.S. Court of International Trade (Court no. 81-10-01412) and which involved a challenge of certain aspects of import relief on mushrooms, the court on June 21, 1983, denied a government motion to dismiss on the ground that the court lacked jurisdiction. The theory for not reviewing ITC sec. 201 recommendations is that they are only recommendations; no case or controversy exists in terms of constitutional law. Given the broad considerations under which the executive acts (see n. 13), it is difficult to contemplate a situation in which the president's actions under sec. 201 could be successfully challenged in court. The doctrine of judicial abstention in political questions would weigh against such a challenge.

In addition to sec. 201, laws written by Congress establish the conditions for according relief from subsidized imports (19 USC 1671), sold at less than fair value, or "dumped" (19 USC 1673), injure U.S. agriculture (7 USC 624), or infringe on intellectual property rights (19 USC 1337 and sec. 341, Trade Act of 1974). There is also a special provision for responding to market disruption by imports from Communist countries (19 USC 1436).

17. See *Certain Motor Vehicles and Certain Chassis and Bodies Therefor*, Report to the President in Inv. TA-201-44 under sec. 201 of the Trade Act of 1974, USITC Pub. 1110 (1080).

18. The Trade and Tariff Act of 1984 amended certain provisions affecting the USITC. Only Title VIII, "Enforcement Authority for a National Policy for the Steel Industry," is tangentially related to the discussion of this essay.

19. For example, in *Birch Plywood Doorskins* (Inv. no. TA-201-1, USITC Pub. 743 (1975), Commissioner Minchew considered the cyclical downturn in the industry a part of the norm against which injury was to be measured. The rest of the commission, however, looked at the cyclical drop in demand as part of the injury, and then weighed the relative importance of causes. In *Bolts, Nuts, and Screws of Iron and Steel* (Inv. no. TA-201-2, USITC Pub. 747 [1975], p. 11), Chairman Leonard stated, "'present' injury must be found by examining a time span that discounts brief and transitory episodes in the performance of the domestic industry and established a realistic performance for the industry in the present." Chairman Leonard made a similar statement in *Stainless Steel and Alloy Tool Steel* (Inv. no. TA-201-5, USITC Pub. 756 (1976), p. 72). In contrast, Vice-Chairman Minchew noted in the same investigation (p. 47): "The two principal causes of injury to the domestic industry are increased imports and the cyclical nature of the industry." Although he concluded imports to be the most important cause of serious injury, Vice-Chairman Minchew clearly analyzed cyclical downturn as part of the serious injury. The variety of approaches was further augmented by Commissioner Ablondi when, in selecting an appropriate period within which to measure injury, he stated that "it has been the established practice of the Commission under section 301 of the Trade Expansion Act as well as under section 201 of the 1974 Trade Act to analyze imports over a period of

time of sufficient length to establish trends and thereby put aberrant or temporary conditions into proper perspective." *See Stainless Steel and Alloy Tool Steel*, Commissioner Ablondi, citing *Ceramic Table and Kitchen Articles, Including Dinnerware*, TEA-1-22, TC Pub. 406 (1971); *Bagatelle, Billiard, and Pool Balls*, TEA-1-19, TC Pub. 347 (1971); *Nonrubber Footwear*, TEA-1-18, TC Pub. 359 (1971), pp. 10–11 (Commissioners Clubb and Moore) and p. 37 (Commissioner Leonard).

20. One function of the views by which the commission explains its votes in investigations is to expose the methodology and reasoning—as well as the conclusions—to public scrutiny. It is for this reason that a textual analysis of them is particularly helpful.

21. *Automobiles* was instituted by the USITC on June 12, 1980, and concluded with a negative commission recommendation on December 6, 1980. No 201 investigations were initiated while *Automobiles* was in progress.

22. Our examination of all commission escape clause, market disruption, countervailing duty, and antidumping determinations between October 1978 and June 1983 shows that the proportions of commission affirmatives in 201 investigations (57 percent) was slightly higher than that for all determinations (55 percent). Some would contend that many potential 201 investigations are never brought because of the poor chances for relief actually being accorded after the ITC sends its recommendation to the White House.

23. The president did not accord relief in the first six instances where the USITC recommended it between December 1977 and September 1978. In the next six investigations in which the commission recommended relief, between September 1978 and August 1980, the president consistently accorded relief. The approaching elections may have had some significance in this turnabout but any such conclusion would require detailed analysis of each case.

24. It is not important to our discussion whether 1980 to 1983 is broken down into two recessions. Certainly, the economic phenomena of concern here had a continuity through the whole period.

25. *Automobiles*, "View of Chairman Bill Alberger," p. 21. The commission members for *Automobiles* were Chairman Bill Alberger, Vice-Chairman Michael Calhoun, Commissioners Catherine Bedell, George Moore, and Paula Stern.

26. Ibid., "View of Vice-Chairman Michael J. Calhoun," p. 83, 86.

27. Ibid., pp. 85–86, 88–89.

28. Ibid., "Views of Commissioner Paula Stern," p. 129.

29. Congress has recognized that the relative weighing of alternate causes of injury is unquestionably subjective. In *World Trade and the Law of the GATT* (New York: Bobbs-Merrill, 1969), sec. 23.1, p. 561, John Jackson states that "serious" investigation of the term serious injury "has occurred only once in practice"—the *Hatters' Fur* case (1950). The GATT working party appointed to investigate that dispute found that even serious injury, no less its causation, "is essentially a matter of economic and social judgment involving a considerable subjective element" (Report on Withdrawal by the United States of a Tariff Concession under Article 19 of the GATT, Geneva, 1951, p. 22). While we agree with the GATT working party on this point, causal considerations are even more subjective in nature than injury considerations.

30. *Automobiles*, "Views of Commissioner Paula Stern," p. 129.

31. *Automobiles*, "Views of Commissioners George M. Moore and Catherine Bedell," p. 172.

32. Ibid., pp. 172–74.

33. *Heavyweight Motorcycles, and Engines and Power Train Subassemblies Therefor*, Report to the President on Inv. no. TA-201-47 under sec. 201 of the Trade Act of 1974, USITC Pub. 1342 (February 1983). Hereafter referred to as *Motorcycles*. See "Views of Chairman Eckes," pp. 5–19; "Views of Commissioner Veronica Haggart," pp. 21–54; and "Views of Commissioner Paula Stern," pp. 55–83.

34. Chairman Eckes had participated in *Fishing Rods and Parts Thereof*, Inv. no. TA-201-45, November 1981, and both he and Commissioner Veronica Haggart took part in *Tubeless Tire Valves*, Inv. no. TA-201-46, September 1982. Both cases resulted in unanimous negative determinations.

35. For instance, the issue of how to define the domestic industry arose. From the outset, the investigation was to center on heavy motorcycles. But how heavy is heavy? Such an inherently subjective question is typical of the ones that the USITC must regularly answer with as an objective approach as possible. Harley-Davidson argued that the commission should look at all cycles over 700 cc as being "like and directly competitive." The competition—the bulk of whose heavy machines hovered between 700 and 900 cc, saw these as "unlike" Harley's larger bikes. Because drawing distinctions on size proved elusive, all bikes over 700 cc were considered.

36. Our examination of all 54 completed sec. 201 investigations reveals no other instance in which the president's action so closely followed the commission's recommendation. Relief recommended

by the commission has virtually always been greater than the relief actually provided by the president, because the ITC is required to look only at the narrowly defined interests of the injured industry while the president must consider other interests as well. The law requires the commission to recommend import restrictions that will fully "remedy such injury" to the domestic industry. On the other hand, sec. 202 of the Trade Act requires the president to consider also any adjustment assistance that is already being provided to the workers or the firms in the industry, efforts being made by the industry to adjust to import competition, possible effects of the import restrictions on consumers and on the international interests of the United States, the effects on other industries and firms of possible compensation that might be given to offset the effects of the import restrictions on other nations, and so on. Any of these other factors could give the president reason for providing less than the full relief recommended by the commission. Since the relief that is finally provided is the result of weighing all of these factors, one would expect full relief to be granted only when these other factors had significant influence. Prior to *Motorcycles*, this had never occurred.

37. For a discussion of these tests, see *Motorcycles*, "Views of Commissioner Paula Stern," pp. 60–61.

38. *Motorcycles*, "Views of Chairman Alfred Eckes," p. 15.

39. Ibid., "Views of Commissioner Veronica Haggart," pp. 43–44.

40. Ibid., "Views of Commissioner Paula Stern," p. 134.

41. The increasing imports of 1982 went into inventory as imports were expanded to accommodate the growth of demand experienced in 1981. But sales declined 28 percent in 1982. Both Eckes and Haggart saw the overhanging import inventories as a threat. Stern saw them as a symptom of a more important cause of injury—decline in demand. A number of factors contributed to this judgment: the established policy of importers of orderly marketing practices, the predominance (80 percent) of cycles under 850 cc in the inventories of heavy motorcycles that did not directly compete with Harley's bigger cycles, and the public commitment of Japanese importers to reduce exports to the United States in 1981. Past practices by these importers lent credibility to these commitments.

There are bizarre aspects to the remedy recommended and applied in *Motorcycles*. First, it ironically applies to future imports while the threat was seen by the majority as coming from inventories already imported!

Second, the import relief was patently advertised as an effort to aid one domestic producer. (In a memorandum to the U.S. trade representative dated April 1, 1983, the president directed the trade representative to monitor the effectiveness of the import relief and "Harley-Davidson's trade adjustment efforts." 19 Presidential Documents 492 [no. 13, Apr. 4, 1983].) But this relief will likely sharpen Harley's domestic competition. All indications are that Harley, under its new ownership, has undertaken an aggressive adjustment program that offers opportunities for success by expanding its model lines and broadening its image to attract new customers. But Harley's difficulties, as we have seen, were not principally import related. To the extent relief restricts the flow of Japanese heavy motorcycles to the United States, it could induce Honda of America to expand its Marysville, Ohio, production, which is already devoted to production of heavy motorcycles. Thus, import relief could very well increase the presently limited overlap of Honda and Harley in the U.S. marketplace, particularly since Harley wishes to broaden its line at the lower end of the heavy motorcycle class where Honda now imports but would most likely switch to domestic production with a large tariff increase. Honda of America, not the petitioner, may have been the prime beneficiary of any import relief.

42. *Stainless Steel and Alloy Tool Steel*, Report to the President on Inv. TA-201-48 under Sec. 201 of the Trade Act of 1974, USITC Pub. 1377 (May 1983). Referred to as *Specialty Steel*.

43. *Specialty Steel*, "Views of the Commission," p. 24.

44. Ibid., "Additional Views of Commissioner Paula Stern," p. 63.

45. This "equal access" principle had first been cited in *Automobiles*. In *Automobiles*, advice of interested parties and the intent of Congress led to the dictum that "cyclical industries should receive no special treatment." But that dictum does not, of course, specify what treatment is special—factoring in or factoring out the "normal" cyclical behavior of an industry. See "Views of Commissioner Stern" p. 129. The underlying logic was not fully fleshed out until *Specialty Steel*.

46. We do not mean to imply that it is simple to establish what is "regular," "normal," or "expected." Each recession is individual in its timing, severity, and recovery. The National Bureau of Economic Research has been cycle-watching for many decades without any definitive conclusions. National economies may move into recessions; individual industries and firms experience those recessions as downturns reflecting both national and particular circumstances. As one moves from the aggregate economic concept of recession to questions of a downturn in an individual industry, one

moves into even more hazardous ground. The law of large numbers no longer provides much assistance and the peculiar circumstances of any one industry's market and production conditions—which may be totally unrelated to national conditions—can swamp recession-related effects. Furthermore, the performance of any particular industry can lead, lag, or move in unison with the national aggregates such as gross national product, etc. line that smoothes out the cycles.

47. In *Automobiles*, Stern noted that the problems of the industry in part manifested themselves over the twenty-years of 1960 to 1980 in which each successive peak in aggregate profit margins was lower than the previous peak. (*Automobiles*, p. 142.) It is extremely rare for the commission to have sufficient data to make an observation such as this about the peak performance of a cyclical industry.

48. *Automobiles*, p. 129.

49. As one commentator has stated:

When a question arises as to whether or how a statute should apply with reference to particular circumstances, as is the case when any other kind of question is to be decided, a decision can be reached only by applying some kind of a criterion, whether it be rational or otherwise. For the interpretation of statutes, 'intent of the legislature' is the criterion, or test, that is most often recited. An almost overwhelming majority of judicial opinions on statutory issues is written in the idiom of legislative intent. The reason for this doubtless lies in an assumption that an obligation to construe statutes in such a way as to carry out the will, real or attributed, of the lawmaking branch of the government is mandated by principles of separation of powers.
[C. Sands, *Sutherland Statutory Interpretation* (Wilmette, Il.: Callaghan, 1973), (§ 45.05). See also *SEC v. Joiner Corp.*, 320 U.S. 344, 355 (1943)].

Although the commission is not a federal court, it is a creature of the Congress. The commission cannot make the law, but must interpret it so as to best carry out congressional intent. As the Supreme Court has stated: "The intent of the law-makers is the law." See *Jones v. Guaranty and Indemnity Co.*, 101 U.S. 622, 626 (1979). The statement was made in reference to the actions of courts constituted under Art. 3 of the Constitution. However, it clearly applies to the work of the commission.

50. S. Rept. no. 93-1298, pp. 120–21.

51. Although dollar appreciation was a fundamental factor in explaining the success of imports, no remedy available under sec. 201 could reach this factor. Rather the relief period could offer innovative U.S. producers some breathing space. As Stern noted in her additional views, "More enlightened public policy—and in its absence, old-fashioned luck—will have to take care of the rest" (*Specialty Steel*, pp. 96). Exchange rate fluctuations can be influenced by many short-term political phenomena. If they are a fundamental part of an import problem, this fact should argue for a shorter rather than longer period of relief so that appropriate adjustments may be made in light of circumstances that can change rather dramatically in the short run.

52. In *Specialty Steel* the definition of the domestic industry was not as problematic as it had been in *Motorcycles* or *Automobiles*. Four industries were considered: stainless steel plate, stainless steel sheet and strip, stainless steel bar and rod, and alloy tool steel.

53. For a discussion of the basis for this conclusion, see "Views of Commissioner Paula Stern on Stainless Steel Plate" in *Specialty Steel*, pp. 33–37.

54. In 1975—the most severe postwar recession prior to 1982—real interest rates had actually been negative because inflation exceeded the cost of borrowing money. In 1982, however, not only were real interest rates positive, but they were higher than in any recent period. Inflation declined to 3 percent from the end of 1981 to the end of 1982 while the nominal prime rate remained at about 15 percent.

55. Net profits declined by over $400 million between 1979 and 1982 while net interest payments increased by $10 million.

56. There may be hidden snares in revising sec. 201 causal standards. For instance, it has been suggested that 201 should be changed to remove the weighing requirements. Imports would have to cause serious injury, but relief would be possible even if other causes were more important (as in *Automobiles*). On its face such a change would seem to lower the standards of sec. 201. However, there are potential situations in which such a change could make relief more difficult for a domestic industry to obtain. Consider a scenario where the serious injury threshold is only marginally met. Each cause—including imports—is responsible for a quantum of injury that is not by itself serious. However, when added together, the total meets the serious standard. Under the present statute a relief recommendation would follow if imports were at least as important as any other cause. Under the proposed change, relief would not be possible because imports by themselves would not be causing serious injury. The present causal standard is more stringent than the proposed one in terms

of the ranking of imports as a cause; it is weaker than the proposed one in allowing serious injury to be an additive result of several causes.

Requiring imports to be "a cause of serious injury" would remove this problem but reduce the necessary injury attributable to imports alone to the material level. The low "material injury" threshold is reserved in the law only for relief against unfair imports. If it were written into a new sec. 201, relief could become virtually automatic in any recession if import share increased in the slightest amount. This raises questions about whether such a change would undermine United States commitments under Article 19 of the GATT.

57. Serious attention to the availability of general import relief and its relation to industrial modernization was reawakened with the ITC's examination of the carbon steel industry in 1984. See *Carbon and Certain Alloy Steel Products,* Report to the President in Inv. TA-201-51 under Sec. 201 of the Trade Act of 1974, USITC Pub. 1553 (1984). For the first time, petitioners raised the notion of conditioning import relief on certain actions by labor and management in the industry. Four commissioners commented on the concept of such conditionality, which goes beyond the traditional bounds of the ITC's statutory mandate and raises more general issues of industrial policy. In the context of providing enforcement authority for negotiated voluntary restraints on steel imports, Congress in the Trade and Tariff Act of 1984 provided for monitoring of the adequacy of labor and management adjustment actions in the steel industry. This limited experiment may form the basis for future conditionality programs that make use of the ITC's expertise. However, it is at present an ad hoc process.

The National Security Clause
of the Trade Expansion Act of 1962:
Import Competition and the
Machine Tool Industry

GARY R. SAXONHOUSE

INTRODUCTION

National security considerations are increasingly being invoked as a reason to restrict imports of Japanese products into the United States. This paper will examine the history of the legal basis for such efforts and will evaluate the use of such arguments by the American machine tool industry. Special attention will be given to the relationship between national security grounds for limiting Japanese imports and the industrial targeting counterparts of such arguments.

HISTORY OF THE NATIONAL SECURITY CLAUSE

Noneconomic factors overturning the implications of economic theory are as old as economics itself.[1] In 1776, Adam Smith observed, "Defense is of much more importance than opulence." In the nineteenth century, John Stuart Mill wrote, "Economic welfare is not the sole goal of life. Political considerations are also important. Thus, it may be necessary to become partially self-sufficient in certain times of activity, even at great cost because of fear of future wars."[2]

This long-understood exception to the policy implications of the theory of comparative advantage was codified in the postwar General Agreements on Tariffs and Trade (GATT). Article 21 of the GATT observes that "[n]othing in this Agreement shall be construed . . . (b) to prevent any contracting party from taking any action which it considers necessary for the protection of its essential security interests. . . . (i.e.) relating to the traffic in arms, ammunition and implements of war and to such traffic in other goods and materials as is carried on directly for the purpose of supplying a military establishment."

In the United States, while the GATT has an ambiguous legal status owing to its never having been formally recognized by Congress, the substance of Article 21 has been taken over explicitly in a number of pieces of legislation.[3] The national security clause was enacted as part of the Trade Agreements Extension Act of 1954. The 1954 act provided that "[n]o action shall be taken . . . to decrease the duty on any article if the President finds that such reductions would threaten domestic production needed for projected national defense requirements."[4]

Congress greatly enlarged the scope of the national security clause the following year when it enacted the Trade Agreements Act of 1955. Only some limited curbs on tariff reductions were provided for in the 1954 act. The new 1955 act strengthened the national security clause by giving the president authority to protect industries threatened by imports under the status quo. The 1955 act allows the president to raise tariff and impose quotas on imports where necessary to protect national security.[5]

The national security clause has been strengthened on a number of occasions since 1955. In 1958, Congress broadened the language of the clause, applying it not only to imported articles but also to their derivatives. The 1958 act also broadened the language of the clause so that it might permit relief when either the quantities or the circumstances of imports threaten to impair the national security.[6] Congress also granted private parties the right to petition for relief under the national security clause and required the executive branch to publish a report in response to each such petition.[7]

This latter element in the 1958 expansion of the national security clause reflects a uniquely American approach to international trade law. Unlike the practices of its major trading partners during the postwar period, private American citizens have had the right to attempt to compel the American government to force foreign governments to live up to their international economic obligations.[8] In the context of the national security clause such standing for private citizens may seem strange. It is one thing to provide a channel for private citizens to bring to the attention of the U.S. government the unfair practices of foreign governments that cause them specific economic injury. It is another matter entirely to use similar channels to convey information about national security from private individuals to the United States government. It is difficult to believe that the Congress in making this expansion actually believed private parties were in a better position to assess national security needs than the executive branch. Rather this expansion is yet another manifestation of the congressional distrust of the executive branch's handling of international economic diplomacy. Perhaps in the 1950s, during the McCarthy era, it was considered appropriate to presume that the executive branch in furtherance of universalist principles might negotiate away national security unless checked by the due process owed to an informed and aroused private sector!

No major changes in the national security clause occurred from 1958 until 1974 when the negotiating authority for the Tokyo Round was being developed. In that year, Congress amended the national security clause, altering the proce-

dures available to private parties seeking relief under its terms.[9] Where formerly
the secretary of the treasury had the exclusive responsibility to make the initial
determinations in response to petitions from private parties, the Trade Act of
1974 now required him to consult with the secretaries of defense and commerce
prior to making such a determination. Finally, in 1979, as part of a broader shift
of international trade administration functions from Treasury and State to Commerce in an obvious effort to make them more responsive to producer interests,
the secretary of commerce was given the responsibility of making the initial
determination on national security clause petitions.[10]

The dangers of the obvious misuse of national security arguments for private
ends go back well before Dr. Johnson's famous eighteenth-century aphorism.
More recently in a section entitled "The Security Exceptions of Article XXI and
the Problems of Politically Motivated Economic Measures," John Jackson noted
that Article 21 can be "a dangerous loophole to the obligations of the GATT."[11] In
1970, Kenneth Dam, who has since served as Deputy U.S. Secretary of State,
similarly wrote:

> One danger is that the national security argument is almost infinitely expandable.
> Protectionist claims based on national security are put forth not only for products
> used by the military but also for civilian products. The arguments favoring such
> restrictions are based on the notion that the product in question is produced by
> industry and that in time of war that industry would be called upon greatly to expand
> its production. In times of competitive pressure, almost every industry can produce
> an argument along national security lines.[12]

Both Jackson and Dam were referring to actions under Article 21. Given the
opportunity for private parties to initiate actions under the national security
clause in U.S. trade law, dangers of the kind envisioned by Jackson and Dam are
still more likely. In a 1956 report the U.S. Congress's Joint Economic Committee noted that the law provides "a new rationale whereby some industries denied
other forms of relief from foreign competition, might advance a 'national defense'
argument as the next solution to their problems.[13] The report observed that as
many industries had applied for relief less than a year after the adoption of the
national security clause as there were pending applications for relief under the
escape clause. The Joint Economic Committee warned against "the real danger
that . . . trade restrictions in the name of defense will really be manifestations of
commercial advantage made sacrosanct against criticisms by the aura of patriotic
need, even though the real effect is to weaken national security."[14] Echoing the
Joint Economic Committee report, a year later in 1957 Charles Kindleberger
wryly noted "Manufacturers of many peacetime products ranging from paper to
candles and thumbtacks have insisted that the country will be unable to defend
itself against aggression from overseas unless they get tariff protection."[15]

Under section 232, petitions have not been as blatant as Kindleberger projected. Since 1962 claims of necessity to national defense have been made on

behalf of manganese and chromium alloys; tungsten mill products; antifriction bearings and parts; watches, movements, and parts; ferroalloys and related products; miniature and instrument precision ball bearings; EHV power circuit breakers; industrial fasteners (bolts, nuts, and large screws, except mini roof bolts); glass-lined chemical processing equipment; ferromanganese, ferrochromium, ferrosilicon, and related materials; bolts, nuts, and large screws of iron and steel; crude oil.[16] Contrary to the fears expressed by Jackson and Dam, with the important exception of crude oil, all the above petitions have been rejected.

In making these administrative decisions, the Treasury and the Commerce departments have appeared to rely on a series of separate criteria for economic injury that are set forth in section (e) of the statute. These factors include "domestic production needed for projected national defense requirements, the capacity of domestic industries to meet such requirements, existing and anticipated availabilities of the . . . products . . . essential to the national defense, the requirements of growth of such industries . . . including the investment . . . necessary to insure such growth, and the importation of goods . . . as effect such industries and the capacity of the United States to meet national security requirements." Additionally, the secretary and the president must consider "the impact of foreign competition on the economic welfare of individual domestic industries [necessary to our national security] and any substantial unemployment . . . , loss of skills or investment."[17]

Characteristically, the meaning and application of these criteria in administrative decisions have been extremely controversial. Under section 232 Treasury and Commerce officials have sought to discover whether an import restriction would substantially improve an industry's capacity to respond to a national security crisis by seeking evidence as to whether an industry's current impairment of such capacity was the result of import competition.[18] Whether there is statutory language that requires such a strict interpretation is unclear. By seeking such evidence, however, Commerce and Treasury officials have prevented the use of section 232 proceedings as a means by which industries, a portion of whose sales are defense-related, can circumvent the requirements of section 201 and make their claims for import relief in closed fora insulated from the public scrutiny associated with the work of the International Trade Commission. In the one instance where relief was granted under section 232, the enormous size of the domestic oil industry relative to any of the other petitioners seems to have been the critical element that allowed the success of its petition.[19] Even this decision was widely regarded at the time it was made as blatantly protectionist.[20]

THE AMERICAN MACHINE TOOL INDUSTRY
AND INTERNATIONAL TRADE STATUTES

In the spring of 1983, the National Machine Tool Builders Association on behalf of its members submitted a petition for import quota protection under section 232. The American machine tool industry, while very small by comparison with the domestic oil industry, is a much larger and more significant industry than most of the other previous petitioners under the national security clause. Furthermore, the submission of this petition was almost simultaneous with the rejection by the Office of Special Trade Representatives of a hotly contested petition by Houdaille Industries, an important constituent member of the National Machine Tool Builders Association.[21] The Houdaille petition attempted to use the hitherto obscure section 103 of the Revenue Act of 1971, which allows the exercise of presidential discretion to withhold the investment tax credit from foreign firms that, among other actions, receive subsidies from their governments. It is significant that in attempting to seek relief from import competition the American machine tool industry has fashioned a strategy that avoids the use of section 201 (relief from injury caused by import competition), section 301 (response to foreign trade practices) and countervailing duty proceedings. Note that both the NMTBA petition and the Houdaille petition were prepared by the same law firm.

Economic Condition at the Time of the Houdaille and Section 232 Petitions

There is no question that in common with many other sectors of the American economy in 1982 and early 1983 the American machine tool industry had become extremely depressed. Shipments of machine tools by the domestic industry in the latter part of 1982 in real terms were little more than 50 percent of what they had been at their peak two-and-one-half years earlier. At the same time in real terms, new orders were one-sixth of what they had been in real terms in the late 1970s. With production down so substantially and new orders so low, it is not surprising that by the end of 1982 total machine tool industry employment was down by 35 percent from what it had been two years earlier. New investment in the industry in 1982 had also dropped in real terms by 55 percent from what it had been two years earlier.

As the demand for new machine tools in the United States accelerated and remained high during the 1970s and early 1981, the share in American consumption of machine tools supplied by foreign producers had risen dramatically from 10.6 percent in 1972 to approximately 27.0 percent in 1982 when measured in value. Ominously, foreign producers of machine tools did not turn out to be marginal suppliers to the American market. The sharp cyclical drop in the demand for machine tools in 1982 did not result in a decline in import market share. If anything, import share of domestic machine tool consumption continued to rise. With recovery, the share of imports reached 39.0 percent in 1984. And more than 50 percent of all machine tools imported into the American market came from Japan.

It is not just that the growing import share of the domestic market continues to grow; what is also significant is imports have come to play a particularly significant role in the most sophisticated end of the machine tool market.

While imports have been particularly successful in penetrating the more sophisticated end of the American machine tool imports, among all imports the Japanese machine tool industry does best in the new, rapidly growing sectors. For example, for the full year 1982, Japan supplied 81 percent of all numerical control (NC) turning machinery and 89 percent of all machining centers imported into the United States (see table 1).[22]

The Houdaille Petition

The Houdaille petition, which was filed in May 1982, alleged the government of Japan had been particularly aggressive in its protection, subsidy, and support of the machine tool industries. It alleged the Japanese Ministry of International Trade and Industry worked closely with the Japan External Trade Organization, the Japan Machinery Exporters' Association, the Japan Society for the Promotion of the Machine Industry, the Japan Development Bank, the Japan Keirin Association, the Japan Motorcycle Racing Association, the Japan Machinery Industry Federation, the Japan Machine Tool Manufacturers Association and other public, quasi-public, and private organizations in sponsoring and directing programs that have specifically benefited Japanese machine tool builders.[23] Examples of such programs and activities are alleged to include: (1) promotion of a Japanese machine tool cartel with explicit exemption from the Antimonopoly Law of Japan; (2) subsidy of the Japanese machinery industry with funds in excess of $100 million a year from proceeds of races sponsored by the Japan Keirin Association and the Japan Motorcycle Racing Association; (3) preferential loans by the Japan Development Bank to Japanese machine tool builders, primarily for

TABLE 1

Imports of Machine Tool Products

(In value and in units as percentage of the total consumption, 1982)

Submarket	In Value	In Units
Horizontal numerical control turning machines	49	70
Vertical numerical control turning machines	28	66
Nonnumerical control turning machines	48	50
Gear cutting machines	29	79
Boring machines	25	80
Forging machines	26	52
Machine centers	38	64
Numerical control punching, shearing, bending, and forming machines	43	23

SOURCE: U.S. Department of Commerce, Census Bureau, Current Industrial Reports, Metalworking Machinery FT 246, FT 446, and Malmgren Associates.

research and development and sales promotion, including below-market interest rates and government guarantees; (4) special tax concessions for Japanese
machine tool capital expenditures, including an accelerated depreciation program designed specifically to subsidize high technology NC machine tools; (5)
technical research and development assistance to the Japanese machine tool
industry provided by the Technical Research Institute of the Japan Society for
the Promotion of the Machinery Industry.[24]

These allegations by Houdaille Industries conform to the language of section
103. This section specifically says that revoking the investment tax credit granted
under the Revenue Act of 1971 can be justified when foreign governments
tolerate international cartels and discriminatory acts.

Because delivery time and quality rather than price have been generally
suggested as the bases for the increase in the imported share of American
machine tool consumption, it is puzzling why Houdaille was willing to engage in
an extremely expensive petition effort whose benefits could be otherwise nullified or won over again by relatively modest movements in the yen-dollar
exchange rate. During the eleven-and-one-half month period during which the
petition was active, in fact, this happened on numerous occasions. Moreover, the
allegations that Houdaille made in its petition might have been argued under
other more familiar statutes. It can only be surmised that on the basis of past
section 201 and related proceedings the kind of evidence available to Houdaille
would not have been sufficient to gain an affirmative decision from the International Trade Commission. Doubtless Houdaille hoped that by seeking administrative action under a new statute its available evidence might help to create a
new standard favorable to the particular predicament the machine tool industry
found itself in. Perhaps it also hoped that an affirmative decision under section
103 would open the way politically for the consideration of other protective
remedies that were economically more useful to the industry. Alternatively,
perhaps there was speculation that, faced with the specter of a rash of new
protective decisions under section 103, the Japanese government might
preemptively take steps to encourage a further voluntary restriction of Japanese
machine tool exports to the United States. For example, toward the end of 1977
some U.S. machine tool manufacturers were accusing the Japanese machine tool
industry of numerous illegal acts. In response MITI established a check-price
system, which had the dual effect of both raising export prices and confirming
that Japanese penetration of the machine tool market had mostly to do with
nonprice factors.

In April of 1983, the Office of the Special Trade Representative rejected the
Houdaille petition in its entirety. It has been alleged by the petitioners that
nothing less than the intervention of Prime Minister Nakasone with President
Reagan was needed before the special trade representative would ignore the
obvious merits of their case in making its decision.

Regardless of whether such high-level pressure was actually brought to bear, it
is fair to say that representatives of major foreign trading partners did regularly
impress upon the executive branch that an affirmative finding for Houdaille

would work to seriously undermine international economic relations by undercutting the painstakingly negotiated Tokyo Round agreements. In place of the detailed standards for section 201, section 301, and countervailing duty proceedings embodied in the Trade Agreements Act of 1979, which accepted the substance of the Tokyo Round negotiations, it was argued that the very same subject matter would be evaluated by the entirely vague standards of a much earlier piece of legislation.

That section 103 was not explicitly repealed by either the Trade Act of 1974 or the Trade Agreements Act of 1979 was probably the result of its obscurity. That it was not immediately considered repealed by implication because later acts deal explicitly with the same subject matter is, at least in part, further evidence of the continuing ambiguous status in the United States of laws pertaining to international commerce under the GATT framework.

Quite apart from whether any affirmative action under section 103 could be taken that would be consistent with explicit and implicit American agreements under the GATT, it did prove most difficult for representatives of Houdaille to argue that any action could be justified even by the terms of section 103. Most of the allegations had comparatively little substance.

Cartel Behavior. Despite a number of clear efforts by MITI to restrict competition, no effective cartel has ever been established in this industry.[25] The number of firms in the industry has never been limited, nor have markets been effectively divided. While this has clearly occurred in other Japanese industries, the Japanese machine tool industry seems almost uniquely competitive. For example, the number of Japanese firms producing NC machine tools more than doubled from 1968 to 1981. Among the top six producers of NC machine tools in 1970, only two were among the top six in 1981. The top producer of this equipment in Japan today was not even among the top ten manufacturers in 1976.[26]

The American machine tool industry is feeling beseiged not because a faceless machine tool cartel is moving in lockstep to conquer world markets, but because it is feeling the same competitive pressure that the older firms in the Japanese machine tool industry are feeling from the industry's upstart members. With a special kind of competitive genius, the old underclass of the Japanese machine tool industry, some of whom are still so close to their "mom and pop" status that they are not publicly held corporations, are turning the world industry inside out. As a by-product of this process the smaller firms of the Japanese machine tool industry face bankruptcy rates that exceed even those in the United States. Among the largest firms, the Ikegai Corporation, which was the leading producer in this industry in the early 1970s, has been forced to go through a painful structural transformation with its market share diminishing sharply.

Subsidies. There is no more evidence of major Japanese government subsidies to the machine tool industry than there is evidence of an effective machine tool industry cartel. Subsidies given directly by the Japanese government to firms in the machinery industry as a whole, of which machine tools are just a small part, in the late 1970s sum to no more than $350,000 at current exchange rates.[27] Indeed, no direct subsidies at all were given firms in the Japan machine tool industry between 1978 and 1982.[28]

While no subsidies have been received by firms in Japan's machine tool industry, subsidies have been received by trade associations to be spent on behalf of the industry. The Japan External Trade Organization (JETRO) receives a special subsidy for promoting and advising on the overseas commerce of a number of industries. One of the industries targeted is the Japanese machine tool industry, but other industries targeted for this special help from JETRO include agricultural and fishery products, light machinery, textiles, machinery for shops, chemical products, ship construction machinery, petroleum products, and miscellaneous goods. For promoting this broad array of products, a subsidy in 1981 of 762 million yen (approximately $3.2 million) was allocated in the Japanese government budget.[29] In 1982, this subsidy was increased to 851 million yen (approximately 3.5 million dollars). In addition to this subsidy from the government, JETRO also receives subsidies from other sources of 573 million yen (or approximately 2.4 million dollars).[30] Given the very broad purposes and scope for which this subsidy must be applied, it seems very small and indeed is little different from many of the programs sponsored by the U.S. Department of Commerce and the U.S. Department of Agriculture.

The JETRO case is very similar to what careful analysis has yielded in connection with the uses of proceeds of the alleged $100 million that Houdaille claims was available annually from the proceeds of racing sponsored by the Japan Keirin Association and the Japan Motorcycle Racing Association. By law these proceeds must go to designated public interest groups or foundations, among which is the Japan Machine Tool Builders Association. In practice, the very broad spectrum of groups supported are mostly those having nothing in particular to do with machine tools. For example, no more than 70.9 million yen (approximately 340,000 dollars) was given last year from this source to the Japan Machine Tool Builders Association.[31] The association used these funds to print brochures, gather statistics, and hold trade shows at which American machine tools were displayed.

Research Grants. What is true for subsidies in general is also true specifically for research grants. Expenditures on Japanese government-sponsored or Japanese government-conducted projects to assist the machine tool industry are quite modest. With the important exception of MITI's Laser Utilizing Complex Manufacturing System Project, which involved fifty-five million dollars spent over six years and which engaged three Agency for Industrial Science and Technology laboratories and twenty Japanese machine tool companies, it is doubtful that the rest of the Japanese government-sponsored or conducted research on behalf of the machine tool industry comes to more than one or two million dollars annually.[32] Despite the cooperative character of this important project, the dramatic changes in the relative fortunes of the various machine tool industry members and the reluctance of the industry leaders to join this project make it difficult to believe that it served as the fulcrum of an industry-wide research and development cartel.

Tax Expenditures. There is only one recent provision of the Japanese tax code that has had particular benefit for the Japanese machine tool industry. Until 1982 Japanese users of new computerized NC machine tools were eligible for a bonus 10 percent depreciation allowance for the first year the machine tool was in operation. Because this depreciation allowance (like a similar depreciation allowance for industrial robots) was user based, discriminating in favor of machine tools in general, it did not particularly favor Japanese machine tools in preference to U.S.-built machine tools. Indeed, in 1986 MITI has proposed a bonus tax credit and bonus special depreciation for small- and medium-sized firms using imported machine tools.

Manipulation of the Capital Market. The only government-supported, below market-rate loans received by the machine tool industry in recent years have come from the Japan Development Bank and the Small Business Finance Corporation. The Japan Development Bank made a total of eleven loans to firms in the machine tool industry between 1977 and 1981 totaling approximately six million dollars at an interest rate savings averaging 0.8 percent under prime. The Small Business Finance Corporation made a total of nine loans to firms in the industry for 3.8 million dollars at interest rate savings between 0.6 percent and 1.3 percent under prime.[33] This is an extremely small proportion of total Japanese machine tool industry financing.

THE AMERICAN MACHINE TOOL INDUSTRY
AND THE NATIONAL SECURITY CLAUSE

The National Machine Tool Builders Association petition starts from the presumption that modern defense policy recognizes that full-scale nuclear war, whose outcome in all likelihood would be decided with armaments on hand at the outset of the war and limited military engagements, such as the Vietnam War, during which sea lanes would remain open and foreign trade would continue, are not the only kinds of wars that the United States must be prepared to fight. It is suggested that a protracted large-scale conventional war, perhaps involving Soviet and Warsaw Pact thrusts into Western Europe and the Persian Gulf, has once again become a realistic possibility.[34] The petition argues that the dramatic build-up of nuclear weapons in the Soviet Union over the past decade has now made it unrealistic for the United States to initiate the use of nuclear weapons. By this reasoning the United States can no longer assume that its "nuclear umbrella" will compensate for deficiencies in local nonnuclear deterrent power to forestall a nonnuclear attack on America's vital interests in Europe or Asia.[35]

A protracted large-scale conventional war would drastically increase the demand for machine tools in the United States. At the same time it is argued it would disrupt sea lanes linking the United States with Europe and Japan and would present a serious risk that the production from overseas machine tool factories would be denied to the United States either as a result of hostile military occupation, attack, or intimidation, or as a result of the use of the overseas capacity for the defense needs of the countries in which it is located.

Having established the possibility of a large-scale conventional war and assuming that only domestic resources can be relied upon, the Machine Tool Builders' petition goes on to estimate, using an input-output model, what demands the requirements of such a war might impose on the domestic machine tool industry.[36] For the purpose of the petition, the National Machine Tool Builders' Association assumes a massive mobilization began in 1983, escalated to a full conflict in 1984, and had manpower requirements similar to World War II, with demobilization finally in 1987. As indicated in table 2, a large conventional war of this assumed duration results in an increase in the aggregate demand for machine tools of over 23 percent average annual rate of increase between 1982 and 1987. The capacity of the machine tool industry to surge to meet these demands under the assumption of a continued substantial import presence until the onset of a war and that the industry operates under emergency mobilization conditions is next examined.[37] As figure 1 illustrates, the National Machine Tool Builders Association finds a substantial gap between large conventional war machine tool demand and projected emergency supply. Within two to three years of the onset of a large-scale conventional war demand is found to exceed supply by some 40 percent.

Since capacity to meet wartime demands for machine tools is assumed to rest entirely on domestic product capacity, any step to increase such productive capacity prior to onset of large-scale conventional war, everything else being equal, will lessen the wartime gap between supply and demand. With this in mind, the National Machine Tool Builders' Association petition asks that imports of foreign machine tools be reduced and limited to no more than 17.5 percent of total American market. Such quota protection will cause American machine tool production capacity to be substituted for foreign machine tool capacity. Specifically, the National Machine Tool Builders' Association estimates that this 17.5 percent of the market quota will induce sufficient new investment to increase the domestic production base for machine tools by 10 percent by 1987 over the base that year in the absence of relief.[38] This same analysis also finds that the imposition of these quotas will have only a very minor domestic inflationary impact.

The National Machine Tool Builders Association analysis is controversial. First, at a strategic level, it is probably not plausible to totally write off the machine tool capacity of Western Europe and Japan as being unavailable to the United States and its allies in time of large-scale conventional war with the Soviet Union. Given present and projected Soviet military capacity, the dominance of ocean routes implied in the National Machine Tool Builders Association analysis sufficient to completely prevent shipment of foreign machine tools to the United States does not seem plausible. In addition, in time of war, air transport could be used to bring foreign machine tools to the aid of the U.S. war effort.

If Soviet domination of ocean route and air space in a large-scale conventional war seems implausible, Soviet domination of Japan and Western Europe under these special assumptions seems still more unlikely. Would the United States really continue a conventional war under these conditions? Commitments to Japan and to the Western European allies suggest that the level of conflict would escalate before the scenario envisioned by the National Machine Tool-Builders Association is reached.

Quite apart from the strategic presumptions of the National Machine Tool Builders' Association, the calculations of large-scale conventional war aggregate demand seem unreasonable. As seen from table 2, the National Machine Tool

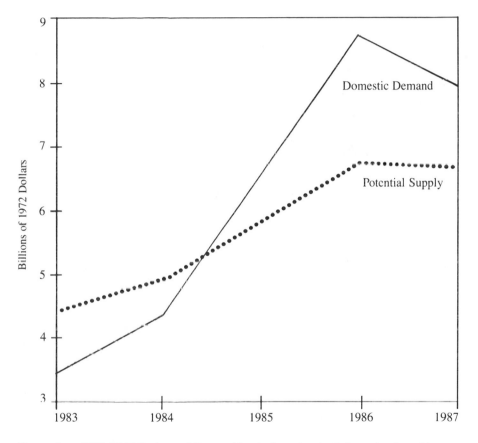

Figure 1.   1983-87 U.S. demand for machine tools and potential supply of machine tools under the "large conventional war" scenario, 1972 dollars. *(U.S. demand is defined as domestic demand with no exports. Potential supply is defined as the maximum output of the domestic machine tool industry under emergency operating conditions, with no imports.)*
SOURCE: Data Resources, Inc. (1983).

TABLE 2

Domestic Machine Tool Demand

"Large Conventional War" Scenario 1982–1987 (billions, 1972 dollars)

	1982	1983	1984	1985	1986	1987	Annual Growth Rate 1982–87
Aggregate Demand	2.819	3.478	4.336	6.485	8.734	7.969	23.094
Metal Cutting	2.354	2.913	3.597	5.297	7.027	6.395	22.126
Metal Forming	0.465	0.565	0.739	1.187	1.706	1.572	27.577
Defense-Related Demand:							
Metal Cutting	0.486	0.939	1.257	2.239	2.768	1.736	28.982
Metal Forming	0.078	0.174	0.249	0.476	0.612	0.356	35.515
Essential Civilian							
Metal Cutting	1.868	1.974	2.340	3.058	4.259	4.659	20.056
Metal Forming	0.387	0.391	0.490	0.711	1.094	1.216	25.732

SOURCE: National Machine Tool Builders Association, p. 97.

Builders Association appears to have made no allowance for the inflexible character of the Department of Defense's Defense Economic Impact Modeling System (DEIMS) when making their demand calculations. Thus, at a time of grave national emergency, DEIMS finds that demand for machinery tools to meet civilian needs, rather than being curtailed, rises at an annual average rate of 21.1 percent a year between 1982–1987. While such a growth rate can be expected in the absence of special government intervention, it seems entirely unreasonable not to assume such intervention. For example, in deciding the section 232 *Nuts, Bolts and Large Screws* case, the government found that civilian needs declined throughout the war period.[40] Given the large initial size of civilian demand relative to defense demand, almost any reasonable assumption about civilian demand for machine tools is sufficient to remove the gap between supply and demand.

At a more fundamental level the whole conception of what the machine tool industry is and what its role might be in time of national emergency may be changing. This whole area of American manufacturing industry is undergoing fundamental changes—particularly in relation to potential defense and national security needs. Traditional concepts of metal working in manufacturing engineering are being replaced by broader concepts of material processing as a result of rapid technological change.[41] This technological change is being driven by rapid progress in two areas: computer technology, which is dramatically altering the design and operation of manufacturing systems that encompass the forming, shaping, cutting, and materials-removal processes; and materials technology, including the development of both new metal alloys and new man-made substitutes for traditional metals that dramatically change the requirements for materials processing equipment. Many, if not most, of these technological breakthroughs are occurring and will be carried forward outside the boundaries of the traditionally defined machine tool sector.

Unfortunately, the National Machine Tool Builders Association modeling of supply response focuses entirely on machine tool producers classified in Standard Industrial Classification Codes 3541 and 3542. Metalworking capacity, in general, and machine tool capacity, in particular, to respond in the present and in the future to emergency mobilization demands, is located more broadly throughout the industrial sectors of the American economy. Indeed, it is likely that most future technological changes will emanate from enterprises located outside the traditional machine tool Standard Industrial Code definition.[42] This is because technological change has become user driven. It has frequently been the case that users devise, design, and build prototypes that are then produced in large numbers by traditional machine builders. In the future, users and other suppliers of producers' equipment and systems are likely to become more and more involved in machine tool production and competition. This will be particularly so in the area of multipurpose and reprogrammable equipment capable of standardized, volume production, the area of greatest importance in the event of mobilization for large-scale conventional war.

THE NATIONAL SECURITY CLAUSE,
INDUSTRIAL TARGETING, AND FUTURE PETITIONS

Many, if not most, of the changes in metal cutting and metal forming technology just indicated have been promoted and supported by the research and development programs of the Department of Defense and other government agencies. Unsurprisingly, this support has been given to further specific national security objectives. Considering the large financial support given the development of manufacturing technology through the years by these agencies, that they should now be playing a major role in stimulating change in metal cutting and metal forming technology cannot be unexpected. The Manufacturing Technologies program of the Department of Defense, which earlier was instrumental in the development of numerically controlled machine tool technology and which underwrote the early diffusion of this technology in the United States, now spends an average of 131 million dollars annually on research and development of manufacturing technology innovation, including CAM/CAD systems, robotics, and flexible manufacturing systems.[43] Quite apart from the Department of Defense programs, the National Aeronautics and Space Administration, the National Science Foundation, and the National Bureau of Standards' Center for Manufacturing Technologies all have substantial manufacturing technology-related programs.

U.S. government aid for manufacturing technologies is so large relative to what the Japanese government is doing for its industry that it seems strange that the machine tool industry should go to the executive branch and Congress complaining about Japanese industrial targeting.[44] In other contexts it might be argued that U.S. government aid for manufacturing technologies, unlike Japanese government aid, is defense-related and therefore not generally useful in shaping international competitiveness. But this is just the point. Aid to American industries for research and development may not be generally useful, but it is targeted to be particularly useful for helping an industry to contribute to national security. This is just the sort of aid that should be pertinent when the executive branch is considering a section 232 petition. How could general import quotas or tariff increases possibly be more effective instruments than carefully targeted direct subsidies and grants?[45] If the future contribution of a particular sector that is already a major beneficiary of such aid is called into question, the character and size of this aid need to be reviewed. Import protection in the interest of improving the national security-related performance of an industry seems an unusual choice of policy instruments when programs for this purpose already exist.

It should be noted that what is true for machine tools is true for many American defense-related industries. In the late 1970s and early 1980s the Japanese government has funded no more than 2 percent of all research and development undertaken by private sector enterprise. By contrast, the U.S. government has been so actively engaged in externally conducted research and development that it has funded fully 35 percent of all research and development undertaken by the private sector in the American economy.[46] U.S. aid for defense-related research and development in the private sector plays a major part in explaining the differing roles of the Japanese and American governments. In the future, it can be expected that any high technology-related industry seeking relief from import competition under the terms of the national security clause will find it particularly difficult to evoke any tangible sympathy from the executive branch when, by international and absolute standards, such industries already receive large amounts of direct aid from the U.S. government precisely on national security grounds!

THE NATIONAL SECURITY CLAUSE
AND THE UNITED STATES–JAPANESE ALLIANCE

An open international economic system is important to the national security of the United States not only because it increases global wealth and therefore global stability, but also because it makes available to the United States the technological advances of its trading partners.[47] At a time when the United States was globally dominant in technology, trade largely substituted for the relative scarcity of unskilled labor in the United States. Today, when technological leadership is more broadly shared, foreign advances in electronics, robotics, shipbuilding, and nuclear engineering, among many other areas, can work to directly bolster the national security of the United States. Walling out potentially superior foreign products seems an odd way to improve domestic production capacity for a time of national emergency. As the Secretary of Defense's *Annual Report to the Congress* notes, "While the Soviet Union must rely primarily on military research and development, the United States is fortunate in possessing a strong private sector that it can draw upon for novel and creative approaches to the improvement of our military forces. We are also fortunate in having as allies advanced industrialized nations, with independent technological capabilities for the development of advanced military material."[48]

Quite apart from the efficacy of denying American industry the benefits of potentially superior Japanese products, such a policy does raise more fundamental issues about the character of the U.S.–Japanese alliance. This alliance is occasionally characterized as one-sided because, unlike the NATO allies, while the United States is legally committed by treaty to defend Japan, Japan is not legally bound to defend the United States.[49] This asymmetry, however, is largely a product of Japan's American occupation-imposed peace constitution and, of course, does not capture the current multifaceted cooperation between Japan and the United States for their mutual security. For example, American forces stationed in Japan are not there just to provide protection for the Japanese. They are there also as part of America's defense strategy in Northeast Asia. Without such stationing of forces, the line of U.S. defense would have to be drawn closer to the Pacific coast of North America. Japan contributes to this forward deployment by providing bases to the United States rent free and by paying for the maintenance and improvement of U.S. facilities.[50]

Prime Minister Nakasone has taken a number of initiatives to augment U.S.-Japan security cooperation. Most importantly, an exception to previous policy has been made to allow military applications-related high technology to be transferred to the United States.[51] Previous policy banned the export of all arms. This step, which was originally requested by the Carter administration, was taken to highlight the harnessing of Japan's technological capabilities for the benefit of the U.S.–Japanese alliance.[52] In addition, at the Williamsburg Summit Conference in 1983, Prime Minister Nakasone specifically endorsed American arms and arms control policies. The specificity of Nakasone's endorsement was without precedent and entailed considerable political risk. In light of these steps the imposing of quota restrictions on machine tool imports with the implication that Japan is an unreliable supplier would serve to undermine the quality and character of the U.S.–Japanese alliance.

FINALE AND SUMMARY

Since its enactment in the mid 1950s, many American industries have sought relief from import competition under the national security clause. While one petition has been granted under the clause, no manufacturing industry has yet successfully argued its case. At the same time, the machine tool industry is the most important American manufacturing industry ever to attempt to use the national security clause to protect itself from import competition.

During the early 1980s, the American machine tool industry did experience an extremely sharp decline in the demand for its products at the same time that imports of machine tools were rising. It is clear, however, that the plight of the American machine tool industry owes more to the sharp cyclical downturn of the American economy and the technological obsolescence of certain of its products than it does to import competition. What import competition the machine tool industry does face comes not from a monolithic Japanese cartel nurtured by large doses of Japanese government aid. Tariff protection, subsidies and grants, tax expenditures, and low interest rate loans from government financial institutions are comparable or less than aid received by the American machine tool industry from the American government.

Because escape clause or countervailing duty proceedings before the United States International Trade Commission are seen as unlikely to lead to a favorable outcome, the members of the American machine tool industry have adopted a strategy that seeks import relief from agencies in the American government not so subject to the burdens of precedent and routinized standards of procedure. The first move in this strategy has not proved successful. The attempt by Houdaille Industries to successfully petition for revoking the eligibility of Japanese made machine tools for the investment tax credit provided for under the Revenue Act of 1971 largely on the grounds that the Japanese machine tool industry was a government aided cartel was rejected in April 1983 by the Office of the Special Trade Representative. While the entire range of considerations that entered into the decision to reject this petition are not known, the great difficulty Houdaille Industries had in establishing not only the existence of substantial Japanese government aid but also any evidence of industry collusion undoubtedly had an important impact on the final outcome. In the same way that established American machine tool manufacturers have been hurt by the competitive strength of a new group of upstart Japanese machine tool manufacturers, so also the established, previously dominant Japanese machine tool companies have been hurt by this same group. Developments in the machine tool industry attest to healthy competition in this sector of the Japanese economy and not to government-inspired collusion.

The second move in the machine tool industry's strategy of seeking import relief has been the National Machine Tool Builders Association's petition under the national security clause. Unfortunately, the industry's argument that present machine tool capacity is insufficient to meet the demands of a mobilization for a large-scale conventional war rests on the assumption (1) that civilian demands on machine tool capacity will not be suppressed in any major way in the event of such a mobilization; (2) that the United States will respond only by conventional means in the event of Soviet domination of Western Europe and Japan; and (3) that the entire locus of future technological progress in the machine tool industry is producer-based and financed rather than user-based and financed.

Even if it were true that present American machine tool industry production and technological capacities were insufficient to meet future national security needs, the quota protection asked by the National Machine Tool Builders Association is a poor instrument to use to build up such capacity. Japanese government aid to the machine tool industry and to many of its other industries looks extremely small when compared with American government programs precisely because so much U.S. aid is defense-related. This suggests that the American government has already assembled a sophisticated array of instruments to prepare the American industrial base to meet national security needs. If a question exists as to American industrial capacity for this purpose, these very large programs need to be reviewed and adjusted. Given the wide array of American government programs this is the likely outcome not only of the machine tool industry petition but also of the future petition of almost any other manufacturing industry seeking protection from imports under the national security clause. Such petitions are unlikely to lead to protection from imports.

NOTES

1. Adam Smith as quoted in Charles Kindleberger, *International Economics* (Homewood, Illinois: Richard Irwin and Co., 1968, 4th ed.), p. 116.
2. John Stuart Mill as quoted in Paul Samuelson *Economics* (New York: McGraw Hill, 1980, 11th ed.), p. 626.

3. See John Jackson, "The General Agreements on Tariffs and Trade in U.S. Domestic Law," *Michigan Law Review* 66 (1967): 268.

4. *Statutes*, 68th Congress (1954) p. 360, codified in United States Code 19, para. 1862 (a).

5. Trade Agreements Extension: Hearing on H.R. 1 before the House Committee on Ways and Means, 84th Congress 1st sess. (1955), p. 151.

6. *Statutes*, 72nd Congress)1958), p. 673.

7. *Statutes*, 72nd Congress (1958) codified in United States Code 19, para. 1862 (c).

8. Trade Agreements Act of 1979, Public Law no. 96-39, para. 901.

9. *Statutes*, 88th Congress (1974) codified in United States Code 19, para. 2101 (1976).

10. United States Code 19, para. 1862 (b) (Supplement V, 1981).

11. John Jackson, *World Trade and the Law of GATT* (Indianapolis: Bobbs-Merrill, 1969), p. 148.

12. Kenneth Dam, *The GATT: Law and International Economic Organization* (Chicago: University of Chicago Press, 1970).

13. Joint Economic Committee, *Defense Essentiality and Foreign Economic Policy, Case Study: Watch Industry and Precision Skills*, S. Rep. no. 2629 84th Congress, 2nd sess. (1956).

14. Ibid., p. 30.

15. Staff of the House Committee on Ways and Means, 85th Congress, 1st sess., *Compendium of Papers on United States Foreign Trade Policy*, p. 645.

16. U.S. Department of Commerce, *The Effect of Imports on the National Security* (Washington, D.C.; Government Printing Office, 1982).

17. United States Code 19, para. 1862(c) (1976).

18. U.S. Department of Commerce, *Report to the President on the Effect of Imports of Nuts, Bolts and Large Screws on the National Security* (Washington, D.C.; Government Printing Office, 1983), pp. 62–63; U.S. Department of Commerce, *Investigation of Imports of Glass-Lined Chemical Processing Equipment* (Washington, D.C.: Government Printing Office, 1983), pp. 746–53.

19. See the discussion in President's Special Committee to Investigate Crude Oil Imports *Report to the President* (Washington, D.C.: Government Printing Office, 1957).

20. See articles in *New York Times*, Feb. 20, 1967, p. 1; *New York Times*, Mar. 22, 1968, p. 69; *Journal of Commerce*, May 20, 1968, p. 4; *Wall Street Journal*, May 14, 1968, p. 32, as cited in John Jackson, *World Trade*, p. 752.

21. *Petition of Houdaille Industries, Inc. to the President for the Exercise of Presidential Discretion Authorized by Section 103 of the Revenue Act of 1971* (May 3, 1981); *Comments by Houdaille Industries, Inc. on the Section 103 Petition* (July 31, 1982).

22. Ibid.

23. Petition of Houdaille Industries.

24. Comments by Houdaille Industries, pp. 21–30.

25. The legal authority for a cartel in the machine tool industry was regularly provided by the Japanese government. The Special Measures Law for Promotion of the Machinery Industry, Art. 6 (1956), which authorizes a cartel, was applied by cabinet order 238 (July 20, 1956) to machine tools. Similarly, the Special Measures Law for Promotion of Specific Electronic Industries and Specific Machinery Industries (1971) exempts the machine tool industry from Japan's Antimonopoly Law. The existence of such legislation and cabinet orders may allow the unwary observer to believe that a ruthless and successful attempt to cartelize this industry was actually undertaken.

26. Nihon kōsaku kikai kōgyō kai (Japan Machine Tool Builders' Association), *Kōsaku kikai tōkei yōran 1982* (Machine tools statistical handbook 1982) (Tokyo, 1983); idem, *Kōsaku kikai kōgyō enkyō chōsa* (Survey of machine tool industry condition) (Tokyo, 1982).

27. Hiroya Ueno and Akira Goto, "Subsidy Schemes for Industry in Japan," Seikei University Discussion Paper and Report to OECD.

28. Okurashō (Ministry of Finance), *Hōjōkin benran* (Compendium of subsidies), *1978–1982*, 5 vols.

29. Ibid., *1981*.

30. Ibid., *1982*, pp. 370–91.

31. Ibid., pp. 397–98.

32. Kagaku gijutsu cho (Science and Technology Agency), *Kuni no shiken kenkyū gyomu keikaku* (National Research and Development Projects) (Tokyo, various issues).

33. Data received from Japan Development Bank and Small Business Finance Corporation.

34. National Machine Tool Builders' Association, *Petition Under the National Security Clause, Section 232 of the Trade Expansion Act of 1962 for the Adjustment of Imports of Machine Tools*, pp. 63–90.

35. Henry Kissinger, "The Future of NATO," in Kenneth A. Myers, ed., *NATO: The Next Thirty Years* (Boulder, Col.: Westview Press, 1980), pp. 3–14.

36. The National Machine Tool Builders' Association uses the U.S. Department of Defense's Defense Economic Impact Modeling System (DEIMS) to assess such demands.

37. Appendix F of National Machine Tool Builders' Association, *Petition*. The supply models of the machine tool industry used in this analysis follow the theoretical framework of N. I. Nadiri and S. Rosen, *A Disequilibrium Model of Demand for Factors of Production* (New York: National Bureau of Economic Research, 1974).

38. National Machine Tool Builders' Association, *Petition*, p. 208.

39. U.S. Department of Commerce, *The Effects of Imports of Nuts, Bolts and Large Screws Report of the President on an Investigation Conducted Under the Authority of Section 232 of the Trade Expansion Act of 1962, As Amended* (Washington, D.C.; Government Printing Office, 1983).

40. Ibid., Appendix F.

41. *American Metal Markets, Metal Working News Edition*, April 25 and May 2, 1983.

42. National Research Council Assembly of Engineering, Manufacturing Studies Board Committee on the Machine Tool Industry *The U.S. Machine Tool Industry and Defense Readiness: An Agenda for Research* (Washington, D.C.: National Academy Press, 1982), pp. 2–3.

43. U.S. Congress, Congressional Budget Office, Federal *Financial Support for High Technology Industries* (Washington, D.C., 1985), p. 31.

44. Ibid. The non-Department of Defense manufacturing technologies projects are in aggregate at least as large and quite possibly several times as large as all Japanese government programs in these areas put together, including MITI's Laser-using Complex Manufacturing Project.

45. While clearly the case in this instance, this is also true in general. See J. Bhagwati and V.K. Ramaswami. "Domestic Distortions, Tariffs and the Theory of Optimum Subsidy," *Journal of Political Economy*, February 1963, pp. 44–51, and W. M. Corden, *Trade Policy and Economic Welfare* (Oxford: Clarendon Press, 1974).

46. Kagaku gijutsu chō (Science and Technology Agency), *Kagaku gijutsu hakushō* (White paper on science and technology) (Tokyo, 1981), p. 4.

47. U.S. Secretary of Defense, *Annual Report to the Congress, Fiscal Year 1984* (Washington, D.C.; Government Printing Office, 1983), p. 15.

48. Ibid., p. 269.

49. National Machine Tool Builders' Association, *Petition*, p. 170.

50. M. Mochizuki and M. Nacht, "Modes of Defense Co-operation" in *U.S.–Japan Relations in the 1980's: Towards Burden Sharing* (Cambridge: Center for International Affairs, Harvard University, 1982), pp. 129–30.

51. Unhappily, this new policy has been implemented only very slowly. See "Japan Inches Towards Sharing Its Technology with the U.S.," *Christian Science Monitor*, Sept. 21, 1984.

52. See T. Aoki, *Nihon no boei gijutsu* (Japan's defense technology) (Tokyo: Kyoikusha, 1979), pp. 69–149. The possibilities and limits of U.S.–Japanese cooperation in defense technology are discussed in Daniel Okimoto, "The Economics of National Defense" in Daniel Okimoto, ed. *Japan's Economy: Coping with Change in the International Environment* (Boulder, Colo: Westview Press, 1982), pp. 272–73.

Japan's Rapid-Growth Policy on Trial:
The Television Case

KOZO YAMAMURA
JAN VANDENBERG

The focus of this study is the examination of linkages between the economic policies Japan adopted in the rapid-growth decades and the "Television Case," a major and as yet unresolved antitrust suit brought, in the early 1970s by two American producers of television sets against every Japanese exporter of television sets to the United States.[1] This complex case, to be detailed in part two, essentially charges that during the 1960s and 1970s Japanese firms, having successfully cartelized their domestic markets for consumer electric and electronic products, collusively fixed the prices of television sets sold in Japan, and, springing from this high-profit base, mounted a predatory campaign to sell their products at below-cost prices on the American market, thereby injuring U.S. producers.

Both the gravity of these allegations against large and well-established Japanese corporations and that sufficient evidence exists to fuel a prolonged legal proceeding in U.S. courts call for a serious reexamination of underlying facts, especially those pertaining to Japanese government policies to promote rapid economic growth.

Our examination of this case has two goals. One is a better understanding of the nature and effects of the economic policies adopted by the Japanese in the 1950s and 1960s to achieve rapid economic growth. We will focus on the policies' impact on firms' market behavior and on the winners and losers thereby created. The other, even more important goal is to gain, through an analysis of the economic and legal issues involved in this case, insights useful in answering several timely and widely debated questions: Should Americans be concerned with Japan's current policies toward its high technology industries, which are

We wish to express our appreciation for valuable criticism and comments made on an earlier version of this manuscript by Gary R. Saxonhouse and John O. Haley. Nonetheless, the authors are responsible for any errors and shortcomings remaining in this study.

largely dominated by the very firms named in the TV case? Could the success of those policies cause the U.S. high technology industries to undergo a painful restructuring similar to that experienced by the producers of television sets? And what implication do our findings have for the current debate on the American adoption of an industrial policy?

In part one, we present (1) a brief analysis of the basic dynamics underlying the Japanese "investment race"—the rapid and sustained investment campaigns undertaken by large industrial firms from the 1950s through the early 1970s; (2) a discussion of the role of the vertically integrated marketing systems built by some oligopolistic firms in their generally successful efforts to restrict competition in a score of major domestic markets; and (3) an analytic overview of the possibly crucial impact of the "investment race" and collusive conduct within domestic markets on market strategies (including "dumping") adopted by oligopolistic firms to increase exports. In brief, this part provides descriptions and analyses of the policy milieu and economic dynamics of Japan during the rapid-growth era critical to an accurate understanding of the issues in the television case, and thus of their implications for broader industrial policy issues.

The second part turns to the specifics of the case. Drawing from the analysis in the first, we discuss the rapid growth of the Japanese home electronics products industry and examine evidence regarding the domestic market behavior of the seven major firms in the industry. We then describe the market strategies these firms adopted to enter the American television market and the legal challenge such strategies invited. We argue that both the analysis and the evidence strongly suggest that the increase in Japanese exports of television sets to the United States was spearheaded by price cuts made feasible, even profitable, by scale economies of products, Japanese firms' high fixed costs, and the effective cartelization of the domestic market.

The final part contains a summary and discussion of the lessons to be learned from this case. The lessons, we contend, have an especially important bearing on the domestic and international implications of current Japanese policies toward high technology industries and on the current debate over the American adoption of an industrial policy (or "targeting") with the "Japanese model" very much in mind.

1. JAPANESE RAPID-GROWTH POLICY
AND MARKETPLACE STRATEGIES

When Japan entered its era of rapid growth (1950–73), it was in many respects a "lesser developed country" and accordingly adopted many of the heavy-handed progrowth strategies seen in LDCs today. Japan was not expected to employ free market policies and open trade practices until 1964, when it was admitted to OECD and became an Article 8 nation under the General Agreement on Tariffs and Trade (GATT). It is gradually being acknowledged that protectionist and interventionist policies continued to characterize the Japanese economy even well after 1964. As openly recognized by virtually all those knowledgeable about the Japanese economy of this era, including many former government officials and business leaders, capital markets were insulated and regulated, oligopolization and collusion among domestic firms was condoned and even encouraged, various discriminatory laws and practices against trading partners were adopted, foreign exchange was bureaucratically allocated, and technology imports were coordinated by government offices.[2]

To what extent these characterizations are inaccurate when applied to Japan of the 1980s—how much liberalization, in the broadest sense of the term, has occurred during the past decade—is the subject of intense debate. For the moment, let us simply state that significant changes have taken place under strong foreign pressure in the Japanese capital market, in trade practices, and in the market behavior of large firms, and turn at this point to an examination of Japanese policies and business behavior during the rapid-growth era.

Growth Policy, the "Investment Race," and Collusion

The rapid growth achieved prior to the first oil crisis of 1973 was based on a frenetic race among Japan's major companies to adopt successively more advanced, large-scale production techniques. The burgeoning world and domestic markets and the ready availability of Western engineering know-how led most large Japanese firms of this period to perceive increased investment, enlarged scale, and mass output as a profitable course of action leading to efficiency and reduced unit cost. This perception was crucially enhanced by the role the Japanese government played in promoting and coordinating the "investment race" and in condoning its anticompetitive consequences.

An important and, some would argue, essential progrowth policy measure contributing directly to the investment race was the regulation of the Japanese capital market. The race was fueled by loan capital flowing from the largest Japanese banks—the thirteen "city banks"—to large firms at subequilibrium interest rates. This disequilibrium created chronic excess demand for loans and gave the Ministry of Finance (MOF) extensive power to ration credit. A policy of providing capital to large firms (and depriving consumers and small firms of funds) was feasible because the Japanese capital market was insulated from international money markets.[3]

MOF allocated credit primarily to assist industries such as shipbuilding, steel, automobile, electronics, and chemicals, considered central to achieving rapid growth. That is, the ministry played a major role in creating strong, oligopolistic firms in each of these industries by providing abundant credit to the large city banks, which in turn were the principal suppliers of credit to these firms. Few scholars dispute that MOF used "administrative guidance" to direct credit to specific industries or even specific firms in need of funds for expansion of their productive capacities. Simply put, MOF policy made possible both the investment race itself and the concurrent oligopolization of Japan's major industries.[4]

Along with MOF policy, a discussion of the government's contributions to the investment race must treat the generous tax incentives designed to promote rapid investment and exports, as well as the trade policies (tariffs, quotas, foreign exchange control, etc.) that crucially influenced the pace of the race. However, we here focus on the role of the Ministry of International Trade and Industry MITI (in the investment race, a role many believe was no less important than that played by MOF.

Little overstatement is involved in saying that MITI made the investment race possible by coordinating or "umpiring" the contest, thereby reducing the risks of rapid investment. Let us briefly explain what is meant by the above, drawing from an earlier, more detailed analysis.[5]

In the rapid-growth period, firms faced what economists call a declining long-run average cost curve, that is, if output expands, unit costs decline and production becomes more efficient. This was principally due to the availability of readily borrowable, successively more advanced, foreign technologies and meant that each firm in an industry could successfully undersell its rivals by investing more and producing more than others in the industry. The structure of such industries is "unstable," to again use economists' jargon. That is, competitive investment to increase productive capacity could not but lead to the bankruptcy of some of the firms in an industry, thereby allowing the market to regain stability with fewer firms, possibly even a monopoly.

However, the costly dislocations of such an unstable situation, which would be detrimental to rapid economic growth, could be avoided if an authority outside the market could coordinate the pace of investments made by competing firms. In postwar Japan, MITI acted as this authority. In a nutshell, MITI "guided" firms to coordinate investment so that each oligopolist in a market made investments roughly proportional to its current market share—no firm was to make an investment so large that it would destabilize the market. The policy was effective in encouraging competition for market share (i.e., preserving the essential competitiveness in the industrial markets) while promoting the rapid investment necessary to increase productive efficiency and output.

This policy, however, could be pursued only if market-share competition did not result in profit eating open price war, especially in periods in which demand declined or failed to keep pace with the rate of increase in productive capacity. MITI's solution to this problem, understandably welcomed by the firms, was cartels. As a result, overt cartels were repeatedly organized, then dissolved, in steel, chemical, and other industries (including the home electric products industry, especially the television market).

This is not to say that these industries fixed prices at all times and were not competitive. Cartels were frequently formed when firms were adopting new technology, the optimal scale of which usually exceeded that of the technology being replaced (rationalization cartels), when recessions occurred in the domestic and/or international market (recession cartels), and when inventories became too large for various reasons including a too-rapid increase in capacity. In some instances the industry took the initiative to create cartels, while at other times MITI did so.[6] Both the "rationalization" and "recession" cartels were permitted under the Antimonopoly Act as amended in 1953; moreover, MITI's extralegal "guidance" cartels went unchallenged by the Fair Trade Commission of Japan (FTCJ), which, during this period, remained only a minor irritant in the national effort to achieve rapid economic growth.[7]

The credit allocation policies of MOF and MITI's coordination of firms' strategies were mutually reinforcing and the results were manifested in many ways. One of the most important consequences was the saddling of large Japanese firms with a high proportion of fixed to variable costs. As a result of MOF policy, large firms borrowed heavily to expand, which resulted in debt/equity ratios much higher than those seen in other industrial nations. Consequently, large interest obligations to banks became the primary capital costs for large Japanese firms, rather than flexible, performance-oriented dividends paid to stockholders; that is, capital costs became essentially fixed.[8]

Another reason for the high fixed costs was the permanent employment system utilized by large Japanese firms.[9] The willingness of firms to assume this invariant labor bill was due in large part to the mutually reinforcing progrowth policies in effect during the high-growth decades, especially the MITI policy allowing recession cartels that reduced the risks of bankruptcy from high costs and low sales during cyclical drops in demand. As seen in the visible erosion of this employment system since the end of rapid growth, even the biggest of firms are unwilling to maintain or increase fixed labor cost outside the environment of rapid growth.[10]

Though often neglected, yet a third reason for the high ratio of fixed to variable costs was the unavoidable cost associated with the creation and maintenance of distribution outlets and production subcontractors affiliated with each large manufacturer. Typically, the costs associated with distribution systems were for administration (coordination, enforcement, etc.), marketing (advertisement, providing assistance for sales promotion, etc.), advancing trade and other credits, and providing capital. Since we later analyze in considerable detail the special role of firm-specific, vertically integrated marketing systems, here we stress only that relationships between these "parent-and-child" firms were not arms'-length, open-market transactions but rather were exclusive and long term, and limited each firm's freedom to move in and out of the vertical hierarchy. Parent firms, when faced with a decline in demand, could not simply "axe" their respective "child" firms, that is, subcontractors and distribution outlets. In short, to the extent the parent firms found it necessary to maintain the parent-child relationship with a number of distribution outlets even when demand slumped, the costs of maintaining such a relationship became fixed.[11]

These three fixed costs combined to make a substantial portion of the costs faced by major Japanese firms very difficult to reduce when sales fell or failed to increase as expected. This fact had two important effects on corporate behavior. One was to motivate firms to operate at, or as close as possible to, full capacity to prevent sharp increases in costs-per-unit that resulted from reductions in output without corresponding reductions in the fixed costs just described. In short, large Japanese firms suffered from an inherent downward inflexibility of output level and a vulnerability to cyclical drops in demand.[12] The other effect is that the desire to minimize the costs of this inflexibility and vulnerability motivated firms to collude during periods of "excess capacity." In light of these facts, we must examine both the domestic and international marketing strategies of many major Japanese corporations, particularly the role in those strategies of vertically integrated groups of distributing affiliates—the distribution *keiretsu*.

Keiretsu *and Marketing Strategy*

While vertically integrated marketing systems controlled by oligopolistic manufacturers are not unknown in any nation—gasoline retailing systems in the United States come to mind—such integrated marketing systems are more prevalent in Japan than in any other major economy.[13] The reasons can be traced back to the environment that produced rapid growth.

While strategic industries essential to Japan's leap into industrial power grew rapidly due to the conditions already described, manufacturing industries that consisted mostly of small firms, the service sector, and, importantly, distribution, retained many characteristics of the prewar years. They remained chronically short of capital, labor intensive, relatively inefficient, and small scale until late in the rapid-growth period. In part, this "dual structure" developed because of the progrowth policy.

This early bifurcation of the national economy resulted in a mismatch between the mass-production capabilities of many of Japan's new industries and the underdeveloped distribution system. As large firms producing consumer goods began to expand, they faced a formidable obstacle in the fragmented marketing system, which was characterized by layers of capital-starved wholesalers and very small, inefficient neighborhood retailers. The emergence of efficient, modern mass merchandisers was slowed by legal obstacles and difficulties in gaining access to capital; volume sellers did not assume importance until the late 1960s.[14]

Several manufacturing industries reacted to the distribution bottleneck by vertically integrating their sales systems. Each manufacturer carved out a complete marketing channel, pumping capital and modern organization expertise into selected, controlled wholesalers and retailers. These groups of affiliated distributors—*keiretsu* channels—were built by the consumer electronics and electric appliance firms, and by the producers of automobiles, pharmeceuticals, cosmetics, and confectioneries. Vertical integration was common in many other markets but these consumer products industries have the largest and most thoroughly organized systems.[15]

The prevalence of this distribution strategy can be judged from the estimates by the Fair Trade Commission of Japan (FTCJ) that in the late 1960s the prices of 2 percent of all goods sold in the nation were set under legalized resale price maintenance and those of another 20 percent by covert upstream control of retail prices, both enforced through vertical restraints on distributors.[16]

The *keiretsu* outlets were drawn into affiliation with a manufacturer through a system of mutually reinforcing business practices reflecting restricted access to capital for small firms and weak enforcement of their legal rights.[17] The most important techniques used to attract and control distributors were the provision of capital and the rebate system, but refusals to deal and other devices were used as well. The provision of capital by a large producer often took the form of the ownership of blocks of wholesalers' stock; also, manufacturers frequently held bank promissory notes from the wholesalers and retailers while goods were moved. Other forms of trade credit, as well as direct loans, were extended by producers to cash-strapped distributors, strengthening the *keiretsu* relationship between them.[18]

Under the industry-wide rebate system, which was likewise important in fostering *keiretsu* ties, retail prices were set by the manufacturer, and price observance by the *keiretsu* outlets was ensured through capital provision and other mutually reinforcing tactics (as outlined below). Manufacturers would also set wholesale prices in such a way that they differed little from retail prices with the intent of providing the intermediate handlers of goods barely enough profits to keep them in business. Some goods had no margin at all.[19] Manufacturers adopted such a strategy to make the *keiretsu* distributors responsive to sporadic, arbitrary rebates manipulated to reward sellers for manufacturer-preferred behavior. There are reportedly 500 names for different types of rebates, the most important relating to the proportion of an outlet's total sales constituted by the affiliated brand and to adherence to the suggested retail price.[20] Rebates were offered to distributors on a case-by-case, confidential basis and were often given for "loyalty," "cooperation," and "effort." In addition, wholesalers were rewarded for joining the company-affiliated wholesalers' organization.[21] A variant of the rebate was the practice of selling merchandise to distributors at varying prices. As all outlets resold at a uniform price, this was an effective way to reward and punish affiliates.[22]

Many manufacturers enforced territorial restriction on their wholesalers and divided Japan into discrete regions, assigning one wholesaler to each area.[23] The *itten itchōai* (literally, one store, one account) system, which specified the retailers to whom a given wholesaler was permitted to sell and similarly restricted the retailer's source of supply, became prevalent in some industries, further solidifying vertical distributional columns.[24] The dominant firms also extended a variety of assistance (promotional aids, demonstration services, and the like) to distributors in a discriminating manner, and transfers of personnel were commonplace between outlets and the manufacturer.[25]

Another of these techniques aimed at dominating outlets was the underwriting of consumer installment purchase plans by the controlling manufacturer. Since credit for private purchases was virtually unavailable from banks in Japan due to the regulation of financial markets, credit extended by large producers (enjoying preferential access to bank loans) to consumers via the marketing channels provided an important booster of retail sales.[26] Even more effective practices, such as refusals to deliver goods to retailers who shaved prices and industry-wide collusion on rebate levels, are examined in the context of the consumer electronics industry in part two.

The cohesive vertical distribution channels obviously provided an ideal setting for effective restriction of the behavior of downstream agents. In Japan, the most important such vertical restraint was retail price maintenance. This practice has not been shown to result necessarily in the loss of economic efficiency.[27] Indeed, it can yield such efficiency gains as the prevention of "free-riding" on national advertising campaigns, the encouragement of post- and presale service, and the prevention of monopoly rent extraction by wholesalers and retailers themselves.[28]

However, in the hands of oligopolistic manufacturers, retail price mainte- nance is a powerful tool for restraint of price competition at the retail level to effectuate horizontal price-fixing agreements. Usually, the producers' interest is best served if fierce competition exists among their distributors. However, if those producers are collusively raising prices, price competition at the retail level can and often does reduce retailers' margins and destabilize upstream collusion as marginal retailers discontinue sale of the high-price, low-profit product. To prevent such a development, manufacturers are forced to reduce prices to increase sales margins to the remaining distributors. Under these circumstances, a manufacturer seeking to increase market share has a strong incentive to cut wholesale prices further to attract retailers from competing brands to its product. Industry-wide retail price maintenance, if effective, can alleviate these destabilizing pressures by protecting retailers' margins or rebate levels.

The *keiretsu* distribution systems offered an additional bonus. The limited mobility of all wholesalers and retailers was the key to greatly reducing the colluding producers' rewards for cheating on price and quantity agreements while increasing the penalty for doing so. It is true of most cartel arrangements that a cheating member can, by shaving price, suddenly capture a substantial portion of the market. Nevertheless, since wholesalers and retail outlets were captive and bought on an exclusive, long-term basis from one producer meant that, in most cases, only the increase in sales achievable *within* the cheater's own *keiretsu* outlets could be captured. The channels could have been expanded, but only so slowly competitors would have retaliated before any appreciable portion of the market could have been overtaken. If the price-fixing agreement collapsed into open price war, the considerable investment made in building the *keiretsu* would no longer earn its expected return. Thus competitive pricing meant an actual loss of return on investment and on administrative expenditures—not simply forgone "extra" profits.

No less important, both theory and empirical evidence support the argument that distribution *keiretsu* made entry into markets difficult, not only for would-be exporters to Japan but also for potential Japanese entrants.[29] How did these barriers enabling entrenched producers to consistently earn comfortable profits work? First, and of considerable significance, was the simple closure of existing wholesalers and, to a large extent, retailers, to new entrants. This resulted in a substantial increase in the initial investment necessary to enter the market.

While the existence of mass merchandisers and department stores facilitated entry to a degree, the control of wholesalers by incumbents could make entry into this distribution sector difficult as well. Also, as the combined market share of these two types of distribution outlets was 15 percent of total retail sales in Japan in 1966, it is unlikely that the volume of sales necessary to support a mass production operation could have been realized by reliance on these non-*keiretsu* outlets during the period we are discussing.[30] Although the gradual emergence of a modern, well-capitalized independent retailing system has become the most serious threat to manufacturers' control of distribution, practically speaking, new entrants to these controlled markets in the 1950s and 1960s would have had to establish and maintain a network of sales outlets. This eliminated all but the largest, most well-capitalized new manufacturers from the ranks of would-be entrants.

According to some theorists, however, requiring a new entrant to do what the incumbents have done—make an investment—is not a barrier to entry. For such a barrier to exist, there must be assymetries between entrenched firms and would-be entrants that work against the newcomer.[31] Even under this more severe standard, we argue, Japan's distribution *keiretsu* created barriers to entry—the structures had characteristics that asymmetrically disadvantaged newcomers. One was that would-be entrants faced significantly higher costs in attracting *keiretsu* members than did entrenched firms. The new firm would have had to develop a distribution empire of its own on a thoroughly colonized continent. In these consumer products industries few independent wholesalers remained to be enlisted, and most of the unattached retail outlets were mass merchandisers or department stores, not small shops.[32] Thus, new distribution chains would have required building from the ground up.

The second major problem for firms that contemplated building a vertically integrated sales system was an exacerbation of the problem faced by any entrant to an industry requiring a large initial investment. That is, the cost per unit sold of making this massive one-time investment decreased as time went by and large volumes of goods were moved through the outlets. This meant that for incumbents who had made these investments in the past (as much as thirty years ago in the electronics industry), this cost could be divided, as it were, over total cumulative output. Thus, in terms of arriving at an approximate additional cost-per-unit to be added to price to cover distribution expenses, entrenched firms had a substantial, if not prohibitive, advantage over the would-be entrant. In short, the entrenched producers could always cooperatively set prices below an entrant's costs, which had to include the recent massive investment required to build a new *keiretsu*.

As for the situation faced by would-be foreign entrants, the necessity of investing huge sums to create their own *keiretsu* marketing mechanism made up only part of the formidable barrier they faced. They were also confronted by various legal and procedural obstacles now widely acknowledged to have effectively protected the Japanese market well into the rapid-growth era.[33] Especially important are that throughout the rapid-growth period ownership in excess of 50 percent of ten or more retail outlets required special approval by the national government[34] and that foreign companies were prohibited from underwriting installment loans for consumer purchases. Nor could foreign manufacturers make arrangements with retailers to restrict their dealings in competing domestic goods as was widely done by Japanese producers.[35] These factors, and the obvious problems associated with wresting away outlets already in one of the Japanese *keiretsu*, combined to create great difficulty in penetrating Japanese markets for goods distributed through manufacturer-controlled distribution channels.

All of the preceding had another very important consequence. The virtually closed domestic markets, the existing anticompetitive systems of vertical restraints (enabling certain industries to engage in nearly institutionalized domestic price fixing), the cost structure (high fixed costs) and the rapid expansion of most large Japanese firms provided the firms with the motivation and means to sell their products on world markets at prices below those commanded at home—possibly below the cost of production. Japanese firms have been accused of using their protected, high-price home market bases to finance export drive, and their low-price market-entry tactics and even predatory campaigns to gain market power in foreign countries. We now offer possible rationales behind the behavior that led to these allegations.

International Implications: A Theoretical Analysis

Selling goods at lower prices abroad than on domestic markets and purposely setting low prices to injure competitors have several things in common, not the least of which is that, at first glance, both seem counterproductive and irrational. Nonetheless, economic rationales for both activities are well established and theories linking the two can be readily presented. Toward this end, we offer four analytic scenarios that can cause export prices to be set below those charged in domestic markets, or "dumping." ("Dumping" is used here to indicate international price discrimination as defined under the Antidumping Act of 1921 and Kennedy Round Agreements on GATT [Art. 6]; i.e., the export of goods at a price less than that charged on the domestic market, not at a price less than the cost of producing the product.)

The four types of dumping are characterized by: (1) the simple inability on the part of a monopolist or oligopolists to sell products abroad at prices above competitive levels, while doing so domestically; (2) export-led expansion campaigns to reduce per-unit-costs of production, thereby increasing profits on goods sold domestically at fixed prices—this profit gain is balanced against any losses necessary to move "excess" goods on export markets; (3) the clearing of inventories accumulated during a decline in domestic demand by offering the products at low prices on the international market (thereby preserving cartel agreements on quantity and/or price in the domestic market); and (4) intent to gain foreign market power through predatory schemes and then recoup losses by increasing prices, that is, simple classic predation carried out across national boundaries.

The first scenario is perhaps the most common form of dumping and involves selling at cost-plus-profit on the world market while charging fixed, higher prices to domestic consumers. In most circumstances, foreign competitors are not harmed by this full-cost international price discrimination. The export prices should be near world market prices, and consistent with fair competition.[36]

However, a large, persistent differential between domestic price and the price prevailing on world markets indicates that dumping firms enjoy market power at home bolstered by barriers to imports from the world market. This is true because if the cheap foreign goods could enter the high-priced domestic market (or if lower-priced products exported into the world market could be re-imported back into the firm's domestic market) these sales would destroy the dumping firms' market power, equalize prices, and eliminate the dumping. Thus, a protected home market is a prerequisite to dumping and a persistent price differential in the absence of overt tariffs and quotas is clear evidence of the existence of effective nontariff barriers (NTBs). Even in this scenario, if economies of scale and learning curve effects are important in the production of an internationally traded commodity, the closure of markets, which underlies dumping, can have a strong negative impact on excluded foreign firms.

The second scenario is perhaps the most important, at least in the context of the rapid-growth era Japanese economy: an "export-led" expansionary campaign to reduce per-unit costs. Japanese firms during the era of rapid growth had strong incentives to reduce per-unit costs by increasing output. The condition created by the desire of each individual firm to expand output within a protected and cartelized domestic market can be readily anticipated. Because increased output means reducd costs per unit, it translates into increased profits on the products sold at high fixed prices in the domestic market, even if a part of increased output has to be sold on the world market at no profit or even at a loss. Therefore, even if increased output yields no profit (economic loss) on export markets, a rapidly expanding firm with a protected home market and facing a declining long-run average total cost curve would actually invest, produce, and sell to achieve the efficiencies and cost savings associated with mass production, despite temporary losses on world markets.

It is important to remember that this situation is not a matter of manufacturers deciding to invest and expand with full knowledge that the resulting production will be sold at no profit or at a loss on the world market, leaving them with only the reduction in production costs on units sold domestically as a return on their investment. Rather, these manufacturers enjoy a margin of error when making these major investment decisions. Essentially, even in the face of a high probability that the increase in output will have to be sold unprofitably on the international market, expansion is still worth the risk. The stronger the "home market cushion"—or the more effective the cartels in a closed market—the smaller the risk.[37] (The detailed microeconomic analyses behind this phenomenon are developed in the Appendix.)

The motivations to engage in the third type of dumping—reduced-price sales abroad to clear an accumulated inventory—are inextricably linked to the high fixed costs typical of Japanese firms in the period under discussion. The associated inflexibility of output level creates a cost pinch in the face of sagging domestic sales as costs-per-unit increase quickly if output is reduced. Reducing domestic prices during a period of slack demand is not an attractive alternative, because if home market prices are set collusively at profit-maximizing levels, the attempt to move more goods would necessarily drive the price from its optimal level and result in a net loss, even if more goods are sold.[38] Therefore, it is reasonable to assume that a firm would be willing to accept any loss on those goods on the international market that is less than the loss associated with selling the goods at home. Indeed, a smaller loss may result from exporting the goods at prices substantially lower than domestic prices—or even at a price less than the cost of production—than from overburdening the domestic market. (For a more precise analytic explanation, see the Appendix.)

It is useful to look at sporadic Japanese export drives in this light. When examining statistics of Japan's postwar export and domestic sales, a tendency for exports to increase in response to domestic recessions is clearly evident. The export drive can be at least partly explained by the difference in American and Japanese firms' responses to flaccid domestic demand. American firms reduce costs (usually the wage bill) and cut output. On the other hand, Japanese firms, burdened by inflexible obligations, face sharply increasing costs per unit if they decrease output; in some sectors, as exemplified by the oligopolized consumer electronics industry, total revenues would fall if prices were cut. Thus, these firms are very likely to maintain relatively high production levels and to attempt to export as much as possible of the accumulating inventory. The exports may or may not be priced so as to fully cover costs.[39]

The fourth type of dumping is merely the international version of an infamous business tactic—predatory pricing. The purpose of low-price sales is to drive competing firms out of the market, thereby gaining market power; losses incurred can be recouped by charging high prices after the elimination of competitors. For obvious reasons, this is a rare phenomenon.[40]

These motivations for dumping are not mutually exclusive; most important, expansionary campaigns in pursuit of economies of scale and export drives to clear inventory build-ups due to recessions can make predation less expensive and thus a more realistic option.

With the insight gained from the preceding analysis, we now turn to an examination of the growth, marketing strategies, and export behavior of the seven major Japanese electronics firms embroiled in a major antitrust litigation arising from their exports of television sets to the United States in the 1960s and 1970s.

2. CONSUMER ELECTRONICS: A CASE STUDY

Along with shipbuilding, steel, chemicals, automobiles, machinery, and several others, the consumer electric and electronic appliance industry is an excellent example of an industry that made the rapid economic growth of Japan possible. The volume of literature and evidence available both in Japanese and

English on the industry's marketing behavior make it possible to undertake a detailed analysis of the industry, revealing the dynamics behind rapid growth and a vertically integrated, cartelized domestic market in a stark, factual light.

This section will first acquaint the reader with the basic facts relating to the Japanese television producers, their industrial structure and marketing strategies, then will present only the essential facts regarding their penetration of the American market and the litigation that ensued. Out intent is not to proffer an opinion on the appropriate outcome of the ongoing antitrust litigation that involves legal issues peculiar to U.S. antidumping and antitrust statutes. Our focus here is on the causal relationship between policy and motivations; that is, to discern whether or not the behavior of the Japanese exporters of television sets to the United States was consistent with the behavior expected of an industry undergoing major expansion within the context of the Japanese rapid-growth policies of the 1950s and 1960s. Stated differently, our intent is to demonstrate that the market behavior, both at home and abroad, of Japanese television set producers was consistent with the pattern that would be anticipated on the basis of the analysis offered in the preceding section.

Growth and Structure of the Consumer Electric Appliances Industry

Starting from very humble beginnings in the prewar period—there were only 3,199 electric washing machines in Japan in 1938—the Japanese consumer electric appliances industry has grown into a world giant. In the mid-1950s, production began to mushroom and by 1968 output had grown twenty-fivefold. By 1971, one-third of world home electric appliance production was Japanese.[41] Because of mass production techniques and progrowth policies, seven major companies enjoying strong ties to the large city banks rose to dominate the industry (see table 1). A primary part of this industry was (and is) made up of the consumer-products arms of huge, multidivisional firms that produce not only a complete line of consumer appliances and electronic products—from refrigerators to video cameras—but also manufacture industrial machinery, scientific equipment, commercial electronics, and recently, computers and other high technology products.

Numerous companies producing electrical goods sprang up during the immediate postwar period; however, the industry experienced virtually no new entry from the late 1950s through the 1970s; a presumably complete list of Japanese electronics firms and firm histories through 1981 shows the entrance of Kensonic into small-scale audio component production in 1972 as the only case of a firm start-up since 1960. The television industry itself has had no new entry. All ten companies producing televisions in 1981 were in business by 1950; three are subsidiaries of other television manufacturers, leaving seven independent producers.[42]

The top seven firms and their subsidiaries dwarf all others, controlling about 96 percent of the home electric appliance and electronics market and 99.9 percent of the television market.[43] Most other Japanese electronics companies—

and there are many small ones—produce commercial products or parts purchased by the majors; many are subcontractors or subsidiaries of larger
companies.[44] Table 2 provides detail on the concentration ratios in the markets
for various consumer electronics products and appliances; while it is clear that
the industry is oligopolistic, the ratios are not extremely high.[45] The seven large
firms that produce televisions as one of many product lines are vital to Japan's
economy: electronics products comprised 10.3 percent of national industrial
production and 17.5 percent of Japan's exports in 1980; Matsushita is Japan's
fourth largest exporter.[46]

The sheer size of the industry and its pivotal position in the national economy

TABLE 1
Japanese Television Receiver Manufacturers

Producer	Total sales[a] (1982, in millions of dollars)	Consumer goods as percent of output (1982)	Export ratio (1982)	Est. Mkt. Share Japan Consumer Goods[b]	Number of keiretsu retailers
Matsushita	10,783	63	32	33.0	25,000
Hitachi	8,878	23	32	13.3	10,000
Toshiba	7,954	32	23	10.7	14,000
Mitsubishi	5,911	25	24	6.3	4–5,000
Sony	4,231(1980)	75(1980)	71(1981)	9.9	NA
Sanyo	2,478	83	54	11.0	6,000
Sharp	2,102	66	55	6.5	3,500
Japan Victor	1,104	95(1980)	NA	6.6	Matsushita subsidiary
Onkyo	1,290(1980)	97(1980)	NA	NA	Toshiba subsidiary
Columbia[c]	270(1980)	46(1980)	NA	0.6	Hitachi subsidiary
Fuji[c]	105(1980)	0	NA	NA	NA

[a]Converted at 230 ¥/$.

[b]The shares of subsidiaries are included with those of the parent company (except Japan
Victor).

[c]Not producing televisions by 1981.

SOURCES: United States International Trade Commission, *Foreign Industrial Targeting and its Effects on U.S. Industries, Phase 1: Japan*, USITC Pub. 1437 (Washington,
D.C.: GPO, 1983), Appendix H. Kawagoe Ryūtsū, "Keiretsuka no jittai" (The realities of
vertical integration), in *Ryūtsū keiretsuka to dokkinho* (Distribution channelization and
the Antimonopoly Law) (Tokyo: Matsushita, 1981), p. 59. *Japan Electronics Almanac,
1981* (Tokyo: Dempa Publications, 1981). Kenasaki Takashi, *Kadengyokai* (Electronics
world) (Tokyo: Kyoikusha, 1982), p. 64.

surely explain at least in part why the Japanese government three times passed laws specifically to promote the industry and why MITI organized and oversaw joint research into solid state technology for television receivers in 1966.[47] Another government action materially aiding electronics and appliance production was the prohibition or restriction of competing imports under the Law Concerning Foreign Investment and the Foreign Exchange and Trade Control Law enacted in 1949 and 1950, respectively. These statutes remained in effect throughout the rapid-growth period, though changes in enforcement policies under both statutes allowed for substantial liberalization beginning in the mid-sixties.[48]

As it grew in size and efficiency, the consumer electronics and appliance industry probably faced one of the most serious distribution bottlenecks experienced by any Japanese industry. In an assertive response, the firms organized an industry-wide set of vertically integrated marketing channels rivaled in size, discipline, and completeness only by the systems built by the automobile producers and the pharmaceutical and cosmetics industries.[49]

Matsushita led the industry into the integration of distribution channels when, in 1949, it organized all its wholesalers in given geographic areas into single companies in which it held 30 to 50 percent of the stock. Each of these wholesalers (totaling 165 in 1970) has exclusive rights to a certain region in Japan.[50] During the recession in 1964–65, this technique spread throughout the industry. Sony, for example, divided Japan into 72 territories and assigned one wholesaler to each. Manufacture control became virtually complete at the wholesale level of this industry.[51]

The number of manufacturer-affiliated retail outlets doubled between 1956 and 1966 as each producer worked to create its own distribution system; by the

TABLE 2

Concentration Ratios
in Selected Consumer Electronics Products, 1980

Product	Number of Companies[a]				
	3	4	5	8	10
Monochrome TV	61.1	73.9	86.3	99.9	100.0[b]
Color TV receivers	47.0	57.6	66.9	91.2	99.9
Electric ranges	65.7	80.1	88.9	99.5	99.9
Hair dryers	86.1	89.4	92.3	98.5	100.0
Radio receivers	43.2	51.8	58.2	65.7	65.9
Tape recorders	45.5	52.9	58.8	71.6	77.9
Stereo sets	42.2	51.8	58.6	76.9	80.2

[a]Subsidiary's output is counted as that of a separate company in this table.
[b]This market has a concentration ratio of 100% at nine companies.
SOURCE: Seno-o Akira, *Gendai Nihon no sangyo shūchū* (Industrial concentration in modern Japan) (Tokyo: Nihon Keizai Shimbunsha, 1983).

mid-1960s, each producer had built a chain of affiliated—*keiretsu*—retailers. As can be seen in table 1, Matsushita had 25,000 affiliated retailers and each of the other companies controlled a set of *keiretsu* outlets proportionate in size to its domestic consumer products sales in the early 1970s. Two-thirds of the appliances stores in Japan are clearly affiliated with a single manufacturer and, despite the existence of discount houses, 73 percent of the products sold in the nation moved through the *keiretsu* outlets as late as 1974.[52] Because important types of rebates were set to reflect the "loyalty" each retailer showed his *keiretsu* producer, the typical *keiretsu* dealer came to derive about 70 percent of its revenue from sales of the products of its *keiretsu* producer, usually carrying one subordinate brand for customer appeal.[53]

Collusion in the Domestic Market

There is considerable evidence that the electronics manufacturers organized to use their distribution channels to control prices and quantities of goods sold on the national market. However, before detailing the effect of vertical restraints on horizontal price fixing, the analytically important facts as to the role of the distribution *keiretsu* in virtually closing the Japanese appliance and electronics market to new entrants, both foreign and domestic, must be ascertained, as price fixing cannot last long if new companies quickly appear and disrupt oligopolistic marketing agreements.

One can readily establish that the large electronics firms have consistently earned profits well above the Japanese average for major industrial companies.[54] Despite this, no company large and diversified enough to build and maintain a full-line *keiretsu* has emerged since the incorporation of Sanyo in 1947,[55] and American producers, who led the world throughout the 1950s and 1960s, have made no headway into the lucrative Japanese market. Imports occupied 0.1 percent of the Japanese color television market as late as 1980.[56]

The level of profit enjoyed by these seven oligopolistic firms was due only in part to effective barriers to entry into their market. They have actively colluded to boost their profits. Evidence directly attesting to their collusive market behavior can be found in the many documents, diaries, and letters seized by the Fair Trade Commission of Japan in a series of investigations begun in 1957; these inquiries led to three antitrust cases against the industry, to be described below.[57] The confiscated documents confirm the existence of a clandestine system of meetings, attended monthly by representatives from high- and middle-echelon management and technical personnel of every firm in the industry over a period of ten to fifteen years. The following summary of the group meetings directly concerned with television receivers provides a glimpse into the activities of these groups.[58]

The Market Stabilization group was organized by Matsushita, Toshiba, Sharp, Hitachi, Mitsubishi, Sanyo, and their subsidiaries during an economic downturn in 1956. In a subsequent investigation by the FTCJ, the firms in this group admitted to crafting an active program to control the prices of TV sets. Allowable profit margins for retailers were set industry wide at 22 percent and for whole-salers at 8 percent.[59] To enforce these profit margins, essential in maintaining the agreed-upon price levels, the colluding firms took pains to closely monitor prices charged by wholesalers and retailers. These participating firms also adopted measures to make certain their products would not go to "disloyal" wholesalers who would make the television sets available to nonaffiliated retailers, which were not bound by the agreed-upon rebate margin and fixed prices. The collud-ing firms are known to have resorted in the mid-1960s to a variety of tactics in their attempt to minimize the "leakage" of their television sets to nonaffiliated or "disloyal" retailers; one example is:

> Recently the following incident occurred: The Kobe Daiei Supermarket revealed to a member of the Committee on Price Controls in the House of Councillors the electric home appliance manufacturers' trick of secretly marking merchandise. On the back of electric washing machines and television sets the identification number of the sales route is written with a special kind of ink, visible only under a special light. By knowing this marking, manufacturers can tell which district distributor is sending goods to stores that sell goods at low prices, and on this basis they impose sanctions on the district distributor such as stopping shipment or abrogating con-tracts.[60]

In 1966, the FTCJ launched an investigation of such activities (which resur-faced during the 1964–65 recession and continued in the mid-1960s). The inquiry resulted in the "Six Company Case" in which the FTCJ charged the six major electronics firms with "unreasonable restraint of trade." Sony alone among the seven majors was not included.[61] Specifically, the charge was engaging in "con-certed activities" to "fix, maintain, or enhance prices, or to limit production . . . thereby causing, contrary to public interest, a substantial restraint of trade."[62]

In a 1970 preliminary decision, the FTCJ found the companies guilty of "agreeing . . . on the bottom prices, margin rates, and distributors' prices for both color and black-and-white televisions" and of "substantially restricting competition." However, the FTCJ decided in 1978 not to take further action on this case on the following ground: "the conduct that was at issue in this case, having ended in January 1967, is ten years old. Thus, even if this case is continued, it is unlikely the facts relating to this case can be clarified. Also seen from the perspective of maintaining competition, no substantial gains can be obtained by continuing the case."[63]

Evidence of the horizontal price fixing of the six-company case was discovered by the FTCJ while investigating illegal vertical price fixing by Matsushita and Sony. In 1968 the commission issued Sony a warning, and agreed with the company that legal action would be halted if Sony would modify written contracts it made with its distributors in reference to price maintenance.[64] Matsushita, however, contested the findings until formal hearings were begun. Then, in 1971, it accepted a Consent Decree whereby it admitted to having instructed its wholesalers to refuse shipment to retailers who cut prices, and agreed to discon-tinue the practice.[65] Thus, despite findings that these companies had engaged in illegal horizontal and vertical price fixing, no structural adjustment or major fines have ever been forced on the industry.[66]

The evidence of collusive conduct seized by the FTCJ (but not released until antitrust proceedings against the seven companies and their subsidiaries were filed in the United States) tells much more. In brief, the companies formed a network of working groups, most of which met monthly from 1964 through at least September 1974. The most important were the TS group, the Tenth-day group, the Palace Preparatory group, the Palace group, and the Okura group. The TS group (the meaning of TS is not explained) was attended by representatives of all seven major companies and smaller ones as well. The Tenth-Day group was similar except that it was limited to mid-level managers in the television divisions of the majors only (possibly excepting Sanyo).[67] The Palace Preparatory group was assigned the task of digesting the material discussed by the Tenth-Day group and preparing a streamlined agenda of the more important unresolved matters for consideration by the Palace group, composed of senior managing directors meeting at the Tokyo Palace Hotel. From there decisions went before the highest executives of the major companies, who met monthly at the Hotel Okura.[68]

An equally important point of contact among the companies was the Electronic Industries Association of Japan (EIAJ)—a legal trade association—to which each manufacturer submitted monthly reports detailing sensitive, current data on television production, shipments, and inventories broken down by screen size and tube type; confiscated reports were dated as early as 1958 and as late as 1975. The association disseminated this information to all the other manufacturers on a monthly basis. Documents indicate that a so-called MD group was the actual point of exchange and discussion of the data and that this group held votes on future production levels and shipments.[69]

The existence of this welter of clandestine groups and overt cooperative activity has never been denied by the companies represented. Moreover, the seized documents in the possession of the FTCJ indicate that the primary goal of all of these groups was price fixing and the cooperative control of distributors. The groups openly discussed and agreed upon bottom prices for each type of receiver as well as wholesale and retail profit margins and rebate levels to *keiretsu* outlets.[70]

The success of the cooperative system, especially in pulling the industry through the 1964–65 recession, has been proudly discussed by some officers of these companies and is openly referred to in Japanese language sources.[71] The following is an excerpt from a speech delivered in 1966 by Konosuke Matsushita, the founder of the dominant firm in the industry, Matsushita Electric:

> The electric appliance industry has grown to be a very large industry today. However, there used to be no opportunity for Presidents from each company to meet and talk. As you know, in other big industries, Presidents constantly meet with each other and discuss the direction that should be followed by the whole industry. Quite naturally, questions also come up as to what quantity to produce. But, where the electric appliance manufacturers are concerned, although there are meetings

such as those of the industrial association, there used to be no summit talks. This is very strange indeed. I think that responsible men should meet at least once a month and talk about management for the purpose of stabilizing the industry at all times. . . . Therefore, such summit talks have been held.[72]

Until the mid-1960s, most Japanese consumers apparently remained unaware that the prices they were paying for television sets were inflated by the producers' price-fixing cartel. This situation changed dramatically, however, when they learned that the American consumers were paying much less for the same Japanese products. In late 1966 the existence of large differentials between domestic and export prices was reported by the major newspapers. For example, a November 10, 1966, article in *Yomiuri Shimbun*[73] reported that

A problem exists in the difference between the prices of exported and domestically sold color television sets. In selling to the U.S., the FOB price averages only 180 dollars, that is, a mere 64,800 yen. Though the makers claim that "no dumping is involved," it is quite natural that many, including the FTCJ, doubt the claim. Miki, the MITI minister, ordered investigation of this price differential and the answer provided by the electronics machinery industry was as follows: The difference of 85,000 yen between the FOB price of about 65,000 yen and the ex-factory domestic price of 150,000 yen is due to:

Differences in quality	15,000 yen	Warranty costs	3,200 yen
Commodity tax	14,000 yen	Spare parts reserve	2,000 yen
Sales costs	19,000 yen	Patent costs	1,500 yen
Advertisement costs	6,500 yen	Interest costs	5,700 yen
Installation costs	2,000 yen	Other costs	16,100 yen

Understandably, the explanation offered by producers to the *Yomiuri* was not readily accepted. Along with the large "Other costs," the item "Differences in quality" drew sharp criticisms such as the following made by Kazuki Daimon in his book *Kuroi bukka* (Black prices):

The manufacturers also recognize that exports are cheaply priced, but explain that exports can be priced cheaply because they can be shipped in large quantities and because they use parts that are fitting for low-priced products." [Daimon is quoting a Toshiba source]

So, this is an explanation. . . . American buyers would no doubt be angry if they heard such a thing. If they were informed that in television sets priced at ¥50,000, only parts befitting such a price were used, and in televisions priced at ¥12,000 or ¥13,000, only correspondingly inexpensive parts were used, then exports would probably be stopped.[74]

As for the industry's attempts to explain that the ex-factory domestic price was higher because of the "maker sales costs," the Zendenshōren (the national association of retail stores of electric home appliances) disagreed, saying it was due to "the large profits of the makers."[75] The unions representing the employees of these companies, in a highly unusual move, went public with their complaints against management's market conduct and demanded the domestic price of television sets be lowered.[76] Such revelations of the inflation of domestic prices led the Shufuren, an organization of Japanese housewives, to lead a nationwide boycott of televisions in 1967. This nationwide boycott has been credited with forcing Matsushita to accept the FTCJ Consent Decree of 1971 on the resale price maintenance case.[77]

Nonetheless, the clandestine meetings between producers were allowed to continue, and the control of distributors and the use of the rebate system persisted. The average price differentials between domestic and export (ex-factory sales) price computed over a broad range of Japanese television receivers (see table 3) collaborates the findings that the *Yomiuri* article reported. The differentials were indeed large, persistent, and characterized the sales of every exporting company (though margins on Sony products were relatively thin).[78] Japanese prices dropped marginally in 1968 but were still substantially above export prices; the differentials had actually increased by the early 1970s, and ranged from 1 to 170 percent. The average domestic set probably remained about 50 percent more expensive than a comparable set in the United States, which makes American firms' lack of sales success on the Japanese market remarkable.[79]

The impact of the Japanese exporters' pricing tactics was not limited to the domestic scene; patterns of sales of television sets incited strong reactions in the United States as well. While American consumers praised Japanese managerial and engineering know-how and purchased low-priced Japanese goods in record quantities, the U.S. television industry reeled under severe price competition. Developments in the American market caused by the successful entry of the Japanese exporters are the subject of the following subsection.

TABLE 3

Television Receiver Export Price Margins (*In percentages*)[a]

Company	Color	Monochrome
Matsushita	74.02	55.16
Hitachi	58.42	43.36
Toshiba	32.34	38.78
Mitsubishi	52.73	81.72
Sony[b]	NA	NA
Sanyo	76.03	64.90
Sharp	61.80	66.72
Average	59.2	58.5

[a]Calculated by dividing export price to the United States by the difference between average export price and average domestic price.

[b]The differences for Sony's products were smaller than those of the other companies.

SOURCE: *Appellants' Brief*, p. 39, In re: Japanese Electronics Products Antitrust Litigation, 723 F.2d 238 (3rd Cir. 1983).

The Japanese in the American Market

Large surges in the imports of inexpensive television sets from Japan during the 1960s and 1970s are said to have caused the near collapse of the American television industry. Though several major U.S. companies survived and are now operating in the black, the industry underwent a major restructuring due to Japanese sales success in the United States. The restructuring resulted in the exit of twenty-one companies (leaving only five American producers), the internationalization of every remaining firm, and in the entry onto the American scene of a major Japanese presence, in the form of both direct imports and of the production of Japanese-owned American subsidiaries. We provide here a brief review of the events that resulted in this transformation.

Japanese import penetration into the U.S. television receiver market began with small black-and-white TVs in the early 1960s. Japanese makers supplied 0.8 percent of American purchases in 1962; this rose to 6.5 percent in 1966 and 25 percent in 1971. Then the Japanese market share declined, while that for total imports climbed steadily to 91 percent in 1981 as noted in table 4.[80] Giving considerable credence to "product cycle" theory,[81] production shifted increasingly to Taiwan, Korea, and Mexico, as U.S. producers moved overseas in search of cheap labor, preferential local government treatment, and cost savings on tariffs under a special statute lowering duties on re-imports.[82] Japanese producers also moved to Taiwan and Korea and TV-related investment there appears to be roughly half American and half Japanese.[83]

Color television receivers followed three to five years behind their monochrome predecessors; though the Japanese presence was relatively small in the color market during the sixties, the downward pressure the imports put on prices appears to have created problems as early as 1962, when labor groups began to petition the Tariff Commission for import relief.[84] U.S. employment in the production of receivers declined by half between 1966 and 1970, while Japanese market share increased from about 2 to 9.4 percent (see table 5).[85] The 1974–75 recession deeply wounded the American industry, and its recovery was largely aborted, in part due to the difference between Japanese and American responses to demand contractions analyzed earlier. A surge of Japanese imports swamped the U.S. color television market in 1976, just as demand began to rise; imports rose by 153 percent in one year. During this recession and recovery, Sears quintupled its purchases of Japanese color televisions (from Sanyo and Toshiba), supplanting Warwick, a U.S. producer. Warwick could not meet the price competition and was acquired by Sanyo in 1977; Matsushita purchased the consumer products division of Motorola, another failing American television manufacturer, in 1974.[86] Not only did the U.S. color TV market share occupied by sets produced in Japan rise from 2.6 percent in 1967 to 9.5 percent in 1975 and 18.9 percent in 1976, the production of the seven Japanese companies' American and third-country subsidiaries also rose rapidly during this period. While direct Japanese imports (as listed in tables 4 and 5) supplied only 14.0 percent of the

American color television consumption in 1977, one estimate of the Japanese firms' actual aggregate market share is 44.2 percent.[87]

Although import penetration in the color television market was not as deep as that into monochrome sales, most U.S. color television manufacturers' profits declined steadily.[88] After dropping 50 percent between 1966 and 1970, employment in American firms producing television receivers fell another 33.7 percent between 1971 and 1975, and by 25 percent between 1977 and 1981.[89] The number of firms in the industry also shrank dramatically, from twenty-seven in 1960 to only five in 1980, and of those five, only three—General Electric, RCA, and Zenith—were large enough to constitute a real competitive force.[90]

The International Trade Commission attributed much of the travail in the American industry to severe and sustained price competition;[91] members of the industry attributed the price competition to collusive, predatory schemes on the part of the seven Japanese firms. And considerable evidence supports the allegations of the American producers. In addition to the evidence of collusion in the domestic market we have already presented, facts demonstrate that the seven firms carefully coordinated their export plans; they notified one another of the intended quantity of shipments and prices, allocated U.S. customers among themselves, and cooperatively concealed a web of illegal, covert activity while charging prices low enough to suddenly and decisively gain a large share of the American market.

The nerve center of the seven firms' export communications was a legal export cartel, the Japan Machinery Exporters Association (JMEA) organized in 1952. All the major producers and many of their subsidiaries joined the association, which remained in existence until 1973.[92] Under the umbrella provided by this association, the industry also formed the Television Export Council attended by the top executives of each television exporter.[93]

The JMEA and the TV Export Council devised the "Five-Company Rule"; this rule required each exporter to specify five U.S. companies as its only and exclusive customers. A member firm was to sell to another company's U.S. customer or change customers only with prior approval of the Television Export Examination Committee (of the JMEA), composed of officials from each company, including, of course, any would-be Japanese competitor. This committee was accorded the power to punish transgressions of the agreed-upon conduct by assessing a penalty equal to one-third the value of the offending shipment.[94] Each member of JMEA was also required to file an "application" with JMEA for each shipment to the United States, detailing the exact parties involved in the transaction as well as the type of television receiver, quantity, and domestic and U.S. price relevant to each shipment.[95] These agreements not to compete with each other for the accounts of major U.S. customers and the full exchange of sales information among themselves allegedly prevented U.S. buyers from playing Japanese firms off one another and ensured that increases in sales would be at the expense of American competitors.

The firms also devised a system of common minimum prices for exports known

TABLE 4

Imports and the U.S. Television Receiver Market: Monochrome
(*All figures are in thousands of dollars*)

Year	U.S. Market[b]	Japanese Imports[d]	Total Imports[c]	Japanese Market Share[a]	Import Market Share
1959	806,000				
1960	750,091				
1961	757,500				
1962	851,000	7,010		0.8	
1963	841,000	22,264		2.6	
1964	896,000	38,878		4.3	
1965	910,000	59,706	59,586	6.5	6.5
1966	756,000	105,706	114,520	14.0	15.1
1967	555,000	65,731	70,644	11.8	12.7
1968	591,000	80,784	97,018	13.7	16.4
1969	523,000	111,928	152,416	21.4	29.1
1970	505,000	119,867	172,869	23.7	34.4
1971	480,000	129,167	208,046	26.9	43.3
1972	514,000	101,427	262,066	19.7	50.9
1973	504,000	60,903	272,404	12.1	53.4
1974	447,000	57,903	277,766	13.0	62.2
1975	313,000	41,995	180,739	13.4	57.8
1976	417,000	87,135	261,166	20.9	62.8
1977[e]	389,822	97,471	293,819	25.0	75.4
1978	434,079	93,521	350,858	21.5	80.8
1979	391,016	42,621	342,644	10.9	87.6
1980	374,152	27,766	531,052	7.4	88.5
1981	366,542	41,017	333,842	11.2	91.1

[a]These market share figures do not include the sales of the subsidiaries of Japanese companies producing in the United States and in third countries; they thus seriously understate Japanese market share but are based on the most complete data set publicly available.

[b]Figures for 1959–69 U.S. market are from *TV Fact Book, 1980*, vol. 49 (Washington, D.C.: TV Digest, Inc., 1980). Figures after 1969 are from United States International Trade Commission, *Television Receivers, Color and Monochrome, Assembled or not Assembled, Finished or not Finished and Subassemblies Thereof*, Report to President on Investigation no. TA-201-19, USITC Pub. 808 (Washington, D.C.: Government Printing Office, 1977); ultimate source is the U.S. Department of Commerce.

[c]SOURCE: Electronic Industries Association, Marketing Services Department, Washington, D.C. "Total U.S. Imports of Consumer Electronic Products," Rpt. no. MS-142-M, Feb. 6, 1978.

[d]SOURCE: U.S. Bureau of the Census, U.S. Imports for Consumption and General Imports, Rpt. FT246, Annual issues, as compiled in "Statistical Analysis: Consumer Electronic Products Imports by Product Category" by plaintiffs in Japanese Electronic Products Antitrust Litigation.

[e]All numbers after 1976 in all columns are from Summary of Trade and Tariff Information, TSUS Items 685.11-685.19, USITC Publication 841, December 1982. Ultimate source of these data is U.S. Department of Commerce.

as "check prices." These minimum prices were agreed upon with the full knowledge and sanction of MITI as part of the legitimate function of the industry's export cartel (JMEA). The rationale for the export cartel, as described in documents requesting MITI approval, was to "prevent disturbance to the U.S. market caused by unfair prices,"[96] and to maintain export prices at a moderate level to prevent legal proceedings against the exporters under the U.S. Antidumping Act of 1921. As this act proscribes exports to the United States at prices less than those charged for the same commodity in the country of manufacture if such exports cause substantial injury to a U.S. industry, the check prices were to be the minimum prices that could prevent export sales from causing major damage to U.S. competitors.[97] These check prices were, nonetheless, far below prices prevailing in Japan.[98]

It appears that the motivations for below-cost export sales, as discussed in part one and in the Appendix, were at least periodically compelling enough that in sanctioning these check prices, MITI was attempting to prevent export-led expansion campaigns and recession-sparked export drives from resulting in injurious, below-cost sales on the U.S. market. It is not difficult to see why MITI, as a government agency, would have wished to avoid the political and legal repercussions arising from such export surges and to insure that "the interest of importers or enterprises concerned at the destination is not injured," as stated in the law authorizing MITI to organize export cartels.[99]

Ironically, had this minimum price system been observed by the Japanese firms, it could have constituted a per se violation of the Sherman Act and would have raised difficult legal issues involving sovereign immunity.[100] In fact, Japanese firms did not adhere to the check prices. Though the "minimum prices" appeared on all official invoices, bills, accounting records, and U.S. customs papers prepared by each Japanese firm and their major U.S. customers for fourteen years, and the firms used the figures on official documents and tax records submitted to their own government, the prices actually paid were consistently lower than the "minimum" check prices.[101]

As reported in the January 10, 1966, issue of The Japan Economic Journal: "Television receivers, electric fans, radios and batteries have been exported at substantially low price levels. Some have been sold even at below-profit levels. . . . Intensive export competition has set off serious underselling operations partly in order to offset poor sales performances in the domestic market. The management of major manufacturers has agreed that if the situation is left uncurbed, no adequate profits will ever be recovered. . . . The industries reconfirmed at a recent meeting to respect the floor export price worked out last year on television receivers and electric fans."[102]

Despite this agreement, the firms continued to "double price" in violation of the intent of the legal export cartel, and in transgression of Japanese tax and U.S. customs laws. To prevent detection of the low prices, the firms were forced to make covert payments to the buyers of their products to make up the difference between the check prices and the actual prices. This "difference money" was transferred back to U.S. mass merchandisers in the form of kickback checks drawn on Hong Kong and Swiss bank accounts, telegraphic transfers, free spare parts, "loyalty discounts," fictitious commissions, "inspection fees," and other clandestine methods.[103] It appears that every Japanese television producer was involved in this double invoicing; the interdependence of each company's behavior in keeping the elaborate system concealed is self-evident and well-documented.[104] Evidence suggests that the bulk of the sales of Japanese television sets before 1973 was characterized by the use of fraudulent prices, and, hence, customs fraud.[105] In short, there is little doubt that the large-scale, clandestine undercutting of the check price subverted the original purpose of the check-price system—the prevention of below-cost exports—to one of concealment of such exports and evasion of U.S. antidumping law.[106]

In this context, the reasons for the "five-company rule" can also be better

TABLE 5

Imports and the U.S. Television Receiver Market: Color

(*All figures are in thousands of dollars*)

Year	Total Market[b]	Japanese Imports[d]	Total Imports[c]	Japanese Market Share[a]	Import Market Share
1959	37,000				
1960	47,000				
1961	56,000	No separate commodity classification			
1962	154,000	existed for color television imports			
1963	258,000	prior to 1967			
1964	488,000				
1965	959,000				
1966	1,861,000				
1967	2,015,000	52,120	53,213	2.6	2.6
1968	2,086,000	102,454	103,572	4.9	5.0
1969	1,653,000	138,689	143,365	8.4	8.7
1970	1,428,000	134,699	141,858	9.4	9.9
1971	1,808,000	191,715	205,271	10.6	11.4
1972	2,109,000	201,528	234,763	9.6	11.1
1973	2,306,000	210,423	263,309	9.1	11.4
1974	2,162,000	185,226	242,429	8.6	11.2
1975	2,025,000	192,805	220,752	9.5	10.9
1976	2,572,000	485,645	560,326	18.9	21.8
1977[e]	2,887,015	405,553	501,118	14.0	17.4
1978	3,245,465	317,715	577,089	9.8	17.8
1979	3,286,392	128,857	302,564	3.9	9.2
1980	3,656,697	108,885	295,595	3.0	8.1
1981	3,907,098	244,452	481,690	6.3	12.3

NOTE: See sources cited in table 4.

understood. Its original intent appears to have been to preserve the minimum price agreements by removing any temptation on the part of Japanese firms to undercut one another. Though the restriction on the price was evaded, the five-company rule appears to have been strictly enforced by cartel members. This is consistent with the allegation by American firms that the rule was used by Japanese firms to ensure that the effect of their low-price tactics would not be dissipated in robbing one another of sales but could enable them to increase their market shares exclusively at the expense of their American competitors.

As the Japanese market share grew, injury to American manufacturers and labor led not only to frantic efforts to adjust—mostly through moves offshore—but also to a series of lawsuits and other legal action against the Japanese exporters.

The American Reaction

The marketing and pricing tactics of the Japanese firms and the resulting damage to American television set producers provoked one of the most rancorous and protracted series of antidumping suits in U.S. history and eventually led to charges against the Japanese under a battery of American antitrust laws. All American statutes for antidumping action rely on executive-branch agencies for their prosecution, except the little-known Antidumping Act of 1916. Thus, many of the legal actions were taken by the appropriate federal agencies in response to petitions filed by industry and labor groups. The U.S. International Trade Commission carried out a total of twenty-two investigations between 1970 and 1981, the Tariff Commission dealt with twenty cases brought by labor groups between 1962 and 1974, and the Labor Department conducted fifteen examinations between 1977 and 1981. The Commerce and Treasury Departments were also deeply involved in the complicated and time-consuming process of enforcing U.S. trade law.[107] In 1976 alone, television imports were being investigated under no fewer than five different U.S. trade laws.[108]

The results from all this activity were mixed. The most important action was the Orderly Marketing Agreement (OMA) in effect between July 1977 and June 1980, limiting Japanese color television imports to 1.56 million units, and 190,000 incomplete units, that is, 146 percent of the 1975 level or 58 percent of the 1976 level. The number of television sets imported from Japan in 1979 actually dropped to a mere 19 percent of the 1976 level as production came on line from the Japanese firms' American subsidiaries and imports from Korea and Taiwan rose sharply.[109]

The other important outcome of the executive-branch activity occurred in 1971, when the Tariff Commission found in favor of a 1968 dumping petition that charged that Japanese television sets were more expensive in Japan than in the United States, a violation of the Antidumping Act of 1921. The petition was sent to the Treasury Department for the determination of price differentials and the corresponding duties; amidst confusion and legal maneuvering, the department grappled for seven years with the question of how much to assess. A decision on duties for 1972–73 was reached in 1978 but was protested and no penalty was collected. Jurisdiction over the problem was transferred to the Department of Commerce in January 1980 and an agreement was reached in April 1980 whereby the Japanese were to pay $66 million, a substantial reduction from the $440 million actually owed, as estimated by the U.S. International Trade Commission. Zenith and COMPACT (Committee for the Preservation of American Color Television) filed suits protesting the settlement, thus further delaying collection. In sum, the Japanese were found guilty of dumping under the 1921 act but the actual collection of duties had not, eleven years later, been made.[110]

In December 1970, National Union Electric Corporation (NUE) filed suit in the District of New Jersey against the seven major Japanese television manufacturers, eight of their subsidiaries, and one Japanese trading company. Four years later, Zenith Radio Corporation filed a similar suit in the Eastern District of Pennsylvania against the same firms, some additional subsidiaries, Motorola, and Sears. Because the facts and legal issues in the two suits were nearly identical, they were consolidated in 1975; the joint suit is known as The Japanese Electronic Products Antitrust Litigation.

The defendant firms were charged with conduct violating several U.S. laws: dumping motivated by predatory intent (under the Antidumping Act of 1916); conspiring to fix minimum prices and allocate customers among themselves (Art. 1 of the Sherman Antitrust Act); attempting to monopolize U.S. trade (Art. 2 of the same); engaging in multiparty conduct affecting importation to restrain trade (the Wilson Tariff Act); practicing price discrimination between Japanese and American customers as well as among different American customers (the Robinson-Patman Act); and, acquiring U.S. firms with an intent to monopolize (Sec. 7, the Clayton Act).[111] NUE is seeking $360 million in damages while Zenith wants $900 million under the provisions of Articles 4 and 16 of the Clayton Act.[112]

Preliminary hearings on the case began in the District Court for the Eastern District of Pennsylvania in 1975. In 1982, the court issued a summary judgment granting the defendants' motion to dismiss all charges made by the plaintiffs. Underlying the dismissal was the district court's judgment that the documents taken from the possession of the Japanese firms by the FTCJ (and relied upon by the FTCJ in making its decisions) failed to meet the tests of the federal rules of evidence, and thus were not reliable; for the same reason, legal documents issued by the FTCJ summarizing its investigations and finding several of the defendants guilty of illegal price stabilization were also judged untrustworthy and prejudicial. The court excluded from consideration official proceedings and decisions of the U.S. International Trade Commission on similar grounds. That is, the court ruled in the defendants' favor in part because it had effectively eliminated much of the evidence presented by the plaintiffs.[113]

The case was appealed by the plaintiffs in 1983 and the Court of Appeals for the Third Circuit overturned nearly every ruling of the District Court, holding that substantial issues of fact existed that warranted a trial. However, the Court of Appeals upheld dismissal of the charges against Sony, Sears, and Motorola. In short, the appellate court held that sufficient evidence existed to warrant a trial to establish whether or not the remaining firms did violate U.S. law.[114]

In June 1984, the Japanese firms sought review by the United States Supreme Court, asking in effect that the decision of the appellate court be voided.[115] The Supreme Court agreed in April 1985 to hear arguments from the parties involved and a decision as to whether the case is to be sent to trial or dismissed entirely is expected in early 1986. Thus, fourteen years after the case was initiated, it has yet to be tried and the legal issues raised by the protection and cartelization of the Japanese market and by the Japanese firms' market conduct in the United States remain unresolved.

Meanwhile, events in the business world moved relentlessly forward; two divergent tendencies had become evident by the late 1970s. While all seven major Japanese companies had set up production in the United States by 1979, sidestepping rising U.S. protectionism, all remaining American producers used some of the breathing space afforded by the OMA to move most subassembly production abroad, repeating the tactics used in producing monochrome sets. Today, both American firms and the consumer electronics arms of Japanese firms have roughly similar structures with respect to sales in the U.S. market— third-country production of basic components and final assembly in the United States. The major losers in these developments have been American workers who lost jobs and those U.S. firms forced out of the market. All in all, the old confrontation has now been muted; the price differentials between Japanese and American television sets have disappeared. Against this backdrop, the billion-dollar civil suit winds slowly through American courts, leaving in its wake many questions to be pondered by students of the Japanese economy, international trade, and industrial policy.

While legal issues remain tangled, it is possible to illuminate some of the economic issues involved by examining the facts of the case in light of the four separable but not mutually exclusive motivations to reduce prices on exports as presented in part one and developed in the Appendix. The pattern of exports of Japanese television sets into the United States in the 1960s and 1970s does not fit into a single category. That the Japanese firms sold large quantities of television receivers in the U.S. market at prices lower than those charged domestically (a violation of the U.S. Antidumping Act of 1921) is indisputable. A major study made under the leadership of Ryutaro Komiya, a prominent Japanese economist, stated: "When the ruling of dumping was made [by the U.S. Tariff Commission in March 1971], the newspapers reported that the Japanese producers were saying that their exports [to the United States] were likely to remain unaffected because export prices were raised after the proceeding against them had been initiated, and, as a result, price differentials [between Japanese and American markets] have now almost disappeared. *Such a statement is nothing but confirmation that dumping was a fact*" [emphasis added].[116]

The case has frequently been made that factor cost advantages, superior management, and advanced technical skills account fully for the Japanese ability to charge these low prices and to defeat the Americans in price competition; thus, it is argued, simple international price discrimination (the first type of dumping described in part one) created the differentials between domestic and export prices.[117] Though few would deny the legitimate competitive strength of the Japanese producers, those holding the view that these advantages alone explain Japanese success in the American market often seem unaware of the domestic/export price differential and of the large number of illegal and anticompetitive acts of the seven firms, in both the Japanese and American markets. If price advantage alone is to be credited, it must be shown that the effective domestic cartel, the subversion of the check-price system, the five-company rule, and other practices had no role in helping the Japanese capture a large share of the American color television market.

We wish to stress here that, beyond the impact of the firms' covert activities, the policies of the Japanese government substantially influenced the structure, marketing practices, and development of the industry. Preferential credit allocation via large banks, lax antitrust enforcement, condoning of de facto recession cartels, MITI-guided investment coordination, and various forms of NTBs were all policies of the Japanese government that promoted and shaped the growth of the industry, policies very different from those under which the American television producers conducted business. The possibility that the interaction of economic forces and government manipulations created incentives for the Japanese firms to engage in below-cost export sales and other activities in violation of U.S. laws must be included in any analysis of the successful penetration of the U.S. television set market by Japanese producers in the rapid growth decades. We contend that the policies did indeed affect domestic market behavior and export strategies of these Japanese firms. One manifestation was export-led expansionary drives to increase productive capacity and to reduce per-unit costs to enlarge profits on goods sold domestically at fixed prices (the second of the four types of dumping postulated earlier).

It can hardly be denied that the industry cartelized its domestic market over an extended period, maintaining stable horizontal price-fixing agreements through vertical restraints on controlled distributors, thus satisfying one of the two conditions necessary for dumping of this kind to occur.

The remaining condition—that the industry was pursuing economies of scale through increased exports—was also met, as evident in the following observation from a recent analysis of the sources of Japanese competitiveness in the production of television sets and tape recorders: "The constant drive to expand exports has contributed to production efficiencies as expanded production volumes permitted firms to move down the learning curve, thereby reducing unit costs, and improve their competitive position against foreign firms."[118] The scale of Japanese television set production multiplied twelve times (increasing from 0.5 million sets to over 6.3 million) between 1966 and 1970.[119] It is not unreasonable to assume that the "margin of safety" provided by the resulting increase in profits on the protected domestic market was a factor in the firms' decisions to expand so courageously and that the new production may have been initially sold at unfavorable prices on the international market.

Circumstances indicate that the Japanese firms in this industry also engaged in the third type of dumping, that which occurs in times of recession to clear inventories accumulated because of Japanese firms' downward inflexibility of output level. Economic analysis of the cost structure of these firms indicate that they were, in fact, saddled with the high fixed costs that create this output inflexibility. [120] Note also that their collusive activities became visible during the downturns of 1956–58 and grew more elaborate in the 1964–65 recession. A closer analysis of the timing of the largest export surges reveals a tendency for increases during the period of recoveries from recessions. Exports of monochrome sets rose by 77 percent following the 1964–65 downturn and shipments of color sets recorded a sudden 152 percent jump on the heels of the 1975–75 recession. Exports of monochrome sets increased by 59 percent during this later period. [121] The suddenness and magnitude of the surge of color set exports, its short duration, and the low-price tactics again adopted in 1976 cannot but suggest that during one of the worst postwar recessions, the firms were engaging in an inventory-clearing export drive to maintain production levels while preserving domestic price-and-quantity agreements.

We stress that all of this rational profit-maximizing behavior occurred under a unique set of constraints; this behavior alone does not imply predatory intent. The Japanese firms could have engaged in below-cost sales in the United States in the simple pursuit of profit, and with no intent to harm American producers and with no plans to overtake and monopolize the U.S. market to recoup losses by raising prices later.

Indications of such predatory intent must be sought in evidence concerning the concerted exporting behavior of the seven firms, particularly the five-company rule and the firms' cooperation in collectively concealing their subversion of the check-price system. Such an intent is suggested by the fact that the cartel appears to have been used to eliminate competition among Japanese companies and to achieve a rapid expansion in their exports of television receivers at the expense of American firms. That is, the firms may have realized that their extended price cutting, directed exclusively at non-Japanese producers, would eventually eliminate their rivals. In an industry such as television production, characterized by economies of scale and high initial investment in plant and equipment, the re-entry of competing firms is expensive and time consuming, and the seven Japanese firms may well have realized this and planned to dominate the U.S. market, raise prices, and recoup the losses of the predatory campaign.

In summary, not only is it incontrovertible that Japanese television sets were exported at price levels far below those charged in Japan, the existence of economic incentives for below-cost exports, as well as contemporaneous reports that such sales occurred, suggest that the seven companies actually took losses on the world market. Furthermore, the plethora of evidence revealing the Japanese producers' concerted and illegal behavior in both domestic and international arenas invites accusations of coordinated predatory intentions against American firms. In short, charges that the seven exporters knowingly colluded to exploit the damage potential of these below-cost exports—though they had other, more basic, structural incentives to export at a loss—must be seriously examined.

This is not to deny that the recognized productive efficiency of the Japanese television manufacturers contributed to their success on the U.S. market. Ascertaining the precise relative importance to this success of cost advantages, as opposed to the impact of the marketing strategies analyzed here, is not, however, the central intent of this essay. Our purpose is to use the Japanese experience to illuminate broader questions of antitrust and industrial policy having significant implications for ongoing debates on the adoption of a U.S. microeconomic policy patterned after Japan's and on global competition in high technology industries.

3. SIGNIFICANCE AND LESSONS OF THE CASE

The television case sheds light on some seldom-mentioned but important aspects of the progrowth policies pursued by the Japanese government during the rapid-growth decades. These policies were intended to promote vigorous economic growth and export expansion by enabling Japan's leading industries to adopt new technology and undertake the construction of large, efficient plants. By all quantitative evidence, the policies were extremely successful; they were, however, far from cost free. While interest rate control kept returns to small savers artificially low, oligopolistic pricing, and politically essential price supports and import quotas benefiting farmers maintained high consumer prices for both manufactured goods and agricultural products.

We are willing to assert that at least in the case of the consumer electronics industry, the costs imposed on Japanese consumers were higher, perhaps substantially higher, than those justified in the name of achieving rapid economic growth. This was the perception, as well, of the housewives who launched a national boycott protesting the high prices of television sets.

On the international scene, Japanese industrial policy has involved export promotion, which, in its most visible forms—subsidies, tax exemptions, and so forth—has long provoked trade friction; furthermore, the difficulty of penetrating Japanese markets has led to allegations that the nation was protected by nontariff barriers and discriminatory legal codes.

The results of Japanese industrial policies most significant to our case study were rapid expansion of productive capacity, high fixed costs, a protected and cartelized market, and collusive conduct; these conditions set in motion economic dynamics that caused below-cost exports to occur. These loss-producing exports benefited American consumers at the expense of Japanese purchasers as they forced U.S. producers of competing goods and their employees to bear costs associated with slumping sales and industrial readjustment.

The character and effects of Japanese industrial policy revealed through this case study have important implications for the ongoing debate on the adoption of an American economic rejuvenation program that goes beyond traditional macroeconomic manipulations. The evidence presented here cannot but create doubts as to the political palatability, both in domestic and international terms, of many Japanese practices if adopted by mature industrial societies. In particular, the costs imposed on consumers by the lax enforcement of antitrust statutes are likely to exceed the benefits such policies provide to firms. Economic analysis tells us that export promotion and protectionism, by overt or covert means, do not yield net benefits to society, although these practices may be profitable to certain sectors. Of course, within the context of catch-up growth, the impact may be different and it is clear that the LDCs have much to learn from the Japanese experience.

Thus the advisability of industrial policy in mature economics rests uneasily on the condition that it be applied judiciously and appropriately by disinterested and even-handed parties. Awarding the power to manipulate microeconomic decision making to agencies vulnerable to capture by industry interests, or conversely, to bodies manned by bureaucrats not fully acquainted with the realities of conducting business, could yield unexpected and costly results. Nevertheless, the evident success of Japanese firms in international competition, coupled with American difficulties, may eventually compel us to institute national programs to counter the Japanese advance.

The dynamics underlying the television case afford valuable insight into the possible effects of Japan's current policies for promotion of its high technology industry. The most important sectors of this industry—semiconductors, computers, and telecommunications—are today in Japan dominated by precisely those firms implicated in the television case, along with a few firms producing mostly computers, such as Fujitsu and Nippon Electric Company. MITI is now organizing and subsidizing joint research projects among the leading Japanese producers of high technology products and we find that companies such as Matsushita, Toshiba, Hitachi, Mitsubishi, and Sharp are being encouraged by the Japanese government to pool their resources and scientific capabilities toward pioneering the development of state-of-the-art computers, software, and integrated circuits. As American and Japanese firms now hotly compete for the leading edge in these technologies, the possibility that these efforts could disadvantage American firms has become a source of serious concern. The argument that the financial contribution made by the Japanese government is not a huge sum provides us little comfort because of the profound impact the organization of the research projects could have on the timing of innovation, on patterns of interfirm competition and cooperation, and on industrial structure.

The National Cooperative Research Act of 1984 exempting cooperative research projects undertaken by American firms from certain prosecution was passed by Congress in reaction to the perceived threat of similar Japanese behavior, but important analytical and practical obstacles lie in the way of the direct adaptation of Japanese techniques by American competitors.[122] Furthermore, the analysis presented here suggests that U.S. producers and government officials should be alert to signs of a repetition of past Japanese export patterns in the new products; specifically we must watch for developments indicating whether, or to what extent, the firms in the Japanese high technology industries are faced with incentives to engage in export drives to expand productive scale or to clear unanticipated inventories.

To be sure, Japan today is not Japan of the rapid-growth decades; its policies have changed substantially for both domestic and international reasons. Japan's capital markets have been significantly liberalized, depriving MOF of much of the power it once possessed. MITI also has become more sensitive to international pressures and today must be more mindful of the effect its guidance has on consumers. The hope is that Japan has abandoned the once-successful export promotion policies of its catch-up days and has become a full-fledged and stable member of the community of mature, industrialized, free-market economies.

However, the pattern of massive investment by Japan's major companies in cost-reducing mass output facilities followed by intense price competition in world markets, as seen in the television industry, is being repeated in semiconductors. As a result, industry sources anticipate intense trade friction over such products as the 64K DRAM to flare up by 1985.[123] As firms have expanded productive capacity rapidly to bring down per-unit cost, evidence suggesting anticompetitive behavior in the marketing of office computers and other final products utilizing microchips has been uncovered by the FTCJ. The commission has released a report on the increasing "capture" of wholesalers, a recent rise in producers' stockholdings in distribution outlets, and the transfer of management personnel between manufacturers and sellers. While the percentage of wholesalers dealing exclusively with one manufacturer is not high (34 percent), the FTCJ discovered that contracts signed between producers and dealers contained "restrictions regarding retail prices, sales area, retailers to whom the products could be sold, and other matters, restrictions which conflict with the intent of the Antimonopoly Act." Accordingly, the FTCJ "advised" the implicated firms to eliminate these clauses.[124]

Clearly, these developments should be watched with care by those firms competing with the Japanese and by government officials charged with enforcing U.S. antidumping and trade laws. For the most important lesson of the television case is that both Americans and Japanese erred in permitting the practices that led to a litigation of more than a dozen years. The same error must not be permitted to recur as our two fully developed and interdependent nations vie for shares of world high technology markets.

NOTES

1. This case is detailed in part two; see also nn. 111 and 112.

2. Two examples among the many writings both by Japanese and Americans who now readily acknowledge the progrowth characteristics of the rapid-growth decades are: Yoshinobu Namiki, *Nihon-gata keizai o toku* (Understanding the Japanese-type economy) (Tokyo: President-sha, 1981), and Edward Lincoln, *Japan's Industrial Policies* (Washington: Japan Economic Institute of America, 1984). The former was once a MITI officer, and his observations regarding what he calls "the Japanese kabushiki-kaisha" (Japan Inc.) and the roles the government played during the rapid growth years are revealing (pp. 236–38). See also: Editorial Staff of *Ekonomisuto*, ed., *Shōgen: Kōdo seichōki no Nihon* (Testimonies: Japan in the rapid-growth period) (Tokyo: Mainichi Shimbun, 1984). The book, published by Mainichi Newspaper in two volumes, contains eighty-three interviews conducted by the editorial staff of *Ekonomisuto* with former officials, leading politicians, business leaders, and others who played key roles in formulating and administering the policies of the rapid-growth era. These interviews contain remarkably candid responses to questions regarding policy formulation and implementation and how they affected various aspects of both the domestic economy and Japan's trade. See especially the interviews with a former high-ranking MITI official on pp. 296–319, and with a former steel company executive on pp. 333–37, in vol. 1; and those with the president of a major business organization on pp. 233–42, with a former bank president on pp. 342–51, and with a former high-ranking officer of the Ministry of Finance on pp. 379–88 in vol. 2.

3. For an analysis of the significance of capital market structure in allowing governments to adopt policies to promote economic growth, see John Zysman, *Governments, Markets and Growth* (Ithaca: Cornell University Press, 1983). See also Ryoichi Mikitani, "Monetary Policy in Japan," in Karel Holbik, ed., *Monetary Policy in Twelve Industrial Countries* (Boston: Federal Reserve Bank of Boston, 1973), pp. 246–81; Yukio Noguchi, "The Government-Business Relationship in Japan; The Changing Role of Fiscal Resources," in Kozo Yamamura, ed., *Policy and Trade Issues of the Japanese Economy* (Seattle: University of Washington Press, 1982), p. 125; and for a more extended discussion of fiscal policy and capital market, see Henry G. Wallich and Mable I. Wallich, "Banking and Finance," in Hugh Patrick and Henry Rosovsky, eds., *Asia's New Giant* (Washington, D.C.: Brookings Institution, 1976), pp. 246–315.

4. We are not unaware of the recent revisionist view that argues in effect that MOF policy had little impact on the dictates of market forces, i.e., MOF's subequilibrium interest rate policy was ineffective. This view is now available in English in such works as Eisuke Sakakibara et al., "The Japanese Financial System in Comparative Perspective," a study prepared for the Joint Economic Committee, Congress of the United States, 1982, and in Akiyoshi Horiuchi, "Economic Growth and Financial Allocation in Postwar Japan," Brookings Discussion Papers, no. 18, 1984.

In our judgment, however, their view, which may appeal to those interested in a theoretical analysis, is seriously flawed because they typically assume away important institutional and behavioral characteristics of Japanese monetary policy, the capital market, and the participants in the market. Instead of extending this essay with specific criticisms, both theoretical and empirical, of the revisionist view, let us only note that we remain convinced by a more widely accepted view of the character and effectiveness of the MOF policy. Murakami, after assessing the revisionist view (or the market school as he called it), summarized this view in the following words: "If all relevant facts are considered in a comprehensive way, it may be a sound judgment that the interest rate was regulated at an artificially low level in the following sense. The effective interest rates in most financial markets would have been significantly higher, and never lower, if the network of financial regulations had been removed." Yasusuke Murakami, "Toward a Socioinstitutional Explanation of Japan's Rapid Growth," in *Policy and Trade Issues of the Japanese Economy*, p. 14.

5. See Kozo Yamamura and Yasusuke Murakami, "A Technical Note on Japanese Firm Behavior and Economic Policy," *Policy and Trade Issues*, pp. 113–22.

6. See Kozo Yamamura, "Structure is Behavior," in Isaiah Frank, ed., *The Japanese Economy in International Perspective* (Baltimore: Johns Hopkins University Press, 1975), pp. 67–100.

7. The agency in charge of enforcing antitrust legislation, the Fair Trade Commission of Japan, was small and exercised very limited powers. Until 1977, the only binding sanctions available to the FTCJ were criminal prosecutions, and in thirty years of investigating, advising, and admonishing business, criminal charges were brought only six times—of which three were in 1949. The maximum fine for noncompliance with FTCJ orders was approximately $25; after 1977 the penalty was increased to $1,000. For more detail, see Kenji Sanekata, *Dokusen kinshi-hō to gendai keizai* (The Antimonopoly Act and the contemporary economy) (Tokyo: Seibundō, 1977).

8. Gary R. Saxonhouse, "The Impact of Japanese Financial and Employment Practices on Japanese Production and Pricing Behavior," unpublished paper, May 1979.

9. Shunsaku Nishikawa, ed., *The Labor Market in Japan* (Tokyo: University of Tokyo Press, 1980).

10. In the 1970s, the risk of being saddled with large fixed labor costs also began to be reduced by making semiannual bonus payments more flexible, i.e., reflective of the profit level of the firm and the rate of increase in productivity. See, for example, Kazutoshi Koshiro, "Development of Collective Bargaining in Postwar Japan," in Taishiro Shirai, ed., *Contemporary Industrial Relations in Japan* (Madison: University of Wisconsin Press, 1983), pp. 205–57.

11. See M. Y. Yoshino, *The Japanese Marketing System* (Cambridge: MIT Press, 1971), especially pp. 121–22, and Mitsuaki Shimaguchi, *Marketing Channels in Japan* (Umi Research Press, 1978), and sources cited in n. 15 below for general information on business groups.

12. Saxonhouse, "Japanese Financial and Employment Practices," and the sources cited in nn. 3 and 5.

13. For example, Masu Uekusa in his major study of Japanese industrial organization, *Sangyō soshikiron* (A study of industrial organization) (Tokyo: University of Tokyo Press, 1982), concluded his analysis of the Japanese distribution system by saying: "Creating the *keiretsu* distribution outlets is not a phenomenon unique to Japan. It is also found in Western nations. However, in Japan this mode of distribution is adopted by many industries, as we have just demonstrated. Furthermore, such systems as the territory system, the *itten-itchōai* system, and the discriminatory rebate system cannot be found in other nations where antimonopoly statutes are strictly enforced. The outlets in other nations are not organized into distributors' associations as prevalently as in Japan. . . . thus, the *keiretsu* distribution system can be seen as a significant characteristic of Japanese industrial organization" (p. 98). These systems referred to by Uekusa are discussed fully in the text below.

14. Mass merchandisers sold 4 percent of total retail sales in 1966, according to Yoshino, *Japanese Marketing System*, p. 134.

15. Ibid., pp. 81–128. It is necessary to note that the Japanese distribution *keiretsu* are not an isolated phenomenon but are merely one variety of *kigyō keiretsu*, a vertical Japanese business group. The most common type of *kigyō keiretsu* is composed not of marketers but of production subcontractors that manufacture subassemblies and parts for the parent firm. It is useful to clearly distinguish between the small, vertical, tightly held *kigyō keiretsu* and the large, loosely organized, bank-centered, horizontal *kinyū keiretsu*, to which most of the published data on business groups in Japan pertain. For discussions of *keiretsu*, see K. Bieda, *The Structure and Operation of the Japanese Economy* (Sydney: John Wiley and Sons Australasia Pty. Ltd., 1970); Dodwell Marketing Consultants, *Industrial Groupings in Japan* (Tokyo: Dodwell Marketing Consultants, 1979); and Misonou Hitoshi et al., *Kokumin no dokusen hakusho: Kigyō shūdan* (People's white paper on monopolies: economic groups) (Tokyo: Ochanomizu Shobō, 1978).

16. Yoshino, *Japanese Marketing System*, p. 120. No date was given for these figures; the estimate was termed "recent" in 1971.

17. For a legal background on this weak enforcement of legal and contractual rights, readers are referred to John Owen Haley, "Sheathing the Sword of Justice in Japan: An Essay on Law Without Sanctions," *Journal of Japanese Studies* 8, no. 2 (Summer 1982): 265–81, and idem, "Myth of the Reluctant Litigant," *Journal of Japanese Studies* 4, no. 2 (Summer 1978): 349–90. He argues, in essence, that because of the limited size and power of the Japanese judiciary, written legal contracts can be enforced only with great difficulty, especially in small concerns with limited resources. This explains why business relations in general must be based on "trust." Such a relationship between a large and a small firm has great potential to work against the bargaining position of the small firm by denying it legal recourse. The various forms of power exerted by large firms over small distributors described in the text must be viewed against this legal reality.

18. Shimaguchi, *Marketing Channels*, p. 51. Many Japanese sources provide details on the organization and operation of the distribution *keiretsu*; the most important are: Fair Trade Commission of Japan, "Ryūtsū keiretsuka ni tsuite" (On the vertical integration of distribution) (Tokyo: FTCJ, 1973); Kanasaki Takashi, *Kadengyōkai* (The home electronic products industry) (Tokyo: Kyōikusha, 1982); Fair Trade Commission of Japan, "Ryūtsū keiretsu-ka ni kansuru dokusen-kinshihōjō no toriatsukai" (The treatment of vertically integrated distribution under the Antimonopoly Act). This last source, a report issued by an internal FTCJ study group in March 1980, is particularly thorough in its description of the business tactics used to cement vertical *keiretsu* bonds and details the operation of territorial restrictions, rebate systems, and retail price maintenance. Also, extensive data are included on the relative volumes of goods passing through various distribution channels. See pp. 392–418.

19. Shimaguchi, *Marketing Channels*, pp. 50–52; Kanasaki, *Kadengyōkai*, pp. 108–10.

20. J. Amanda Covey, "Vertical Restraints under Japanese Law: The Antimonopoly Law Study Group Report," *Law in Japan: An Annual* 14 (1981): 55. This article provides an overview of the FTCJ group report issued in March 1980; see n. 18 above.

21. Shimaguchi, *Marketing Channels*, pp. 49, 87.

22. Kanasaki, *Kadengyōkai*, p. 108.

23. Yoshino, *Japanese Marketing System*, pp. 114, 117.

24. Ishida Hideto, "Anticompetitive Practices in the Distribution of Goods and Services in Japan: The Problem of Distribution *Keiretsu*," *Journal of Japanese Studies* 9, no. 2 (Summer 1983): 324.

25. Shimaguchi, *Marketing Channels*, pp. 52–58; Kanasaki, *Kadengyōkai*, p. 109.

26. Yoshino, *Japanese Marketing System*, p. 231.

27. For an overview of analytic articles relating to vertical integration and its efficiency implications, see David L. Kaserman, "Theories of Vertical Integration: Implications for Antitrust Policy," *Antitrust Bulletin*, no. 23 (Fall 1978), pp. 483–510. See also G. A. Hay, "An Economic Analysis of Vertical Integration," *Industrial Organization Review* 1 (1973): 188–98; J. M. Vernon and D. A. Graham, "Profitability of Monopolization by Vertical Integration," *Journal of Political Economy* 79 (July/August 1971): 924–25; and F. M. Westfield, "Vertical Integration: Does Product Price Rise or Fall?" *The American Economic Review* 71, no. 3 (June 1981): 334–36. Readers interested in a "model" of how effectively upstream collusion can be enforced at the retail level may wish to read *Shinketsu* (Decision) rendered by FTCJ on August 30, 1966 (1966, Decision no. 11) against Nagano Electric Machinery Commercial Association (a trade association of retailers of 174 stores in Nagano prefecture). FTCJ ordered the association to desist from agreeing to use the producer-suggested prices as the bases from which retail prices were determined (i.e., adding 15 percent to the prices the producers charged them), charging that this had the effect of price cartelization.

28. One characteristic of the "distribution bottleneck" faced by rapidly growing Japanese consumer products firms was the existence of regionally dominant wholesalers. Many Japanese firms in the prewar period bought all raw materials from, and sold all output to, trading firms or wholesalers, which in turn supplied all the wares sold by specialized retail outlets. These intermediaries could enjoy considerable local market power. Even today, this system survives in the Japanese textile and apparel industries.

As mass manufacturers grew larger and gained command of some position in their respective markets, the presence of layers of rent-extracting agents exacerbated distribution inefficiencies. The gains realized from eliminating this waste were one incentive leading manufacturers to capture and control wholesalers. Interestingly, however, this development also increased consumer surplus.

The rationale for this outcome can be quickly grasped. Imagine but one monopolist intermediary between the manufacturer and the final consumer. This intermediary agent would have a marginal revenue curve, derived with respect to final consumers' demand, which traces the combinations of prices and quantities at which it would be willing to buy from the manufacturer. This curve would be the manufacturer's effective demand curve, and the monopolist manufacturer would equate the marginal cost of production to the marginal revenue derived with respect to that secondary curve (which is both the wholesaler's marginal revenue curve and the manufacturer's demand curve). As each agent—the manufacturer and the wholesaler—would limit quantity to equate its marginal revenue and marginal cost, price would be "twice inflated" and consumer surplus would be limited accordingly. With vertical integration the manufacturer can eliminate the market-distorting impact of the rent-extracting middleman and equate the marginal cost of manufacture directly to marginal revenue derived with respect to final consumer demand, thereby increasing sales, reducing price, and increasing consumer surplus.

29. See pp. 250–53 for a discussion of entry into the electronics industry.

30. Yoshino, *Japanese Marketing System*, p. 134.

31. We are aware of the view of William J. Baumol outlined in "Contestable Markets: An Uprising on the Theory of Industry Structure," *American Economic Review* 72, no. 1 (March 1982): 1–15. The capital requirement for entry into a market effectively organized into *keiretsu* outlets *would* constitute a barrier to free entry under Baumol's criteria, making such a market "noncontestable." However, the "asymmetry" test for barriers to entry as posited by Michael Waterson, "On the Definition and Meaning of Barriers to Entry," *The Antitrust Bulletin*, no. 26 (1981), pp. 521–39, is employed here to demonstrate that *keiretsu* distribution structures can be shown to constitute a barrier even under this more stringent standard.

274   KOZO YAMAMURA AND JAN VANDENBERG

32. Yoshino, *Japanese Marketing System*, p. 114.

33. The importance of effective import barriers to Japanese industrial policy during the 1950s and 1960s is acknowledged even in publications funded by the Japanese government, such as Lincoln, *Japan's Industrial Policies*, p. 14.

34. Also, restrictions remained even after "full" liberalization of foreign investment in 1973. See Dan Fenno Henderson, *Foreign Enterprise in Japan: Laws and Policies* (Chapel Hill: University of North Carolina Press, 1973), appendix 11, p. 401.

35. Iyori Hiroshi and Uesugi Akinori, *The Antimonopoly Laws of Japan* (Federal Legal Publications, 1983), appendix 1, pp. 271–74.

36. If sales under these conditions injure an American industry, the selling firms are vulnerable to legal action under the Antidumping Act of 1921. It must be said that this possibility of suits against "fairly priced" imports is the source of much of the debate on U.S. antidumping law. See John J. Barcelo, "Subsidies, Countervailing Duties and Antidumping After the Tokyo Round," *Cornell International Law Journal* 13 (1980): 257–88; and Wesley K. Caine, "A Case for Repealing the Antidumping Provisions of the Tariff Act of 1930," *Law and Policy in International Business* 13, no. 3 (1981): pp. 682–701.

37. Also see Zysman, *Governments, Markets and Growth*, p. 41.

38. Price theory posits a profit-maximizing quantity for a given demand curve—that quantity at which a monopolist's marginal revenue equals marginal cost. Selling a greater quantity lowers price and the reduction in price multiplied by the quantity that would have been sold at the higher price is a loss. When this is deducted from the increase in revenues resulting from selling the additional units, a net loss always occurs.

39. Yamamura and Murakami, "Technical Note," pp. 99–100; see also H. W. de Jong, "The Significance of Dumping in International Trade," *Journal of World Trade Law* 2, no. 2 (March/April, 1969): 171.

40. Predatory dumping is expressly forbidden under the Antidumping Act of 1916; however, this little-known act has never been successfully invoked.

41. Yoshino, *Japanese Marketing System*, pp. 93–94.

42. This guide to Japanese electronics firms lists forty-eight companies; twenty-nine produced only parts or products with commercial applications; six produced parts, commercial products, and/or consumer audio equipment; and nine produced any combination of the above plus televisions. Fuji, an independent television producer in the 1950s and 1960s, appears to have been absorbed or exited from the market sometime before this *Almanac* was compiled. *Japan Electronics Almanac* (Tokyo: Dempa Publications, 1981), pp. 221–305.

43. This figure was computed from 1980 output quantities in Kanasaki, *Kadengyōkai*, p. 64, and is supported by market shares used as representative of the last few decades in Ishida, "Anti-competitive Practices," p. 328. See table 1 for more detail; subsidiaries output is included with that of the parent company when the relationship can be determined (except Japan Victor).

44. *Japan Electronics Almanac*, 1981, pp. 221–305, and n. 42 above.

45. The output of subsidiaries is by all indications counted as that of a separate company in the compilation of this table.

46. Kanasaki, *Kadengyōkai*, pp. 29, 39; and United States International Trade Commission, *Foreign Industrial Targeting and its Effects on U.S. Industries, Phase I: Japan*, Report to the Subcommittee on Trade, Committee on Ways and Means, U.S. House of Representatives on Investigaion no. 332–162, USITC Pub. 1437 (Washington, D.C.: Government Printing Office, 1983), appendix H-2.

47. "Integrated Circuits for Television Receivers," I.E.E.E. *Spectrum*, May 1969 as cited in James E. Millstein, "Decline in an Expanding Industry: Japanese Competition in Color Television," in John Zysman and Laura Tyson, eds., *American Industry in International Competition* (Ithaca: Cornell University Press, 1983), p. 107.

48. Henderson, *Foreign Enterprise*, pp. 195, 218–36.

49. Yoshino, *Japanese Marketing System*, pp. 91–128.

50. Rowland Gould, *The Matsushita Phenomenon* (Tokyo: Diamond Sha, 1970), pp. 108–11; Kanasaki, *Kadengyōkai*, p. 108.

51. *Nihon keizai shimbun* (Japan economic news), Oct. 23, 1970; Yoshino, *Japanese Marketing System*, pp. 114, 117.

52. Kanasaki, *Kadengyōkai*, p. 110. The presence and role of distributors selling consumer electronics products at prices below high cartelized levels deserves a more detailed explanation here. Japanese producers practiced "dual pricing" or discriminatory selling on their domestic market, that

is, *keiretsu* outlets were charged a higher price by the producers for goods than certain volume sellers, who paid in cash (for example, ¥199,000 vs. ¥145,000 for a 19-inch color TV). The role of these cut-rate distributors is explained by the president of one of these outlets: staff from the *Asahi Journal* asked: "If we go to discount sales outlets, we find that the products of high-cost producers such as Sharp and Sanyo are sold cheaply in comparison to those of the low-cost producers'—Toshiba, National [Matsushita], and Hitachi—products. Why?" To this, Nobui Yamasaki, the president of Maya Trading, responded: "For the three largest makers, the domestic market is a very important treasure box. They don't want to cause 'confusions' in prices there, so they make sure there is absolutely no decline in the prices. But, the agreed upon export price FOB is [for example] $180 . . . it is lower, but they get paid in cash immediately if they export. So, treating exports to the U.S. as a 'place to get quick cash,' they export to the U.S. as much as they can. In the domestic market, they sell on credit . . . but by maintaining high prices, they earn high profits. . . . The high-cost producers have to sell in the domestic market to get cash."

The unavoidable implication is that the producers used the high-volume dealers judiciously, when necessary, to raise cash. The low-cost producers were careful not to "bust the cartel," while the high-cost producers had a greater need and incentive to "leak" their products to the mass merchandisers. See *Zenkoku denshōren Kaihō, 36-go* (Report of National Association of Electrical Appliance Stores no. 36) (Tokyo: NAEAS, Jan. 6, 1967), p. 12: for further descriptions supporting the above observations, see *Yomiuri Shimbun*, Oct. 13, 1970, *Sankei*, Oct. 16, 1970, *Asahi Shimbun*, Sept. 18, 1970, and *Asahi Journal*, Nov. 27, 1966. However, such "leakage" of products to the large volume cut-rate outlets for the reason described above and others failed to exceed 10 percent of the total sales as late as the early 1970s because "despite the emergence of these non-*keiretsu* distributors, they have not yet grown to a power that can successfully challenge the makers' *keiretsu* system and their oligopolistic control of the distributional stage . . . the makers' watchful eyes are effective, and they take steps to prevent cut-rate sales. The oligopolistic system continues to control both wholesale and retail prices. The barriers to entry in the distribution system remain effective." Ryutaro Komiya et al., "Kaden sangyo" (The home electric industry), *Chūō Kōron*, Business Topics Special Seasonal Issue, Summer 1971, pp. 396–97. See pp. 386–98 for a useful discussion of the non-*keiretsu* outlets. This long article (pp. 360–412) is a good study, both empirical and analytical, of this industry during the 1960s.

53. Yoshino, *Japanese Marketing System*, p. 116; Kanasaki, *Kadengyōkai*, p. 169.

54. Kanasaki, *Kadengyōkai*, p. 111.

55. *Japan Electronics Almanac*, 1981, pp. 221–305.

56. Kanasaki, *Kadengyōkai*, p. 172.

57. For details on this raid, see the weekly *Nihon no jitsugyō*, Feb. 15, 1967, pp. 20–31.

58. See FTCJ, *Kōsei torihiki iinkai nenji hōkoku 1970* (FTCJ Annual Report, 1970) (Tokyo: FTCJ, 1970), pp. 251–56, and FTCJ Annual Report, 1971, pp. 249 and 250.

59. Case Against Home Appliance Market Stabilization Council and One Other Person, Fair Trade Commission of Japan, Decison no. 5, filed Oct. 17, 1957, as prepared by Horace J. DePodwin Associates, Inc., in its *Economic Study of the Japanese Television Industry*, for Plaintiffs' Counsel in the Japanese Electronic Products Antitrust Litigation, M.D.L. 189, Sept. 1979, vol. 1, appendix exhibit 1 (hereafter, *DePodwin Report*).

60. Kazuki Daimon, *Kuroi bukka* (Black prices) (Tokyo: Shakai-Shimpo Publishing Co., 1968), pp. 41–42.

61. The activity charged ("unreasonable restraint of trade"), as defined in chap. 1, sec. 6 of the Japanese Antimonopoly Act, is proscribed by chap. 2, sec. 3 of the same act. *Initial Decision, Case No. 6, 1966*, Office of the Fair Trade Commission of Japan, filed June 9, 1970, as published in *DePodwin Report*, vol. 1, appendix exhibit 2.

62. Art. 3 of the Antimonopoly Act, see Iyori and Uesugi, *Antimonopoly Laws* p. 215.

63. FTCJ, *Kosei torihiki iinkai nenji hōkoku* (The annual report of the Fair Trade Commission) (Tokyo: FTCJ, 1979), p. 57.

64. Yoshino, *Japanese Marketing System*, p. 123.

65. FTCJ, *Kosei torihiki iinkai shinketsu shū* (Collection of judicial decisions of the Fair Trade Commission, 1971), no. 17, pp. 187–208.

66. As late as 1980, the FTCJ found it necessary to organize a group to study the problem of distribution *keiretsu*; the group released a report indicating the need for more restrictive treatment of the vertical restraints that still characterized the channels; see n. 18. For an English-language overview of this report, see Covey, n. 20, above.

67. *Asahi Shimbun*, Jan. 26, 1967.

68. *Mainichi Shimbun*, Mar. 16, 1966, and Komiya et al., "Kadensangyo," pp. 370–71. See also the summary of original documents as published in *Appellants' Brief*, pp. 37–38, in re: Japanese Electronic Products Antitrust Litigation, 723 F.2d 238 (3rd Cir. 1983) (hereafter, *Appellants' Brief*). Students of Japanese management will appreciate the evidence of *ringi*-style decision-making processes in the organization of this clandestine system.

69. *DePodwin Report*, vol. 1, pp. V-1 through V-17. The material used is a summary of the documents seized by the FTCJ.

70. Komiya et al., "Kadensangyo," pp. 373–76, 388–91, and *Appellants' Brief*, p. 36.

71. Gould, *Matsushita Phenomenon*, pp. 108–11, Kanasaki, *Kadengyōkai*, p. 106.

72. Konosuke Matsushita, "The Road to Co-existence and Co-prosperity," Commemorative Lecture at the Appreciation Sale for the Attainment of Six Million National TV Sets (Jan. 1, 1966) as reproduced in the *DePodwin Report*, 1: IV-19.

73. *Yomiuri Shimbun*, Nov. 10, 1966. See also *Mainichi Shimbun*, Aug. 30, 1970.

74. Daimon, *Kuroi bukka*, p. 7.

75. Komiya et al., "Kaidensangyo," pp. 368–69.

76. *Yomiuri Shimbun*, Dec. 16, 1970.

77. Van Zandt, "Learning to do Business with 'Japan, Inc.,'" *Harvard Business Review* 50, no. 4 (July/August 1972): 90; and Yamamura, "Structure Is Behavior," p. 86.

78. Komiya et al., "Kaidensangyo," pp. 368–69; and *Appellants' Reply Brief*, pp. 138–42, in re: Japanese Electronic Products Antitrust Litigation, 723 F.2d 238 (3rd Cir. 1983) (hereafter, *Appellants' Reply Brief*).

79. Data used are from the *DePodwin Report*, vol. 1, table VI-1 to VI-12; the figures were compiled by the accounting firm of Morris R. Cohen and Co. from the answers of defendants in the Japan Electronic Products Antitrust Litigation to interrogatories. Also see Komiya et al., "Kaidensangyo," pp. 367–68.

80. Japanese market shares figured from information reported by the Electronics Industry Association in *TV Fact Book, 1980*, vol. 49, published annually by TV Digest, Inc., Washington, D.C., vary from those figured using data as reported by the Department of Commerce in U.S. International Trade Commission, *Television Receivers, Color and Monochrome, Assembled or Not Assembled, Finished or Not Finished and Subassemblies Thereof*, Report to the President on Investigation no. TA-201-19, USITC Pub. 808 (Washington, D.C.: Government Printing Office, 1977), and from those used by the plaintiffs in the Japanese Electronic Products Antitrust Litigation. There are problems with the inclusion of subassemblies and parts, the subtraction of U.S. exports from U.S. market totals, Japanese falsification of prices on U.S. customs documents, and rounding. Many sources quote market shares in terms of sets, or units, rather than value, which exaggerates the Japanese firms' U.S. market share. The most important source of discrepancy, however, is the inclusion or exclusion of the production of the Japanese companies' American and third-country subsidiaries in the "Japanese market share." This introduces major discrepancies into any figures quoted for years after 1977, though the divergence begins in 1972, when Sony began American production. Figures in this article, unless otherwise noted, are for imports directly from Japan, figured using Department of Commerce data (whenever available) and quoted on a value basis; they thus represent conservative estimates but are based on the most complete data set.

81. See Raymond Vernon, "International Investment and International Trade in the Product Cycle," *Quarterly Journal of Economics*, vol. 80, no. 2 (1966).

82. This article allows American-owned companies to re-import subassemblies constructed from U.S.-produced parts, paying duty only on the value added abroad.

83. While imports directly from Japan accounted for only 11.2 percent of the American market for black-and-white televisions in 1981, it is impossible to determine the actual market share held by Japanese firms due to the inextricable mix of American and Japanese offshore production, and, also important, Japanese production in the United States.

84. Millstein, "Decline in an Expanding Industry,"

85. Employment change was computed using figures from USITC Pub. 808, and Bart S. Fisher, "The Antidumping Law of the United States: A Legal and Economic Analysis," *Law and Policy in International Business* 5, no. 1 (1973): 120. For import figures see table 5.

86. *Appellants' Reply Brief*, pp. 77, 99, and Opinion of Appeals Court, in re: Japanese Electronic Products Antitrust Litigation, 723 F.2d 238, 312, 313 (3d Cir. 1983) (hereafter, *Opinion of Appeals Court*).

87. *Opinion of Appeals Court*, p. 316. The unit used to arrive at this figure—value or number of TV sets—was unspecified in the source document. A 1977 Japanese market share of 37 percent on a

number-of-sets basis was reported in Ira C. Magaziner and Robert F. Reich, *Minding America's Business: The Decline and Rise of the American Economy* (New York: Vintage Books, 1983), p. 170. This estimate, however, excludes Japanese companies' imports into the United States from third countries.

88. United States International Trade Commission, *Summary of Trade and Tariff Information on TSUS Items 685.11-685.19*, USITC Pub. 841, Control no. 6-5-33 (Washington D.C.: Government Printing Office, 1982), pp. 11–12.

89. USITC Pub. 808, p. A-44; Fisher, "Antidumping Law," p. 120; and USITC Pub. 841, p. 12.

90. Magaziner and Reich, *Minding America's Business*, p. 171.

91. USITC Pub. 841, p. 12.

92. *Appellants' Reply Brief*, p. 77.

93. *DePodwin Report*, 1: V-17.

94. JMEA "Rules," Art. 9, para. 4 and Art. 14; also, JMEA "Agreement" of 1963 as cited in *DePodwin Report*, 1: IV-37.

95. *DePodwin Report*, 1: V-17, V-19; the information used consists of a summary of original documents accepted as legal evidence.

96. *Appellants' Reply Brief*, p. 19.

97. Ibid.

98. Table 3 lists the differentials between domestic price and the check price—not the actual export price, which would be even lower.

99. *Appellants' Brief*, p. 18.

100. "Sovereign immunity"—the immunity from U.S. law granted any foreign government's action—has raised thorny issues in the television case. Under this doctrine, if a cartel is organized under the compulsion of a sovereign national power or its agent—such as MITI—it is exempt from prosecution under U.S. laws.

101. That the firms attempted to conceal their subversion of the check-price system from the Japanese government is attested to by a meeting held in 1966 by the Statistics Committee of the Electronic Industries Association of Japan where measures to change methods of reporting data to the government to prevent discovery of the size of the export price margins were discussed and adopted. *Appellants' Brief*, p. 39; *Opinion of Appeals Court*, p. 146. For information on the check-price system in general, see *Appellants' Brief*, pp. 11–34, *Appellants' Reply Brief*, pp. 100–103.

102. *The Japan Economic Journal*, Jan. 10, 1966.

103. *Appellants' Brief*, pp. 24–28.

104. An example of this documentation is the following handwritten cryptic note found in the possession of Sears: "Phone call from Tokyo: Iijima, Tokyo—Toshiba Murao says he heard customs was questioning Sanyo on double invoicing? Sanyo top level says no—not at present time. Sanyo feels we should wait on divulging system, Trigger off new investigation, last for years. Very dangerous—would re-open whole new case. . . . Re Toshiba: will have to divulge how we over and under bill them—would we have to reveal system if asked by customs?" (*Appellants' Brief*, p. 30).

105. Sears, which purchased 60 percent of Japan's television exports between 1963 and 1973, was served with a 13-count customs fraud conspiracy indictment in 1980; 37 persons were identified as coconspirators in a series of illegal activities occurring between 1966 and 1975. *Appellants' Reply Brief*, pp. 96–103.

106. Documents seized during later court proceedings indicate that, for the firms involved, an important reason for maintenance of the system was the avoidance of U.S. antidumping scrutiny, and in the event of such scrutiny, the understatement of price differentials that would allow for partial evasion of antidumping duties. *Appellants' Brief*, p. 33. The assessment of duties, to be discussed below, was materially delayed by the confusion resulting from multiple prices.

107. USITC Pub. 841, pp. 4–6, and Millstein, "Decline in an Expanding Industry," pp. 122–24.

108. Yoshio Ohara, "Nichi-bei-ō kankei no sōgōteki kōsatsu" (A comprehensive analysis of Japan-U.S.-European relations), *Japan-EC Studies Association Annual Report*, no. 3 (1983), p. 38.

109. USITC Pub. 841, pp. 5, 6, and 35; for market-share figures, see Table 5.

110. USITC Pub. 841, pp. 4–6; Millstein, "Decline in an Expanding Industry," p. 125; and Ohara, "A Comprehensive Analysis," p. 38.

111. See *Opinion of Appeals Court*, pp. 310, 316–19, for a summary description. Also see Phillips B. Keller, "Zenith Radio Corp. v Matsushita Electrical Industrial Co.: Interpreting the Antidumping act of 1916," *Hastings International and Comparative Law Review* 6 (1982): 137.

112. Ohara, "A Comprehensive Analysis," p. 38; and *Opinion of Appeals Court*, p. 318.

113. See Keller, "Zenith Radio Corp.," and Kermit W. Almstedt, "International Price Dis-

crimination and the 1916 Antidumping Act—Are Amendments in Order?" *Law and Policy in International Business* 13, no. 3 (1981): 747–80.

114. Of the charges filed, only the allegations of price discrimination between Japanese and American customers was explicitly voided. For Robinson-Patman Act charges to have merit, both parties to the price discrimination must be American. *Opinion of Appeals Court*, pp. 310–18.

115. This appeal was accompanied by a statement prepared by the Japanese government stating that all export behavior of the defendants was carried out according to the instructions issued by, and under the express compulsion of, MITI and the Japanese government (see n. 100 above). *Brief of the Government of Japan as Amicus Curiae in Support of the Petition for a Writ of Certiorari*, filed July 6, 1984, in re: Japanese Electronic Products Antitrust Litigation, 723 F.2d 238 (3d Cir., 1983).

116. Komiya et al, "Kaidensangyo," p. 29.

117. For analyses of the situation based on this assumption, see Magaziner and Reich, *Minding America's Business*, pp. 169–80, and Zysman, *Governments, Markets and Growth*, pp. 278–79.

118. "Sources of Competitiveness in the Japanese Color Television and Tape Recorder Industry," paper prepared by World Developing Industry and Technology Inc., for the U.S. Department of Labor (October 1978), p. 72.

119. *Japan Economic Yearbook, 1971* (Tokyo: The Oriental Economist, 1971), p. 208.

120. Saxonhouse, "Japanese Financial and Employment Practices," pp. 1–8.

121. The OMA expired in 1980, so the 1981 increase cannot be correctly attributed to cyclical movements. For export figures, see tables 4 and 5.

122. A full treatment of antitrust issues arising from the MITI-led joint research projects in the Japanese high technology industry is available in Kozo Yamamura, "Joint Research and Antitrust: Japanese vs. American Strategies," a paper presented at the Conference on Japanese Industrial Policy in Comparative Perspective, New York City, March 17–19, 1984.

123. Tetsuro Wada, "Trilateral Friction in Microchip Business Seen among Japan, U.S. and Korea," *The Japan Economic Journal*, Tuesday, July 24, 1984, p. 20. A "64K DRAM" is a 64 kilobyte direct random access memory chip.

124. FTCJ, *Office computer no ryūtsu jittai chōsa ni tsuite* (A survey of the reality of office computer distribution), a nonclassified internal study, Sept. 28, 1984.

APPENDIX

NOTES ON BELOW-COST EXPORTS

The text (part one) posited four situations that could lead to export sales at prices below those charged on the exporting firms' domestic market. Leaving aside the first, which involves export sales at or near marginal cost while monopoly rents are extracted on a protected home market (probably the most common type of international price discrimination), and the fourth, which is nothing more than classic predation carried out across national boundaries, we turn here to examine more analytically the other two situations: export-led expansion and recession-sparked export drives. In analyzing both of these, a worldwide industry is posited in which all firms have identical cost functions; some have protected, cartelized, domestic markets while others sell on global markets only.

Export-led campaigns to achieve economies of scale rest on a firm's perception of declining long-run average total cost (LRATC, i.e., variable plus fixed costs) and the command of a cartelized domestic market; such a firm is diagrammed in figure 1. (The figure is not drawn to scale; it is exaggerated for ease of exposition.) The firm is faced by two demand curves—a low-elasticity domestic curve and a highly elastic but downward sloping world demand curve. (The origin with respect to the world demand curve is $(q_d, 0)$.) Initially, the firm equates domestic marginal revenue (MR_d) and short-run marginal cost (SRMC), selling quantity q_d for price p_d on the cartelized domestic market. It then exports the balance of its output $(q_t - q_d)$ at price p_w, which is equal to its marginal cost of production (SRMC). The firm is engaging, thus, in the previously mentioned "simple" international price discrimination.

The firm is in equilibrium at this production level (q_t). As firms worldwide have identical costs functions, and face a common global demand schedule, if the extraction of rent in the cartelized domestic market is stabilized by barriers to entry, the industry as a whole is in global equilibrium, both short-run and long-run, provided the particular type of increase in productive capacity associated with export-led campaigns does not occur. This is because any increase will force prices below long-run costs.

However, those firms that control protected domestic markets with fixed prices have a special incentive to invest and to increase production from q_t to q_t' and to drive global prices permanently to below-cost levels, as indicated by p_w'. The firms will expand to move down their declining LRATC curves (following arrow), and increasing the profit made on units sold domestically by a sum proportionate to rectangle ABCD as production costs-per-unit decrease on goods sold on the home market at a fixed price. (The adjustment in domestic price and quantity that would result as the SRMC curve shifts due to an increase in capacity is not shown on the diagram as it does not materially affect the outcome of the strategy.) This gain must be balanced against the losses incurred

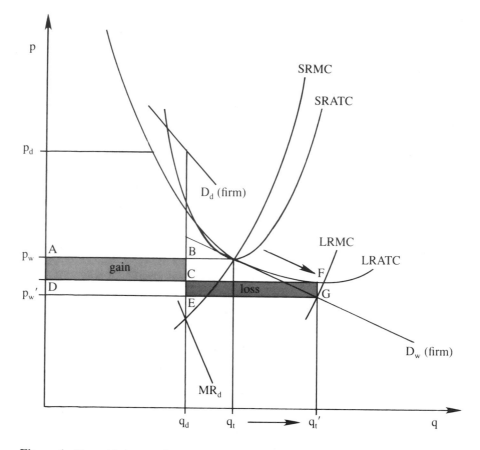

Figure 1. Export-led expansion

q_d =   sales on domestic market (at p_d)

q_t =   initial level of production

             $q_t - q_d$ exported (at p_w)

q_t' =   expanded level of production

             $q_t' - q_d$ exported (at p_w')

ABCD   =   gain on domestic sales associated with expansion

CEFG   =   loss on increased export sales

NOTE: The SRATC curve in this diagram is drawn so that a portion falls below the LRATC curve, due to the fact that if any minimum point on an SRATC curve is also to fall on the LRATC curve, the long-run curve cannot always be below the short-run curve. This paradox was first confronted by Jacob Viner, "Cost Curves and Supply Curves," *Readings in Price Theory* (Chicago: Richard D. Irwin, Inc., 1952) pp. 198-232.

on international markets, which would be equal to rectangle CEFG, as increased sales are possible only through price reductions to levels below average total cost.

The firms with protected home market bases would restabilize output at level q_t' and price p_w' or at such point that the area of ABCD was equal to the area of CEFG. If all firms had identical costs functions, this price level would destroy the profit margins of firms that have no protected home market. The exit of these firms could conceivably shift firm-specific global demand schedules so as to allow remaining firms to make world-market sales at profitable prices.

This necessarily schematic rendition of the theoretical mechanics underlying a certain type of vigorous expansion of exports of a commodity that exhibits significant economies of scale points out one feasible way in which a protected home market can benefit an internationally oriented firm.

As made clear in the text, this type of expansion campaign is probably not engaged in in the face of full knowledge that the resulting increase in production will have to be sold at below-cost prices on the international market. Rather, the cost savings on goods sold domestically acts as a buffer, making firms willing to expand courageously into world markets even with a high probability that global demand conditions may at some point force such below-cost sales. That is to say, the command of a protected home market affords these firms a margin of safety, and thus encourages risk taking in the penetration of foreign markets.

The economic motivations behind a recession-sparked export drive can be easily analyzed with the aid of figure 2. Once again, two demand curves of differing elasticity are posited and the firm is in short-run equilibrium when producing so as to equate SRMC and MR_d on its national market and selling at SRMC on the world market. The firm would, thus, sell quantity q_d (at price p_d) at home and export q_w (at price p_w), for a total output of q_t. The firm is characterized by high fixed costs as evidenced by the steep rise of the short-run average total cost (SRATC) curve as total production varies from q_t. (The reasons for Japanese firms having these fixed costs are discussed in the text.)

Equilibrium is disturbed by a drop in domestic demand. (A concurrent drop in global demand is not posited here to simplify the analysis; such a drop would exacerbate the decrease in world-market prices associated with an export drive.) Adjustment to this slump in domestic demand causes the firm to reduce its sales to q_d' to re-equate SRMC and domestic marginal revenue; domestic price will fall to p_d'. With a constant level of export sales, total production would fall to q_t^*, an output associated with an increase in SRATC (following arrow) to a level indicated by line AE. This increase in costs-per-unit would cause a decrease in profit on domestic sales in the amount indicated by the area of rectangle ABCD and losses in the amount of DCFE on export sales.

However, a decrease in export price could enable the firm to increase exports enough to maintain output at or near the cost-minimizing level. That is, rather than decrease production from q_t to q_t^* and incur losses (shown as ABFE), the firm could export at a below-cost price, such as p_w', leading to an increase in world-market sales equal to $q_t - q_t^*$ (or $q_w' - q_w$) and incurring a loss (CGHI).

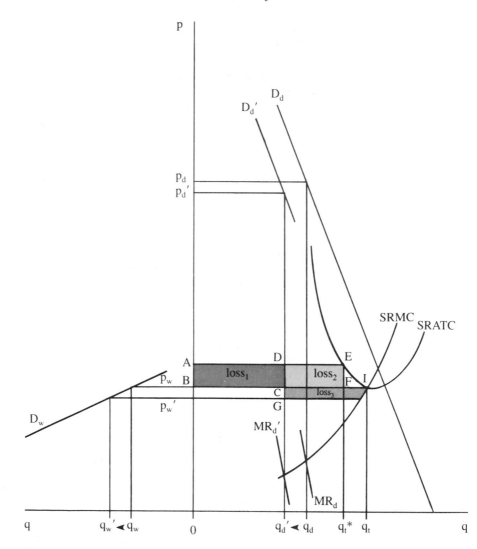

Figure 2. Recession export drive

q_t	=	initial level of production in short-term equilibrium
q_d	=	initial level of sales on domestic market (at p_d)
q^w	=	initial level of sales on international market (at p_w)
		—domestic demand falls—
q_d'	=	new profit-maximizing level of domestic sales (at p_d')
q_t^*	=	total output without below-cost exports
q_w'	=	expanded level of exports at below-cost price
ABCD	=	potential loss on domestic sales
CDEF	=	potential loss on export sales
CGHI	=	loss associated with below-cost export drive (at p_w')

The ratios between the size of the price reduction necessary (as related to the elasticity of global demand), the rate of increase in cost-per-unit as output falls and the percentage of production sold on the respective markets will determine which loss would be smaller; high fixed costs, highly elastic global demand, and moderate export ratios imply that a smaller loss would result from export drives than production cuts.

The amount of inventory on hand will necessarily affect the timing of such export surges as producers hold goods for a period of time going into an economic downturn, hoping for a quick recovery that would revive domestic demand and obviate the necessity of below-cost exports to clear inventories.

Thus, for a firm having high fixed costs and control of domestic cartelized domestic market, an export drive, even when pursued by selling their product at a below-cost price, may be a profit-maximizing (or loss-minimizing) response to a prolonged decline in demand. The below-cost sales can do sudden damage to foreign competitors (who may also be suffering from the recession) but prices will not be permanently depressed; when demand recovers, prices should return to levels permitting normal profit.

The Contributors

TERUO DOI is professor of law at Waseda University.

JOHN O. HALEY is professor of law and associate dean of the University of Washington School of Law.

KOICHI HAMADA is professor of economics at the University of Tokyo.

DAN F. HENDERSON is professor of law at the University of Washington School of Law.

HIDETOH ISHIDA is a special investigator of the Fair Trade Commission of Japan.

HIROSHI IYORI is the chief administrative officer (Jimu kyokuchō) of the Fair Trade Commission of Japan.

MASAHIRO MURAKAMI is a special investigator of the Fair Trade Commission of Japan.

KAZUO SATO is professor of economics at Rutgers University.

GARY SAXONHOUSE is professor of economics at the University of Michigan.

PAULA STERN is chairwoman of the United States International Trade Commission since June 1984. She has served as commissioner since 1978.

JAN L. VANDENBERG was a research assistant to Kozo Yamamura at the University of Washington where she majored in economics and Japanese studies and is a graduate student in economics at Stanford University.

ANDREW WECHSLER has served as senior economic advisor to Chairwoman Paula Stern of the U.S. International Trade Commission since 1979. He is completing his doctorate in economics at Stanford University.

KOZO YAMAMURA is professor of East Asian Studies and Economics and chairman of the Japanese Studies Program at the University of Washington.

Index

Administrative guidance (*gyōsei shidō*), 60, 69–71, 108, 109–10; and competition, 61, 69–71, 108; compliance with, 71, 110–11; and product liability, 87; definition of, 107–8, 109. *See also* Ministry of International Trade and Industry

Alcoa case (1945), 67

Allied Occupation, 63, 115–16. *See also* Shoup Mission

Antidumping Act of 1921 (U.S.), 263, 265

Antimonopoly Law (Japan), 56, 61–62, 66–69, 75n; and MITI, 57; exemptions to, 65, 68, 79–81; violations of, 65–66, 70, 81–82; mentioned, 60, 71–72, 138, 164, 187. *See also* Fair Trade Commission

Antitrust law, 56, 57

Antitrust policy (U.S.), 62, 110–11, 115, 238–49, 255, 263–65

Automobile industry (U.S.), 201–3

Bank of Japan, 140, 145, 151, 154

Capital: accumulation of, 6, 7; flow of, 41, 132, 134, 141, 240. *See also* Ministry of Finance

Cartels, 65, 66–67, 69–70, 133; recession, 60, 79–81, 241; and trade associations, 61; prewar, 62; surcharges on, 81–82; in the oil industry, 111; in the machine tool industry, 225, 236n; in television industry, 238, 253–57 passim, 259–63, 265–68 passim; rationalization, 241. *See also* Ministry of International Trade and Industry

Check-price system, 121, 125n

Civil Code, 88, 91; remedies for product liability, 84, 88–93, 100–101; provisions for patent violations, 166–70; and know-how protection, 189n

Clayton Act, 68

Commercial Code, 163, 168, 170, 186

Consumer electric appliances industry (Japan), 250

Consumer loans, 37–40

Consumer Product Safety Commission, 96

Convention Establishing the World Intellectual Property Organization, 157

Copyright Act (U.S.), 171, 172

Copyright Law, 171–78, 190; protection for computer software, 170–77; revision of, 176–77; protection for semiconductors, 178; merchandising rights under, 178–83; penalties imposed by, 179; and "right of publicity," 181–82

Council for Foreign Exchange, 142–43, 153

Criminal code, 85, 168

Cultural Affairs Agency, 171, 176

Daiichi Kangyō group, 64

Dam, Kenneth, 220

Davis, Paul, 109–10

Designated Industries Promotion Temporary Measures Bill (Japan 1963), 58, 74n, 117, 118

Deutsche Werft Aktiengesellschaft v. Chūetsu Waukesha Yūgen Kaisha, 165–66

Distribution system (*keiretsu*), 64, 144, 145, 242, 243–47, 272n, 273n; as trade barriers, 245–47, 253; anticompetitive nature of, 245, 247; of the television industry, 252–53, 255; and price level, 274n

Dumping, 239, 267; definition of, 247; four types of, 247–49; of television sets, 263–64, 265

Economic Planning Agency (EPA), 93; investigation by, 85–86, 88–89, 92, 100; and seal system, 87; survey by, 93–95

Egg-Tōfu case, 89, 91

Electronic Industries Association of Japan (EIAJ), 255

Exports: role of FECL, 132, 134; U.S. criticism of, 134